ASPEN PUBLISHERS

D1370985

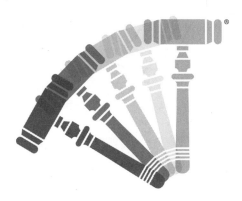

Casenote™ Legal Briefs

BUSINESS ORGANIZATIONS

Keyed to Courses Using

O'Kelley and Thompson's
Corporations and Other Business Associations

Sixth Edition

Wolters Kluwer
Law & Business

AUSTIN   BOSTON   CHICAGO   NEW YORK   THE NETHERLANDS

© 2010 Aspen Publishers. All Rights Reserved.
www.AspenLaw.com

No part of this publication may be reproduced or transmitted in any form or by any means, electronic or mechanical, including photocopy, recording, or any information storage and retrieval system, without permission in writing from the publisher. Requests for permission to make copies of any part of this publication should be mailed to:

Aspen Publishers
Attn: Permissions Dept.
76 Ninth Avenue, 7th Floor
New York, NY 10011-5201

To contact Customer Care, e-mail customer.service@aspenpublishers.com, call 1-800-234-1660, fax 1-800-901-9075, or mail correspondence to:

Aspen Publishers
Attn: Order Department
P.O. Box 990
Frederick, MD 21705

Printed in the United States of America.

1 2 3 4 5 6 7 8 9 0

ISBN 978-0-7355-8979-7

About Wolters Kluwer Law & Business

Wolters Kluwer Law & Business is a leading provider of research information and workflow solutions in key specialty areas. The strengths of the individual brands of Aspen Publishers, CCH, Kluwer Law International and Loislaw are aligned within Wolters Kluwer Law & Business to provide comprehensive, in-depth solutions and expert-authored content for the legal, professional and education markets.

CCH was founded in 1913 and has served more than four generations of business professionals and their clients. The CCH products in the Wolters Kluwer Law & Business group are highly regarded electronic and print resources for legal, securities, antitrust and trade regulation, government contracting, banking, pension, payroll, employment and labor, and health-care reimbursement and compliance professionals.

Aspen Publishers is a leading information provider for attorneys, business professionals and law students. Written by preeminent authorities, Aspen products offer analytical and practical information in a range of specialty practice areas from securities law and intellectual property to mergers and acquisitions and pension/benefits. Aspen's trusted legal education resources provide professors and students with high-quality, up-to-date and effective resources for successful instruction and study in all areas of the law.

Kluwer Law International supplies the global business community with comprehensive English-language international legal information. Legal practitioners, corporate counsel and business executives around the world rely on the Kluwer Law International journals, loose-leafs, books and electronic products for authoritative information in many areas of international legal practice.

Loislaw is a premier provider of digitized legal content to small law firm practitioners of various specializations. Loislaw provides attorneys with the ability to quickly and efficiently find the necessary legal information they need, when and where they need it, by facilitating access to primary law as well as state-specific law, records, forms and treatises.

Wolters Kluwer Law & Business, a unit of Wolters Kluwer, is headquartered in New York and Riverwoods, Illinois. Wolters Kluwer is a leading multinational publisher and information services company.

Format for the Casenote Legal Brief

Nature of Case: This section identifies the form of action (e.g., breach of contract, negligence, battery), the type of proceeding (e.g., demurrer, appeal from trial court's jury instructions), or the relief sought (e.g., damages, injunction, criminal sanctions).

Fact Summary: This is included to refresh your memory and can be used as a quick reminder of the facts.

Rule of Law: Summarizes the general principle of law that the case illustrates. It may be used for instant recall of the court's holding and for classroom discussion or home review.

Facts: This section contains all relevant facts of the case, including the contentions of the parties and the lower court holdings. It is written in a logical order to give the student a clear understanding of the case. The plaintiff and defendant are identified by their proper names throughout and are always labeled with a (P) or (D).

Palsgraf v. Long Island R.R. Co.

Injured bystander (P) v. Railroad company (D)

N.Y. Ct. App., 248 N.Y. 339, 162 N.E. 99 (1928).

Party ID: Quick identification of the relationship between the parties.

NATURE OF CASE: Appeal from judgment affirming verdict for plaintiff seeking damages for personal injury.

FACT SUMMARY: Helen Palsgraf (P) was injured on R.R.'s (D) train platform when R.R.'s (D) guard helped a passenger aboard a moving train, causing his package to fall on the tracks. The package contained fireworks which exploded, creating a shock that tipped a scale onto Palsgraf (P).

🏛 RULE OF LAW
The risk reasonably to be perceived defines the duty to be obeyed.

FACTS: Helen Palsgraf (P) purchased a ticket to Rockaway Beach from R.R. (D) and was waiting on the train platform. As she waited, two men ran to catch a train that was pulling out from the platform. The first man jumped aboard, but the second man, who appeared as if he might fall, was helped aboard by the guard on the train who had kept the door open so they could jump aboard. A guard on the platform also helped by pushing him onto the train. The man was carrying a package wrapped in newspaper. In the process, the man dropped his package, which fell on the tracks. The package contained fireworks and exploded. The shock of the explosion was apparently of great enough strength to tip over some scales at the other end of the platform, which fell on Palsgraf (P) and injured her. A jury awarded her damages, and R.R. (D) appealed.

ISSUE: Does the risk reasonably to be perceived define the duty to be obeyed?

HOLDING AND DECISION: (Cardozo, C.J.) Yes. The risk reasonably to be perceived defines the duty to be obeyed. If there is no foreseeable hazard to the injured party as the result of a seemingly innocent act, the act does not become a tort because it happened to be a wrong as to another her. If the wrong was not willful, the plaintiff must show that the act as to her had such great and apparent possibilities of danger as to entitle her to protection. Negligence in the abstract is not enough upon which to base liability. Negligence is a relative concept, evolving out of the common law doctrine of trespass on the case. To establish liability, the defendant must owe a legal duty of reasonable care to the injured party. A cause of action in tort will lie where harm,

though unintended, could have been averted or avoided by observance of such a duty. The scope of the duty is limited by the range of danger that a reasonable person could foresee. In this case, there was nothing to suggest from the appearance of the parcel or otherwise that the parcel contained fireworks. The guard could not reasonably have had any warning of a threat to Palsgraf (P), and R.R. (D) therefore cannot be held liable. Judgment is reversed in favor of R.R. (D).

DISSENT: (Andrews, J.) The concept that there is no negligence unless R.R. (D) owes a legal duty to take care as to Palsgraf (P) herself is too narrow. Everyone owes to the world at large the duty of refraining from those acts that may unreasonably threaten the safety of others. If the guard's action was negligent as to those nearby, it was also negligent as to those outside what might be termed the "danger zone." For Palsgraf (P) to recover, R.R.'s (D) negligence must have been the proximate cause of her injury, a question of fact for the jury.

Concurrence/Dissent: All concurrences and dissents are briefed whenever they are included by the casebook editor.

▶ ANALYSIS
The majority defined the limit of the defendant's liability in terms of the danger that a reasonable person in defendant's situation would have perceived. The dissent argued that the limitation should not be placed on liability, but rather on damages. Judge Andrews suggested that only injuries that would not have happened but for R.R.'s (D) negligence should be compensable. Both the majority and dissent recognized the policy-driven need to limit liability for negligent acts, seeking, in the words of Judge Andrews, to define a framework "that will be practical and in keeping with the general understanding of mankind." The Restatement (Second) of Torts has accepted Judge Cardozo's view.

Analysis: This last paragraph gives you a broad understanding of where the case "fits in" with other cases in the section of the book and with the entire course. It is a hornbook-style discussion indicating whether the case is a majority or minority opinion and comparing the principal case with other cases in the casebook. It may also provide analysis from restatements, uniform codes, and law review articles. The analysis will prove to be invaluable to classroom discussion.

Quicknotes

FORESEEABILITY A reasonable expectation that change is the probable result of certain acts or omissions.

NEGLIGENCE Conduct falling below the standard of care that a reasonable person would demonstrate under similar conditions.

PROXIMATE CAUSE The natural sequence of events without which an injury would not have been sustained.

Issue: The issue is a concise question that brings out the essence of the opinion as it relates to the section of the casebook in which the case appears. Both substantive and procedural issues are included if relevant to the decision.

Holding and Decision: This section offers a clear and in-depth discussion of the rule of the case and the court's rationale. It is written in easy-to-understand language and answers the issue presented by applying the law to the facts of the case. When relevant, it includes a thorough discussion of the exceptions to the case as listed by the court, any major cites to the other cases on point, and the names of the judges who wrote the decisions.

Quicknotes: Conveniently defines legal terms found in the case and summarizes the nature of any statutes, codes, or rules referred to in the text.

Aspen Publishers is proud to offer *Casenote Legal Briefs*—continuing thirty years of publishing America's best-selling legal briefs.

Casenote Legal Briefs are designed to help you save time when briefing assigned cases. Organized under convenient headings, they show you how to abstract the basic facts and holdings from the text of the actual opinions handed down by the courts. Used as part of a rigorous study regimen, they can help you spend more time analyzing and critiquing points of law than on copying bits and pieces of judicial opinions into your notebook or outline.

Casenote Legal Briefs should never be used as a substitute for assigned casebook readings. They work best when read as a follow-up to reviewing the underlying opinions themselves. Students who try to avoid reading and digesting the judicial opinions in their casebooks or online sources will end up shortchanging themselves in the long run. The ability to absorb, critique, and restate the dynamic and complex elements of case law decisions is crucial to your success in law school and beyond. It cannot be developed vicariously.

Casenote Legal Briefs represents but one of the many offerings in Aspen's Study Aid Timeline, which includes:

- *Casenote Legal Briefs*
- *Emanuel Law Outlines*
- *Examples & Explanations* Series
- *Introduction to Law* Series
- Emanuel *Law in a Flash* Flash Cards
- Emanuel *CrunchTime* Series

Each of these series is designed to provide you with easy-to-understand explanations of complex points of law. Each volume offers guidance on the principles of legal analysis and, consulted regularly, will hone your ability to spot relevant issues. We have titles that will help you prepare for class, prepare for your exams, and enhance your general comprehension of the law along the way.

To find out more about Aspen Study Aid publications, visit us online at *www.AspenLaw.com* or email us at *legaledu@wolterskluwer.com*. We'll be happy to assist you.

Get this Casenote Legal Brief as an AspenLaw Studydesk eBook today!

By returning this form to Aspen Publishers, you will receive a complimentary eBook download of this Casenote Legal Brief and AspenLaw Studydesk productivity software.* Learn more about AspenLaw Studydesk today at *www.AspenLaw.com/Studydesk*.

Name	Phone ( )

Address	Apt. No.

City	State	ZIP Code

Law School	Graduation Date Month _____ Year _____

Cut out the UPC found on the lower left corner of the back cover of this book. Staple the UPC inside this box. Only the original UPC from the book cover will be accepted. (No photocopies or store stickers are allowed.)

> **Attach UPC**
> **inside this box.**

Email (Print legibly or you may not get access!)

Title of this book (course subject)

ISBN of this book (10- or 13-digit number on the UPC)

Used with which casebook (provide author's name)

Mail the completed form to: Aspen Publishers, Inc.
Legal Education Division
130 Turner Street, Bldg 3, 4th Floor
Waltham, MA 02453-8901

* Upon receipt of this completed form, you will be emailed a code for the digital download of this book in AspenLaw Studydesk eBook format and a free copy of the software application, which is required to read the eBook.

For a full list of eBook study aids available for AspenLaw Studydesk software and other resources that will help you with your law school studies, visit *www.AspenLaw.com*.

Make a photocopy of this form and your UPC for your records.

For detailed information on the use of the information you provide on this form, please see the PRIVACY POLICY at *www.AspenLaw.com*.

A. Decide on a Format and Stick to It

Structure is essential to a good brief. It enables you to arrange systematically the related parts that are scattered throughout most cases, thus making manageable and understandable what might otherwise seem to be an endless and unfathomable sea of information. There are, of course, an unlimited number of formats that can be utilized. However, it is best to find one that suits your needs and stick to it. Consistency breeds both efficiency and the security that when called upon you will know where to look in your brief for the information you are asked to give.

Any format, as long as it presents the essential elements of a case in an organized fashion, can be used. Experience, however, has led *Casenotes* to develop and utilize the following format because of its logical flow and universal applicability.

NATURE OF CASE: This is a brief statement of the legal character and procedural status of the case (e.g., "Appeal of a burglary conviction").

There are many different alternatives open to a litigant dissatisfied with a court ruling. The key to determining which one has been used is to discover *who is asking this court for what.*

This first entry in the brief should be kept as *short as possible.* Use the court's terminology if you understand it. But since jurisdictions vary as to the titles of pleadings, the best entry is the one that addresses who wants what in this proceeding, not the one that sounds most like the court's language.

RULE OF LAW: A statement of the general principle of law that the case illustrates (e.g., "An acceptance that varies any term of the offer is considered a rejection and counteroffer").

Determining the rule of law of a case is a procedure similar to determining the issue of the case. Avoid being fooled by red herrings; there may be a few rules of law mentioned in the case excerpt, but usually only one is *the* rule with which the casebook editor is concerned. The techniques used to locate the issue, described below, may also be utilized to find the rule of law. Generally, your best guide is simply the chapter heading. It is a clue to the point the casebook editor seeks to make and should be kept in mind when reading every case in the respective section.

FACTS: A synopsis of only the essential facts of the case, i.e., those bearing upon or leading up to the issue.

The facts entry should be a short statement of the events and transactions that led one party to initiate legal proceedings against another in the first place. While some cases conveniently state the salient facts at the beginning of the decision, in other instances they will have to be culled from hiding places throughout the text, even from concurring and dissenting opinions. Some of the "facts" will often be in dispute and should be so noted. Conflicting evidence may be briefly pointed up. "Hard" facts must be included. Both must be *relevant* in order to be listed in the facts entry. It is impossible to tell what is relevant until the entire case is read, as the ultimate determination of the rights and liabilities of the parties may turn on something buried deep in the opinion.

Generally, the facts entry should not be longer than three to five *short* sentences.

It is often helpful to identify the role played by a party in a given context. For example, in a construction contract case the identification of a party as the "contractor" or "builder" alleviates the need to tell that that party was the one who was supposed to have built the house.

It is always helpful, and a good general practice, to identify the "plaintiff" and the "defendant." This may seem elementary and uncomplicated, but, especially in view of the creative editing practiced by some casebook editors, it is sometimes a difficult or even impossible task. Bear in mind that the *party presently* seeking something from this court may not be the plaintiff, and that sometimes only the cross-claim of a defendant is treated in the excerpt. Confusing or misaligning the parties can ruin your analysis and understanding of the case.

ISSUE: A statement of the general legal question answered by or illustrated in the case. For clarity, the issue is best put in the form of a question capable of a "yes" or "no" answer. In reality, the issue is simply the Rule of Law put in the form of a question (e.g., "May an offer be accepted by performance?").

The major problem presented in discerning what is *the* issue in the case is that an opinion usually purports to raise and answer several questions. However, except for rare cases, only one such question is really the issue in the case. Collateral issues not necessary to the resolution of the matter in controversy are handled by the court by language known as *"obiter dictum"* or merely *"dictum."* While dicta may be included later in the brief, they have no place under the issue heading.

To find the issue, ask *who wants what* and then go on to ask *why did that party succeed or fail in getting it.* Once this is determined, the "why" should be turned into a question.

The complexity of the issues in the cases will vary, but in all cases a single-sentence question should sum up the issue. *In a few cases,* there will be two, or even more rarely, three issues of equal importance to the resolution of the case. Each should be expressed in a single-sentence question.

Since many issues are resolved by a court in coming to a final disposition of a case, the casebook editor will reproduce the portion of the opinion containing the issue or issues most relevant to the area of law under scrutiny. A noted law professor gave this advice: "Close the book; look at the title on the cover." Chances are, if it is Property, you need not concern yourself with whether, for example, the federal government's treatment of the plaintiff's land really raises a federal question sufficient to support jurisdiction on this ground in federal court.

The same rule applies to chapter headings designating sub-areas within the subjects. They tip you off as to what the text is designed to teach. The cases are arranged in a casebook to show a progression or development of the law, so that the preceding cases may also help.

It is also most important to remember to *read the notes and questions* at the end of a case to determine what the editors wanted you to have gleaned from it.

HOLDING AND DECISION: This section should succinctly explain the rationale of the court in arriving at its decision. In capsulizing the "reasoning" of the court, it should always include an application of the general rule or rules of law to the specific facts of the case. Hidden justifications come to light in this entry: the reasons for the state of the law, the public policies, the biases and prejudices, those considerations that influence the justices' thinking and, ultimately, the outcome of the case. At the end, there should be a short indication of the disposition or procedural resolution of the case (e.g., "Decision of the trial court for Mr. Smith (P) reversed").

The foregoing format is designed to help you "digest" the reams of case material with which you will be faced in your law school career. Once mastered by practice, it will place at your fingertips the information the authors of your casebooks have sought to impart to you in case-by-case illustration and analysis.

B. Be as Economical as Possible in Briefing Cases

Once armed with a format that encourages succinctness, it is as important to be economical with regard to the time spent on the actual reading of the case as it is to be economical in the writing of the brief itself. This does not mean "skimming" a case. Rather, it means reading the case with an "eye" trained to recognize into which "section" of your brief a particular passage or line fits and having a system for quickly and precisely marking the case so that the passages fitting any one particular part of the brief can be easily identified and brought together in a concise and accurate manner when the brief is actually written.

It is of no use to simply repeat everything in the opinion of the court; record only enough information to trigger your recollection of what the court said. Nevertheless, an accurate statement of the "law of the case," i.e., the legal principle applied to the facts, is absolutely essential to class preparation and to learning the law under the case method.

To that end, it is important to develop a "shorthand" that you can use to make marginal notations. These notations will tell you at a glance in which section of the brief you will be placing that particular passage or portion of the opinion.

Some students prefer to underline all the salient portions of the opinion (with a pencil or colored underliner marker), making marginal notations as they go along. Others prefer the color-coded method of underlining, utilizing different colors of markers to underline the salient portions of the case, each separate color being used to represent a different section of the brief. For example, blue underlining could be used for passages relating to the rule of law, yellow for those relating to the issue, and green for those relating to the holding and decision, etc. While it has its advocates, the color-coded method can be confusing and time-consuming (all that time spent on changing colored markers). Furthermore, it can interfere with the continuity and concentration many students deem essential to the reading of a case for maximum comprehension. In the end, however, it is a matter of personal preference and style. Just remember, whatever method you use, underlining must be used sparingly or its value is lost.

If you take the marginal notation route, an efficient and easy method is to go along underlining the key portions of the case and placing in the margin alongside them the following "markers" to indicate where a particular passage or line "belongs" in the brief you will write:

N   (NATURE OF CASE)
RL   (RULE OF LAW)
I   (ISSUE)
HL   (HOLDING AND DECISION, relates to the RULE OF LAW behind the decision)
HR   (HOLDING AND DECISION, gives the RATIONALE or reasoning behind the decision)
HA   (HOLDING AND DECISION, APPLIES the general principle(s) of law to the facts of the case to arrive at the decision)

Remember that a particular passage may well contain information necessary to more than one part of your brief, in which case you simply note that in the margin. If you are using the color-coded underlining method instead of marginal notation, simply make asterisks or checks in the margin next to the passage in question in the colors that indicate the additional sections of the brief where it might be utilized.

The economy of utilizing "shorthand" in marking cases for briefing can be maintained in the actual brief writing process itself by utilizing "law student shorthand" within the brief. There are many commonly used words and phrases for which abbreviations can be substituted in your briefs (and in your class notes also). You can develop abbreviations that are personal to you and which will save you a lot of time. A reference list of briefing abbreviations can be found on page xii of this book.

C. Use Both the Briefing Process and the Brief as a Learning Tool

Now that you have a format and the tools for briefing cases efficiently, the most important thing is to make the time spent in briefing profitable to you and to make the most advantageous use of the briefs you create. Of course, the briefs are invaluable for classroom reference when you are called upon to explain or analyze a particular case. However, they are also useful in reviewing for exams. A quick glance at the fact summary should bring the case to mind, and a rereading of the rule of law should enable you to go over the underlying legal concept in your mind, how it was applied in that particular case, and how it might apply in other factual settings.

As to the value to be derived from engaging in the briefing process itself, there is an immediate benefit that arises from being forced to sift through the essential facts and reasoning from the court's opinion and to succinctly express them in your own words in your brief. The process ensures that you understand the case and the point that it illustrates, and that means you will be ready to absorb further analysis and information brought forth in class. It also ensures you will have something to say when called upon in class. The briefing process helps develop a mental agility for getting to the *gist* of a case and for identifying, expounding on, and applying the legal concepts and issues found there. The briefing process is the mental process on which you must rely in taking law school examinations; it is also the mental process upon which a lawyer relies in serving his clients and in making his living.

Abbreviations for Briefs

acceptance	acp	offer	O
affirmed	aff	offeree	OE
answer	ans	offeror	OR
assumption of risk	a/r	ordinance	ord
attorney	atty	pain and suffering	p/s
beyond a reasonable doubt	b/r/d	parol evidence	p/e
bona fide purchaser	BFP	plaintiff	P
breach of contract	br/k	prima facie	p/f
cause of action	c/a	probable cause	p/c
common law	c/l	proximate cause	px/c
Constitution	Con	real property	r/p
constitutional	con	reasonable doubt	r/d
contract	K	reasonable man	r/m
contributory negligence	c/n	rebuttable presumption	rb/p
cross	x	remanded	rem
cross-complaint	x/c	res ipsa loquitur	RIL
cross-examination	x/ex	respondeat superior	r/s
cruel and unusual punishment	c/u/p	Restatement	RS
defendant	D	reversed	rev
dismissed	dis	Rule Against Perpetuities	RAP
double jeopardy	d/j	search and seizure	s/s
due process	d/p	search warrant	s/w
equal protection	e/p	self-defense	s/d
equity	eq	specific performance	s/p
evidence	ev	statute	S
exclude	exc	statute of frauds	S/F
exclusionary rule	exc/r	statute of limitations	S/L
felony	f/n	summary judgment	s/j
freedom of speech	f/s	tenancy at will	t/w
good faith	g/f	tenancy in common	t/c
habeas corpus	h/c	tenant	t
hearsay	hr	third party	TP
husband	H	third party beneficiary	TPB
injunction	inj	transferred intent	TI
in loco parentis	ILP	unconscionable	uncon
inter vivos	I/v	unconstitutional	unconst
joint tenancy	j/t	undue influence	u/e
judgment	judgt	Uniform Commercial Code	UCC
jurisdiction	jur	unilateral	uni
last clear chance	LCC	vendee	VE
long-arm statute	LAS	vendor	VR
majority view	maj	versus	v
meeting of minds	MOM	void for vagueness	VFV
minority view	min	weight of authority	w/a
Miranda rule	Mir/r	weight of the evidence	w/e
Miranda warnings	Mir/w	wife	W
negligence	neg	with	w/
notice	ntc	within	w/i
nuisance	nus	without	w/o
obligation	ob	without prejudice	w/o/p
obscene	obs	wrongful death	wr/d

Table of Cases

CHAPTER 1

Economic and Legal Aspects of the Firm

Quick Reference Rules of Law

Community Counselling Service, Inc. v. Reilly

Employer (P) v. Employee (D)

317 F.2d 239 (4th Cir. 1963).

NATURE OF CASE: Appeal from denial of a request for an accounting.

FACT SUMMARY: After submitting a letter of resignation, but while still employed by Community Counselling Service, Inc. (CCS) (P), Reilly (D) solicited three potential CCS (P) clients for himself.

> ## 🏛 RULE OF LAW
> Prior to severing the employment relationship, an employee cannot solicit for himself future business which his employment requires him to solicit for his employer.

FACTS: Community Counselling Service, Inc. (CCS) (P), a professional fund-raising organization, employed Reilly (D) as a regional sales representative in its sales division. His job was to seek out likely prospects and to convince them of the desirability of using CCS's (P) services. After Reilly (D) submitted a formal letter of resignation, but while he was still employed by CCS (P), he reached agreements with three potential CCS (P) clients to personally conduct their fund-raising campaigns when his employment with CCS (P) ended. CCS (P) filed suit, seeking an accounting from Reilly (D) and alleging disloyal promotion of his conflicting interests prior to the termination of his employment. The trial court ruled in favor of Reilly (D), and CCS (P) appealed.

ISSUE: Prior to severing the employment relationship, can an employee solicit for himself future business which his employment requires him to solicit for his employer?

HOLDING AND DECISION: (Haynsworth, J.) No. Prior to severing the employment relationship, an employee cannot solicit for himself future business which his employment requires him to solicit for his employer. Reilly's (D) primary duty as an employee was to sell the services of CCS (P) and to promote its interests. When, during his employment, he solicited the business of the three parishes for himself, he was untrue to his employment obligation and disloyal to his employer. It is irrelevant that Reilly (D) did not actually begin those campaigns until after the effective date of his resignation from CCS (P). The substantial fees he collected were partly due to his disloyal conduct during his employment when he owed an unequivocal duty to solicit those contracts for his employer. Thus, CCS (P) was entitled to an accounting. Reversed and remanded.

▶ ANALYSIS

The court of appeals noted that difficulties arise when employment continues after an employee has made a determination to leave his employment, for then his interests and those of his employer may conflict. Further, if prospective customers undertake the opening of negotiations which an employee could not initiate, he must decline to participate in them. Above all, he should withhold no information from his employer which would be useful to the employer in the protection and promotion of its interests.

■━■

Quicknotes

ACCOUNTING The evaluation of assets for the purpose of assigning relative interests.

■━■

Hamburger v. Hamburger

Owner of company (P) v. Nephew and employee of company (D)

Mass. Super. Ct., 1995 WL 579679 (1995).

NATURE OF CASE: Action for violation of fiduciary duty.

FACT SUMMARY: While employed by Ace Wire and Burlap, Inc. (Ace), David (D) made financing and leasehold arrangements for a company he planned to start. Immediately upon his resignation, he began to solicit many of Ace's customers.

> ## 🏛 RULE OF LAW
> An employee is free to make logistical arrangements, such as financing and lease plans, for a new company, while he is still employed by another company. He is also entitled to use his general knowledge, experience, memory, and skill in establishing his new company.

FACTS: Ted (P) and Joseph were brothers and owned Ace Wire and Burlap, Inc. (Ace). They had a strained relationship. Joseph's son, David (D), worked at Ace throughout high school, college, and after graduation from college. David (D) built Ace from about 300 suppliers and $500,000 in sales to over 700 accounts and over $1,000,000 in sales. Ted (P) became resentful of David's (D) ascent to sales manager and general manager of the business. After inquiring with Ted (P) about his long-term future at Ace, David (D) believed that if his father Joseph passed away before his uncle Ted (P), then David (D) would be fired from Ace. One of Ace's four suppliers agreed to loan David (D) capital to start his own wire business, New England Baling Wire, Inc. (NEBW). David (D) subsequently deposited money in an account under the name of his new company and also leased space for the company. Shortly thereafter, David (D) resigned from Ace without proper notice, formally incorporated NEBW, and began working the following day at his new business. Upon his resignation, David (D) immediately began to actively solicit many of Ace's customers, resulting in several hundred of them becoming customers of NEBW. Ted (P) sued David (D) alleging that David (D) violated his fiduciary relationship to Ace and to Ted (P).

ISSUE: Were David's (D) arrangements for financing and a lease for NEBW and his solicitation of Ace's customers wrongful not only because such actions had commenced while David (D) was still an Ace employee but also because the customer solicitation was facilitated by David's (D) appropriation of Ace's customer lists and pricing information?

HOLDING AND DECISION: (Fremont-Smith, J.) No. David's (D) financing and lease arrangements for NEBW, conducted while he was still an Ace employee, were not illegal because an employee is free to make such logistical arrangements while still an employee. Furthermore, there is no evidence that David (D) solicited Ace customers in any significant way prior to his resignation from Ace. He was entitled to use his general knowledge, experience, memory, and skill in establishing his new company, including knowledge about Ace's customers and pricing with which he had been familiar as Ace's sales manager. Customer lists are not considered trade secrets if the information is readily available from published sources, such as business directories, as they were in this case. Ace should have used a non-competition agreement if it wished to restrict David's (D) post-employment activities. Judgment in favor of David (D).

▶ ANALYSIS

Fiduciary duty imposes a general obligation to act fairly.

■=■

Quicknotes

FIDUCIARY DUTY A legal obligation to act for the benefit of another, including subordinating one's personal interests to that of the other person.

■=■

Foley v. Interactive Data Corp.

Employee (P) v. Employer (D)

Cal. Sup. Ct., 47 Cal. 3d 654, 765 P.2d 373 (1988).

NATURE OF CASE: Appeal from demurrer without leave to amend in action for damages for wrongful termination.

FACT SUMMARY: After Foley (P) was given the choice of resigning or being fired, despite his exemplary employment record at Interactive Data Corp. (D), Foley (P) brought this action for wrongful discharge.

🏛 RULE OF LAW
The presumption that an employment relationship of indefinite duration is intended to be terminable at will may be overcome by evidence of contrary intent, either express or implied.

FACTS: During the almost seven years Foley (P) was employed by Interactive Data Corp. (D) (Interactive) he compiled an exemplary employment record. After Foley (P) told his former supervisor that Foley's (P) present supervisor was currently under investigation by the FBI for embezzlement from his former employer, Foley (P) was advised not to discuss "rumors." Later, Foley (P) was told that he was being replaced for "performance reasons" and that he could transfer to a position in another division. Although Foley (P) agreed to all changes stipulated by Interactive (D), he was nevertheless subsequently given the choice of resigning or being fired. Foley (P) filed this action for wrongful discharge, alleging that Interactive (D) maintained written "Termination Guidelines," setting forth express grounds for discharge and a mandatory seven-step pretermination procedure. The trial court sustained Interactive's (D) demurrer without leave to amend, and the court of appeal affirmed. Foley (P) appealed.

ISSUE: May the presumption that an employment relationship of indefinite duration is intended to be terminable at will be overcome by evidence of contrary intent, either express or implied?

HOLDING AND DECISION: (Lucas, C.J.) Yes. The presumption that an employment relationship of indefinite duration is intended to be terminable at will may be overcome by evidence of contrary intent, either express or implied. Foley (P) alleged repeated oral assurances of job security and an exemplary employment record, contributing to his reasonable expectation that he would not be discharged except for good cause. Further, an agreement to limit the grounds for termination can be inferred from the employee's reasonable reliance on the company's personnel manual or policies. Finally, Foley (P) signed an agreement whereby he promised not to compete with Interactive (D) for one year after termination. The noncompetition agreement may be probative evidence that the parties intended a continuing relationship, with limitations upon the employer's dismissal authority. On demurrer, these facts must be assumed to be true, and Foley (P) is entitled to his opportunity to prove those allegations. Regarding Foley's (P) cause of action for tortious breach of the implied covenant of good faith and fair dealing, it must first be noted that the distinction between tort and contract is well grounded in common law. Here, Foley (P) seeks to extend the tort remedy to a situation where the implied covenant is breached in an employment contract. Courts traditionally have awarded damages for breach of contract to compensate the aggrieved party rather than to punish the breaching party. Traditionally, breach of the implied duty has been remedied by contract damages determined by the nature of the breach and standard contract principles. An exception to this general rule has developed in the context of insurance contracts where, for a variety of policy reasons, courts have held that breach of the implied covenant will provide the basis for an action in tort. One of the bases for permitting this exception is that an insurer is a purveyor of a vital service that is quasi-public in nature. Another is that the relationship of insurer and insured is inherently unbalanced in favor of the insurer, which has the superior bargaining position. A thorough review of scholarship on this subject, however, does not lead to the conclusion that a special relationship analogous to that between insurer and insured should be deemed to exist in the usual employment relationship and should warrant recognition of a tort action for breach of the implied covenant. A breach in the employment context does not place the employee in the same economic dilemma that an insured faces when an insurer in bad faith refuses to pay a claim or to accept a settlement offer within policy limits. When an insurer takes such actions, the insured cannot turn to the marketplace to find another insurance company willing to pay for the loss already incurred. The wrongfully terminated employee, on the other hand, can (and must, in order to mitigate damages make reasonable efforts to seek alternative employment). Therefore, judicial extension of the proposed additional tort remedies for breaches of the implied covenant of good faith and fair dealing in employment contracts is rejected. Affirmed as to this issue.

▶ ANALYSIS

At trial, Foley (P) asserted three distinct theories: (1) a tort cause of action alleging a discharge in violation of public policy, (2) a contract cause of action for breach of an implied-in-fact promise to discharge for good cause only, and (3) a cause of action alleging a tortious breach of

Continued on next page.

the implied covenant of good faith and fair dealing. The California Supreme Court concluded that Foley (P) failed to show a violation of a fundamental public policy, that he had sufficiently alleged a breach of an implied-in-fact contract, and that the covenant of good faith and fair dealing may give rise to contract but not tort damages.

■━■

Quicknotes

DEMURRER The assertion that the opposing party's pleadings are insufficient and that the demurring party should not be made to answer.

IMPLIED COVENANT OF GOOD FAITH AND FAIR DEALING An implied warranty that the parties will deal honestly in the satisfaction of their obligations and without intent to defraud.

PUBLIC POLICY Policy administered by the state with respect to the health, safety and morals of its people in accordance with common notions of fairness and decency.

WRONGFUL TERMINATION Unlawful termination of an individual's employment.

■━■

Blackburn v. Witter

Investor (P) v. Investment advisor (D)

Cal. Dist. Ct. App., 201 Cal. App. 2d 518 (1962).

NATURE OF CASE: Appeal from judgment for plaintiff in an action to recover damages for fraud.

FACT SUMMARY: Blackburn (P) brought this action to recover financial losses suffered due to a fraudulent investment recommended by her financial adviser while he was employed by Walston (D) and by Witter (D).

🏛 RULE OF LAW
A principal who puts an agent in a position that enables the agent, while apparently acting within his authority, to commit a fraud upon third persons is subject to liability for the fraud.

FACTS: While employed by Walston & Company (D) and Dean Witter & Company (D), Long (D) had acted as investment adviser for Blackburn (P). Long (D) had been a trustworthy counselor for Blackburn (P) until he persuaded her to invest in a nonexistent company by selling him some of her stock in exchange for his personal note. Although Blackburn (P) questioned Long (D) about discrepancies in the transactions, he allayed her concerns by telling her that he was acting for his employers and that the investment was recommended by their research. When Long's (D) fraudulent action came to light, Blackburn (P) filed this action to recover her losses. The trial court entered judgment in favor of Blackburn (P), on the basis of ostensible authority, finding that Walston (D) and Witter (D) placed Long (D) in a position to defraud their customers. This appeal followed.

ISSUE: Is a principal who puts an agent in a position that enables the agent, while apparently acting within his authority, to commit a fraud upon third persons subject to liability for the fraud?

HOLDING AND DECISION: (Stone, J.) Yes. A principal who puts an agent in a position that enables the agent, while apparently acting within his authority, to commit a fraud upon third persons is subject to liability for the fraud. If there is liability here, it must rest on the theory of ostensible agency since Long (D) clearly had no authority as an employee of either Walston (D) or Witter (D) to borrow money for his personal use or to take money from a client and give his personal note rather than a security for it. Walston (D) and Witter (D) cannot accept the benefits of the sale of the stock by Long (D) as their agent while at the same time denying liability for the fraudulent misuses of the money obtained by the sale of the stock. Further, Walston (D) knew Long (D) was drinking to excess, gambling heavily, and encouraging customers to buy and sell stock merely for the purpose of promoting volume so that his commissions would be greater, yet it did nothing to advise his customers of this. Affirmed.

▶ ANALYSIS

The principle outlined in the above rule is expressed in § 261 of the Restatement of the Law of Agency. The comment to § 261 provides, "The principal is subject to liability under the rule although he is entirely innocent, although he has received no benefit from the transaction, and although the agent acts solely for his own purposes. Liability is based upon the fact that, from the point of view of the third person, the transaction seems regular on its face and the agent appears to be acting in the ordinary course of the business confided to him."

Quicknotes

FRAUD A false representation of facts with the intent that another will rely on the misrepresentation to his detriment.

Sennott v. Rodman & Renshaw

Investor (P) v. Securities brokerage house (D)

474 F.2d 32 (7th Cir. 1973).

NATURE OF CASE: Appeal of judgment of vicarious liability.

FACT SUMMARY: Sennott (P) alleged Rodman (D) was vicariously liable for the fraudulent actions of one of its partners and his son.

🏛 RULE OF LAW
A partnership will not be vicariously liable for the actions of its partner if the partner did not knowingly assist and participate in efforts to defraud and the fraud victim did not rely on the apparent authority of the defrauder.

FACTS: Rothbart (D), a securities dealer, had been an employee of Rodman & Renshaw (D), for a time, after 1958. Rothbart (D) was a member of the Chicago Board of Trade engaged as a trader for his own account in commodities. At the Board, he met Sennott (P) who was also an active trader. In January 1964, in response to Rothbart's (D) assertions that Rothbart's father, a partner at Rodman (D), thought a particular stock was good, Sennott (P) asked Rothbart (D) to purchase a limited number of shares for him. Rothbart (D) thus arranged for the purchase of Sennott's (P) order through Rodman (D). Seven trading accounts with Rodman were subsequently opened for Sennott (P). Sennott's (P) trading volume with Rodman (D) between 1964 and 1965 totaled more than $2,000,000, and about seventy percent of this trading was done through accounts opened by Rothbart (D) at the recommendation of Rothbart (D) or his father. In February 1964, Sennott (P) bought 2,000 shares of Skyline stock through Rodman (D) at Rothbart's (D) recommendation. Shortly there-after, Rothbart (D) approached Sennott (P) about purchasing additional shares of Skyline stock through stock options allegedly available to Rothbart (D) through his father's dealings with Skyline. Sennott (P) agreed to purchase Skyline stock through the option plan, and his order totaled $142,000. No such stock options ever existed, however. Instead of depositing the payments into an escrow account as promised, Rothbart (D) placed the money into his wife's personal checking account and used the funds to pay off his own losses. Sennott (P) was subsequently summoned to a meeting with the managing partner of Rodman (D). Prior to the meeting, Rothbart (D) and his father had told Sennott (P) that the managing partner wanted to meet with him to discuss the options but that the options were none of the managing partner's business. Sennott (P) was then advised not to cooperate with the managing partner and was reassured by Rothbart's (D) father that he would be getting the options. At a meeting later that day, the managing partner produced several checks, which Sennott (P) had given Rothbart (D) for the

options, and the manager questioned Sennott (P) as to why the checks were endorsed by Rothbart's (D) wife and deposited into her account. Sennott (P) said it was none of his business and refused to disclose the nature of his dealings with Rothbart (D). Sennott (P) later signed a letter of indemnity protecting Rodman (D) from liability for any failure on its part to investigate fully the signatures on the checks. Sennott (P) then became aware of Rothbart's (D) alleged fraudulent activities with another trader, his expulsion from the securities market, and his dismissal from Rodman (D). Sennott (P) still, however, refused to cooperate with the Business Conduct Committee's investigation of Rothbart (D). Sennott (P) finally spoke to Rothbart's (D) father about the nondelivery, but the father said there was nothing he could do. The district court found Rodman (D) vicariously liable for the losses caused to Sennott (P) by the fraudulent securities manipulations of Rothbart (D). Rodman (D) appealed.

ISSUE:
(1) Did Rothbart's (D) father knowingly assist and participate in the efforts of his son to defraud Sennott (P)?
(2) Did Sennott (P) rely on Rothbart's (D) apparent authority?

HOLDING AND DECISION: (Pell, J.)
(1) No. Rothbart's (D) father did not knowingly assist and participate in the fraud. It is clear that Rodman (D) had knowledge of all the securities transactions which Rothbart (D) solicited for his father prior to the inception of the fraudulent stock option scheme. Under general principles of agency, therefore, that knowledge is imputed from Rothbart's (D) father to the partnership, Rodman (D). The record, however, is silent as to how Rothbart's (D) father had knowledge of his son's stock option deception. The first contact Sennott (P) had with Rothbart's (D) father with regard to the options was the meeting with the managing partner after all of the payments for the stock had been made. There is no evidence that prior to this meeting Rothbart's (D) father did anything to induce Sennott (P) to subject himself to Rothbart's (D) fraud nor that the father had any knowledge of what was transpiring until after the fact. There is also no evidence that Sennott (P) considered Rothbart's (D) father to be in on any part of the transaction, other than that he had been the original offeree of the options. Sennott (P) was not to speak about the options deal to anyone except Rothbart (D), he believed that the options were coming directly from Skyline and not through Rodman (D), and he had testified that he had no knowledge that Rothbart's (D) father had conspired with Rothbart (D) to perpetuate the options fraud.

Continued on next page.

(2) No. Sennott (P) did not rely on Rothbart's (D) apparent authority. Furthermore, it is not evident that Sennott (P) relied on Rothbart's (D) apparent authority, and hence on Rodman (D), when Sennott (P) decided to purchase the Skyline options. The fraudulent representations never involved Rodman (D) because Rothbart (D) and Sennott (P) tried to prevent Rodman (D) from discovering the option transactions. Sennott (P) refused to cooperate with Rodman's (D) investigation into the endorsements of Sennott's (P) checks, and Sennott (P) made statements that he believed the entire transaction would have gone undetected by Rodman (D). Reversed and remanded.

▶ ANALYSIS

Apparent authority occurs when an agent is without actual authority but the principal manifests his consent directly to the third party who is dealing with the agent.

■■■■

Quicknotes

APPARENT AUTHORITY The authority granted to an agent to act on behalf of the principal in order to effectuate the principal's objective, which is not expressly granted but which is inferred from the principal's conduct.

ESCROW A written contract held by a third party until the conditions therein are satisfied, at which time it is delivered to the obligee.

INDEMNITY The duty of a party to compensate another for damages sustained.

■■■■

Partnerships

Quick Reference Rules of Law

Byker v. Mannes

Business co-owner (P) v. Business co-owner (D)

Mich. Sup. Ct., 641 N.W.2d 210 (2002).

NATURE OF CASE: Appeal from reversal of judgment finding a general partnership.

FACT SUMMARY: Byker (P) contended that his association with Mannes (D) to carry on as co-owners of a business for profit, regardless of their intent to form a partnership, established a general partnership between them.

🏛 RULE OF LAW
In ascertaining the existence of a partnership, the proper focus is on whether the parties intended to, and in fact did, "carry on as co-owners a business for profit" and not on whether the parties subjectively intended to form a partnership.

FACTS: Over several years, Byker (P) and Mannes (D) had pursued various business enterprises and had created several business entities. With regard to these, Byker (P) and Mannes (D) shared equally in commissions, financing fees, and termination costs. They also personally guaranteed loans from several financial institutions. Their relationship deteriorated after the creation of an unsuccessful entity that encountered serious financial difficulties. Eventually, Mannes (D) refused to make monetary contributions to address these difficulties. Byker (P), without Mannes's (D) knowledge, however, continued to make loan payments and incurred fees on behalf of the entity, and even took out several loans for the entity's benefit. The business ventures between the two ceased, and Byker (P) then approached Mannes (D) with regard to equalizing payments as a result of the losses incurred from the various entities. This was the first time that Mannes (D) received notice from Byker (P) concerning any outstanding payments and was absolutely dumbfounded by this request. After unsuccessfully seeking reimbursement from Mannes (D), Byker (P) filed suit for the recovery of the money on the basis that the parties had entered into a partnership. Specifically, he asserted that the obligations between them were not limited to their formal business relationships established by the individual partnerships and corporate entities, but that there was a "general" partnership underlying all their business affairs. Based on its reading of the state's Uniform Partnership Act, the trial court determined that the parties had created a general partnership. An intermediate appellate court reversed, and the state's highest court granted review.

ISSUE: In ascertaining the existence of a partnership, is the proper focus on whether the parties intended to, and in fact did, "carry on as co-owners a business for profit" and not on whether the parties subjectively intended to form a partnership?

HOLDING AND DECISION: (Markman, J.) Yes. In ascertaining the existence of a partnership, the proper focus is on whether the parties intended to, and in fact did, "carry on as co-owners a business for profit" and not on

whether the parties subjectively intended to form a partnership. The trial court had determined that parties must merely have intent to carry on a business for profit, not a subjective intent to create a partnership, for there to be a partnership. The appellate court concluded that the mutual intent of the parties to create a partnership is of prime importance in ascertaining whether a partnership exists. The issue is one of law and statutory interpretation. The Uniform Partnership Act (UPA) was amended by the National Conference of Commissioners, whereby the amended definition of a partnership stated that "the association of two or more persons to carry on as co-owners a business for profit forms a partnership, whether or not the persons intend to form a partnership." This amendment codified the universal judicial construction of the pertinent UPA section that a partnership is created by the association of persons whose intent is to carry on as co-owners a business for profit regardless of their subjective intention to be "partners." Although the state has not adopted this amendment, its statute is consistent with that amendment. In this state, partnership is statutorily defined as "an association of 2 or more persons . . . to carry on as co-owners a business for profit. . . ." That is, if the parties associate themselves to "carry on" as co-owners a business for profit, they will be deemed to have formed a partnership relationship regardless of their subjective intent to form such a legal relationship. The statutory language is devoid of any requirement that the individuals have the subjective intent to create a partnership. Thus, the statute does not require partners to be aware of their status as "partners" in order to have a legal partnership. A review of prior case law confirms this understanding. Remanded.

▶ ANALYSIS

In some jurisdictions, most prominently New York, an agreement to share losses appears indispensable to the existence of a partnership. However, in many jurisdictions, such an agreement to share losses also is indispensable to the existence of a joint venture. The UPA provides that, unless otherwise agreed, partners share partnership losses in the same proportion as they share partnership profits.

■═■

Quicknotes

GENERAL PARTNERSHIP A voluntary agreement entered into by two or more parties to engage in business whereby each of the parties is to share in any profits and losses therefrom equally and each is to participate equally in the management of the enterprise.

■═■

Hynansky v. Vietri

Business venturer (P) v. Business venturer (D)

Del. Ct. Ch., 2003 WL 21976031 (2003).

NATURE OF CASE: Cross-motions for summary judgment in action to obtain initial capital contribution and pro rata share of a business venture's losses.

FACT SUMMARY: Hynansky (P) contended that the agreement he and Vietri (D) entered into unambiguously created a partnership, and that, therefore, Hynansky (P) was entitled to summary judgment in his action to obtain Vietri's (D) initial capital contribution and pro rata share of the partnership losses.

🏛 **RULE OF LAW**

An unambiguous agreement to form a general partnership by itself does not establish as a matter of law that the parties to that agreement have formed a general partnership.

FACTS: Hynansky (P) and Vietri (D) entered into a business venture to purchase and develop land. They executed a document (the Agreement) that purportedly established JHV Associates (the Partnership). When the venture experienced substantial losses, Hynansky (P) brought suit to obtain Vietri's (D) initial capital contribution and pro rata share of the partnership losses, claiming that the two had established a general partnership. Although the Agreement expressly created a general partnership and was fully integrated, and although Vietri (D) signed other documents that referred to the entity as a partnership, Vietri (D) claimed that his understanding was that the business would be conducted under some kind of limited liability entity and that his contribution to the venture would not be cash but, instead, would be his experience and expertise. Hynansky (P) and Vietri (D) cross moved for summary judgment.

ISSUE: Does an unambiguous agreement to form a general partnership by itself establish as a matter of law that the parties to that agreement have formed a general partnership?

HOLDING AND DECISION: (Noble, V. Chan.) No. An unambiguous agreement to form a general partnership by itself does not establish as a matter of law that the parties to that agreement have formed a general partnership. A key issue is whether the parol evidence rule applies. This rule prevents the use of extrinsic evidence of an oral agreement to vary a fully integrated agreement that the parties have reduced to writing. In order for the parol evidence rule to apply, one must first present a fully integrated agreement. The factors to be assessed in ascertaining whether a contract is fully integrated include: "whether the writing was carefully and formally drafted, whether the writing addresses the questions that would naturally arise out of the subject matter, and whether it expresses the final intentions of the parties." Here, the Agreement was a formal document,

evidencing the typical degree of care associated with establishing a relatively straightforward partnership arrangement. Nothing in the Agreement suggested that it was establishing anything but a general partnership. In addition, there was no indication that the fulfillment of a condition precedent was necessary for Vietri (D) to become a partner. Indeed, the text of the Agreement demonstrated that it was the intention of the parties to execute an integrated agreement. The Agreement's integration clause and other text demonstrated that it was the intention of the parties to execute an integrated agreement. Accordingly, the Agreement is to be interpreted in light of the parol evidence rule and extrinsic evidence of an oral agreement contradicting the terms of the Agreement may not be considered, unless one of the exceptions to the application of the parol evidence rule is present. One of these exceptions is where fraud or misrepresentation as alleged. Another is where mutual mistake is alleged. Here, Vietri (D) cannot demonstrate that he relied upon any misrepresentation of Hynansky (P). Because he knew that he was signing as a "partner," any reliance would not have been reasonable. He also has failed to provide any basis for a conclusion that the agreement was the product of mutual mistake. For summary judgment purposes, Vietri (D) may have demonstrated that as he went to closing he did not anticipate that the business venture would be conducted as a general partnership. However, he signed the Agreement, after having had fair opportunity to review it and after having noted the word "Partner" in the Agreement. In addition, at about the same time, he signed loan closing documents as "Partner." To find mutual mistake in the face of this conduct would be to allow the disappointed party to assert mutual mistake whenever events did not unfold as anticipated. More specifically, there is no reason to believe that the mistake, if any, was mutual. Therefore, the argued exceptions to the parole evidence rule are inapplicable. This, however, does not end the inquiry. The creation of a partnership is a question of intent. To prove the existence of a partnership, one must show the intent to divide the profits of the venture. In demonstrating that a partnership exists, the acts, dealings, conduct, admissions and declarations of the purported partners, in addition to other direct evidence, may be utilized. Because the fundamental inquiry in determining whether the parties created a general partnership is the intention of those parties, evidence in the form of a partnership agreement is strong, but not conclusive proof of such an intention. Instead, the entire agreement and all the attendant circumstances must be taken into consideration in reaching a determination that a partnership has actually materialized. Thus, a judicial determination of whether a partnership was created must not be confined to an analysis solely of the terms of the agreement.

Continued on next page.

Because of the broad scope of the intensely factual review of all the attendant circumstances involved, it is inappropriate at this point to grant summary judgment. In addition, Vietri (D) has presented evidence which conflicts with the evidence presented by Hynansky (P). Because any conclusion as to the parties' intent to form a partnership would require the court to balance the conflicting evidence, summary judgment on the issue of whether JHV Associates is a general partnership is denied. Motion for summary judgment denied.

▶ ANALYSIS

When the controversy is between two alleged partners, as it was in this case, stricter proof of the intention to create a partnership is required. This stricter standard was, in part, the reason that the court in this particular case declined to grant summary judgment on the issue of whether a partnership had been formed, and left for trial the factual determinations necessary for ascertaining the parties' intent.

Quicknotes

EXTRINSIC EVIDENCE Evidence that is not contained within the text of a document or contract but which is derived from the parties' statements or the circumstances under which the agreement was made.

GENERAL PARTNERSHIP A voluntary agreement entered into by two or more parties to engage in business whereby each of the parties is to share in any profits and losses therefrom equally and each is to participate equally in the management of the enterprise.

PAROL EVIDENCE RULE Doctrine precluding parties to an agreement from introducing evidence of prior or contemporaneous agreements in order to repudiate or alter the terms of a written contract.

SUMMARY JUDGMENT Judgment rendered by a court in response to a motion by one of the parties, claiming that the lack of a question of material fact in respect to an issue warrants disposition of the issue without consideration by the jury.

Kovacik v. Reed

Investor (P) v. Superintendent (D)

Cal. Sup. Ct., 49 Cal. 2d 166, 315 P.2d 314 (1957).

NATURE OF CASE: Suit for an accounting and appeal to recover one-half the losses sustained by the parties' joint venture.

FACT SUMMARY: Kovacik (P) asked Reed (D) to be his superintendent on several remodeling jobs; when the jobs were unprofitable, Kovacik (P) asked Reed (D) to share equally in the losses and Reed (D) refused.

🏛 RULE OF LAW
In a joint venture in which one party contributes funds and the other labor, neither party is liable to the other for contribution for any loss sustained.

FACTS: Kovacik (P) asked Reed (D) to be his superintendent on several remodeling jobs. Kovacik (P) told Reed (D) that he had approximately $10,000 to invest and that if Reed (D) would superintend and estimate the jobs, he would share the profits with him on a 50-50 basis. They did not discuss the apportionment in the event of any losses. Reed (D) accepted the proposal and began working. Several months later Kovacik (P) informed Reed (D) that the venture lost money, and demanded Reed (D) contribute to the losses. Reed (D) refused and Kovacik (P) filed suit for an accounting and to recover from Reed (D) one-half the losses. The trial court concluded the parties were to "share equally all their joint venture profits and losses" and, following an accounting, awarded plaintiff $4,340, representing one-half the losses found to have been incurred by Kovacik (P). Reed (D) appealed.

ISSUE: In a joint venture, in which one party contributes funds and the other labor, is either party liable to the other for contribution for any loss sustained?

HOLDING AND DECISION: (Schauer J.) No. In a joint venture in which one party contributes funds and the other labor, neither party is liable to the other for contribution for any loss sustained. The general rule is that in the absence of an agreement to the contrary the law presumes partners and joint venturers intended to participate equally in profits and losses of the common enterprise, irrespective of the amounts contributed, each sharing in the loss in the same proportion as he would in the profits. However, that presumption applies only in cases in which each party had contributed capital or was to receive compensation to be paid to them before computation of the losses or profits. This was not such a case. Reversed.

▶ ANALYSIS

The court also stated that the party who contributed money or other capital to the venture was not entitled to recovery

from the party who contributed his labor. The rationale for the rule is that in the event of a loss, each party would lose his investment—one money and one labor. Another basis for the rule is that each party valued his contributions to be equal and thus have sustained equivalent losses.

■=■

Quicknotes

CONTRIBUTION The right of a person or party who has compensated a victim for his injury to seek reimbursement from others who are equally responsible for the injury in proportional amounts.

JOINT VENTURE Venture undertaken based on an express or implied agreement between the members, common purpose and interest, and an equal power of control.

■=■

Shamloo v. Ladd

Partner (P) v. Partner (D)

Cal. Ct. App., 2d Dist., 2003 WL 68054 (2003).

NATURE OF CASE: Appeal from judgment awarding compensation and denying interest on a loan as part of a partnership's dissolution.

FACT SUMMARY: Ladd (D) argued that as part of the dissolution of the Ginnytex Company, Inc. (Ginnytex) partnership he had with Shamloo (P), Shamloo (P) should not have been awarded $40,000 as "sweat equity," and Ladd (D) should have been awarded interest on a loan he had made to Ginnytex.

🏛 RULE OF LAW

(1) Upon dissolution of a partnership, and in the absence of an express agreement to the contrary, a partner is not entitled to remuneration for rendering services to the partnership other than profits.

(2) Upon dissolution of a partnership, and absent an express agreement to the contrary, a partner who has made a loan to the partnership in excess of his capital contribution is entitled to interest on the loan from the date the advance was made.

FACTS: Ladd (D) and Shamloo (P), who had planned to incorporate Ginnytex Company, Inc. (Ginnytex) but failed to do so, operated the business as a partnership pursuant to an oral partnership agreement. Ladd (D) contributed a $75,000 interest-free loan to the partnership, and Shamloo (P) contributed "sweat equity," i.e., his labor, knowledge, and expertise. Shamloo (P) devoted about half his time to running Ginnytex. Eventually, Shamloo (P) brought suit seeking the partnership's dissolution, claiming that Ladd (D) had breached his fiduciary duties and the partnership agreement by failing to pay Shamloo (P) his share of partnership assets; converting partnership assets; and failing to pay creditors. The trial court awarded Shamloo (P) over $40,000 (later reduced to around $27,000 due to lack of partnership assets) for his services, but denied Ladd (D) interest on his loan to Ginnytex. The intermediate appellate court granted review.

ISSUE:

(1) Upon dissolution of a partnership, and in the absence of an express agreement to the contrary, is a partner entitled to remuneration for rendering services to the partnership other than profits?

(2) Upon dissolution of a partnership, and absent an express agreement to the contrary, is a partner who has made a loan to the partnership in excess of his capital contribution entitled to interest on the loan from the date the advance was made?

HOLDING AND DECISION: (Turner, J.)

(1) No. Upon dissolution of a partnership, and in the absence of an express agreement to the contrary, a partner is not entitled to remuneration for rendering services to the partnership other than profits. Ginnytex was a de facto partnership governed by the state's Uniform Partnership Act. That Act provides that no partner is entitled to remuneration for acting in the partnership business, except that a surviving partner is entitled to reasonable compensation for his or her services in winding up partnership affairs. Case law has explained that the general rule applicable to dissolution in such cases is that in the absence of an express agreement to the contrary, the person advancing capital is entitled to its return before there is a division of income or profits. The general rule is that each partner is entitled to the amount of capital that he contributed. Absent an agreement, a partner is not entitled to compensation for rendering services for the partnership other than profits. Here, there was no substantial evidence that the parties contemplated, much less resolved, the issue of whether Shamloo (P) was to be compensated upon dissolution of the partnership for his contribution of services to the enterprise in lieu of actual capital compensation. Therefore, the general rules are applicable so that Shamloo (P) should not have been remunerated for his services. Reversed as to this issue.

(2) Yes. Upon dissolution of a partnership, and absent an express agreement to the contrary, a partner who has made a loan to the partnership in excess of his capital contribution is entitled to interest on the loan from the date the advance was made. Ladd (D) claimed he was entitled to interest on the $75,000 loan he made to Ginnytex. Statutory law provides that subject to any agreement between the parties, a partner who in aid of the partnership makes any payment or advance beyond the amount of the capital which he agreed to contribute "shall be paid interest from the date of the payment or advance." Shamloo (P) argues there was no agreement that interest would be paid on the loan. This argument is based on the rule that no interest is paid on capital contributions. However, a distinction must be made between interest paid on a loan and interest paid on a capital contribution. Interest on a capital contribution is not due unless the parties otherwise agree or until payment of the capital is due. Here, however, Ladd (D) is not asking for interest on his capital contribution. Because there was no evidence of an agreement to the contrary, the general rule applies, and Ladd (D) is entitled to interest on the loan he made to

Continued on next page.

Ginnytex from the date of the advance. Reversed on this issue.

 **ANALYSIS**

This case demonstrates the application of default rules in the absence of a partnership agreement. Typically, where a partnership agreement has been executed, the parties replace the default rules with negotiated terms, which, unless contrary to law, will be given effect by the courts.

■══■

Quicknotes

BREACH OF FIDUCIARY DUTY The failure of a fiduciary to observe the standard of care exercised by professionals of similar education and experience.

■══■

Meinhard v. Salmon

Co-adventurer (P) v. Adventurer (D)

N.Y. Ct. App., 164 N.E. 545 (1928).

NATURE OF CASE: Award of an interest in a lease.

FACT SUMMARY: Meinhard (P) and Salmon (D) were coadventurers in a lease on a hotel, but prior to the expiration of that lease, Salmon (D) alone, without Meinhard's (P) knowledge, agreed to lease the same and adjacent property.

🏛 RULE OF LAW
Joint adventurers owe to one another, while their enterprise continues, the duty of finest loyalty, a standard of behavior most sensitive.

FACTS: Salmon (D) leased from Gerry a New York hotel on Fifth Avenue for a period of 20 years. Later, Salmon (D) entered into a joint adventure with Meinhard (P), who contributed money while Salmon (D) was to manage the enterprise. Near the end of the lease, Gerry, who owned adjacent property as well as the hotel, desired to raze those buildings and construct one large building. Gerry, unable to find a new lessee to carry out his intentions, approached Salmon (D) with the idea when there was less than four months to run on his and Meinhard's (P) lease. The result was a 20-year lease to Midpoint Realty Company, wholly owned and controlled by Salmon (D). Meinhard (P) was never informed of the planned project or the negotiations for a new lease. After he learned of it, he made demand on Salmon (D) that the lease be held in trust as an asset of the venture, which was refused. This suit followed with an award to Meinhard (P) of a 25% interest in the lease, one-half of his value in the hotel lease proportionate to the new lease, while on appeal it was increased to 50%. Salmon (D) appealed, arguing that he breached no duty to Meinhard (P).

ISSUE: Do joint adventurers owe to one another, while their enterprise continues, the duty of finest loyalty?

HOLDING AND DECISION: (Cardozo, J.) Yes. Joint adventurers owe to one another, while their enterprise continues, the duty of finest loyalty, a standard of behavior most sensitive. Many forms of conduct permissible in a workday world for those acting at arm's length are forbidden to those bound by fiduciary ties. Here, Salmon (D) excluded his coadventurer from any chance to compete and from any chance to enjoy the opportunity for benefit that had come to him alone by virtue of his agency. It was likely that Salmon (D) thought that with the approaching end of the lease he owed no duty to Meinhard (P), but, here, the subject matter of the new lease was an extension and enlargement of the subject matter of the old one. As for Meinhard's (P) remedy, he should have been awarded one share less than half of the shares in Midpoint Realty Company. As modified, affirmed.

DISSENT: (Andrews, J.) This was not a general partnership. Rather, Meinhard (P) and Salmon (D) entered into a venture for a limited purpose. The interest terminated when the joint adventure expired. There was no intent to renew the joint adventure after its expiration.

▶ ANALYSIS

One of the most important aspects of the partnership relation is the broad fiduciary duty between partners. Judge Crane says, "The unique feature is their symmetry; each partner is, roughly speaking, both a principal and an agent, both a trustee and a beneficiary, for he has the property, authority and confidence of his co-partners, as they do of him. He shares their profits and losses, and is bound by their actions. Without this protection of fiduciary duties, each is at the others' mercy."

■=■

Quicknotes

FIDUCIARY DUTY A legal obligation to act for the benefit of another, including subordinating one's personal interests to that of the other person.

GENERAL PARTNERSHIP A voluntary agreement entered into by two or more parties to engage in business whereby each of the parties is to share in any profits and losses therefrom equally and each is to participate equally in the management of the enterprise.

■=■

Vigneau v. Storch Engineers

Partner (P) v. Partnership (D)

Conn. Super. Ct., 1995 WL 767984 (1995).

NATURE OF CASE: Action to recover the value of a partnership interest.

FACT SUMMARY: Vigneau (P), who during his tenure as a partner in Storch Engineers (Storch) (D) secretly participated in other business ventures, sued Storch (D) to recover the value of his partnership interest pursuant to the retirement provisions of the partnership agreement; Storch (D) counterclaimed for damages from Vigneau's (P) self-dealing.

🏛 **RULE OF LAW**

(1) A partner's violation of his fiduciary duty does not deprive him of his right to be paid for his vested partnership interest.

(2) A partnership is entitled to recover secret profits made by a partner during his breach of fiduciary duties owed to the partnership.

(3) A disloyal partner is entitled to compensation and profit-sharing benefits earned at the partnership during the period of disloyalty.

FACTS: Vigneau (P) was a partner in Storch Engineers (Storch) (D). The partnership agreement expressly provided that partners would devote their entire time and loyalty to the partnership. During his tenure at Storch (D), Vigneau (P) secretly entered into other business ventures and, on behalf of those other ventures, entered into business arrangements with Storch (D). He made a profit from some of his secret business interests and never revealed or accounted for these profits to Storch (D). He also engaged in deliberate, calculated deceptions to conceal his conflicts of interest. After Storch (D) discovered Vigneau's (P) self-dealing, Vigneau (P) resigned from Storch (D). The partnership agreement provided that the partnership would purchase a retired partner's interest. Accordingly, Vigneau (P) demanded that his 3.071% interest be purchased by Storch (D) at a stipulated value of about $168,000. Storch (D) refused to pay him on the grounds that Vigneau's (P) breach of the partnership agreement released its obligation to pay. Vigneau (P) then sued for payment under the agreement.

ISSUE:

(1) Does a partner's violation of his fiduciary duty deprive him of his right to be paid for his vested partnership interest?

(2) Is a partnership entitled to recover secret profits made by a partner during his breach of fiduciary duties owed to the partnership?

(3) Is a disloyal partner entitled to compensation and profit-sharing benefits earned at the partnership during the period of disloyalty?

HOLDING AND DECISION: (Satter, J.)

(1) No. A partner's violation of his fiduciary duty does not deprive him of his right to be paid for his vested partnership interest. A partner has a fiduciary duty to not engage in self-dealing, and a partner is obligated to his partners to render a true accounting and full information about everything that affects the partnership. Here, Vigneau (P) clearly violated his fiduciary duties to Storch (D). It is no excuse that Storch (P) may have benefited from such disloyalty (in the form of extra business from Vigneau's (P) undisclosed business ventures); the rule is prophylactic in nature, based on the need not only to compensate but to deter conduct that poses a risk of damage to the partnership. The real issue here is whether Vigneau's (P) violation of his fiduciary duty deprives him of his right to be paid for his vested partnership interest. Precedent from other jurisdictions indicates that disloyal partners are nonetheless entitled to their interest in partnership reserves and capital accounts, as well as income earned but not distributed. The theory underlying such precedent is that capital contributions are not a form of liquidated damages to which partners can resort in the event of a breach. Therefore, here, Vigneau (P) is entitled to the value of his vested partnership interest—around $168,000.

(2) Yes. A partnership is entitled to recover secret profits made by a partner during his breach of fiduciary duties owed to the partnership. Storch (D) counterclaimed for breach of fiduciary duty. The measure of damages for fiduciary breach includes profits earned as a result of the breach. Therefore, one consequence of Vigneau's (P) violation is that Storch (D) is entitled to recover from him any secret profit he realized from his disloyal business ventures, with interest.

(3) Yes. A disloyal partner is entitled to compensation and profit-sharing benefits earned at the partnership during the period of disloyalty. Storch (D) claimed damages for all compensation and profit-sharing paid to Vigneau (P) during the period of disloyalty, amounting to around $164,000. The Restatement of Agency, Second, at § 469 provides that "an agent is entitled to no compensation for conduct . . . which is a breach of his duty of loyalty; if such conduct constitutes a willful and deliberate breach of his contract of service, he is not entitled to compensation even for properly performed services for which no compensation is apportioned." However, other courts examining the reasoning behind the provisions of the Restatements of Agency and Trusts, have found that the basis for refusal of compensation to a trustee is not in the nature of a penalty, but because

Continued on next page.

payment is not due for services not properly performed. Thus, application of the rule that a failed fiduciary may be denied compensation or be required to return compensation paid is within the court's discretion. Here, because apart from his disloyalty, Vigneau (P) performed well for Storch (D) and contributed to its success, requiring him to repay his entire compensation would constitute undue enrichment to Storch (D) and amount to an unjust penalty. Therefore, the court denies such a result.

▶ *ANALYSIS*

The court in this case made additional rulings. First, it determined that Vigneau's (P) conduct breached the state's unfair trade practices act, under which punitive damages were available. Accordingly, the court awarded Storch (D) $50,000 in punitive damages. The court also awarded Storch (D) reasonable attorney's fees, which amounted to $110,000. Thus, at least in this case, the disloyal conduct was costly even though the breaching partner [Vigneau (P)] did not have to forego the value of his partnership interest or his earned compensation.

■━━■

Quicknotes

BREACH OF FIDUCIARY DUTY The failure of a fiduciary to observe the standard of care exercised by professionals of similar education and experience.

COUNTERCLAIM An independent cause of action brought by a defendant to a lawsuit in order to oppose or deduct from the plaintiff's claim.

FIDUCIARY DUTY A legal obligation to act for the benefit of another, including subordinating one's personal interests to that of the other person.

VESTED INTEREST A present right to property, although the right to the possession of such property may not be enjoyed until a future date.

■━━■

Covalt v. High

Partner (P) v. Partner (D)

N.M. Ct. App., 675 P.2d 999 (1983).

NATURE OF CASE: Appeal from award of damages in an action seeking an accounting as to former partnership property.

FACT SUMMARY: After High (D) refused to assent to Covalt's (P) demand that High (D) increase the monthly rent for real estate owned under their oral partnership agreement, Covalt (P) filed this suit seeking an accounting.

🏛 RULE OF LAW
Except where partners expressly agree to the contrary, all partners have equal rights in the management and conduct of the business of the partnership.

FACTS: Covalt (P) and High (D) orally agreed to the formation of a partnership which purchased real estate and constructed an office and warehouse building on the land. The partnership leased the building to CSI, a corporation of which Covalt (P) and High (D) were the only corporate officers and shareholders. After resigning his corporate position but remaining as a shareholder in the corporation and as a partner with High (D), Covalt (P) wrote to High (D), demanding that the monthly rent for the partnership real estate leased to CSI be increased. High (D) disagreed. Covalt (P) filed this action, seeking the sale of real property in lieu of partition, an accounting, and both actual and punitive damages. The trial court awarded damages to Covalt (P). High (D) appealed.

ISSUE: Except where partners expressly agree to the contrary, do all partners have equal rights in the management and conduct of the business of the partnership?

HOLDING AND DECISION: (Donnelly, J.) Yes. Except where partners expressly agree to the contrary, all partners have equal rights in the management and conduct of the business of the partnership. However, if the parties are evenly divided as to a business decision affecting the partnership and have made no written provision providing for such a contingency, then the power to exercise discretion on behalf of the partners is suspended so long as the division continues. One partner may not recover damages for the failure of the copartner to acquiesce in a demand to negotiate and execute an increase in the monthly rentals of partnership property. Thus, there was no breach of a fiduciary duty in this case. In the absence of a mutual agreement, or a written instrument detailing the rights of the parties, the remedy for such an impasse is dissolution of the partnership. Reversed.

▶ ANALYSIS

The problems which have arisen here emphasize the importance of formulating written partnership agreements detailing the rights and obligations of the partners. As specified in the Uniform Partnership Act, § 18(h), "any difference arising as to ordinary matters connected with the partnership business may be decided by a majority of the partners." According to Lindley, on the *Law of Partnership*, Chapter 14 at 354 (E.H. Scamell, 12th ed., 1962), "If the partners are equally divided, those who forbid a change must have their way."

Quicknotes

ACCOUNTING The evaluation of assets for the purpose of assigning relative interests.

FIDUCIARY DUTY A legal obligation to act for the benefit of another, including subordinating one's personal interests to that of the other person.

PARTITION The division of property held by co-owners granting each sole ownership of his or her share.

Starr v. Fordham

Law firm partner (P) v. Law firm partner (D)

Mass. Sup. Jud. Ct., 648 N.E.2d 1261 (1995).

NATURE OF CASE: Appeal from judgment for plaintiff and award of damages in action for breach of partnership agreement.

FACT SUMMARY: Starr's (P) law firm partners (D) claimed the trial court erred in: imposing on them the burden of proving the fairness of their profit distribution to Starr (P); concluding the business judgment rule precluded review of their profit distribution to Starr (P); and finding that they breached their fiduciary duties and the implied covenant of good faith and fair dealing in their allocation of firm profits to Starr (P).

 RULE OF LAW

(1) It is not erroneous to place the burden on a partnership of proving the fairness of its profit distribution to a departing partner.

(2) The business judgment rule does not preclude review of a partnership's profit distribution to a departing partner where the departing partner has proved that the remaining partners have engaged in self-dealing.

(3) Partners breach their fiduciary duties and the implied covenant of good faith and fair dealing when they make a profit distribution to a departing partner that is unfair.

FACTS: Starr (P) joined the law firm Fordham & Starrett (the Firm) as a partner after receiving assurances from a founding partner, Fordham (D), that client origination would not be a significant factor for allocating profits. Despite these assurances, the partnership vested the power to determine profit distributions in the founding partners, and although Starr (P) voiced his concern about these provisions, Starr (P) signed the agreement despite his concerns. The first year Starr (P) was with the Firm, profits were equally divided among the Firm's five partners. The next year, the Firm's financial fortunes improved significantly. At the end of that year, Starr (P) withdrew from the Firm. The remaining partners determined that his share of the Firm's profits for that year were 6.3% of the total profits, even though his billable hours and billable dollar amounts constituted around 16% of the total billable hour and billable dollar amounts for all of the partners as a group. Starr (P) brought suit to recover amounts he alleged he was entitled to under the partnership agreement, and for damages for the remaining founding partners' (D) breach of fiduciary duty. The trial court found that the founding partners had decided to exclude billable hour figures in order to justify the lowest possible payment to Starr (P), and that Fordham (D) had fabricated a list of negative factors that the founding partners

(D) had used in determining Starr's (P) share of the Firm's profits. The court thus determined that the founding partners (D) breached their fiduciary duties to Starr (P) as well as the implied covenant of good faith and fair dealing when they determined Starr's (P) share of the Firm's profits for the year. The court concluded that Starr (P) was entitled to 11% of the Firm's profits and awarded him around $75,000 in damages. The state's highest court granted review.

ISSUE:

(1) Is it erroneous to place the burden on a partnership of proving the fairness of its profit distribution to a departing partner?

(2) Does the business judgment rule preclude review of a partnership's profit distribution to a departing partner where the departing partner has proved that the remaining partners have engaged in self-dealing?

(3) Do partners breach their fiduciary duties and the implied covenant of good faith and fair dealing when they make a profit distribution to a departing partner that is unfair?

HOLDING AND DECISION: (Nolan, J.)

(1) No. It is not erroneous to place the burden on a partnership of proving the fairness of its profit distribution to a departing partner. Partners owe each other a fiduciary duty of the highest degree of good faith and fair dealing. When a partner has engaged in self-dealing, that partner has the burden to prove the fairness of his actions and to prove that his actions did not result in harm to the partnership. Here, the founding partners (D) engaged in self-dealing, because the percentage of the profits which they had assigned to Starr (P) directly impacted their own share of the profits. Therefore, the trial court did not err in imposing on the founding partners (D) the burden of proving that their distribution of the Firm's profits to Starr (P) was fair and reasonable. Affirmed as to this issue.

(2) No. The business judgment rule does not preclude review of a partnership's profit distribution to a departing partner where the departing partner has proved that the remaining partners have engaged in self-dealing. The test to be applied when one partner alleges that another partner has violated his duty of strict faith is whether the allegedly violating partner can demonstrate a legitimate business purpose for his action. Nevertheless, the business judgment rule does not apply if the plaintiff can demonstrate self-dealing on the part of the allegedly wrongdoing partner. Having concluded that the founding partners (D) had engaged in self-dealing, the trial court did not err in concluding that the business judgment rule was

Continued on next page.

inapplicable to the founding partners' (D) actions. Affirmed as to this issue.

(3) Yes. Partners breach their fiduciary duties and the implied covenant of good faith and fair dealing when they make a profit distribution to a departing partner that is unfair. An unfair determination of a partner's respective share of the partnership's earnings is a breach not only of one's fiduciary duty, but also of the implied covenant of good faith and fair dealing. Here, the judge had found that Starr's (P) billable hour and billable dollar amounts constituted around 16% of the total billable hour and billable dollar amounts for all of the partners in the group. In addition, the other partners received substantially greater shares of the profits. Therefore, in light of all the evidence, it was not clearly erroneous for the trial court to determine that distributing only 6.3% of the Firm's profits to Starr (P) constituted a breach of fiduciary duty and the implied covenant of good faith and fair dealing. Affirmed as to this issue.

▶ *ANALYSIS*

This case demonstrates a compromise position on the issue of fiduciary duty. At one extreme is the view that fiduciary duty is an immutable feature of partnership law, whereby judges are empowered to ensure that partners exercise the utmost honesty, candor, and good faith when dealing with the partnership and other partners. At the other extreme is the view that fiduciary duty is a fully mutable feature of partnership law that must yield to contractual agreements that limit or eliminate a role for ex post judicial intervention. This case takes the middle ground. Although the partnership agreement provided that the founding partners (D) could determine profit distributions, and although Starr (P) entered into that agreement knowingly and willingly, the court nevertheless imposed fiduciary duties on the founding partners (D) when they exercised their contractual rights.

■■■

Quicknotes

BREACH OF FIDUCIARY DUTY The failure of a fiduciary to observe the standard of care exercised by professionals of similar education and experience.

BUSINESS JUDGMENT RULE Doctrine relieving corporate directors and/or officers from liability for decisions honestly and rationally made in the corporation's best interests.

DUTY OF GOOD FAITH AND FAIR DEALING An implied duty in a contract that the parties will deal honestly in the satisfaction of their obligations and without intent to defraud.

FIDUCIARY DUTY A legal obligation to act for the benefit of another, including subordinating one's personal interests to that of the other person.

■■■

Ferguson v. Williams

Partners (D) v. Investor (P)

Tex. Ct. App., 670 S.W.2d 327 (1984).

NATURE OF CASE: Review of damage award for negligent joint venture management.

FACT SUMMARY: Williams (P) invested funds in a venture running short on cash; the venture failed, and Williams (P) lost his invested funds.

🏛 RULE OF LAW
Negligence in the management of the affairs of a general partnership or joint venture does not create any right of action against that partner by other members of the partnership.

FACTS: Ferguson (D) and Welborn (D), doing business as F & W Development Company, intended to purchase and move two apartment buildings to a new location, rehabilitate them, lease the apartments, and finally sell the properties. Short on cash, they contacted Williams (P) and offered to sell him a one-fourth interest for $15,000. Ferguson (D) secured land to which they would move the apartments, but could not get interim financing. When the partners needed more money, Williams (P) advanced another $5,000 to the project. Williams (P) remained active in the project, paying bills, securing loans, inspecting building sites, and regularly speaking with the other partners on the matter. However, the venture failed due to lack of construction financing, the buildings were dismantled, and the materials sold to pay debts. Williams (P) sued for negligence and won a judgment in the amount of his investment plus costs and damages; the trial court held that Williams (P) was a secured passive investor and thus able to recover his investment. Ferguson (D) and Welborn (D) then appealed.

ISSUE: Does negligence in the management of the affairs of a general partnership or joint venture create any right of action against that partner by other members of the partnership?

HOLDING AND DECISION: (Brady, J.) No. Negligence in the management of the affairs of a general partnership or joint venture does not create any right of action against that partner by other members of the partnership. In a partnership, when one partner holds assets of another and then converts them for his own use, an action will lie. However, poor management by one partner will not give rise to an action by the other partners. Each active partner is responsible to police the venture and to minimize poor decisions. Here, Williams (P) was an active member, not a passive investor. He participated throughout most of the venture, making financial decisions and the like. Therefore, he cannot claim that he was unaware of the decisions of the other partners and thus recover for negligent management. Reversed.

▶ ANALYSIS

In preparing to draft the Revised Uniform Partnership Act, many commentators argued that a duty of care between partners should not be imposed. They argued that partners had adequate incentive to monitor the use of their funds, and the courts should not be involved in the process. Case law is also virtually silent on any duty of care owed between partners.

■■■

Quicknotes

GENERAL PARTNERSHIP A voluntary agreement entered into by two or more parties to engage in business whereby each of the parties is to share in any profits and losses therefrom equally and each is to participate equally in the management of the enterprise.

JOINT VENTURE Venture undertaken based on an express or implied agreement between the members, common purpose and interest, and an equal power of control.

■■■

McCormick v. Brevig

Partner (P) v. Partner (D)

Mont. Sup. Ct., 322 Mont. 112, 96 P.3d 697 (2004).

NATURE OF CASE: Appeal from order of partnership dissolution and accounting.

FACT SUMMARY: Joan (P), a 50% owner of Brevig Land Live and Lumber (the Partnership), contended that the trial court erred, after it ordered dissolution of the Partnership, by failing to order liquidation of the Partnership assets, and instead granting Clark (D), the other 50% owner, the right to purchase Joan's (P) Partnership interest at a price determined by the court.

🏛 RULE OF LAW
(1) When a partnership is judicially dissolved, and when it is no longer reasonably practicable to carry on partnership business, it must be liquidated by a sale of partnership assets and distribution in cash of any surplus to the partners.
(2) When a partnership is judicially dissolved, a full accounting must be ordered.

FACTS: Joan (P) and Clark (D), who were siblings, were each 50% owners of Brevig Land Live and Lumber (the Partnership). Eventually, they began disagreeing on how to run the Partnership, and Joan (P) brought suit seeking an accounting, or, alternatively, dissolution and winding up of the Partnership. The trial court entered an order dissolving the Partnership, and ordering its business wound up, pending a hearing before a special master and a determination of the proper method for dissolution. A special master conducted a limited accounting, and the trial court, which concluded that the Partnership agreement was inapplicable, ordered judicial dissolution. Although the court recognized that statutorily any surplus assets after paying creditors had to be paid to the partners in cash in accordance with their distribution rights, it nonetheless ruled that it would be inequitable to order the liquidation of the Partnership assets to satisfy Joan's (P) interest in the Partnership. Therefore, in keeping with its desire to preserve the family farm, the court ordered Joan (P) to sell her interest in the Partnership to her brother following an appraisal and determination of the value of her share. With the assistance of a special master, and following an accounting of Partnership assets, the trial court fixed a price of $1,107,672 on Joan's (P) 50% interest in the Partnership. Joan (P) appealed, Clark (D) cross-appealed, and the state's highest court granted review.

ISSUE:
(1) When a partnership is judicially dissolved, and when it is no longer reasonably practicable to carry on partnership business, must it be liquidated by a sale of partnership assets and distribution in cash of any surplus to the partners?

(2) When a partnership is judicially dissolved, must a full accounting be ordered?

HOLDING AND DECISION: (Rice, J.)
(1) Yes. When a partnership is judicially dissolved, and when it is no longer reasonably practicable to carry on partnership business, it must be liquidated by a sale of partnership assets and distribution in cash of any surplus to the partners. This conclusion derives from the state's Uniform Partnership Act, which is based on the national Revised Uniform Partnership Act (RUPA). Under RUPA, a judicial dissolution of a partnership requires that partnership assets to be liquidated and the proceeds distributed between the partners proportionately. Using Black's Law Dictionary definition of "liquidate" to mean an assembling and mobilizing of assets, the trial court concluded that a judicially ordered buy-out of Joan's (P) interest was an acceptable alternative to liquidation of the partnership assets through a compelled sale. Here, the trial court did not have to resort to using a dictionary to define "liquidate." The statute itself provides a clear, plain meaning of the term "liquidation" which involves reducing the partnership assets to cash, paying creditors, and distributing to partners the value of their respective interest. By adopting a judicially created alternative, the trial court erred. Reversed and remanded as to this issue.

(2) Yes. When a partnership is judicially dissolved, a full accounting must be ordered. Here given the trial court's conclusion that the special master should determine the parties' respective capital contributions and Partnership assets, the special master performed a limited accounting. Every partner is generally entitled to have an accounting of the partnership's affairs, even in the absence of an express contract so providing. The purpose of an accounting is to determine the rights and liabilities of the partners, and to ascertain the value of the partners' interests in the partnership as of a particular date. When an action for an accounting is being used to wind up the partnership's affairs, the court is obligated to provide for a full accounting of the partnership assets and obligations and distribution of any remaining assets or liabilities to the partners in accordance with their interests in the partnership. Here, the special master performed a detailed accounting of those matters to which the court limited the scope of his investigation. By reviewing tax returns, and by holding several extensive meetings with the parties in which he heard oral arguments and received evidence, the special master performed a sufficient accounting given the issues that were presented for his review, and given that his testimony was subject to cross-examination. However,

Continued on next page.

because the Partnership's assets must be liquidated, on remand the trial court will have to conduct a full accounting of the Partnership's affairs. Once again, this requires a detailed accounting of all the Partnership's assets and liabilities, as well as distributions of assets and liabilities to the partners in accordance with their respective interests in the Partnership. The special master's reports may very well be of assistance in this process, but on their own are insufficient as a complete accounting for liquidation purposes. Remanded as to this issue.

▶ ANALYSIS

The court in this case declined Clark's (D) invitation to take a liberal reading of the state's UPA, based on cases that had held that there are judicially acceptable alternatives to compelled liquidation in a dissolution situation. The court distinguished those cases on the way the partners exited the entity. In the cases where an in-kind distribution was permitted, the partner had died, whereas, here, Joan (P) sought a court-ordered dissolution. Under RUPA, the death of a partner allows for the purchase of the dissociated partner's interest in the partnership, whereas, conversely, a court-ordered dissolution, as in this case, results in the dissolution and winding up of the partnership. The court in this case was adhering to these RUPA standards.

■═■

Quicknotes

DISSOLUTION Annulment or termination of a formal or legal bond, tie or contract.

LIQUIDATION The reduction to cash of all assets for distribution to creditors.

■═■

Drashner v. Sorenson

Partner (P) v. Partner (D)

S.D. Sup. Ct., 75 S.D. 247, 63 N.W.2d 255 (1954).

NATURE OF CASE: Appeal from order dissolving a partnership.

FACT SUMMARY: In Drashner's (P) action against Sorenson (D) seeking an accounting, dissolution, and winding up of the partnership in which Drashner (P) was associated with Sorenson (D), Sorenson (D) contended that Drashner (P) caused dissolution of the partnership wrongfully and was, therefore, not entitled to receive any partnership property upon dissolution.

RULE OF LAW
A partner causes dissolution of a partnership wrongfully by willfully and persistently committing a breach of the partnership agreement and by conducting himself in matters relating to partnership business so as to render impracticable the carrying on of the business in partnership with him.

FACTS: Drashner (P) and Sorenson (D) entered into a partnership with each other. They purchased a real estate and insurance agency with money advanced by Sorenson (D), a sum of $7,500. Differences arose among the partners when Drashner (P) drew out money for his own personal use from funds held in escrow by the partnership. Drashner (P) then requested that Sorenson (D) advance Drashner $100 personally. When Sorenson (D) refused, Drashner (P) brought an action to dissolve the partnership. At trial, Sorenson (D) contended that Drashner (P) caused the dissolution of the partnership wrongfully and was, therefore, not entitled to receive any partnership property upon dissolution. The court found that Drashner (P) had violated the terms of the partnership agreement in that he had demanded a larger share of the income of the partnership than he was entitled to receive under the terms of the agreement. The court also valued the partnership property at $4,498.90, and that this belonged to Sorenson (D) because he had not yet been reimbursed for his investment in the partnership. Drashner (P) appealed.

ISSUE: Does a partner cause dissolution of a partnership wrongfully by willfully and persistently committing a breach of the partnership agreement and by conducting himself in matters relating to the partnership business so as to render impracticable the carrying on of the business in partnership with him?

HOLDING AND DECISION: (Smith, J.) Yes. A partner causes dissolution of a partnership wrongfully by willfully and persistently committing a breach of the partnership agreement and by conducting himself in matters relating to partnership business so as to render impracticable

the carrying on of the business in partnership with him. Here, evidence presented tends to show that Drashner (P) neglected the business and spent too much time in a nearby bar during business hours. At a time when Drashner (P) had overdrawn his partner and was also indebted to Sorenson (D) for personal advances, he requested $100, and his request was refused. Drashner (P) then threatened to dissolve the partnership and brought this action to do just that. It cannot be said that the trial court acted unreasonably in concluding that the insistent and continuing demands of Drashner (P) and his attendant conduct rendered it reasonably impracticable to carry on the business in partnership with him. It follows, then, that Drashner (P) caused the dissolution wrongfully. Affirmed.

ANALYSIS

When partnership dissolution is caused by the wrongful act of a partner, the innocent partners have an election of remedies. They may wind up the partnership business and seek damages from the wrongful partner. They may continue the business in the same name, either by themselves or jointly with others. Finally, they may continue the business and seek damages.

■■■

Quicknotes

DISSOLUTION Annulment or termination of a formal or legal bond, tie or contract.

■■■

McCormick v. Brevig

Partner (P) v. Partner (D)

Mont. Sup. Ct., 322 Mont. 112, 96 P.3d 697 (2004).

NATURE OF CASE: Appeal from denial of petition requesting expulsion of a partner from a partnership.

FACT SUMMARY: Joan (P), a 50% owner of Brevig Land Live and Lumber (the Partnership), contended that the trial court erred in concluding that her brother Clark (D), the other 50% owner, had not dissociated from the Partnership and, therefore, should not be expelled as requested by Joan (P).

RULE OF LAW
A court does not clearly err in determining that a partner has not dissociated by withdrawing from a partnership where it finds that the partner continues to benefit the partnership, that other partners are partially at fault for the deterioration of the partnership, and that the partner has taken actions necessitated by the parties' inability to communicate about partnership business.

FACTS: Joan (P) and Clark (D), who were siblings, were each 50% owners of Brevig Land Live and Lumber (the Partnership). Eventually, they began disagreeing on how to run the Partnership, and Joan (P) brought suit seeking an accounting, or, alternatively, dissolution and winding up of the Partnership. As part of her suit, Joan (P) petitioned the court for an order expelling Clark (D) from the Partnership as a result of his allegedly wrongful conduct of converting Partnership assets to his own personal use. Following a non-jury trial, the trial court concluded that neither party had dissociated from the Partnership, and denied Joan's (P) request for an order of expulsion. On appeal, she claimed that the court failed to consider evidence that Clark (D) had denied the existence of the Partnership and had taken steps to transfer legal title of the Partnership's primary asset—the ranch—to his name, and had converted over $400,000 of Partnership funds to his own personal use. She further maintained that the court erred in denying her request for expulsion in light of the fact that Clark (D) had instigated criminal theft charges against her that later proved frivolous. The state's highest court granted review.

ISSUE: Does a court clearly err in determining that a partner has not dissociated by withdrawing from a partnership where it finds that the partner continues to benefit the partnership, that other partners are partially at fault for the deterioration of the partnership, and that the partner has taken actions necessitated by the parties' inability to communicate about partnership business?

HOLDING AND DECISION: (Rice, J.) No. A court does not clearly err in determining that a partner has not dissociated by withdrawing from a partnership where it finds that the partner continues to benefit the partnership, that other partners are partially at fault for the deterioration of the partnership, and that the partner has taken actions necessitated by the parties' inability to communicate about partnership business. Under the state's Uniform Partnership Act (UPA), one of the ten events causing a partner's dissociation is expulsion by judicial decree, made upon application by the partnership or another partner, where the partner has engaged in wrongful conduct that has adversely and materially affected the partnership business; has committed a material breach of the partnership agreement or a duty owed to partnership or other partners; or has engaged in conduct that makes it not reasonably practical to carry on business in the partnership. Here, the trial court found that Clark (D) had not given notice of his express will to withdraw as a partner, that the partnership agreement did not apply, and that Clark (D) had continued to work the ranch since his alleged dissociation, which Joan (P) and the Partnership had benefited from. The trial court further noted that, although Clark (D) had obtained loans in his individual name since he allegedly dissociated from the firm, this did not constitute dissociation since it was a necessary action in light of the parties' inability to communicate about ranch finances. Others of Joan's (P) allegations were not raised at trial, and so are disregarded on appeal. Additionally, Joan's (P) contention that Clark (D) dissociated from the Partnership by instigating criminal theft charges against her fails. The trial court weighed this evidence at trial and rejected it, finding that both parties were at least partially at fault for the deterioration of the Partnership. The court also noted that the act of taking alternate legal positions during the course of the dispute did not amount to dissociation. Because Joan (P) has not established that the trial court's findings were clearly erroneous, that court did not err in concluding that Clark (D) did not dissociate from the Partnership. Affirmed as to this issue.

ANALYSIS

The term "dissociation" was introduced by RUPA. Dissociation occurs upon the happening of any one of ten events specified in the statute. Examples of events leading to dissociation include bankruptcy of a partner and death, but dissociation does not include a judicially ordered dissolution of the partnership. Wrongful dissociation, as the name suggests—and the kind that Joan (P) was alleging had occurred in this case—must be "wrongful." Sometimes it is clear whether conduct has been "wrongful," e.g., a breach of the partnership agreement,

Continued on next page.

whereas sometimes what is wrongful is left to the court's judgment.

■━■

Quicknotes

DISSOLUTION Annulment or termination of a formal or legal bond, tie or contract.

■━■

Page v. Page

Partner (P) v. Partner (D)

Cal. Sup. Ct., 359 P.2d 41 (1961).

NATURE OF CASE: Action for a declaratory judgment.

FACT SUMMARY: Page (P) sought a declaratory judgment that the partnership he had with Page (D) was a partnership at will which he could dissolve.

🏛 RULE OF LAW
A partnership may be dissolved by the express will of any partner when no definite term or particular undertaking is specified.

FACTS: Page (P) and Page (D) were partners in a linen supply business they had entered into in 1949, pursuant to an oral agreement. Each had contributed about $43,000 to purchase linen, equipment, and land. It was not until 1958 that business began to show a profit. Page (P) was the sole owner of the corporation which was the partnership's major creditor, holding a $47,000 demand note, and in 1959, he sought a declaratory judgment that it was a partnership at will which he could terminate. The trial court found the partnership to be for a term, namely such reasonable time as was necessary to repay from profits the original outlays of Page (P) and Page (D) for equipment, etc.

ISSUE: Can a partnership be dissolved by the express will of any partner when no definite term or particular undertaking is specified?

HOLDING AND DECISION: (Traynor, J.) Yes. When no definite term or particular undertaking is specified, a partnership may be dissolved by the express will of any partner. Partners may impliedly agree to continue in business until certain debts are paid, until one or more partners recoup their investments, etc., but there is no evidence in this case to support any implied agreement of that nature. All partnerships are ordinarily entered into with the hope they will be profitable, but that alone does not make them all partnerships for a term and obligate the partners to continue in the partnerships until all of the losses over a period of many years have been recovered or original investments recouped. In holding that this is a partnership terminable at will, it is noted that the power to dissolve it must be exercised in good faith and not to "freeze out" a copartner. Reversed.

▌ ANALYSIS

An important aspect of this leading case is the introduction of the concept that a partner holds his dissolution power as a fiduciary. That means he owes his partners fraternal duties of good faith and fair dealing in exercising his dissolution rights.

■=■

Quicknotes

DECLARATORY JUDGMENT A judgment of the courts establishing the rights of the parties.

DISSOLUTION Annulment or termination of a formal or legal bond, tie or contract.

FIDUCIARY DUTY A legal obligation to act for the benefit of another, including subordinating one's personal interests to that of the other person.

PARTNERSHIP-AT-WILL A voluntary agreement entered into by two or more parties to engage in business and to share any attendant profits and losses, which lasts for an unspecified time period and may be terminated by either of the parties at any time and for any reason.

■=■

Bohatch v. Butler & Binion

Former associate (P) v. Law firm (D)

Texas Sup. Ct., 977 S.W.2d 543 (1998).

NATURE OF CASE: Review of appeals court award of lost earnings and reversal of punitive damages award.

FACT SUMMARY: Bohatch (P), an attorney who was expelled from a partnership because she had reported suspected overbilling by another partner, successfully sued for lost earnings and punitive damages, alleging breach of fiduciary duty. The court of appeals found that the law partnership had breached the partnership agreement, but had not breached any fiduciary duty.

> **RULE OF LAW**
> A law firm does not owe a partner a fiduciary duty not to expel her for reporting unethical conduct.

FACTS: Bohatch (P) was a partner in a law firm and she suspected that the managing partner was overbilling a client. Convinced that she was obliged by the Code of Professional Responsibility to report her concerns to the firm's management, she did so. The next day, Bohatch (P) was told that the client was dissatisfied with her work and she was never assigned any work for the client again. Bohatch (P) feared that she was not given the work in retaliation for reporting the alleged unethical conduct because she had not been aware of any criticism of her work prior to her contacting the firm's management with her suspicions. The client investigated the charges of overbilling and found that the firm's bills were reasonable. When Bohatch (P) was informed that no evidence of overbilling had been found, she was also advised to seek employment elsewhere since it would be difficult for her to continue with the law firm under the circumstances. Bohatch (P) sued Butler & Binion (D) for breach of the firm partnership agreement and breach of fiduciary duty. A jury found for her on both counts, but the court of appeals held that Butler & Binion's (D) only duty to Bohatch (P) was not to expel her in bad faith. "Bad faith" meant only that the partners could not expel another partner for self-gain. Finding no evidence that Bohatch (P) was expelled for self-gain, the appeals court concluded that Bohatch (P) could not recover for breach of fiduciary duty. Bohatch (P) appealed.

ISSUE: Does a law firm owe a partner a fiduciary duty not to expel her for reporting unethical conduct?

HOLDING AND DECISION: (Enoch, J.) No. A law firm does not owe a partner a duty not to expel her for reporting unethical conduct. A partner may be expelled for accusing another partner of overbilling without subjecting the partnership to tort damages. While Bohatch's (P) claim that she was expelled in an improper way is governed by the partnership agreement, her claim that she was expelled for an improper reason is not. A partnership exists solely because the partners chose to place personal confidence and trust in one another. The fiduciary duty that partners owe one another does not encompass a duty to remain partners or else answer in tort damages. A partnership is under no duty to retain a "whistleblowing" partner. Affirmed.

DISSENT: (Spector, J.) Partners violate their fiduciary duty to one another by punishing compliance with the Disciplinary Rules of Professional Conduct. The majority views the partnership relationship among lawyers as strictly business. The practice of law is a profession first, then a business. Moreover, it is a self-regulated profession subject to the Rules promulgated by the court. The fiduciary relationship among law partners should incorporate the rules of the profession promulgated by this Court. Although, as the majority stated, partners have a right not to continue a partnership with someone against their wills, partners may still be liable for damages directly resulting from terminating that relationship.

▶ **ANALYSIS**

The common law does not provide any remedy for termination of "at will" employment. Some courts have found a public policy exception for whistleblowers who report misconduct in a firm. The terms of the partnership agreement control the partner's legal rights. Some partnership agreements permit expulsions only for "cause."

■=■

Quicknotes

BAD FAITH Conduct that is intentionally misleading or deceptive.

BREACH OF CONTRACT Unlawful failure by a party to perform its obligations pursuant to contract.

FIDUCIARY DUTY A legal obligation to act for the benefit of another, including subordinating one's personal interests to that of the other person.

PARTNERSHIP A voluntary agreement entered into by two or more parties to engage in business and to share any attendant profits and losses.

■=■

Meehan v. Shaughnessy

Partner (P) v. Law firm (D)

Mass. Sup. Jud. Ct., 535 N.E.2d 1255 (1989).

NATURE OF CASE: Appeal from denial of relief on a counterclaim for breach of a partnership agreement in a partnership action.

FACT SUMMARY: After leaving Parker Coulter (D), the law firm in which they were partners, Meehan (P) and Boyle (P) filed this suit to recover amounts owed to them under the partnership agreement. Parker Coulter (D) counterclaimed, alleging violation of fiduciary duties and breach of the partnership agreement.

🏛 RULE OF LAW
Partners owe each other a fiduciary duty of the utmost good faith and loyalty.

FACTS: Meehan (P) and Boyle (P), partners in the law firm of Parker Coulter (D), planned to start their own firm. In the meantime, they continued to work full schedules and to generally maintain their usual standard of performance at Parker Coulter (D). After giving notice, Meehan (P) and Boyle (P) spoke with a majority of referring attorneys and obtained authorizations from a majority of clients whose cases they planned to take with them. The partnership agreement provided that a partner could remove a case upon payment of a "fair charge," subject to the right of the client to stay with the firm. Boyle (P) did not provide Parker Coulter (D) with the list of those cases until two weeks after it had been requested. Meehan (P) brought this action after Parker Coulter (D) refused to return the capital contributions made by Meehan (P) and Boyle (P) or to return their share of the dissolved firm's profits. Parker Coulter (D) counterclaimed that Meehan (P) and Boyle (P) violated their fiduciary duties and breached the partnership agreement when they unfairly acquired consent from client and attorneys to remove their cases from Parker Coulter (D). The trial court rejected all of Parker Coulter's (D) claims for relief. Parker Coulter (D) appealed.

ISSUE: Do partners owe each other a fiduciary duty of the utmost good faith and loyalty?

HOLDING AND DECISION: (Hennessey, C.J.) Yes. Partners owe each other a fiduciary duty of the utmost good faith and loyalty. While affirmatively denying any plans to leave the partnership, Meehan (P) and Boyle (P) made secret preparations to obtain removal authorizations from clients. Boyle (P) also delayed providing his partners with a list of clients he intended to solicit until he had obtained authorization from a majority of those clients. Finally, the content of the letter sent to the clients was unfairly prejudicial to Parker Coulter (D) because it did not clearly present to the clients the choice they had between remaining at Parker Coulter (D) or moving to the new firm. By engaging in these preemptive tactics, Meehan (P) and Boyle (P) violated the duty of utmost good faith and loyalty that they owed their partners. Thus, they have the burden of proving that the clients would have consented to removal in the absence of any breach of duty. The trial judge erred in finding that they did not unfairly acquire consent from clients and referring attorneys to withdraw cases but correctly found that they did not breach their duty by improperly handling cases for their own benefit or by secretly competing with the partnership. Reversed in part and remanded.

▶ ANALYSIS

The ABA Committee on Ethics and Professional Responsibility, in Informal Opinion 1457 (April 29, 1980), set forth ethical standards for attorneys announcing a change in professional association. The standard provides that any notice must explain to a client that he or she has the right to decide who will continue the representation. Further, the court noted that a partner has an obligation to render on the demand of any partner true and full information of all things affecting the partnership. Here, Meehan (P) and Boyle (P) continued to use their position of trust and confidence to the disadvantage of Parker Coulter (D).

■══■

Quicknotes

FIDUCIARY DUTY A legal obligation to act for the benefit of another, including subordinating one's personal interests to that of the other person.

■══■

P.A. Properties, Inc. v. B.S. Moss' Criterion Center Corp.

Contracting party (P) v. Joint venturer with other contracting party (D)

2004 WL 2979984 (S.D.N.Y. 2004).

NATURE OF CASE: Breach of contract action.

FACT SUMMARY: P.A. Properties, Inc. (PAP) (P) claimed that B.S. Moss' Criterion Center Corp. (Moss) (D) was liable on a consulting agreement that PAP (P) had entered into with United Artists Theatre Circuit, Inc. (UA), by virtue of UA having been the manager of a joint venture with Moss (D), and on the theory that the agreement was the joint venture's obligation.

🏛 RULE OF LAW
A general partnership joint venturer, who is not named in an agreement between a co-venturer and a third party, is liable on the agreement to the extent that the agreement was for the benefit of the joint venture.

FACTS: United Artists Theatre Circuit, Inc. (UA) entered into a joint venture with B.S. Moss' Criterion Center Corp. (Moss) (D) and other entities for the purpose of managing, operating, leasing, and otherwise "dealing with" movie theatres of the joint venturers. UA was designated as the Managing Venturer, with complete authority for the day-to-day business of the theatres, including management and financial matters. The joint venture agreement provided that the members were liable for all debts, liabilities and obligations of the joint venture in proportion to their allocable shares. The joint venture was a "joint venture general partnership under and pursuant to the . . . [Uniform Partnership] Act." Four years after the joint venture was formed, UA entered into a consulting agreement with P.A. Properties, Inc. (PAP) (P) to discover possible overcharges on a theatre lease. The only named entities on the consulting agreement were UA and PAP (P); the joint venture was not mentioned. Six years after that, PAP (P) brought suit against UA in state court for breach of contract and to get paid for its services. Two years after that, UA filed for bankruptcy protection, and PAP (P) received a fraction of the amount owed to it. PAP (P) then brought suit in federal district court against Moss (D) on the theory that UA's consulting agreement with PAP (P) was an obligation of the joint venture, so that Moss (D), the remaining solvent joint venturer, was liable thereon.

ISSUE: Is a general partnership joint venturer, who is not named in an agreement between a co-venturer and a third party, liable on the agreement to the extent that the agreement was for the benefit of the joint venture?

HOLDING AND DECISION: (Swain, J.) Yes. A general partnership joint venturer, who is not named in an agreement between a co-venturer and a third party, is liable on the agreement to the extent that the agreement was for the benefit of the joint venture. The applicable state Uniform

Partnership Act (UPA) provides that every partner is an agent of the partnership for the purpose of its business, and the act of every partner; partners are jointly liable for all partnership debts and obligations. The general law of agency applies, and provides that a principal may be liable to a third party on a transaction conducted by its agent if the agent was actually or apparently authorized to enter into the transaction, or the agent had authority based on the agency relation. A general agent for an undisclosed principal authorized to conduct transactions subjects his principal to liability for acts done on his account, if usual or necessary in such transactions, although forbidden by the principal to do them (inherent agency power). In such a situation, the liability of the undisclosed principal turns on the agent's intent. An agent with inherent agency power is a "general agent." A general agent thus has the power to bind an undisclosed principal as to matters within the general scope of the agency. Therefore, although Moss (D) is correct as a matter of contract law that it is not a party to the consulting agreement between PAP (P) and UA, it may nonetheless be liable under general agency principles. That is because the consulting agreement was an obligation of the joint venture (and thus of its component partners) by virtue of the doctrine of inherent liability of an undisclosed principal for acts within the scope of a general agency, at least with respect to PAP's (P) claim relating to periods during which the theatre for which PAP's (P) services were engaged was operated by and for the benefit of the joint venture. The facts show that UA intended to benefit the joint venture by virtue of the arrangement, the goal being to reduce the joint venture's lease payments. Even if, as Moss (D) contends, UA was prohibited by the joint venture agreement from unilaterally retaining or replacing independent accountants to review and audit the books and records of the joint venture and its theatres, the doctrine of inherent authority would still apply, because this doctrine is operative as to matters within the broad scope of a general agency even if, as between principal and agent, the particular action has been forbidden. Motion for summary judgment denied.

▶ ANALYSIS

Here, Moss (D) would not be liable under the consulting agreement on the agency law principle of apparent authority, because no conduct of Moss (D) or of UA or of the joint venture led PAP (P) to believe that UA was authorized to bind the joint venture. That is, the principal here did not give the appearance of authority in the agent to conduct the challenged transaction.

■━■

Continued on next page.

Quicknotes

BANKRUPTCY A legal proceeding whereby a debtor, who is unable to pay his debts as they become due, is relieved of his obligation to pay his creditors either by liquidation and distribution of his remaining assets or through reorganization and payment from future income.

BREACH OF CONTRACT Unlawful failure by a party to perform its obligations pursuant to contract.

GENERAL PARTNERSHIP A voluntary agreement entered into by two or more parties to engage in business whereby each of the parties is to share in any profits and losses therefrom equally and each is to participate equally in the management of the enterprise.

JOINT VENTURE Venture undertaken based on an express or implied agreement between the members, common purpose and interest, and an equal power of control.

■━■

Haymond v. Lundy

Partner of law firm (P) v. Partner of law firm (D)

2002 WL 1972101 (E.D. Pa. 2002).

NATURE OF CASE: Review of Receiver's treatment of partner's referral fee payment.

FACT SUMMARY: Haymond (P) objected to how the Receiver for his dissolved partnership chose to treat a referral fee paid by Lundy (D).

▥ RULE OF LAW
Absent evidence contrary to the plain language of a partnership agreement, the plain language will be relied upon in determining whether a partner violated the agreement when he dispersed material assets of the partnership.

FACTS: Post dissolution of their firm, Haymond & Lundy, partners Haymond (P) and Lundy (D) could not agree on the payment of a referral fee agreed to and paid by Lundy (D) on behalf of the firm. Haymond (P) objected to the Receiver's proposed treatment of the referral fee as a $150,000 partnership expense paid in the form of a referral fee to Fitzpatrick. The referral fee came about when a client retained Fitzpatrick to represent him in a personal injury action. Fitzpatrick filed the client's complaint, and then the client retained Lundy (D). Lundy (D) promised Fitzpatrick reimbursement for his costs and a referral fee if Lundy (D) were successful. Once the underlying case had been settled, Lundy (D) agreed with Fitzpatrick to pay him a referral fee of $150,000 out of the attorney's fees portion of the settlement. Haymond & Lundy had a partnership agreement that stated that a partner may bind the partnership to a disposal of any material asset over $10,000, if he gets the permission of a majority of the partners.

ISSUE: Did Lundy's (D) commitment to pay the referral fee exceed his authority to bind Hammond & Lundy under the Partnership Agreement?

HOLDING AND DECISION: (Shapiro, J.) Yes. Lundy's (D) commitment to pay the referral fee exceeded his authority to bind Hammond & Lundy under the Partnership Agreement. In the absence of evidence establishing the partnership's customary practice respecting referral fees, it is inappropriate to disregard the plain language of the contract regarding attorney's fees from settlements which are considered material assets of the firm, by holding that the referral fee portion of a settlement is an exception. Lundy (D) made a decision to bind Hammond & Lundy to pay Fitzpatrick when the underlying matter settled. This agreement disposed of a material asset of the partnership exceeding $10,000 and required partners' consent before making the agreement. Only $10,000, therefore, of the $150,000 referral fee should be attributable to Hammond & Lundy. Reversed.

▶ *ANALYSIS*

The court took a strict constructionist approach in evaluating the Partnership Agreement to resolve the issue in this case.

■━■

Dow v. Jones

Law firm client (P) v. Law firm partnership (D)

311 F. Supp. 2d 461 (D. Md. 2004).

NATURE OF CASE: Motion for summary judgment in legal malpractice action.

FACT SUMMARY: Dow (P), who had been convicted of criminal charges, asserted that his attorney, Jones (D), and Jones's (D) firm at the time, Seals Jones Wilson Garrow & Evans (SJWGE) (D)—a Limited Liability Partnership (LLP)—were liable to Dow (P) for legal malpractice, and SJWGE (D) moved for summary judgment, arguing that only Jones (D) could be held liable.

> 🏛 **RULE OF LAW**
> Summary judgment must not be granted to a registered limited liability partnership on the issue of its liability for the acts of an individual where the plaintiff has raised genuine issues of material fact as to whether the individual was a partner, had apparent authority to act on behalf of the partnership, and the partnership, although dissolved, had not wound up its affairs.

FACTS: Sexual abuse charges were brought against Dow (P), who retained attorney Jones (D) to defend him. Jones (D) was a partner with Seals Jones Wilson Garrow & Evans (SJWGE) (D), a Limited Liability Partnership (LLP) law firm. The retainer agreement Dow (P) had with Jones (D) was on SJWGE (D) letterhead, but the agreement did not mention that Dow (P) was retaining the firm. It only indicated Dow (P) was retaining Jones (D). Dow (P) was also defended by a Public Defender. Jones (D) sent a letter to the Assistant State's Attorney, which was also on SJWGE (D) letterhead, stating that he represented Dow (P). Approximately one month before Dow's (P) trial, the firm's status as an LLP was terminated. Dow (P) asserted he was not aware of the firm's dissolution, or that Jones (D) might not have the authority to act for the firm, or that Jones (D) might not even be a partner of the firm. A jury found Dow (P) guilty, but on a petition for post-conviction relief, on the basis of ineffective assistance of counsel, his conviction was vacated and a new trial was granted. Afterward, Dow (P) filed legal malpractice claims against Jones (D), SJWGE (D), and the firm's four other partners. Summary judgment was entered as to the other partners, but not as to Jones (D) or as to the firm.

ISSUE: Must summary judgment be granted to a registered limited liability partnership on the issue of its liability for the acts of an individual where the plaintiff has raised genuine issues of material fact as to whether the individual was a partner, had apparent authority to act on behalf of the partnership, and the partnership, although dissolved, had not wound up its affairs?

HOLDING AND DECISION: (Blake, J.) No. Summary judgment must not be granted to a registered limited liability partnership on the issue of its liability for the acts of an individual where the plaintiff has raised genuine issues of material fact as to whether the individual was a partner, had apparent authority to act on behalf of the partnership, and the partnership, although dissolved, had not wound up its affairs. SJWGE (D) was formed under the Registered Limited Liability Partnership Amendment Act (RLLPAA), which limits the liability of individual partners in registered LLPs. The RLLPAA provides that a partner in a registered LLP is not individually liable for debts and obligations of the partnership arising from errors, omissions, negligence, incompetence, or malfeasance committed in the course of the partnership business by a second partner or a representative of the partnership not working under the supervision or direction of the first partner at the time the errors, omissions, negligence, incompetence, or malfeasance occurred. An exception is where a partner was directly involved in or had written notice or knowledge of the specific conduct at issue. In addition, these provisions do not limit the liability of partnership assets for partnership debts and obligations. Because general agency and partnership law principles apply to LLPs, whether an attorney-client relationship was formed by Dow (D) with the partnership is based on a subjective standard, i.e., Dow's (P) subjective belief that such a relationship had been formed. In addition, because general principles of partnership law are applicable, every partner of an LLP has the power to bind the partnership as an agent. Thus, a partner who is acting within the actual or apparent authority of the partnership can bind the partnership to an agreement with a third party. Apparent authority is created when a principal represents that a party is his agent, and a third party actually and reasonably relies on this representation. Here, Dow (P) has raised genuine issues of material fact as to whether Jones (D) had apparent authority to enter into a retainer agreement on behalf of SJWGE (D) as a partner of the firm. SJWGE (D) listed Jones (D) as a partner in its application for a limited liability partnership and included his last name and the designation of "partnership" in the firm's operating name. By holding Jones (D) out publicly as a partner in SJWGE (D), the firm may have vested Jones (D) with apparent authority to perform those acts customarily performed by law firm partners. Jones (D), by entering into the retainer agreement with Dow (P), was "apparently carrying on in the usual way the business of the partnership." Even if Jones (D) was not a partner of the firm, a person who represents himself or is represented by others as a partner in an existing partnership "is an agent of the persons consenting

Continued on next page.

to such representation to bind them to the same extent and in the same manner as though he were a partner in fact, with respect to persons who rely upon the representation." Here, too, there were public indicia that Jones (D) was a partner in SJWGE (D), and that SJWGE (D) was a partnership. Thus, Dow (P) has raised genuine issues of material fact as to whether the firm made public representations that Jones (D) was a partner in the firm. In cases involving similar public indicia of partnership and no contrary representations, courts have relied on the doctrine of partnership by estoppel to impose liability on entities that appeared to be operating as law firm partnerships. Moreover, SJWGE's (D) argument that it cannot be held liable for Jones's (D) alleged malpractice, because the firm had dissolved prior to Dow's (P) trial, is unavailing. Again, because principles of partnership law apply to an LLP, an LLP does not terminate immediately upon dissolution, but, instead, continues until the winding up of the partnership affairs is complete. In some cases, it may be appropriate to impose liability for legal malpractice claims arising after dissolution because the conduct at issue is appropriate for winding up the law partnership. Thus, a former partner's malpractice that occurs after dissolution but in a case that was pending prior to dissolution still can bind a dissolved law firm partnership, under the theory that the former partner's conduct is appropriate for winding up partnership affairs. Or, such conduct can be binding under the agency theory that the client [here, Dow (P)] had dealt with the partnership and had no notice of its dissolution. Motion for summary judgment is denied.

▶ ANALYSIS

In this case, the court also rejected SJWGE's (D) argument that the only purpose served by suing the firm—which had no remaining assets—would be to pierce the former partnership's veil and pursue claims against the individual partners. The court noted that under the RLLPAA, the firm was required to maintain liability insurance of at least $100,000 to cover the kinds of errors and omissions for which the liability of the individual partners was limited under the act. Accordingly, the court held that Dow (P) was entitled to pursue a judgment against the firm and then pursue any available relief under the firm's insurance policy. Thus, while the RLLPAA changes the balance of risk between innocent partners and third parties, it does not leave third parties without recourse where the partnership or an insolvent liable partner is without assets.

■=■

Quicknotes

APPARENT AUTHORITY The authority granted to an agent to act on behalf of the principal in order to effectuate the principal's objective, which is not expressly granted but which is inferred from the principal's conduct.

DISSOLUTION Annulment or termination of a formal or legal bond, tie or contract.

ESTOPPEL An equitable doctrine precluding a party from asserting a right to the detriment of another whom justifiably relied on the conduct.

LEGAL MALPRACTICE Conduct on the part of an attorney falling below that demonstrated by other attorneys of ordinary skill and competency under the circumstances, resulting in damages.

LIMITED LIABILITY An advantage of doing business in the corporate form by safeguarding shareholders from liability for the debts or obligations of the corporation.

SUMMARY JUDGMENT Judgment rendered by a court in response to a motion by one of the parties, claiming that the lack of a question of material fact in respect to an issue warrants disposition of the issue without consideration by the jury.

■=■

The Corporate Form and Specialized Roles

Quick Reference Rules of Law

Hoschett v. TSI International Software, Ltd.

Stockholder (P) v. Corporation (D)

Del. Ct. Ch., 683 A.2d 43 (1996).

NATURE OF CASE: Cross-motions for summary judgment in an action to force an annual stockholder meeting and publication of stock list.

FACT SUMMARY: Hoschett (P), a stockholder in TSI (D), moved to force TSI (D) to hold an annual meeting of its stockholders so that directors could be elected.

> 🏛 **RULE OF LAW**
> A consent action, which duly designates directors of a company, does not satisfy the corporation's obligation to hold an annual meeting at which the company's directors are to be elected, in conformity with the certificate of incorporation.

FACTS: Hoschett (P) holds shares of common stock in TSI (D). TSI (D) is a privately held corporation. Pursuant to TSI's certificate of incorporation, holders of TSI's (D) stock, vote together on all matters, including the election of directors. TSI (D) has never had an annual meeting for the election of its directors. Hoschett (P) sought an order requiring TSI (D) to hold an annual meeting of its stockholders for the election of directors and to make publicly available to shareholders a stock list. After the action was filed, TSI (D) received a written consent representing a majority of the voting power of the corporation that elected five individuals each to serve as a director of TSI (D) until his or her successor is duly elected and qualified. The parties filed cross-motions for summary judgment.

ISSUE: Does a stockholder's written consent taken after the filing of a complaint and purporting to elect directors for TSI (D), satisfy the requirement to hold an annual meeting?

HOLDING AND DECISION: (Allen, Chan.) No. The consent action which duly designated directors of TSI (D) does not satisfy the corporation's obligation to hold an annual meeting at which time the company's directors are to be elected, in conformity with the certificate of incorporation. Delaware has few mandatory corporate law requirements, and the obligation to hold an annual meeting, at which time the directors will be elected for a term according to the charter, is one of them. Annual meetings and shareholder voting are central to corporate governance. Creating a consent to designate directors in lieu of having an annual meeting does not produce a more practical and efficient system. The formality of notice to all shareholders and a meeting could have an effect on how the majority of shareholders vote. In addition, other matters which shareholders might want to bring before the shareholder body, such as bylaw changes, are not made irrelevant by a consent designation of directors. At a noticed annual meeting a form of discourse among investors and between shareholders and managers is possible. There has to be unanimous consent for a meeting not to occur. Shareholders may, if the certificate of incorporation and bylaws provide, remove holdovers and fill vacancies on the board through an exercise of the consent power, but doing so does not affect the obligation to hold an annual meeting. Such directors would only hold office until the next meeting of shareholders, when the whole body of shareholders could participate. TSI (D) is ordered to hold an annual meeting and to publish a stock list.

▶ ANALYSIS

Annual meetings are required, in part, to minimize the risk that directors will try to thwart shareholders' voting rights to elect different directors or changes in corporate structure.

■═■

Quicknotes

SUMMARY JUDGMENT Judgment rendered by a court in response to a motion by one of the parties, claiming that the lack of a question of material fact in respect to an issue warrants disposition of the issue without consideration by the jury.

■═■

Adlerstein v. Wertheimer

Director/controlling shareholder (P) v. Director (D)

Del. Ct. Ch., 2002 WL 205684 (2002).

NATURE OF CASE: Action seeking a determination that meeting of directors was not properly convened, and thus actions at meeting were null and void.

FACT SUMMARY: Adlerstein (P) sued directors of the company of which he had been Chairman and CEO for not giving him notice of a meeting that would result in the removal of him from his corporate position.

🏛 RULE OF LAW
Advance notice of a meeting's agenda, which is to scheme against a director/controlling shareholder, cannot be withheld from that director/controlling shareholder in order to prevent the director/controlling shareholder from exercising his contractual right to put a halt to the other directors' schemes.

FACTS: Adlerstein (P), who was the Chairman and CEO of SpectruMedix Corporation (SpectruMedix or the Company), sued the Company and the current directors. Prior to the suit, on July 9, 2001, a meeting was held in which a board majority issued to a Reich Partnership a number of shares of a new class of supervoting preferred stock that conveyed to the Reich Partnership a majority of the voting power of the Company's stock. The majority then voted to remove Adlerstein (P) for cause and appointed Reich (D) as CEO and Chairman. The Reich Partnership then delivered to SpectruMedix a written consent purporting to remove Adlerstein (P). Prior to the meeting, Adlerstein (P) had controlled 73.27% of the voting power of the Company. SpectruMedix, however, was in financial trouble, and Wertheimer (D) and Mencher (D) became increasingly concerned. They viewed Adlerstein's (P) actions at the Company as purposefully thwarting the progress of consultants who were attempting to improve the Company's situation. Wertheimer (D) contacted Reich (D) about getting Reich to be an investor and manager of SpectruMedix. Reich (D) was only interested in investing in the Company if he, and not Adlerstein (P), were in charge. As time went on, SpectruMedix began to operate on the brink of insolvency. Wertheimer (D) would later testify at the trial that on July 5, 2001, he and Adlerstein (P) spoke on the telephone about the deteriorating financial conditions of the Company, and Adlerstein (P) agreed to convene a meeting of the board of directors on July 9th. Karl Fazler, the Company's business manager, testified that he spoke with Adlerstein (P) the morning of July 9th, and Adlerstein (P) told Fazler that he was on his way to a meeting of the board of directors. None of the directors received written notice of the meeting; however, not all past meetings had been formally noticed. Adlerstein (P) was deliberately kept unaware of Reich's (D) acquisition

proposal until the meeting. The proposal was that the Reich Partnership would invest $1 million in SpectruMedix, Reich (D) would assume the active management of SpectruMedix, and SpectruMedix would issue shares of its Series C Preferred Stock carrying with them voting control of the Company to the Reich Partnership. Adlerstein (P) moved for a court determination that the meeting was not properly convened, and, therefore, any actions taken at the meeting were null and void.

ISSUE: Was the meeting held on July 9, 2001, a meeting of the board of directors and did the actions of the directors in keeping Alderstein uninformed invalidate the board's actions at the meeting?

HOLDING AND DECISION: (Lamb, V. Chan.) Yes. Although the meeting of July 9th was a board meeting, the actions taken at it must be invalidated. Adlerstein (P) called the July 9th meeting. The bylaws of SpectruMedix set forth the procedure for giving notice of a board meeting. They provide that special meetings of the board may be called by the president by giving 48-hours notice to each director either personally or by telegram. Wertheimer's (D) account of his July 5th telephone call with Adlerstein (P), that Adlerstein (P) agreed to have the meeting in view of the urgent problems confronting the company, is credible. Fazler's testimony that Adlerstein (P) called him on the morning of the meeting and said that he was on his way to a board meeting also supports Wertheimer's (D) position. The bylaws of the company do not require written notice or an advanced distribution of an agenda, and meetings of the directors had been previously held without them. The decision, however, of Wertheimer (D), Mencher (D) and Selbst, the Company's attorney, to keep Adlerstein (P) uninformed about their plan to present the Reich proposal for consideration at the meeting invalidates the board's approval of that proposal at the meeting. In the context of the set of the legal rights that existed with SpectruMedix at the time of the July meeting, Adlerstein (P) was entitled to know ahead of time of the plan to issue new Series C Preferred Stock with the purposeful effect of destroying his voting control over the Company. This right comes from corporate law which requires boards of directors to conduct their affairs in a manner that satisfies minimum standards of fairness. The decision to not let Adlerstein (P) know about the plan to introduce the Reich (D) proposal was significant, because Adlerstein (P) had the contractual power to prevent the issuance of the Series C Preferred stock by executing a written consent to remove one or both of Wertheimer (D) and Mencher (D) from the board. He was entitled to

Continued on next page.

the opportunity to exercise such power. This court cannot condone such a deprivation. In this case, there was a meeting, and Adlerstein (P) had some notice of the Reich (D) proposal before it was approved by the SpectruMedix board of directors. However, he did not have an adequate opportunity to protect his interests. Adlerstein (P) was, therefore, disadvantaged by the other directors' failure to communicate their plans to him. Had he known about the agenda, he could have exercised his legal right to remove one or both of Wertheimer (D) or Mencher (D) and thus prevented them from approving the Reich (D) proposal and removing him from office. The actions taken at the meeting must therefore be undone.

▶ *ANALYSIS*

Shareholders can remove directors with or without cause by a majority vote. This general rule, however, is accompanied by statutory rules which limit shareholders' removal power when the corporation has instituted cumulative voting, staggered terms for directors, or class election of directors. If cause has to be shown, it is usually a high hurdle to overcome.

■════■

Quicknotes

BYLAWS Rules promulgated by a corporation regulating its governance.

■════■

Centaur Partners, IV v. National Intergroup, Inc.

Investment partnership (P) v. Corporation (D)

Del. Sup. Ct., 582 A.2d 923 (1990).

NATURE OF CASE: Appeal from judgment in a declaratory action brought to amend bylaws.

FACT SUMMARY: Attempting to take over National Intergroup, Inc. (National) (D), Centaur Partners, IV (Centaur) (P) proposed an amendment to National's (D) bylaws, providing for enlargement of the board of directors and requiring only a majority vote, which was in direct conflict with the supermajority vote required by both National's (D) certificate of incorporation and its bylaws.

🏛 RULE OF LAW
A charter or bylaw provision, which alters the principle that a majority of the votes cast at a stockholders meeting is sufficient to elect directors, must be positive, explicit, clear, and readily understandable.

FACTS: To achieve a takeover of National Intergroup, Inc. (National) (D), Centaur Partners, IV (Centaur) (P) sought to amend National's (D) bylaws to enlarge the board of directors from nine to fifteen members. Centaur (P) then planned to install a new slate of directors to be selected by Centaur (P) and to be voted on at the next annual shareholder meeting. In its filing with the Securities and Exchange Commission, Centaur (P) stated that, under state law, only a majority shareholder vote was required in order to amend the bylaws. National (D) argued that both its certificate of incorporation and its bylaws required an 80% supermajority vote to enlarge the board. To resolve this dispute, Centaur (P) brought a declaratory action in the Court of Chancery. The vice chancellor ruled in National's (D) favor, and Centaur (P) appealed.

ISSUE: Must, a charter or bylaw provision, which alters the principle that a majority of the votes cast at a stockholders meeting is sufficient to elect directors, be positive, explicit, clear, and readily understandable?

HOLDING AND DECISION: (Walsh, J.) Yes. A charter or bylaw provision, which alters the principle that a majority of the votes cast at a stockholders meeting is sufficient to elect directors, must be positive, explicit, clear, and readily understandable. In the present case, National's (D) charter and bylaw provisions are not unclear or ambiguous. National's (D) charter provision clearly establishes a classified board with no more than a third of the board subject to replacement in any one year. Moreover, both the charter provisions and the bylaw provisions give the power to fix the number of directors on the board solely to the directors themselves and clearly require a vote of 80% or more to amend those provisions. Centaur's (P) argument for a 50% threshold is contrary to the clear purpose in the language of the amended certificate of incorporation and would, therefore, be a nullity if adopted. Affirmed.

▶ ANALYSIS

The court noted that the classification of the board and the 80% supermajority vote were designed to insure continuity in the board of directors and avoid hostile attempts to take over the corporation. By requiring a greater percentage of stockholders to approve a proposed action, stockholders are given more power to defeat actions adverse to their interests. However, such supermajority provisions also protect minority shareholders, giving them the power to veto the will of the majority.

■■■

Quicknotes

BYLAWS Rules promulgated by a corporation regulating its governance.

CERTIFICATE OF INCORPORATION The written instrument that gives rise to the existence of a corporation when filed with the appropriate governmental agency.

■■■

Securities and Exchange Commission v. Edwards

Federal agency (P) v. Company principal (D)

540 U.S. 389 (2004).

NATURE OF CASE: Appeal from reversal of judgment in an SEC civil enforcement action under the federal securities laws.

FACT SUMMARY: The Securities and Exchange Commission (SEC) (P) asserted that an investment scheme offered by Edwards (D) and his company, which offered a contractual entitlement to a fixed rather than variable rate of return, was an "investment contract" subject to the federal securities laws.

🏛 **RULE OF LAW**

An investment scheme offering a contractual entitlement to a fixed rather than variable rate of return can properly be considered an "investment contract," and, therefore, a "security" for purposes of the federal securities laws.

FACTS: Edwards (D) was the chairman, CEO, and sole shareholder of ETS Payphones, Inc. (ETS), which sold payphones to the public via independent distributors. The payphones were offered with an agreement under which ETS leased back the payphone from the purchaser for a fixed monthly payment, thereby giving purchasers a fixed 14% annual return on their investment. Although ETS's marketing materials trumpeted the "incomparable payphone" as "an exciting business opportunity," the payphones did not generate enough revenue for ETS to make the payments required by the leaseback agreements, so the company depended on funds from new investors to meet its obligations. After ETS filed for bankruptcy protection, the Securities and Exchange Commission (SEC) (P) brought a civil enforcement action, alleging, inter alia, that Edwards (D) and ETS had violated registration requirements and antifraud provisions of the Securities Act of 1933 and the Securities Exchange Act of 1934, and Rule 10b-5 thereunder. The district court concluded that the sale-and-leaseback arrangement was an "investment contract" within the meaning of, and therefore subject to, the federal securities laws. The court of appeals reversed, holding that (1) this Supreme Court precedent required an "investment contract" to offer either capital appreciation or a participation in an enterprise's earnings, and thus exclude schemes offering a fixed rate of return; and (2) the requirement that the return on the investment be derived solely from the efforts of others was not satisfied in this case when the purchasers had a contractual entitlement to the return. The Supreme Court granted certiorari.

ISSUE: Can an investment scheme offering a contractual entitlement to a fixed rather than variable rate of return properly be considered an "investment contract,"

and therefore, a "security" for purposes of the federal securities laws?

HOLDING AND DECISION: (O'Connor, J.) Yes. An investment scheme offering a contractual entitlement to a fixed rather than variable rate of return can properly be considered an "investment contract," and therefore, a "security" for purposes of the federal securities laws. The test for determining whether a particular scheme is an investment contract is "whether the scheme involves an investment of money in a common enterprise with profits to come solely from the efforts of others." This definition embodies a flexible, rather than a static, principle that is capable of adaptation to meet the countless and variable schemes devised by those seeking to use others' money on the promise of profits. The term "profits" as used in this Court's precedent, means the income or return that investors seek on their investment, not the profits of the scheme in which they invest, and may include, for example, dividends, other periodic payments, or the increased value of the investment. Using this definition of "profits," there is no reason to distinguish between promises of fixed returns and promises of variable returns for purposes of the test. In both cases, the investing public is attracted by representations of investment income. Moreover, investments pitched as low risk (such as those offering a "guaranteed" fixed return) are particularly attractive to individuals more vulnerable to investment fraud, including older and less sophisticated investors. Under the reading Edwards (D) advances, unscrupulous marketers of investments could evade the securities laws by picking a rate of return to promise. This Court will not read into the securities laws a limitation not compelled by the language that would so undermine the laws' purposes. Moreover, contrary to Edwards's (D) assertion, nothing in this Court's precedent distinguishes between fixed and variable returns, nor is there precedent to the contrary. Also, the SEC (P) has consistently maintained that a promise of a fixed return does not preclude a scheme from being an investment contract. The court of appeals' perfunctory alternative holding, that the scheme here fell outside the definition because purchasers had a contractual entitlement to a return, is incorrect and inconsistent with this Court's precedent. Reversed.

▶ **ANALYSIS**

Congress's purpose in enacting the federal securities laws was to regulate investments, in whatever form in which investments are made and by whatever name a particular

Continued on next page.

investment is called. It was to that end that Congress enacted a broad definition of "security" that is sufficient to encompass virtually any instrument that might be sold as an investment. The decision in this case is consistent with, and gives effect to, that purpose.

■■■

Quicknotes

INTER ALIA   Among other things.

SECURITIES ACT OF 1933 § 4 C(2)   Exempts private offerings from registration requirements.

SECURITIES EXCHANGE ACT OF 1934   Federal statute regulating stock exchanges and trading and requiring the disclosure of certain information in relation to securities traded.

■■■

Securities and Exchange Commission v. Ralston Purina Co.

Government agency (P) v. Corporation (D)

346 U.S. 119 (1953).

NATURE OF CASE: Action to enjoin the unregistered offerings of stock under the Securities Act of 1933.

FACT SUMMARY: Ralston Purina Co. (D) offered treasury stock to their key employees which the Securities and Exchange Commission (SEC) (P) attempted to enjoin.

🏛 RULE OF LAW
The exemption in § 4(1) of the Securities Act of 1933, which exempts transactions by an issuer not involving any public offering from the registration requirement, applies only when all the offerees have access to the same kind of information that the Act would make available if registration were required.

FACTS: Since 1911, Ralston Purina Co. (D) has had a policy of encouraging stock ownership among its employees and, since 1942, has made unissued common shares available to some of them. Ralston Purina (D) had sold nearly $2,000,000 of stock to employees between the years of 1947 and 1951. They had attempted to avoid the registration requirements of the Securities Act of 1933, under the exemption contained in § 4(1) of the Act which exempted transactions by an issuer not involving any public offering. Each year between 1947 and 1951, Ralston Purina (D) authorized the sale of common stock to employees who, without any solicitation by the company or its officers or employees, inquired as to how to purchase common stock of Ralston Purina (D). The branch and store managers were advised that only the employees who took the initiative and were interested in buying stock at the present market prices would be able to purchase the stock. Among those taking advantage of the offer were employees with the duties of artist, bakeshop foreman, chow-loading foreman, clerical assistant, copywriter, electrician, stock clerk, mill office clerk, order credit trainee, production trainee, stenographer, and veterinarian. The buyers resided in fifty widely separated communities scattered throughout the United States. The record shows that in 1947, 243 employees bought stock, 20 in 1948, 414 in 1949, and 411 in 1950. In 1951, 165 made applications to purchase the stock. No actual records were kept showing how many employees were offered the stock, but it is estimated that, in 1951, at least 500 employees were offered the stock. Ralston Purina (D) had approximately 7,000 employees during the years in question. Ralston Purina (D) based its exemption claim on the classification that all the offerees were key employees in its organization. Its position at trial was that a key employee included an individual who is eligible for promotion; an individual who especially influences others or who advises others; a person whom the employees look to in some special way; one who

carries some special responsibility and who is sympathetic to management; and one who is ambitious and who the management feels is likely to be promoted to a greater responsibility. They admit, however, that an offering to all of its employees would be a public offering. The district court held that the exemption applied and dismissed the suit, and the court of appeals affirmed the decision.

ISSUE: Does an offer of stock by a company to a limited number of its employees automatically qualify for the exemption for transactions not involving any public offering?

HOLDING AND DECISION: (Clark, J.) No. The Securities Act does not define a private offering or a public offering. It is clear that an offer need not be open to the whole world to qualify as a public offering. If Ralston Purina (D) had made the stock offer to all of its employees, it would have been a public offering. The court looked at the intent of the Securities Act, which is to protect investors by promoting full disclosure of information thought to be necessary for informed investment decisions. When the Act grants an exemption, the class of people involved was not considered as needing the disclosure that the Act normally requires. Therefore, when an offering is made to people who can fend for themselves, the transaction is considered to be one not involving a public offering. Most of the employees purchasing the stock from Ralston Purina (D) were not in a position to know or have access to the kind of information which registration under the Act would disclose and, therefore, were in need of the protection of the Act. Stock offers made to employees may qualify for the exemption if the employees are executive personnel who, because of their position, have access to the same kind of information that the Act would make available in the form of a registration statement. Absent such a showing of special circumstances, employees are just as much members of the investing public as any of their neighbors in the community. The burden of proof is on the issuer of the stock, who is claiming an exemption to show that he qualifies for the exemption. Also, since the right to an exemption depends on the knowledge of the offerees, the issuer's motives are irrelevant. It didn't matter that Ralston Purina's (D) motives may have been good because they didn't show that their employees had the requisite information. Judgment reversed.

▶ ANALYSIS

The exemption discussed above is now found in § 4(2) instead of § 4(1). This case is considered to be the leading

Continued on next page.

case in this area. The test established in this case is still used in determining whether an offering qualifies for the nonpublic offering exemption of § 4(2). Some of the factors used in determining whether the offerees have sufficient access to information concerning the stock are the number of offerees, the size of the offering, the relationship of the offerees, the manner of the solicitation of the offerees, and the amount of investment experience of the offerees.

■━━■

Quicknotes

ENJOIN The ordering of a party to cease the conduct of a specific activity.

PRIVATE OFFERING An offering of securities in a corporation for sale to a limited number of investors and which is not subject to the requirements of the Securities Act of 1933.

PUBLIC OFFERING The offer to sell securities to the public.

■━━■

Lovenheim v. Iroquois Brands, Ltd.

Shareholder (P) v. Corporation (D)

618 F. Supp. 554 (D.D.C. 1985).

NATURE OF CASE: Motion for preliminary injunction related to a corporation's refusal to include a shareholder proposal in its proxy materials.

FACT SUMMARY: After Iroquois Brands (Iroquois/Delaware) (D) refused to include Lovenheim's (P) proposed resolution in the proxy materials being sent to shareholders prior to the annual meeting, Lovenheim (P) sought to compel the inclusion of his resolution in the proxy materials.

RULE OF LAW
An issuer may omit a security holder's proposal for action if it relates to operations accounting for less than 5% of the issuer's total assets and of its net earnings and gross sales and is not otherwise significantly related to the issuer's business.

FACTS: Lovenheim (P), owner of common stock in Iroquois Brands (Iroquois/Delaware) (D), sought to include a proposed resolution in the proxy materials being sent to all shareholders prior to the upcoming annual meeting. The resolution concerned the inhumane method of force-feeding geese to produce pâté de foie gras and whether such methods were used by the French supplier of the pâté imported by Iroquois/Delaware (D). Less than .05 percent of Iroquois/Delaware's (D) assets were involved in the importation of pâté. When the corporation refused to include Lovenheim's (P) proposal in its proxy materials, he sought to compel its inclusion through this action.

ISSUE: May an issuer omit a security holder's proposal for action if it relates to operations accounting for less than 5% of the issuer's total assets and its net earnings and gross sales and is not otherwise significantly related to the issuer's business?

HOLDING AND DECISION: (Gasch, J.) Yes. An issuer may omit a security holder's proposal for action if it relates to operations accounting for less than 5% of the issuer's total assets and its net earnings and gross sales and is not otherwise significantly related to the issuer's business. This is an exception to the general requirement of SEC Rule 14a-8, mandating that issues set forth all proposals. Lovenheim (P) relied on the word "otherwise," suggesting that it indicated that the drafters of the rule intended that other noneconomic—i.e., ethical or social—tests of significance be used. The Securities and Exchange Commission (SEC) has in fact stated it did not believe that the exception to the rule should hinge solely on the economic relativity of a proposal. Without a preliminary injunction, Lovenheim (P) will suffer irreparable harm by losing the opportunity to communicate with those shareholders not attending the meeting. Inclusion of the proposal in the proxy statement will not cause undue harm to Iroquois/Delaware (D) since it has not claimed any harm from inclusion of the proposal in its 1983 proxy materials. Finally, granting the preliminary injunction would be consistent with the public interest. Motion granted.

ANALYSIS

The purpose of Rule 14a-8 is to assure that shareholders exercise their right to control the important decisions which affect them in their capacity as stockholders and owners of the corporation. Prior to the 1983 amendments, Rule 14a-8(c)(5) did not contain the objective economic significance test specified in the first part of the current version. The SEC has required inclusion in many situations in which the related business comprised less than 1% of a company's revenues, profits, or assets where the proposal raised policy questions important enough to be considered significantly related to the issuer's business.

Quicknotes

PRELIMINARY INJUNCTION A judicial mandate issued to require or restrain a party from certain conduct; used to preserve a trial's subject matter or to prevent threatened injury.

PROXY A person authorized to act for another.

CA, Inc. v. AFSCME Employees Pension Plan

[No adversarial parties.]

Del. Sup. Ct., 953 A.2d 227 (2008) (*en banc*).

NATURE OF CASE: Certified questions to the state's highest court.

FACT SUMMARY: The Securities and Exchange Commission was asked to provide a no-action letter to a corporation, stipulating that it would not recommend an enforcement action against the company if the company accepted a shareholder proposal to amend the company's bylaws. The shareholders proposed to amend the bylaws to require the company to reimburse shareholders for expenses incurred in certain elections of directors.

🏛 RULE OF LAW

(1) A proposal seeking to require a company to reimburse shareholders for expenses incurred in the elections of directors is a proper subject for inclusion in proxy statements as a matter of Delaware law.

(2) A proposal seeking to require a company to reimburse shareholders for expenses incurred in the elections of directors, if adopted, would cause the company to violate any Delaware law to which it is subject.

FACTS: [This decision answers certified questions to the Delaware Supreme Court that were submitted by the Securities and Exchange Commission (SEC). There are no plaintiffs or defendants.] AFSCME, a CA stockholder associated with the American Federation of State, County and Municipal Employees, submitted a proposal for inclusion in proxy materials for CA Inc.'s annual shareholders meeting. The proposal sought to require CA to reimburse expenses incurred by stockholders in elections of directors, provided that at least one nominee was elected. CA argued that the proposal could be excluded pursuant to 1934 Securities Exchange Act Rule 14a-8 because it related to an election of directors, conflicted with Delaware law, was inconsistent with SEC proxy rules, and conflicted with the company's certificate of incorporation, which provided that the management of the company was vested in its board of directors. A no-action request was submitted by the company to ensure that acceptance of the proposal would not result in SEC enforcement action. AFSCME then submitted a response to CA's no-action request, saying that the proposal is a proper action for shareholders and the proposed bylaw, if enacted, would be permissible under Delaware law. The SEC received conflicting opinions from Delaware law firms on a question of Delaware law, and therefore asked the Delaware high court to weigh in on the topic.

ISSUE:

(1) Is a proposal seeking to require a company to reimburse shareholders for expenses incurred in the elections of directors a proper subject for inclusion in proxy statements as a matter of Delaware law?

(2) Would a proposal seeking to require a company to reimburse shareholders for expenses incurred in the elections of directors, if adopted, cause the company to violate any Delaware law to which it is subject?

HOLDING AND DECISION: (Jacobs, J.)

(1) Yes. A proposal seeking to require a company to reimburse shareholders for expenses incurred in the elections of directors is a proper subject for inclusion in proxy statements as a matter of Delaware law. Both the board of directors and the shareholders of a corporation are empowered by law to adopt, amend or repeal the corporation's bylaws. However, such power is not coextensive, because only the board has management powers. Well-established Delaware law provides that a proper function of bylaws is not to mandate how the board should decide specific substantive business decisions, but to define the process and procedures by which those decisions are made. Such bylaws are appropriate for shareholder action. Contrary to CA's argument, it cannot be that any bylaw that in any respect might be viewed as limiting or restricting the power of the board of directors automatically falls outside the scope of permissible bylaws. That reasoning, taken to its logical extreme, would result in eliminating altogether the shareholders' statutory right to adopt, amend or repeal bylaws. Applying these principles here, the AFSCME bylaw, even though couched as a substantive-sounding mandate to expend corporate funds, has both the intent and the effect of regulating the process for electing directors of CA. Therefore, the bylaw is a proper subject for shareholder action.

(2) Yes. A proposal seeking to require a company to reimburse shareholders for expenses incurred in the elections of directors, if adopted, would cause the company to violate any Delaware law to which it is subject. The bylaw would prevent the directors from exercising their full managerial power in circumstances where their fiduciary duties would otherwise require them to deny reimbursement. The challenged bylaw contains no language or provision that would reserve to CA's directors their full power to exercise their fiduciary duty to decide whether or not it would be

Continued on next page.

appropriate, in a specific case, to award reimbursement at all. AFSCME's argument that it is unfair to claim that the bylaw prevents the CA board from discharging its fiduciary duty where the effect of the bylaw is to relieve the board entirely of those duties in this specific area must be rejected as more semantical than substantive, since it concedes the very proposition that renders the bylaw, as written, invalid: the bylaw mandates reimbursement of election expenses in circumstances that a proper application of fiduciary principles could preclude. This is significant given that one of the most basic tenets of Delaware corporate law is that the board of directors has the ultimate responsibility for managing the business and affairs of a corporation.

▶ *ANALYSIS*

Following this case, the Delaware legislature enacted new sections 112 and 113 to the Delaware G.C.L. specifying that bylaws can include provisions requiring a corporation's proxy and proxy solicitation to include individuals nominated by shareholders (§ 112) and providing for the reimbursement by the corporation of expenses incurred in connection with the election of directors (§ 113). The statute is permissive, rather than mandatory, and includes a list of procedures or conditions that may be included. The American Bar Association (ABA) has passed similar provisions in amendments to MBCA § 2.06 that authorize both shareholder-expense-reimbursement bylaws and shareholder-proxy access bylaws.

■■■■

Quicknotes

ACTION LETTER A letter issued by an attorney of a governmental agency stating that if the facts are as stated, he or she would not advise the agency to prosecute.

BYLAWS Rules promulgated by a corporation regulating its governance.

PROXY A person authorized to act for another.

PROXY STATEMENT A statement, containing specified information by the Securities and Exchange Commission, in order to provide shareholders with adequate information upon which to make an informed decision regarding the solicitation of their proxies.

■■■■

Kistefos AS v. Trico Marine Services, Inc.

Minority shareholder (P) v. Corporation (D)

Del. Ct. Ch., 2009 WL 1124477 (2009).

NATURE OF CASE: Motion for expedited proceedings in action for declaratory relief.

FACT SUMMARY: Kistefos AS (P), a minority shareholder of Trico Marine Services, Inc. (Trico) (D), sought expedited proceedings in its action to have its proposed bylaw, which provided that an incumbent director who "fails to receive the number of votes required to elect directors at any meeting of stockholders at which such person is to be elected" would be ineligible to continue to serve and his or her term would expire immediately, go to a shareholder vote at the company's fast-approaching annual meeting.

🏛 RULE OF LAW
Where a bylaw proposal has been rejected on grounds that if adopted it would be inconsistent with state law and a corporation's governing documents, expedited proceedings may be avoided where the corporation's legal position is judicially preserved pending the outcome of a shareholder vote on the proposed bylaw.

FACTS: Kistefos AS (P), a substantial minority stockholder of Trico Marine Services, Inc. (Trico) (D), filed suit against Trico (D) seeking a declaration that Trico (D) improperly rejected a proposed bylaw on grounds that if adopted, the proposed bylaw would be inconsistent with Delaware law and Trico's (D) certificate of incorporation. The bylaw proposal provided that an incumbent director who "fails to receive the number of votes required to elect directors at any meeting of stockholders at which such person is to be elected" would be ineligible to continue to serve and his or her term would expire immediately, creating a vacancy on the board. Trico's (D) bylaws provided that directors were elected by a majority vote of stockholders, but Trico's (D) governing documents provided that an incumbent director who received only a plurality of votes could continue to serve as a "holdover" director until a successor had been elected or until the director's resignation or removal. Kistefos's (P) proposed bylaw would thus "give teeth" to Trico's (D) otherwise illusory majority voting requirement. Because the record date for the annual meeting was fast approaching, Kistefos (P) moved to expedite the case. During a teleconference with the court, Kistefos (P) represented that expedition would not be necessary if the stockholders were permitted to vote on Kistefos's (P) proposed bylaw at the annual meeting. In response, Trico (D) offered to collect and preserve the proxies submitted for and against Kistefos's (P) proposal so that it could later be determined if the proposal received

the required vote, but maintained that it would have to disregard the proposed bylaw, lest it be presented to the stockholders at the meeting as a valid proposal for a vote.

ISSUE: Where a bylaw proposal has been rejected on grounds that if adopted it would be inconsistent with state law and a corporation's governing documents, may expedited proceedings be avoided where the corporation's legal position is judicially preserved pending the outcome of a shareholder vote on the proposed bylaw?

HOLDING AND DECISION: (Chandler, Chan.) Yes. Where a bylaw proposal has been rejected on grounds that if adopted it would be inconsistent with state law and a corporation's governing documents, expedited proceedings may be avoided where the corporation's legal position is judicially preserved pending the outcome of a shareholder vote on the proposed bylaw. To resolve this dispute, the court takes judicial notice of Trico's (D) legal position, which is thus judicially preserved. Because Trico's (D) legal position has been preserved, the company has no reason to prevent a stockholder vote on the proposal. The proposal will be presented for a stockholder vote at the annual meeting in the same manner as other proposals presented to the stockholders for a vote. Also, because of the now pending stockholder vote on the proposal, Kistefos (P) will face no irreparable injury warranting expedited proceedings. If the proposal receives the required number of votes, then the legal issue of its validity will be preserved and ripe for judicial review. If, on the other hand, the proposal fails to receive shareholder approval, the issue will be moot. Absent some compelling reason to do otherwise, the court should refrain from rendering an advisory opinion where adjudication of the issue is not needed for there to be an informed stockholder vote on the proposal. Accordingly, the motion to expedite is denied.

▶ ANALYSIS

The Securities and Exchange Commission (SEC) has proposed new Rule 14a-11, which would change the federal proxy rules to remove impediments to the exercise of shareholders' rights to nominate and elect directors to company boards of directors. The new rules would require, under certain circumstances, a company to include in the company's proxy materials a shareholder's, or group of shareholders', nominees for director. The proposal includes certain requirements, key among which are a requirement that use of the new procedures be in accordance with state law, and provisions regarding the disclosures required to be made

Continued on next page.

concerning nominating shareholders or groups and their nominees. In addition, the new rules would require companies to include in their proxy materials, under certain circumstances, shareholder proposals that would amend, or that request an amendment to, a company's governing documents regarding nomination procedures or disclosures related to shareholder nominations, provided the proposal does not conflict with the SEC's disclosure rules—including the proposed new rules. In this case, for example, Kristefos (P) had to incur the cost of soliciting and mailing proxies. Rule 14a-11 would obviate such shareholder costs, which would be borne by the corporation.

■══■

Quicknotes

BYLAWS Rules promulgated by a corporation regulating its governance.

■══■

Conservative Caucus v. Chevron Corp.

Stockholder (P) v. Corporation (D)

Del. Ct. Ch., 525 A.2d 569 (1987).

NATURE OF CASE: Request for a corporation's stockholder list.

FACT SUMMARY: Concerned about the possibility that Chevron Corp. (D) was likely to suffer economic loss due to its business operations in Angola, stockholder Conservative Caucus (P) sought to obtain access to Chevron's (D) stockholder list to inform the other stockholders of its concerns.

🏛 RULE OF LAW
Any stockholder shall, upon written demand under oath stating the purpose thereof, have the right during the usual hours for business to inspect for any proper purpose a list of the corporation's stockholders and to make copies or extracts therefrom.

FACTS: Conservative Caucus (P), an owner of Chevron Corp. (D) stock, made a demand under oath for a copy of Chevron's (D) stockholder list. Conservative Caucus (P) planned to use the list to inform the other stockholders that Chevron (D) was likely to suffer economic loss as a result of its business operations in Angola. Conservative Caucus (P) brought suit after Chevron (D) refused to provide the list.

ISSUE: Shall any stockholder, upon written demand under oath stating the purpose thereof, have the right during the usual hours for business to inspect for any proper purpose a list of the corporation's stockholders and to make copies or extracts therefrom?

HOLDING AND DECISION: (Harnett, V. Chan.) Yes. Any stockholder shall, upon written demand under oath stating the purpose thereof, have the right during the usual hours for business to inspect for any proper purpose a list of the corporation's stockholders and to make copies or extracts therefrom. A communication with other stockholders about specific matters of corporate concern has consistently been held to be a proper purpose for a stockholder to obtain a stock list. In addition, Conservative Caucus (P) testified that it would only communicate with the stockholders by mail, thus preserving their privacy. Since Conservative Caucus (P) complied with the form and manner of making a demand for a stockholder list, the burden was upon Chevron (D) to establish that the inspection would be for an improper purpose. Chevron (D) has not carried its burden. Conservative Caucus (P) is entitled to the list.

▶ ANALYSIS

The rule adopted here by the Court of Chancery is found in Title 8, Del. C. § 220(b). Title 8, Del. C. § 220(c) states in part that, where the stockholder seeks to inspect the corporation's stock ledger or list of stockholders and he has complied with this section respecting the form and manner of making demand for inspection of such documents, the burden of proof shall be upon the corporation to establish that the inspection he seeks is for an improper purpose. The court declared that: "A proper purpose having been stated, all others are irrelevant."

Quicknotes

8 DEL. C. § 220(b) Any stockholder shall have the right to inspect for any proper purpose the stock ledger of a corporation.

BURDEN OF PROOF The duty of a party to introduce evidence to support a fact that is in dispute in an action.

City of Westland Police & Fire Retirement System v. Axcelis Technologies, Inc.

Shareholder (P) v. Corporation (D)

Del. Ct. Ch., 2009 WL 3086537 (2009).

NATURE OF CASE: Action to compel inspection of books and records.

FACT SUMMARY: The City of Westland Police & Fire Retirement System (Westland) (P), a shareholder in Axcelis Technologies, Inc. (Axcelis) (D), brought suit to compel inspection of Axcelis's (D) books and records, claiming as a proper purpose that the Axcelis (D) board had breached its fiduciary duties by (1) rebuffing the attempts by another company, SHI, to negotiate an acquisition of Axcelis (D) for more than 18 months; (2) subsequently rejecting two above-market acquisition proposals from SHI as inadequate; (3) retaining three candidates for the board after a majority of the shareholders refused to support them, allegedly for their failure to negotiate with SHI; and (4) selling to SHI one of Axcelis's (D) most important assets, its stake in a joint venture with SHI, known as SEN.

> ### 🏛 RULE OF LAW
> A demand for a books and records inspection will be denied where the plaintiff cannot demonstrate any basis from which it can be inferred that a corporation's board of directors has engaged in any wrongdoing and cannot demonstrate any other proper purpose for the inspection.

FACTS: The City of Westland Police & Fire Retirement System (Westland) (P) was a shareholder in Axcelis Technologies, Inc. (Axcelis) (D), which was an equal partner with SHI, a Japanese company, in a joint venture called SEN. At some point, SHI made an unsolicited bid to acquire Axcelis (D) for $5.20 per share. Shares of Axcelis (D) closed at a price of $4.18 per share that day. After consulting with advisers, the Axcelis (D) board rejected SHI's proposal, finding that the offer failed to compensate shareholders adequately for the synergistic value of the SEN joint venture and ignored the substantial business opportunity to take market share back from Axcelis (D) competitors. Thereafter, SHI made another offer at $6.00 per share, on a day that Axcelis (D) stock was trading at $5.45, but the board again rejected the offer as not in the shareholders' best interest. The Axcelis (D) board indicated that confidential merger discussions would be in both companies' interest, but SHI declined to enter into any confidentiality agreements with Axcelis (D) at that point. Two months later, Axcelis (D) held its annual shareholders' meeting, at which three unopposed directors were up for reelection. Although none of the three received a majority of the votes—presumably because shareholders wanted to

send a message that they wanted the board to accept SHI's offer—they were reelected because Axcelis (D) followed the plurality voting provisions of Delaware law, pursuant to which a director may be elected without receiving a majority of the votes cast in a given election. Nevertheless, the directors' failure to receive at least a majority of the votes cast triggered one of Axcelis's (D) corporate governance policies. Pursuant to this policy (the "Policy"), directors failing to receive a majority of the stockholder vote must submit their resignations to the board's Nominating and Corporate Governance Committee, which must then consider and recommend to the board whether such resignations should be accepted or rejected. The ultimate decision to accept or reject any resignations submitted by its directors rests with the board. Following the Policy, the three directors offered to resign their positions, but the board decided not to accept those resignations, finding it was not in the corporation's best interest to do so, given the directors' extensive experience and knowledge, service on a number of key committees, and the ability to move forward negotiations with SHI. The board also expressed its intention to be responsive to the shareholders' concerns that gave rise to the withheld votes by continuing to seek to engage in confidential discussions with SHI. Such discussions were entered into a month later, and extensive due diligence occurred. Nevertheless, SHI placed an acquisition of Axcelis (D) on hold. After Axcelis's (D) announcement of these developments, its shares closed at a price of $1.43 per share. After these events, Westland (P) delivered to Axcelis (D) a demand for the inspection of books and records, pursuant to 8 Del. C. § 220. Westland (P) sought various categories of documents pertaining to the negotiations with SHI, as well as documents related to the board's decision not to accept the resignations of the three directors that were reelected by less than a majority, but the Axcelis (D) board rejected the demand, claiming that Westland (P) had failed to satisfy the standard of § 220 and the corresponding Delaware case law interpreting § 220. Subsequently, Axcelis (D), which was in need of capital, agreed to sell its ownership in SEN to SHI for $136.6 million. The day the deal closed, Axcelis's (D) shares were trading at $0.41 per share. A few days later, Westland (P) filed suit to compel inspection of Axcelis's (D) books and records pursuant to § 220. Westland (P) alleged that the board had breached its fiduciary duties in its decision to retain the three directors and in its handling of SHI's bids. Westland (P) alleged as its "proper purpose" that the board had breached its fiduciary duties by (1) rebuffing the

Continued on next page.

attempts by SHI to negotiate an acquisition of Axcelis (D) for more than 18 months; (2) subsequently rejecting two above-market acquisition proposals from SHI as inadequate; (3) retaining three candidates for the board after a majority of the shareholders refused to support them, allegedly for their failure to negotiate with SHI; and (4) selling one of Axcelis's (D) most important assets, its stake in SEN, to SHI.

ISSUE: Will a demand for a books and records inspection be denied where the plaintiff cannot demonstrate any basis from which it can be inferred that a corporation's board of directors has engaged in any wrongdoing and cannot demonstrate any other proper purpose for the inspection?

HOLDING AND DECISION: (Noble, V. Chan.) Yes. A demand for a books and records inspection will be denied where the plaintiff cannot demonstrate any basis from which it can be inferred that a corporation's board of directors has engaged in any wrongdoing and cannot demonstrate any other proper purpose for the inspection. With regard to the board's retention of the three directors, Westland (P) has failed to demonstrate any credible basis from which it can be inferred that the board's decision to retain the three directors was motivated either by entrenchment or was a defensive measure. Instead, the three directors had been properly reelected under the state's plurality voting provisions, but the corporation's retention Policy was triggered. The Policy, in turn, vested discretion whether to accept the resignations of the three directors in the board. By refusing to accept these resignations, the board effectuated the results of a valid shareholder election, and there was no evidence that the board identified, and then sought to thwart, the will of the shareholder franchise by refusing to accept the resignations. Additionally, the board's justifications for retaining the three directors, e.g., to facilitate negotiations with SHI, were not materially inconsistent with the record. Thus, the board's actions in this regard did not demonstrate a credible basis from which to infer wrongdoing. Also rejected is Westland's (P) argument that the board's exercise of discretion under the Policy warrants heightened scrutiny and a suspicion of wrongdoing, since the logical conclusion of such an argument is that mere shareholder reliance upon a board-enacted governance policy could effectively rewrite the voting provisions contained in a corporation's bylaws— and subject Axcelis (D) to the burden of a § 220 request merely for having adopted the Policy, and exercising its discretion under it in fidelity with Axcelis's (D) bylaws. Merely pointing out the board's exercise of discretion under the Policy—an exercise which ultimately effectuated the shareholder franchise—is not credible evidence of wrongdoing on record at bar. Because Westland (P) has not asserted a proper purpose, its action is dismissed.

ANALYSIS

The court also ruled that the retention of the three directors was not a defensive measure since there was no threat to corporate control at the time of the election, and there was no evidence that the board disloyally wanted to fend off SHI's advances. In fact, the record demonstrated the opposite, since the board attempted to engage SHI in further acquisition discussions. Merely because those efforts failed did not support a finding of wrongdoing, since "[f]ailed negotiations, without more, do not form a credible basis supporting an inference of wrongdoing." Likewise the court found that there was no credible evidence that rejecting SHI's two acquisition proposals was a defensive action requiring the application of the enhanced judicial scrutiny: "Rejecting an acquisition offer, without more, is not 'defensive action' under *Unocal*." (*Unocal Corp. v. Mesa Petroleum Co.,* 493 A.2d 946 (Del. 1985)). Further, the court determined there was no credible basis from which wrongdoing could be inferred from the board's rejection of the two proposals from SHI, or that the board in any way acted in bad faith in exercising its business judgment. These additional reasons also supported the court's finding that Westland (P) had not asserted a proper purpose for its inspection demand.

Quicknotes

8 DEL. C. § 220(b) Any stockholder shall have the right to inspect for any proper purpose the stock ledger of a corporation.

BREACH OF FIDUCIARY DUTY The failure of a fiduciary to observe the standard of care exercised by professionals of similar education and experience.

Fiduciary Duty, Shareholder Litigation, and the Business Judgment Rule

Quick Reference Rules of Law

Shlensky v. Wrigley

Stockholder (P) v. Corporation (D)

Ill. App. Ct., 237 N.E.2d 776 (1968).

NATURE OF CASE: Appeal from dismissal of a stockholder derivative suit.

FACT SUMMARY: Shlensky (P) sued as a stockholder to compel the installation of lights in Wrigley Field.

🏛 RULE OF LAW
To overcome the presumption of business judgment, a stockholder derivative suit must rely on fraud, illegality, or conflict of interest.

FACTS: Shlensky (P) was a minority stockholder of the corporation that owned and operated the Chicago Cubs and Wrigley Field, the Cubs's home park. Wrigley (D), president of the corporation, owned approximately 80% of the stock. At the time of suit, 19 of 20 major league teams had facilities to play night games, with the Cubs as the lone holdout. In years 1961–1965, the Cubs sustained losses from their baseball operations. Shlensky (P) alleged that the losses were due to the lack of lights to play night games. Shlensky (P) alleged that Wrigley (D) felt baseball to be a daytime sport and that night games would have a deteriorating effect on the neighborhood around the park and that Wrigley was not concerned with revenue. Shlensky (P) sued in a derivative action to compel the directors to install lights.

ISSUE: May a stockholder base a derivative suit on a claim of negligent mismanagement of corporate affairs or waste of assets?

HOLDING AND DECISION: (Sullivan, J.) No. To overcome the presumption of business judgment, a stockholder derivative suit must rely on one of three bases: fraud, illegality, or conflict of interest. The role of the directors of a corporation is to manage the affairs of the corporation. Generally, the directors have great discretion in managing. However, surrounding that discretion are certain standards of conduct. The corporation may not act in an illegal or fraudulent manner. There is no requirement that the directors must consider only financial concerns in mapping a course for the corporation. In this case, Wrigley (D) feels that it is reasonable to consider the long run impact of night games on the neighborhood and its subsequent impact on the corporation. Whether this is the best decision is a question for the board of directors, not the courts. Wrigley's (D) consideration of nonfinancial factors does not give rise to a new cause of action based on negligence. Order of dismissal affirmed.

▶ *ANALYSIS*

Shareholders have no power to make ordinary business decisions. Without this protection, directors would be perpetually second guessed. However, the business judgment rule is a presumption that can be overcome. The court will simply start with the presumption that the directors are better situated to make appropriate decisions.

■━■

Quicknotes

BUSINESS JUDGMENT RULE Doctrine relieving corporate directors and/or officers from liability for decisions honestly and rationally made in the corporation's best interests.

DERIVATIVE SUIT An action asserted by a shareholder in order to enforce a cause of action on behalf of the corporation.

■━■

Dodge v. Ford Motor Co.

Stockholder (P) v. Corporation (D)

Mich. Sup. Ct., 170 N.W. 668 (1919).

NATURE OF CASE: Suit seeking an injunction and other relief.

FACT SUMMARY: Dodge (P) objected to Ford Motor Co.'s (D) election not to declare a special dividend despite large profits and a considerable amount of cash on hand.

🏛 RULE OF LAW
A corporation may be compelled to declare a dividend if its directors' failure to do so constitutes fraud, lack of good faith, or an abuse of discretion.

FACTS: For many years, Ford Motor Co. (Ford) (D) declared regular dividends amounting to 60% of the par value of its outstanding stock. Beginning in 1911, the company (D) also declared sizable special dividends. At the end of the fiscal year which concluded July 31, 1916, Henry Ford announced that the special dividends would cease, and that all profits in excess of the regular dividends would thereafter be reinvested in the business. At the time of this announcement, company (D) profits were approximating $60 million per year, cash on hand exceeded $52 million, and the total surplus approached $112 million. The Dodge brothers (P), owners of 10% of the Ford (D) stock, filed suit to enjoin Ford (D) from carrying out the announced policy. The Dodges (P) also sought a decree requiring at least 75% of the accumulated cash surplus to be distributed to stockholders, and an order binding the company (D) to distribute all future earnings which were not reasonably necessary for emergency purposes in conducting the business. The circuit court ordered Ford's (D) directors to declare a special dividend equivalent to 50% of the accumulated cash surplus, less any special dividends declared during the fiscal year ending July 31, 1917. An appeal followed.

ISSUE: May a court of equity require the directors of a corporation to declare and pay a dividend?

HOLDING AND DECISION: (Ostrander, C.J.) Yes. A corporation may be compelled to declare a dividend if its directors' failure to do so constitutes fraud, lack of good faith, or an abuse of discretion. At the time the Dodges (P) made their request for the special dividend, Ford (D) was enjoying immense profits and had a large cash surplus. In short, Ford (D) was an extremely profitable concern. In fact, the company (D) was able to make regular price reductions, although future reductions were to be sacrificed temporarily in order to expand Ford's (D) productive capacity. In the short-run at least, stockholders' returns on their investment will decrease and the Dodges (P) argued that Ford (D) would

soon be, in effect, an eleemosynary institution. Certainly, it is entirely proper for a corporation to behave charitably toward the public if it can do so without compromising the interest of its shareholders. Unfortunately, to an extent at least, Ford (D) seems to have adopted the view that its shareholders should be content with the generous gains which they have realized to date. It would not be proper for the court to interfere with Ford's (D) expansion, especially since it may ultimately result in increased returns for the Dodges (P) and other shareholders. On the other hand, Ford (D) has accumulated cash vastly in excess of its short-term liabilities and expenses. Therefore, the lower court's order compelling a partial distribution is fair to both the company (D) and its shareholders and should be affirmed.

▶ ANALYSIS

The rule of this case is consistent with the weight of authority. Under ordinary circumstances, the directors of a corporation are entitled to exercise considerable discretion in determining whether or not to declare dividends, but they are not permitted limitless latitude. For instance, massive accumulations of earnings may goad a court into ordering a dividend. In such a situation, the conduct of the directors may be characterized as arbitrary, an abuse of discretion, or inconsistent with good business judgment. Courts will also intercede when a controlling faction regulates dividend distribution in a manner calculated to insure excessive profits for itself to the exclusion of others. In ordering a dividend under such a circumstance, a court may base its ruling upon a finding of bad faith, oppression, or even fraud.

■═■

Quicknotes

COURT OF EQUITY A court that determines matters before it consistent with principles of fairness and not in strict compliance with rules of law.

DIVIDEND The payment of earnings to a corporation's shareholders in proportion to the amount of shares held.

ELEEMOSYNARY INSTITUTION An institution established for charitable purposes.

INJUNCTION A court order requiring a person to do or prohibiting that person from doing a specific act.

■═■

Northeast Harbor Golf Club, Inc. v. Harris

Sports club (P) v. President of sports club (D)

Me. Sup. Jud. Ct., 661 A.2d 1146 (1995).

NATURE OF CASE: Appeal from defense judgment in an action for breach of fiduciary duty.

FACT SUMMARY: Harris (D), president of the Northeast Harbor Golf Club (P), personally bought and developed adjoining property without advising the remaining board members.

🏛 RULE OF LAW
Corporate officers and directors must disclose all relevant information prior to taking personal advantage of any potentially corporate opportunity.

FACTS: Harris (D) was the president of Northeast Harbor Golf Club (the Club) (P) from 1971 to 1990. In 1979, a real estate broker informed Harris (D) that property adjoining the golf course was for sale. Harris (D) bought the property in her own name, disclosing this information to the Club's (P) board after the transaction was completed. Subsequently, Harris (D) obtained other adjoining property and eventually sought to develop homes on these properties. The Club's (P) board of directors opposed this development and asked Harris (D) to resign. The Club (P) then filed suit against Harris (D) for breaching her fiduciary duty by taking a corporate opportunity without disclosing it to the board. The trial court ruled for Harris (D), holding that acquiring property was not in the Club's (P) line of business. The Club (P) appealed.

ISSUE: Must corporate officers and directors disclose all relevant information prior to taking personal advantage of any potentially corporate opportunity?

HOLDING AND DECISION: (Roberts, J.) Yes. Corporate officers and directors must disclose all relevant information prior to taking personal advantage of any potentially corporate opportunity. Corporate officers bear a duty of loyalty to their corporation. This duty must be discharged in good faith with a view toward furthering the interests of the corporation. The American Law Institute (ALI) has offered the most recently developed version of the corporate opportunity doctrine for this loyalty duty. ALI § 5.05 essentially states that a director may take advantage of a corporate opportunity only after meeting a strict requirement of full disclosure. This ALI standard should be adopted by the courts. In the present case, the case must be remanded to develop the factual record with regard to the principles of the ALI standard. Vacated and remanded.

▶ ANALYSIS

The trial court ruled for Harris (D) based largely on her good faith. The court found that she had made great financial and time contributions to the Club (P). The court also noted the Club's (P) inability to purchase the real estate.

■══■

Quicknotes

BREACH OF FIDUCIARY DUTY The failure of a fiduciary to observe the standard of care exercised by professionals of similar education and experience.

CORPORATE OPPORTUNITY DOCTRINE Prohibits fiduciaries from usurping business opportunities that rightly belong to the corporation.

DUTY OF LOYALTY A director's duty to refrain from self-dealing or to take a position that is adverse to the corporation's best interests.

■══■

Broz v. Cellular Information Systems, Inc.

Officer/shareholder (D) v. Corporation (P)

Del. Sup. Ct., 673 A.2d 148 (1996).

NATURE OF CASE: Appeal from a judgment for Cellular Information Systems, Inc. (P) in an action alleging Broz (D) usurped a corporate opportunity.

FACT SUMMARY: Broz (D) utilized a business opportunity for his wholly owned corporation instead of Cellular Information Systems, Inc. (P) for which he served as a member of the board of directors.

🏛 RULE OF LAW
The corporate opportunity doctrine is implicated only in cases where the fiduciary's seizure of an opportunity results in a conflict between the fiduciary's duties to the corporation and the self-interest of the director as actualized by the exploitation of the opportunity.

FACTS: Broz (D) was the president and sole stockholder of RFB Cellular, Inc. (RFBC), a Delaware corporation engaged in the business of providing cellular telephone service in the Midwestern United States. At the time of the conduct at issue, Broz (D) was also a member of the board of directors of Cellular Information Systems, Inc. (CIS) (P). CIS (P) was a publicly held Delaware corporation and a competitor of RFBC. The conduct before the court involves the purchase by Broz (D) of a cellular telephone service license for the benefit of RFBC. RFBC owns and operates an FCC license area, known as the Michigan-4. The license entitles RFBC to provide cellular telephone service to a portion of rural Michigan. In April of 1994, Mackinac Cellular Corp. sought to divest itself of Michigan-2, the license area immediately adjacent to Michigan-4. Mackinac thus contacted Broz (P) through a representative and broached the subject of RFBC's possible acquisition of Michigan-2. Michigan-2 was not, however, offered to CIS (P) in light of CIS's (P) recent financial difficulties. During the period from early 1992 until the time of CIS's (P) emergence from bankruptcy in 1994, CIS (P) divested itself of 15 separate cellular license systems. CIS (P) contracted to sell four additional license areas on May 27, 1994, leaving CIS (P) with only five remaining license areas, all of which were outside of the Midwest. Broz (D) spoke separately with CIS's (P) CEO and two of its directors concerning his interest in acquiring Michigan-2. Each indicated that CIS (P) was not interested in Michigan-2. The Court of Chancery decided that Broz (D) breached his fiduciary duty and usurped a corporate opportunity by purchasing a cellular telephone service license for the benefit of RFBC. Broz (D) appealed.

ISSUE: Is the corporate opportunity doctrine implicated only in cases where the fiduciary's seizure of an opportunity results in a conflict between the fiduciary's duties to the corporation and the self-interest of the director as actualized by the exploitation of the opportunity?

HOLDING AND DECISION: (Veasey, C.J.) Yes. The corporate opportunity doctrine is implicated only in cases where the fiduciary's seizure of an opportunity results in a conflict between the fiduciary's duties to the corporation and the self-interest of the director as actualized by the exploitation of the opportunity. Here, the totality of the circumstances indicates that Broz (D) did not usurp an opportunity that properly belonged to CIS (P). Broz (D) was entitled to utilize a corporate opportunity for the benefit of RFBC, his wholly owned corporation, instead of for CIS (P), for which he served as an outside director because: (1) the opportunity became known to him in his individual and not corporate capacity, (2) the opportunity was related more closely to the business conducted by RFBC than to that engaged in by CIS (P), (3) CIS (P) did not have the financial capacity to exploit the opportunity, and (4) CIS (P) was aware of Broz's potentially conflicting duties towards RFBC and did not object to his actions on RFBC's behalf. Reversed.

▶ ANALYSIS

In Klein and Ramseyer's hornbook on Business Associations, the authors note that a common argument made by executives accused of usurping corporate opportunities is that the corporation lacked the financial capacity to effectively exploit it. However, courts generally reject this defense unless the defendant has explicitly disclosed the corporate opportunity and the corporation rejects it. This case, however, represents the Delaware View that, if a corporation does not have the financial ability to utilize the opportunity, its financial incapacity will weigh against a court finding that the director was required to offer the opportunity to the corporation.

━■

Quicknotes

BREACH OF FIDUCIARY DUTY The failure of a fiduciary to observe the standard of care exercised by professionals of similar education and experience.

CORPORATE OPPORTUNITY DOCTRINE Prohibits fiduciaries from usurping business opportunities that rightly belong to the corporation.

━■

Globe Woolen Co. v. Utica Gas & Electric Co.

Mill owner (P) v. Electricity supplier (D)

N.Y. Ct. App., 224 N.Y. 483, 121 N.E. 378 (1918).

NATURE OF CASE: Appeal of action to compel specific performance of a contract.

FACT SUMMARY: Globe Woolen Co. (Globe) (P) sued Utica Gas & Electric Co. (D), which had rescinded a contract to supply electricity to Globe (P), for specific performance.

🏛 RULE OF LAW
The refusal of a chairman to vote at a meeting of the board of directors, held to ratify a contract, does not nullify any influence the chairman might have exerted without voting. Such a trustee has a duty not to take advantage of those in his trust but rather to warn those who trust him that what might be happening is unfair.

FACTS: Globe Woolen Co. (Globe) (P) owns two mills and Utica Gas & Electric Co. (Utica) (D) generates and sells electricity. Maynard is Globe's (P) chief stockholder, president, and a director. He was also a director of Utica (D) and chairman of its executive committee. Maynard wanted Utica (D) to supply Globe (P) with electricity, but only if Utica (D) could guarantee that if Globe (P) switched from steam to electricity Globe (P) would save money in operating costs. Greenidge, general manager of Utica's (D) electrical department, and Maynard formulated a contract whereby Utica (D) would supply to one of Globe's (P) mills electricity at a maximum rate of $.0104 per kilowatt hour. Utica (D) also guaranteed that the cost for heat, light, and power would show a savings each month of $300, as compared with the cost for the corresponding month in the year previous to the changeover from steam to electrical power. After a trial period ending July 1, 1907, and at Globe's (P) option, the contract was to run for five years with renewal for the same term. When the proposed contract was laid before Utica's (D) executive committee, Maynard did not speak about whether the contract was a profitable one for Utica (D). Maynard presided at the meeting, put forward the resolution to ratify the contract, but was excused from voting. Another contract, similar with the exception of a few additional provisions, was also ratified for another one of Globe's (P) mills. Changes in how the mills would be operated were not taken into consideration when the contract was formed, and such changes led to losses for Utica (D). In February 1911, Utica (D) gave notice of rescission. Globe (P) sued to compel the specific performance of the contracts. The lower courts found in favor of Utica (D).

ISSUE: Are the contracts voidable because although Maynard, a director of Globe (P) and chairman of Utica (D), did not vote to ratify the contracts he still crafted them to his benefit and Utica's (D) detriment and

thus had a duty to warn Utica's (D) executive committee about the possible pitfalls of the contracts, prior to ratification, but did not do so?

HOLDING AND DECISION: (Cardozo, J.) Yes. Utica (D) can void the contracts because Maynard's actions violated his duty as a trustee. Maynard could not divest himself of his duties as a trustee for Utica (D) simply by refusing to vote and shifting the responsibilities to his associates and then reap a profit from their error. The trustee's duty of constant and unqualified fidelity is not just something of form but also carries substance. A trustee can be quiet if everything is fair; however, he cannot be quiet, and must warn, if he knows of some oppression. A trustee can assert a dominating influence in other ways than voting. Maynard exerted persuasive influence over the transaction. Greenidge was subordinate to him and was trying to please him. There was no proper separation between Maynard acting as Globe's (P) president requesting certain things and Maynard as Utica's (D) chair offering advice. Maynard and Greenidge wrote the contract, and all that remained when it came before the executive committee was ratification, a mere formality. The members of the committee knew that the contract, which they were looking at for the first time, had been drafted by Maynard, the chairman, and they relied on his faith and loyalty to assume that the contract was just and equitable. The contract, however, was ripe with unfairness to Utica (D), because the guaranty was not limited by a statement of the conditions under which the mills were to be run. No matter how high the business grew, thus resulting in a greater fuel demand, Utica (D) would still have to provide the fuel for a certain price so that there would be savings to Globe (P). Maynard had to know about these possible changes to the business, which could not have also been known by the other directors. Affirmed.

▶ ANALYSIS

Most jurisdictions will not void a conflicting interest transaction solely on that basis if a majority of disinterested directors authorize it or the shareholders approve it in good faith or if it is fair to the corporation at the time it is authorized.

▬═▬

Quicknotes

RESCISSION The canceling of an agreement and the return of the parties to their positions prior to the formation of the contract.

▬═▬

Sinclair Oil Corp. v. Levien

Corporation (D) v. Shareholder (P)

Del. Sup. Ct., 280 A.2d 717 (1971).

NATURE OF CASE: Derivative suit for an accounting by a parent company.

FACT SUMMARY: A minority stockholder in Sinven, Levien (P), accused Sinclair (D), the parent company, of using Sinven assets to finance its operations.

🏛 RULE OF LAW
Where a parent company controls all transactions of a subsidiary, receiving a benefit at the expense of the subsidiary's minority stockholders, the intrinsic fairness test will be applied, placing the burden on the parent company to prove the transactions were based on reasonable business objectives.

FACTS: Sinclair (D) is a holding company that markets, produces, and explores for oil. Sinclair (D) owned 97% of the stock of Sinclair Venezuelan Oil Company (Sinven), a company engaged in petroleum operations in South America. Levien (P) owned about 3,000 of Sinven's 120,000 publicly held shares. Sinclair (D) controlled the directors of Sinven. From 1960 to 1966, Sinclair (D) caused Sinven to pay out excessive dividends of $108,000,000, $38,000,000 above its earnings. In 1961, Sinclair (D) created Sinclair International (International) to coordinate Sinclair's (D) foreign operations, and then caused Sinven to contract to sell crude oil to International at specified rates and minimum quantities. When International failed to live up to the contract, Levien (P) and other minority shareholders of Sinven brought this derivative action requiring Sinclair (D) to account for damages sustained by Sinven as a result of the excessive dividends and causing Sinven not to enforce the contract with International. The Court of Chancery found for Levien (P), and Sinclair (D) appealed.

ISSUE: Does the business judgment rule protecting fiduciaries from judicial scrutiny also protect a parent company where it exerts such complete control over its subsidiary that the parent receives a benefit at the subsidiary's expense?

HOLDING AND DECISION: (Wolcott, C.J.) No. Under the business judgment rule, a court will not interfere with a board of directors' judgment unless there is a showing of gross and palpable overreaching. But this rule does not apply to a situation where a parent company appears to have benefited from its control over a subsidiary to the detriment of the subsidiary's minority stockholders. In such a situation, any transactions will be tested by their intrinsic fairness if there is evidence of breach of the parent company's fiduciary duty coupled with self-dealing. For instance, in the present case, the allegation that Sinclair (D) caused excessive dividends to be paid out of Sinven is not enough to create a cause of action against the parent company for intrinsic unfairness. Levien (P) must meet the burden of proving the dividend was not based on a reasonable business objective. However, the court found that the dividends were not self-dealing since Sinclair (D) had received nothing to the exclusion of Sinven and its minority shareholders. Thus, as to the dividends, the business judgment rule applied. As to the allegations that the dividends had prevented Sinven from expanding, the court held that Levien (P) had proved no loss of business opportunities due to the drain of cash from Sinven. So, again, the business judgment rule protected Sinclair (D). However, the court held that there was self-dealing by Sinclair (D) in contracting with its dominated subsidiary, International. Sinclair (D) caused International to breach its contract with Sinven to the detriment of Sinven's minority shareholders. But Sinclair (D) received products from Sinven through International and thus benefitted from the transaction. However, Sinclair (D) failed to cause Sinven to enforce the contract. Therefore, Sinclair's (D) inherent duty to its subsidiary, Sinven, coupled with its self-dealing, shifted the burden to it to show its breach of the International-Sinven contract was intrinsically fair. The court found that Sinclair (D) failed to meet the burden. Reversed in part, affirmed in part, and remanded.

▶ ANALYSIS

The business judgment rule is an expression of the court's reluctance to interfere with corporate decision-making. It is a rule of evidence rather than a rule of law, and the standard of intrinsic fairness is an extension of the business judgment rule in this respect. For instance, in the present case, the court applied the business judgment rule and refused to interfere with Sinclair's (D) decisions on the dividends. In short, the burden to prove overreaching in order to knock down the business judgment rule was on Levien (P), and it was not met. But as to the breach of the International-Sinven contract, the burden shifted to Sinclair (D) to prove it was intrinsically fair, a burden it failed to meet. In such cases, the shift of burden of proof from the controlling stockholder management to the accusing minority pivots on evidence of overreaching and self-dealing by the majority.

■■■

Quicknotes

ACCOUNTING The evaluation of assets for the purpose of assigning relative interests.

Continued on next page.

BUSINESS JUDGMENT RULE Doctrine relieving corporate directors and/or officers from liability for decisions honestly and rationally made in the corporation's best interests.

DERIVATIVE SUIT An action asserted by a shareholder in order to enforce a cause of action on behalf of the corporation.

INTRINSIC FAIRNESS TEST A defense to a claim that a director engaged in an interested director transaction by showing the transaction's fairness to the corporation.

■═■

Shapiro v. Greenfield

Officers and directors (D) v. Minority shareholders (P)

Md. Ct. Spec. App., 764 A.2d 270 (2000), *reconsideration denied* (2001).

NATURE OF CASE: Appeal of derivative suit.

FACT SUMMARY: Greenfield (P) sued Shapiro (D) for usurping a corporate opportunity which belonged to College Park Woods, Inc. (D), an entity of which they were both officers.

🏛 RULE OF LAW
(1) When a director's involvement in a project demonstrates a conflict of interest but he does not capitalize on an opportunity that should have been presented to the corporation, then there is no usurpation.
(2) When a director does not personally benefit from a transaction, the appropriate inquiry into determining whether a director is to be considered an interested director is to focus on the director's ability to exercise independent judgment and the expected influence of a particular relationship on the director.

FACTS: Shapiro (D) is the operating officer for College Park Woods, Inc. (College) (D). Smith (D) is Shapiro's (D) sister and an officer of College (D). Greenfield (P) is Shapiro's (D) cousin. College (D) owned Clinton Plaza shopping center. Shapiro (D) entered into a joint venture with Jaffe in which three new entities were created: Clinton Crossings Limited Partnership (D), Clinton Crossings Inc. (D), and TSC/Clinton Associates Limited Partnership (D). College (D) transferred its fee simple interest in Clinton Plaza to Clinton Crossings Partnership (D), the owner of the redeveloped center, in exchange for a 50% limited partnership. As a limited partner, College (D) would have no right to manage, direct, or control the affairs of Clinton Crossings Partnership (D). Greenfield (P) was not present at the meeting of College's (D) shareholders when College (D) was authorized to enter into the limited partnerships. Greenfield (P) subsequently brought a derivative suit against College (D) and its officers and directors (D) alleging usurpation of a corporate opportunity of College (D). He also sought an accounting and dissolution of the corporation. The trial court found usurpation, and Shapiro (D) appealed.

ISSUE:
(1) Did the transaction constitute usurpation of a corporate opportunity?
(2) Was the appropriate inquiry made below into determining whether a director is an interested director by focusing on the director's ability to exercise independent judgment and the expected influence of a particular relationship of the director?

HOLDING AND DECISION: (Kenney, J.)
(1) No. The transaction did not constitute usurpation of corporate opportunity. Shapiro's (D) involvement in the redevelopment project demonstrates a conflict of interest, but he did not capitalize on an opportunity that should have been presented to the corporation (D). The corporation (D) entered into a business arrangement with other entities in which certain directors had a direct financial interest.
(2) No. The case needs to be remanded for a redetermination as to whether there were any disinterested directors. The case must be remanded for reconsideration as to the interested director transaction because the findings of fact on which the court relied are not clear. It did not direct the findings of the Report of the Special Master to an interested director analysis and to a determination of whether the Clinton Crossings transaction was fair and reasonable. Part of the analysis will involve a determination of who are the interested directors. The Model Business Corporations Act (MBCA) and the American Law Institute (ALI) define interested director. Maryland has not rejected the MBCA and the ALI definition that a director, who may be related to a party with a material financial interest in the transaction, would also be classified as an interested party. Delaware, New York, and California do not define the term interested director. The focus in their statutes, however, is on a director's ability to exercise independent judgment and the expected influence of a particular relationship on the director. When a director's loyalty is questioned, courts must seek to ascertain whether the conflict has deprived stockholders of a neutral decision-making body. The question is whether the relationship would reasonably be expected to exert an influence on the director's judgment. When the director has no direct interests in the conflicting transaction, neither the MBCA nor the ALI create a per se rule based on a familial or business relationship, because a relationship, between the parties does not necessarily destroy an individual's independent judgment. The case will be remanded to determine whether Smith (D) was an interested director or not. Remanded, and the judgment is vacated.

▶ ANALYSIS

After remand, if it is determined that there were no disinterested directors, the court will then evaluate the transaction from the fair and reasonable perspective. A

Continued on next page.

nondisclosed, interested director transaction may be valid if it is found to be fair and reasonable to the corporation.

■══■

Quicknotes

DERIVATIVE SUIT An action asserted by a shareholder in order to enforce a cause of action on behalf of the corporation.

DISSOLUTION Annulment or termination of a formal or legal bond, tie or contract.

FEE SIMPLE An estate in land characterized by ownership of the entire property for an unlimited duration and by absolute power over distribution.

INTERESTED DIRECTOR TRANSACTION A transaction between the corporation and another party in which the director has a personal interest.

LIMITED PARTNERSHIP A voluntary agreement entered into by two or more parties whereby one or more general partners are responsible for the enterprise's liabilities and management and the other partners are only liable to the extent of their investment.

■══■

Joy v. North

[Parties not identified.]

692 F.2d 880 (2d Cir. 1982).

NATURE OF CASE: Appeal.

FACT SUMMARY: The case excerpt contains no factual discussion.

⚖ RULE OF LAW
A corporate officer who makes a mistake in judgment as to economic conditions, consumer tastes, or production line efficiency will rarely, if ever, be found liable for damages suffered by the corporation.

FACTS: The case excerpt contains no factual discussion.

ISSUE: Will a corporate officer who makes a mistake in judgment as to economic conditions, consumer tastes, or production line efficiency rarely, if ever, be found liable for damages suffered by the corporation?

HOLDING AND DECISION: (Winter, J.) Yes. A corporate officer who makes a mistake in judgment as to economic conditions, consumer tastes, or production line efficiency will rarely, if ever, be found liable for damages suffered by the corporation. First, shareholders to a very real degree voluntarily undertake the risk of bad business judgment. Second, courts recognize that after-the-fact litigation is an imperfect device to evaluate corporate business decisions. The entrepreneur's function is to encounter risks and to confront uncertainty, and a reasoned decision at the time may seem a wild hunch viewed years later against a background of perfect knowledge. Third, because potential profit often corresponds to potential risk, it is very much in the interest of shareholders that the law, not create incentives for overly cautious corporate decisions. Shareholders can reduce the volatility of their risk by diversifying their holdings. In the case of the diversified shareholder, the seemingly more risky alternatives may well be the best choice since great losses in some stocks will over time be offset by even greater gains in others. Thus, a rule which penalizes the choice of seemingly riskier alternatives may not be in the interest of shareholders.

▌ *ANALYSIS*

The rule enunciated in the instant case has been doctrinally labeled the business judgment rule. For whatever its merit, the business judgment rule, extends only as far as the reasons which justify its existence. Thus, it does not apply in cases in which the corporate decision lacks a business purpose, is tainted by a conflict of interest, is so egregious as to amount to a no-win decision, or results from an obvious and prolonged failure to exercise oversight or supervision.

Quicknotes

BUSINESS JUDGMENT RULE Doctrine relieving corporate directors and/or officers from liability for decisions honestly and rationally made in the corporation's best interests.

Smith v. Van Gorkom

Shareholder (P) v. Corporation (D)

Del. Sup. Ct., 488 A.2d 858 (1985).

NATURE OF CASE: Appeal in class action to rescind cash-out merger.

FACT SUMMARY: The trial court held, despite allegations to the contrary by Smith (P) and other stockholders, that Van Gorkom (D) and the other directors of Trans Union (D) had acted in an informed manner and they were thus entitled to the protection of the business judgment rule in approving a cash-out merger.

🏛 RULE OF LAW
A decision made by a board of directors must be an informed one to be protected by the business judgment rule.

FACTS: Smith (P) and other shareholders of Trans Union Corporation (D) brought a class action suit to rescind a cash-out merger that had been approved by Van Gorkom (D) and other members of the board of directors and ultimately approved by an overwhelming majority of the stockholders. After listening to the evidence, the court held that the business judgment rule applied to raise the presumption that the action taken by the board was an informed one made in good faith in the honest belief it was in the corporation's best interests. Renewed allegations that the board of directors acted without sufficient information and that the stockholders were also not sufficiently informed prior to their vote of approval formed the basis of the appeal by Smith (P).

ISSUE: Must a decision made by the board of directors be an informed one in order for it to be protected by the business judgment rule?

HOLDING AND DECISION: (Horsey, J.) Yes. The business judgment rule affords protection for informed decisions made by a board of directors. The concept of gross negligence is the proper standard for making that determination. Here, it is evident the board did not make a deliberate determination whether to approve the merger. A director cannot abdicate his duty by leaving the decision to the shareholders alone, and even they were not adequately informed. Reversed and remanded.

DISSENT: (McNeilly, J.) My dissent is based solely on my diametrical opposition to the evidentiary conclusions of the majority. The majority incorrectly assessed the directors' knowledge and their ability to act under the protection of the business judgment rule. There were five inside directors and five outside directors. The five insiders had extensive experience with the corporation, and with one exception, the five outsiders were all CEOs, and all of them also had considerable experience with the corporation. And the outside director who was not a CEO also served on the boards of several of the nation's largest companies and was a leading business academician. Directors of this caliber are not ordinarily taken in by a "fast shuffle," as the majority believes they were. Instead, they were not taken in by this multi-million dollar corporate transaction without being fully informed and aware of the state of the art as it pertained to the entire corporate panorama of the corporation. These men knew Trans Union (D) like the back of their hands and were more than qualified to make on-the-spot decisions about its affairs, including a 100% sale of the corporation.

▶ ANALYSIS

A settlement agreement was arrived at subsequent to the announcement of this decision. A sum of $23.5 million was paid to the plaintiff class; $10 million came from the liability insurance carrier for Trans Union's (D) directors and officers, that amount being the policy limit. The remaining $13.5 million came from the group that had used the merger to "buy" Trans Union (D), even though none of them was a party to the suit.

Quicknotes

BUSINESS JUDGMENT RULE Doctrine relieving corporate directors and/or officers from liability for decisions honestly and rationally made in the corporation's best interests.

CASH-OUT MERGER Occurs when a merging company prematurely redeems the securities of a holder as part of the merger.

CLASS ACTION A suit commenced by a representative on behalf of an ascertainable group that is too large to appear in court, who shares a commonality of interests and who will benefit from a successful result.

Malpiede v. Townson

Shareholder (P) v. Directors (D)

Del. Sup. Ct., 780 A.2d 1075 (2001).

NATURE OF CASE: Appeal from dismissal of breach of duty of care claim.

FACT SUMMARY: Shareholders of Frederick's of Hollywood (Frederick's) (P) contended that an exculpatory provision in Frederick's charter that precluded money damages for directors' breaches of the duty of care did not bar their claim that the board was grossly negligent in failing to implement a routine defensive strategy that could enable the board to negotiate for a higher bidder in a merger situation, or otherwise create a tactical advantage to enhance stockholder value.

🏛 RULE OF LAW
A breach of the duty of care claim must be dismissed where a corporation has an exculpatory provision in its charter that precludes money damages for directors' breaches of the duty of care.

FACTS: Frederick's of Hollywood (Frederick's) agreed to merge with Knightsbridge Capital (Knightsbridge) for $6.14 per Frederick's share. The merger agreement limited Frederick's board (D) from soliciting competing bids, unless doing so would violate the board's fiduciary duties. Two months after signing, Milton Partners offered $7 per share. Knightsbridge promptly increased its offer to $6.90. A week later, another bidder, Veritas Capital (Veritas), offered $7.75 per share. Knightsbridge also matched that bid, and bought some shares on the open market for $8.21 each. Finally, Veritas increased its bid to $9.00, but the Frederick's board (D) rejected that bid, and moved forward with the Knightsbridge at $7.75. Frederick's shareholders (P) sued, alleging, inter alia, that the board had breached its duties of care and loyalty. Specifically, the shareholders (P) alleged that the board (D) had been grossly negligent in failing to implement a routine defensive strategy that could enable the board to negotiate for a higher bidder in a merger situation, or otherwise create a tactical advantage to enhance stockholder value. Frederick's charter contained an exculpatory provision that precluded money damages for directors' breaches of the duty of care. The trial court granted the board's (D) motion to dismiss. The state's highest court granted review.

ISSUE: Must a breach of the duty of care claim be dismissed where a corporation has an exculpatory provision in its charter that precludes money damages for directors' breaches of the duty of care?

HOLDING AND DECISION: (Veasey, C.J.) Yes. A breach of the duty of care claim must be dismissed where a corporation has an exculpatory provision in its charter

that precludes money damages for directors' breaches of the duty of care. Construing the complaint most favorably to the shareholders (P), it can be read to allege that the board was grossly negligent in immediately accepting the Knightsbridge offer and agreeing to various restrictions on further negotiations without first determining whether Veritas would issue a counteroffer. Although the board had conducted a search for a buyer over one year, the shareholders (P) seem to contend that the board (D) was imprudently hasty in agreeing to a restrictive merger agreement on the day it was proposed—particularly where other bidders had recently expressed interest. Without deciding the issue of whether the shareholders (P) actually state a due care claim, it is assumed that they do state such a claim for relief based on gross negligence during the board's (D) auction process, based on the inferences most favorable to the shareholders (P) that flow from these allegations. The issue then becomes whether these claims may be dismissed by reason of the existence and the legal effect of the exculpatory provision in Frederick's charter. The shareholders (P) argue that the exculpatory provision should not bar their claim because the claim is very closely intertwined with, and therefore indistinguishable from, their duty of loyalty and bad faith claims. However, the shareholders (P) do concede that if a complaint unambiguously and solely asserts only a due care claim, the complaint is dismissible once the corporation's exculpatory provision is invoked. Contrary to the shareholders' (P) assertions, they have asserted such a claim. Their complaint fails properly to invoke loyalty and bad faith claims, so the only claim left is a due care claim. The board (D) had the burden of raising the exculpatory provision as a defense, and it did so. For these reasons, the trial court did not err in dismissing the shareholders' (P) due care claim. Also, here, at the pleading stage, rather than at trial, the board (D) does not bear the burden of proving each of the elements of the exculpatory provision. Thus, if the shareholders (P) at this pleading stage had managed to adequately plead loyalty or bad-faith claims, those claims could have proceeded to trial and would not have been barred by the exculpatory provision. But, because they did not, their only remaining claim (due care) is blocked by the exculpatory provision—and that is the end of the shareholders' (P) case. Affirmed.

▶ ANALYSIS

The exculpatory provision in this case was adopted pursuant to 8 Del. C. § 102(b)(7). That section was adopted following a directors and officers' insurance liability crisis.

Continued on next page.

The purpose of this statute was to permit stockholders to adopt a provision in the certificate of incorporation to free directors of personal liability in damages for due care violations, but not duty of loyalty violations, bad-faith claims and certain other conduct. Such a charter provision, when adopted, would not affect injunctive proceedings based on gross negligence. Once the statute was adopted, stockholders usually approved charter amendments containing these provisions because it freed up directors to take business risks without worrying about negligence lawsuits. Thus, it can be seen that in this case, the statute had its intended effect.

■━■

Quicknotes

BAD FAITH Conduct that is intentionally misleading or deceptive.

BREACH The violation of an obligation imposed pursuant to contract or law, by acting or failing to act.

DUE CARE The degree of care that can be expected from a reasonably prudent person under similar circumstances; synonymous with ordinary care.

DUTY OF CARE Duty that an officer or director owes to the corporation, by virtue of his fiduciary relationship, to act for the benefit of the corporation.

DUTY OF LOYALTY A director's duty to refrain from self-dealing or to take a position that is adverse to the corporation's best interests.

EXCULPATORY CLAUSE A clause in a contract relieving one party from liability for certain unlawful conduct.

GROSS NEGLIGENCE The intentional failure to perform a duty with reckless disregard of the consequences.

■━■

In re Caremark International, Inc. Derivative Litigation

Health care company's board of directors (D) v. Shareholders (P)

Del. Ct. Ch. 698 A.2d 959 (1996).

NATURE OF CASE: Motion to approve a settlement of a consolidated derivative action.

FACT SUMMARY: Caremark, a managed health-care provider, entered into contractual arrangements with physicians and hospitals, often for "consultation" or "research," without first clarifying the unsettled law surrounding prohibitions against referral fee payments.

🏛 RULE OF LAW
A board of directors has an affirmative duty to attempt in good faith to assure that a corporate information and reporting system exists and is adequate.

FACTS: Caremark was involved in providing patient health care and managed health care services. Much of Caremark's revenue came from third-party payments, insurers, and Medicare and Medicaid reimbursement programs. The Anti-Referral Payments Law (ARPL) applied to Caremark, prohibiting payments to induce the referral of Medicare or Medicaid patients. Caremark had a practice of entering into service contracts, including consultation and research, with physicians who at times prescribed Caremark products or services to Medicare recipients. Such contracts were not prohibited by the ARPL, but they raised the issue of unlawful kickbacks. Caremark's board of directors (D) attempted to monitor these contracts internally, seeking legal advice and devising guidelines for employees. However, the government began investigating Caremark. Caremark began making structural changes in response to the investigation, centralizing management. In spite of this, Caremark and two officers were indicted. Several shareholder derivative actions were subsequently filed, charging the board of directors (D) with failure to adequately monitor as part of its duty of care. Settlement negotiations began. Caremark agreed in the settlement to cease all payments to third parties that referred patients to Caremark and to establish an ethics committee, which it had, in effect, already done. Caremark also agreed to make reimbursement payments to private and public parties totaling $250 million. All other claims were waived in the proposed settlement. The proposed settlement was submitted to the court for approval.

ISSUE: Does a board of directors have an affirmative duty to attempt in good faith to assure that a corporate information and reporting system exists and is adequate?

HOLDING AND DECISION: (Allen, Chan.) Yes. A board of directors has an affirmative duty to attempt in good faith to assure that a corporate information and reporting system exists and is adequate. Directors generally do not monitor day-to-day operations in a company. The Supreme Court has said where there is no basis for suspicion, directors cannot be liable. However, it would be extending this holding too far to say that directors have no obligation whatsoever to determine whether they are receiving accurate information. The duty of care implies that a board will make a good faith effort to ensure that the corporate information and reporting system is adequate. In this case, acts that resulted in indictments do not, by themselves, prove that the Caremark board (D) was not adequately monitoring corporate behavior. On the contrary, the board (D) appears to have been making structural changes all along to gain greater centralized control of the company; and an ethics monitoring group was in place well before the settlement was reached. Given that the evidence on the record suggests that success in the derivative suit was unlikely, but that Caremark is giving up little in the way of concessions not already in place, the settlement is fair.

▶ ANALYSIS

A duty to monitor does not require a board to be aware of all the details of corporate activity. In fact, such oversight would be physically impossible in a large company. The duty does, however, require the board to be aware of major activities and related issues that could pose a threat to the company. The choice of what structure to use in informational gathering is still subject to the safe harbor of the business judgment rule; therefore, a claim that the duty to monitor has been breached is tremendously difficult to prove successfully.

■═■

Quicknotes

BUSINESS JUDGMENT RULE Doctrine relieving corporate directors and/or officers from liability for decisions honestly and rationally made in the corporation's best interests.

■═■

Brehm v. Eisner

Stockholders (P) v. Board of directors (D)

Del. Sup. Ct., 746 A.2d 244 (2000).

NATURE OF CASE: Appeal from dismissal of a stockholder derivative complaint.

FACT SUMMARY: Brehm (P) sued Eisner (D) for approving an employment agreement and subsequent non-fault termination of Disney's president, Ovitz.

🏛 RULE OF LAW
A complaint which is mostly conclusory does not meet the rules required for a stockholder to pursue a derivative remedy.

FACTS: Disney hired Ovitz as its president. He was a friend of Disney's Chairman, Eisner (D). Ovitz lacked experience managing a diversified public company. Ovitz's Employment Agreement with Disney was unilaterally negotiated by Eisner (D) and approved by Disney's board of directors (D). The Agreement had an initial term of five years and required Ovitz to devote his full time and best efforts exclusively to the company. In return he received a base salary of $1 million, a discretionary bonus, and options to purchase 5 million shares of Disney's common stock. Certain options would vest immediately upon termination. Per the Agreement, Ovitz's employment could end by his contract not being renewed in five years; Disney's terminating him for good cause prior to the five years expiring; or Ovitz's resigning voluntarily. Non-fault termination would entitle Ovitz to the present value of his remaining salary payments through September 2000, a $20 million severance payment, an additional $7.5 million, for each fiscal year remaining under the agreement, and the immediate vesting of the first $3 million stock options. Problems arose soon after Ovitz began to work, and Brehm (P) alleged that these problems were sufficient to let Ovitz go for cause. Eisner (D) and Ovitz, however, agreed to arrange for Ovitz to leave Disney on the non-fault basis provided in the Agreement, and the New Disney Board (D) approved his decision. Brehm (P) alleges that the Old Disney Board of Directors (D) breached its fiduciary duty in approving the wasteful Agreement; that the New Disney Board (D) breached its fiduciary duty by agreeing to a non-fault termination of the Agreement, and that the directors (D) were not disinterested and independent. Brehm (P) alleged that the Old Disney Board (D) failed to properly inform itself about the total costs and incentives of the Agreement, especially the severance package. The Board (D) had relied on a corporate compensation expert in connection with its decision to approve the Agreement. The expert, however, had not quantified for the Board (D) the maximum payout to Ovitz under the non-fault termination scenario. The expert later stated that

he should have done so at the time. Brehm (P) also charges the Board (D) with waste in that the severance package was over $140 million when Disney really owed Ovitz nothing because he either resigned or could have been fired for cause.

ISSUE: Do the particularized facts alleged in the complaint provide a reason to believe that the conduct of the New and Old Disney Boards (D) constituted a violation of their fiduciary duties?

HOLDING AND DECISION: (Veasey, C.J.) No. The particularized facts as alleged in the complaint do not provide a reason to believe that the conduct of the New and Old Disney Boards (D) constituted a violation of their fiduciary duties. Although the Boards' (D) actions probably did not demonstrate good business judgment of directors in that the compensation and termination payout to Ovitz was lucrative compared to his value to Disney, and the Boards' handling of the termination of the Agreement was sloppy, the 88-page complaint is conclusory, inartfully drafted, and was properly dismissed because it didn't meet the pleading standards for derivative suits. The pleading standards required are particularized factual statements that are essential to the claim, and they must be simple, concise, and direct. The plaintiff must allege with particularity facts raising a reasonable doubt that the corporate action being questioned was properly the product of business judgment. Conclusory allegations are not considered as expressly pleaded facts or factual inferences. In this case, the complaint does not comply with these fundamental pleading mandates as it is full of conclusory language. First, Brehm's (P) theory that the New Disney Board (D) was not disinterested because it was beholden to Eisner (D), and a lavish contract to Ovitz would result in Eisner's (D) own compensation increasing, is not supported by well-pleaded facts, only illogical and counterintuitive conclusory allegations. No reasonable doubt can exist as to Eisner's (D) disinterest in the approval of the Agreement, and Brehm (P) thus has not demonstrated a reasonable doubt that Eisner (D) was disinterested in granting Ovitz a non-fault termination. A majority of the New Disney Board (D) was therefore disinterested and independent. Second, the complaint does not set forth particularized facts creating a reasonable doubt that the decisions of the Boards (D) were not protected by the business judgment rule. Brehm (P) contends that the directors (D) did not avail themselves of all material information reasonably available in approving the Agreement and they, therefore, violated their fiduciary duty of care. The particularized facts in the complaint must create a reasonable doubt

Continued on next page.

that the informational component of the directors' (D) decisionmaking, measured by concepts of gross negligence, included consideration of all material information reasonably available. The economic exposure of Disney to the payout scenarios of the Agreement was material for purposes of the directors' (D) decisionmaking and the dollar exposure numbers were reasonably available. The complaint charges that the expert admitted that neither he nor the directors (D) made the calculation, although all the necessary information was at hand to do so. The trial court's reading of the complaint, that only the expert and not the Board (D) itself failed to bring to bear all the necessary information, was too restrictive, but such error was harmless. The directors (D) relied in good-faith on a qualified expert and therefore have the presumption that they exercised proper business judgment. Brehm (P) must rebut the presumption that the directors (D) properly exercised their business judgment, including their good-faith reliance on his expertise. The trial court's error is harmless because it is not a sufficient rebuttal to say what the expert now believes in hindsight as to what he and the Board (D) should have done in 1995. The complaint was therefore subject to dismissal. Brehm (P), however, should be provided the opportunity to properly replead this issue. Third, the complaint failed to set forth particularized facts creating a reasonable doubt that the directors' (D) decision to enter into the Agreement was a product of the proper exercise of business judgment. The Agreement was not a wasteful transaction for Disney. It was not an exchange that is so one-sided that no business person of ordinary, sound judgment could conclude that the corporation has received adequate consideration. The Boards' (D) decision on executive compensation is entitled to great deference. There are outer limits, but those are confined to unconscionable cases when directors irrationally squander or give away corporate assets. Fourth, the complaint as currently pled does not set forth particularized facts that Ovitz resigned or unarguably breached his Agreement. There are no facts that show he actually resigned before the Board (D) acted on his non-fault termination. Also, the complaint is inconsistent because it states that Ovitz would not actually resign before he could achieve a lucrative payout under the generous terms of his Agreement. Fifth, the complaint also alleges that it was waste to pay Ovitz under non-fault termination when the Boards could have fired him for cause. The facts in the complaint show that Ovitz's performance as president was disappointing at best and arguable grounds existed to fire him for cause. However, what is alleged is only an argument that his conduct constituted negligence or malfeasance. Disney would have had to persuade a trier of fact in litigation which would have been expensive, distracted executives and company resources, caused lost opportunity costs, bad publicity, and an uncertain outcome. The complaint does not show that no reasonable business person would have made the decision that the New Disney Board (D) made under these circumstances. Brehm (P) therefore will have another opportunity on remand to replead. The lower court's ruling is reversed, only as to its ruling of dismissal with prejudice as to claims for breach of fiduciary duty and waste which shall now be dismissed without prejudice. Remanded.

▶ *ANALYSIS*

Absent properly pled seriously egregious conduct on a board's behalf, it is evident from this case that it is unlikely that a court will hold a board liable for approving an employment agreement, and subsequent termination agreement, which costs the company a tremendous amount of money.

■■■■

Quicknotes

BREACH OF FIDUCIARY DUTY The failure of a fiduciary to observe the standard of care exercised by professionals of similar education and experience.

BUSINESS JUDGMENT RULE Doctrine relieving corporate directors and/or officers from liability for decisions honestly and rationally made in the corporation's best interests.

MALFEASANCE The commission of an unlawful act.

PLEADING A statement setting forth the plaintiff's cause of action or the defendant's defenses to the plaintiff's claims.

STOCKHOLDER'S DERIVATIVE SUIT Action asserted by a shareholder in order to enforce a cause of action on behalf of the corporation.

■■■■

In re Walt Disney Company Derivative Litigation

[Parties not identified.]

Del. Sup. Ct., 906 A.2d 27 (2006).

NATURE OF CASE: Appeal from judgment that no breaches of the fiduciary duties of due care and good faith have occurred.

FACT SUMMARY: Shareholders (P) of the Walt Disney Company (Disney) contended that Disney's compensation committee directors (D) violated the fiduciary duties of due care and good faith by approving an employment agreement for Ovitz, the OEA, which contained Non-Fault Termination (NFT) provisions that could potentially result in an enormous payout, without informing themselves of what the full magnitude of that payout could be.

RULE OF LAW

(1) Directors do not breach their duty of due care where, although they do not follow best practices, they are sufficiently informed about all material facts regarding a decision they make.
(2) "Intentional dereliction of duty, a conscious disregard for one's responsibilities" is an appropriate legal definition of bad faith.

FACTS: The directors (D) of the Walt Disney Company (Disney) entered into an employment agreement (OEA) with Ovitz that provided he would receive millions of dollars in severance, foregone bonuses, remaining salary payments and stock options if he were terminated without cause. Ovitz had left a very lucrative position with CAA to join Disney. The board (D) terminated Ovitz without cause not long after entering the OEA because the relationship was not working for the parties, and Disney shareholders (P) brought suit claiming that the directors (D) breached their fiduciary duties of loyalty, good faith, and due care by entering into the employment agreement and then by terminating Ovitz without cause. Specifically, the shareholders contended that Disney's compensation committee directors (D) violated the fiduciary duties of due care and good faith by approving the OEA, which contained Non-Fault Termination (NFT) provisions that could potentially result in an enormous payout, without informing themselves of what the full magnitude of that payout could be. After trial, the Delaware Chancery Court held that the directors had not breached their duties of due care or good faith. The Delaware Supreme Court granted review.

ISSUE:

(1) Do directors breach their duty of due care where, although they do not follow best practices, they are sufficiently informed about all material facts regarding a decision they make?

(2) Is "intentional dereliction of duty, a conscious disregard for one's responsibilities" an appropriate legal definition of bad faith?

HOLDING AND DECISION: (Jacobs, J.)

(1) No. Directors do not breach their duty of due care where, although they do not follow best practices, they are sufficiently informed about all material facts regarding a decision they make. The Chancery Court acknowledged that the compensation committee's decision-making process fell far short of corporate governance best practices, but nevertheless ruled that they were adequately informed about the OEA before approving it, so that they did not breach their duty of care. The shareholders (P) claim that the Chancery Court's decision was erroneous because the evidence showed that the compensation committee members did not properly inform themselves of the material facts, so that they were grossly negligent in approving the NFT provisions of the OEA. Under a best practices scenario, the committee members would have considered a matrix of alternative scenarios under the OEA. Instead, they considered a term sheet that summarized the material terms of the OEA. The term sheet disclosed what would happen in the case of a non-fault termination. Although this knowledge was not imparted in one tidy source, such as a spreadsheet—which would have been desirable under a best practices scenario—the information was made available to the compensation committee in various spreadsheets that had been prepared for the committee's meetings. The compensation committee members derived their information about the potential magnitude of an NFT payout from two sources. The first was the value of the "benchmark" options previously granted to other officers, along with their valuations, and the second was the amount of downside protection Ovitz was demanding. The committee members knew that by leaving CAA and coming to Disney, Ovitz would be sacrificing "booked" CAA commissions of $150 to $200 million—an amount that Ovitz demanded as protection against the risk that his employment relationship with Disney might not work out. Ovitz wanted at least $50 million of that compensation to take the form of an "up-front" signing bonus. Because it was decided to not grant such a bonus, the committee members knew that the value of the options had to be greater. They also knew that under the NFT, the earlier in the contract that Ovitz was terminated without cause, the

Continued on next page.

greater the severance payment would be. For these reasons, the Chancery Court did not err in concluding that there was sufficient evidence that the compensation committee members were adequately (if, albeit, not ideally) informed about the potential magnitude of an early NFT severance payout. Affirmed as to this issue.

(2) Yes. "Intentional dereliction of duty, a conscious disregard for one's responsibilities" is an appropriate legal definition of bad faith. This is the definition the Chancery Court used in assessing whether the directors (D) and compensation committee had not acted in good faith, and in holding that they had not acted in bad faith. The Chancery Court noted that this standard of bad faith is not the only one that can be used, but is an appropriate definition. The shareholders (P) argue that this is not an appropriate standard. The Chancery Court did not err in using this definition, because there are at least three different categories of fiduciary conduct that can give rise to a bad faith claim. The first is "subjective bad faith," which is fiduciary conduct motivated by an actual intent to do harm. Such conduct is not claimed to have occurred here. The second category involves lack of due care, which does not involve malevolent intent, but taken by reason of gross negligence (here, the Chancery Court did not find gross negligence). In any event, gross negligence by itself cannot constitute bad faith, as these are clearly distinguished in common law and by statute. In fact, the legislature has provided for exculpation of liability for the breach of due care duty. To adopt a definition that conflates the duty of care with the duty to act in good faith by making a violation of the former an automatic violation of the latter, would nullify those legislative protections. The third category falls between the first two, and this is the category intended to be captured by the Chancery Court's definition. The question is whether such misconduct is properly treated as a non-exculpable, non-indemnifiable violation of the fiduciary duty to act in good faith; the answer is "yes." That is because fiduciary misconduct is not limited to self-interested disloyalty or to gross negligence, but may lie somewhere in between these extremes. For example, the fiduciary may intentionally act with a purpose other than that of advancing the best interests of the corporation, may act with the intent to violate applicable positive law, or may intentionally fail to act in the face of a known duty to act, demonstrating a conscious disregard for his duties. Such an intermediate category of bad faith is also recognized statutorily, whereby gross negligence may be exculpated, but acts not in good faith may not. The Chancery Court's definition of bad faith encompasses this intermediate bad faith category, and, therefore, is appropriate. Affirmed as to this issue.

ANALYSIS

This case demonstrates, among other things, how the duty of directors to act in good faith is an independent duty that is on the same footing as the duties of care and of loyalty, and how that duty interacts with the other independent duties. Although the duty to act in good faith has always been part of corporate governance jurisprudence, it has been only relatively recently that the duty has been viewed as an independent duty, rather than as a duty subsumed within the other fiduciary duties.

■■■

Quicknotes

BAD FAITH Conduct that is intentionally misleading or deceptive.

BREACH OF FIDUCIARY DUTY The failure of a fiduciary to observe the standard of care exercised by professionals of similar education and experience.

DUTY OF CARE Duty that an officer or director owes to the corporation, by virtue of his fiduciary relationship, to act for the benefit of the corporation.

GOOD FAITH An honest intention to abstain from taking advantage of another.

STOCKHOLDER'S DERIVATIVE SUIT Action asserted by a shareholder in order to enforce a cause of action on behalf of the corporation.

■■■

Miller v. U.S. Foodservice, Inc.

Former director/officer (P) v. Corporation (D)

361 F. Supp. 2d 470 (D. Md. 2005).

NATURE OF CASE: Action for breach of employment agreement and countersuit for breach of fiduciary duties.

FACT SUMMARY: Miller (P), a former officer and director of United States Foodservice, Inc. (USF) (D), and a director of its parent, Royal Ahold (D), sued both companies for breach of his employment agreement. The companies counterclaimed that because Miller (P) had breached his fiduciary duties, they were not obligated to provide him benefits under the agreement.

🏛 RULE OF LAW

A claim of breach of the fiduciary duties of care and good faith is stated where it is alleged that an officer/director intentionally misled the corporation's audit committee about the implementation of corrective internal controls.

FACTS: Miller (P) was an officer and director of United States Foodservice, Inc. (USF) (D), and a director of its parent, Royal Ahold (D). He resigned from these positions after an accounting scandal involving an USF's (D) income from promotional allowances, which are payments made by vendors to the company to promote their goods. Internal investigations revealed that USF (D) accounting irregularities had resulted in an overstatement of USF's (D) income by nearly $900 million for two fiscal years. Miller (P) averred that he had absolutely no involvement in the purported wrongful conduct and that the companies treated him as a scapegoat for the problem. The companies claimed that Miller (P) had knowledge of the problems and was responsible for them over a period of three years. They also asserted that Miller (P) knew ineffective tracking of promotional allowances had the potential to cause USF (D) to overstate its income and thus to show phantom profits, and that Miller's (P) incentive-based compensation depended on the net profitability of USF (D). They asserted that he was alerted to the internal control problems by the company's external auditor and that he intentionally misrepresented to the USF Audit Committee that corrective measures were being implemented several times during the audit process. In fact, no significant progress had been made on implementing the necessary changes. Miller (P) resigned from his positions at Royal Ahold's (D) request, and then sued the companies in federal district court for failing to provide him with post-termination benefits he claimed he was entitled to under his employment agreement. The companies countersued, claiming that Miller (P) had breached his fiduciary duties and that, therefore, they were not obligated to provide him with the benefits he sought.

ISSUE: Is a claim of breach of the fiduciary duties of care and good faith stated where it is alleged that an officer/director intentionally misled the corporation's audit committee about the implementation of corrective internal controls?

HOLDING AND DECISION: (Blake, J.) Yes. A claim of breach of the fiduciary duties of care and good faith is stated where it is alleged that an officer/director intentionally misled the corporation's audit committee about the implementation of corrective internal controls. Miller (P) claimed his actions were protected by the business judgment rule. However, although the companies' allegations did not directly suggest that Miller (P) should have suspected wrongdoing, he nonetheless had a duty to ensure that, an adequate information and reporting system, existed. First and foremost, directors and officers must assure that a reporting system exists that is "in concept and design adequate" to provide appropriate and timely information to them so that they may satisfy their monitoring responsibility. Therefore, questions as to whether a director had grounds to suspect wrongdoing by other officers or directors presume the existence of an adequate reporting system. The most critical support for the companies' claims that Miller (P) breached fiduciary duties of care and good faith, however, is the allegation that Miller (P), for a period of almost three years, intentionally misrepresented to the USF Audit Committee (and consequently to the parent company) that the internal controls were being corrected. If these allegations are true, they may constitute persuasive evidence that Miller (P) acted in bad faith, thereby violating duties of both care and good faith. Additionally, Miller's (P) dual role as director and officer magnifies the importance of the duties he owed and allegedly violated. Construing the allegations in the light most favorable to the counterclaiming companies, they have stated claims against Miller (P) for breach of the fiduciary duties of care and good faith.

▶ ANALYSIS

Under the Sarbanes-Oxley Act of 2002, the corporation's chief executive officer (CEO) and chief financial officer (CFO) must certify in each quarterly and annual filings with the SEC, among other things, that based on their knowledge the reports are not misleading and fairly present the company's financial situation, and that they have disclosed to the auditors and the audit committee any material deficiencies in the designer operation of the company's financial controls. Knowingly making a false certification exposes the CEO or CFO to criminal penalties, including up to 20 years in prison.

Continued on next page.

This raises the issue of whether a CEO or CFO should face liability for breach of fiduciary duty if their conduct does not violate the Sarbanes-Oxley Act. Arguably, the fiduciary duties of officers and directors are broader than the duties imposed by the Act, as they cover conduct that is broader in scope than that covered by the Act.

■═■

Quicknotes

BREACH The violation of an obligation imposed pursuant to contract or law, by acting or failing to act.

BREACH OF FIDUCIARY DUTY The failure of a fiduciary to observe the standard of care exercised by professionals of similar education and experience.

BUSINESS JUDGMENT RULE Doctrine relieving corporate directors and/or officers from liability for decisions honestly and rationally made in the corporation's best interests.

■═■

Aronson v. Lewis

Corporation (D) v. Shareholder (P)

Del. Sup. Ct., 473 A.2d 805 (1984).

NATURE OF CASE: Interlocutory appeal to review denied motion to dismiss a derivative suit.

FACT SUMMARY: Lewis (P), a shareholder, filed a derivative action based upon the excessiveness of certain management salary contracts, but Lewis (P) made no demand on the board for redress due to his conclusion that such action was futile.

🏛 RULE OF LAW
A stockholder must make a demand upon the board of directors to redress a wrong prior to the filing of a derivative suit, unless he can allege facts, with particularity, which creates a reasonable doubt that the directors' action was entitled to protections of the business judgment rule.

FACTS: Meyers Parking Systems, Inc. (Meters) was formed in 1979 as a subsidiary company spun off from its parent. Leo Fink, a director of Meyers, owned 47% of Meyers's stock. Fink was paid a consulting fee which was shared by Meyers and its old parent corporation. In 1981, Fink entered into an employment contract with Meyers for five years, automatically renewable each year thereafter. Fink was to receive $150,000 plus a 5% bonus of pretax profits over $2,400,000. At termination, Fink was to be paid a consulting salary of at least $100,000 a year for life. Fink was 75 years old when the contract was approved. Large interest-free loans were also made to Fink. Lewis (P), a shareholder, challenged the entire arrangement as "grossly excessive" and a "waste of corporate assets." However, Lewis (P) did not make a demand on the board of directors to correct the alleged wrong due to a belief that the directors, chosen by Fink, could not make an untainted decision. Lewis (P) filed a derivative action before the Court of Chancery. Defendants appealed the denial of their motion to dismiss.

ISSUE: Must a stockholder make a demand upon the board of directors to redress a wrong prior to the filing of a derivative suit?

HOLDING AND DECISION: (Moore, J.) Yes. A stockholder must make a demand upon the board of directors to redress a wrong prior to the filing of a derivative suit unless he can allege facts, with particularity, which creates a reasonable doubt that the directors' action was entitled to protections of the business judgment rule. The board of directors is charged with the management of the corporation. To protect the managerial discretion of the board, the law requires that a shareholder demand action from the board to correct a wrong to the corporation before filing suit. However, where demand would be futile, the shareholder need not seek redress

before filing suit Mere board approval of a challenged action does not prove that the demand requirement would be meaningless. To show demand futility, particular facts must raise a reasonable doubt that the directors are independent. If such a doubt cannot be raised, then definite facts must raise a reasonable doubt that the transaction was otherwise a valid exercise of business judgment. The entire review is factual in nature. In the instant case, no such particular facts have been alleged. Fink owns less than a majority of stock, so he is not in total control of the corporation. Even majority stock control does not strip directors of the presumption of independence. No facts are offered to show that Fink will not merit the payments he is to receive. Lewis (P) has not shown a factual setting in which demand upon the board is excused. Reversed and remanded with leave to amend.

▶ ANALYSIS

The decision in this case has also affected cases where a demand was made on the board. In cases where demand has been made, the plaintiff is deemed to have tacitly conceded that the board is independent. Thus, the only inquiry left to be made when the demand is refused by the board rests on the analysis of good faith in the board's inquiry into the matter.

■━■

Quicknotes

BUSINESS JUDGMENT RULE Doctrine relieving corporate directors and/or officers from liability for decisions honestly and rationally made in the corporation's best interests.

DERIVATIVE SUIT An action asserted by a shareholder in order to enforce a cause of action on behalf of the corporation.

INTERLOCUTORY APPEAL The appeal of an issue that does not resolve the disposition of the case, but is essential to a determination of the parties' legal rights.

■━■

In re The Limited, Inc. Shareholders Litigation

[Parties not identified.]

Del. Ch. Ct., 2002 WL 537692 (2002).

NATURE OF CASE: Motion to dismiss in shareholder derivative action.

FACT SUMMARY: Shareholders (P) of The Limited sued the Company (D) and its Board Directors (D) for committing waste and breaching their fiduciary duty of loyalty and due care.

RULE OF LAW

There is a reasonable doubt as to a director/largest shareholder's disinterestedness in connection with a company's rescission of an agreement which he negotiated for the benefit of his children. Moreover, directors who are so beholden to that shareholder so as to create a reasonable doubt about their independence are also not disinterested. To constitute waste, the transactions must be shown to have served no corporate purpose.

FACTS: The Limited (D) authorized a self-tender offer for up to 15 million shares of stock and also rescinded an agreement that included a call option to purchase 18.75 million shares of common stock from a trust set up for the benefit of Wexner's (D), The Limited's (D) founder and its largest shareholder/director, children. Under the terms of the tender offer, The Limited (D) agreed to purchase those shares at a premium over their preannouncement closing price. The Board (D) concluded that the stock repurchase was the most attractive method for utilizing the Company's (D) excess cash and would demonstrate how much confidence it had in the business. Under the Agreement, the Trust had acquired the right through January 2006 to require The Limited (D) to redeem all or a portion of the 18.75 million shares of common stock it held at $18.75 per share or through July 2006 at $25.07. $350 million was to remain in a restricted account to satisfy the obligations under the now rescinded Agreement. Stockholders (P) of The Limited (D) brought a derivative suit, on behalf of The Limited (D), against The Limited (D) and its Board (D). They alleged that the Board (D) committed corporate waste and breached its fiduciary duties of loyalty and due care by rescinding the Agreement and funding, in part with monies made available as the result of rescission of the Agreement, a self-tender offer that resulted in no consideration to the Company. They allege that such transactions were done only to benefit Wexner (D) in that he could avoid the Agreement. There was thus no legitimate business purpose for the transactions, and the transactions also came as a detriment to the Company (D) because, had the Company (D) purchased the Trust's shares, it would have saved $280 million due to the Trust's shares being sold

for less than the Company's (D) current trading price of $40. The breach of the fiduciary duty of loyalty arises from at least half of the Board members (D) having a disqualifying self-interest in the transactions due to their relationships with Wexner (D). The Directors (D) brought a motion to dismiss.

ISSUE:

(1) Have the stockholders (P) met the pre-suit demand requirements?

(2) Have the stockholders (P) stated an actionable claim for breach of fiduciary duty?

(3) Have the shareholders (P) failed to state an actionable claim for corporate waste?

HOLDING AND DECISION: (Noble, V. Chan.)

(1) Yes. The stockholders (P) have met the pre-suit demand requirements. When a plaintiff initiates a shareholder derivative action without first making a demand on the company's board, the complaint must allege with particularity the reasons justifying the plaintiff's failure to do so. The stockholders (P) have alleged sufficient particularized facts to raise a reasonable doubt as to the disinterestedness of at least six of the twelve directors (D). Since Wexner (D), in his individual capacity and as trustee for the Trust, negotiated the Agreement that was for the benefit of his children, the complaint has alleged sufficiently particularized facts creating a reasonable doubt as to his disinterestedness in the Company's (D) rescission of that Agreement. Mrs. Wexner (D) similarly stood to benefit. Four of the other directors, although not themselves financially interested in the transactions, were so beholden to Wexner (D), or so under his influence, as to create a reasonable doubt about their independence. One's position as a director for a number of years, the receipt of director's fees, or receiving revenues from The Limited (D) that are not material, are not facts which raise a doubt as to independence. An individual's receiving material compensation from principle employment at The Limited (D) or its subsidiary; material consulting fees from The Limited (D); and gifts given from Wexner (D) to a university because of that individual's solicitation raises a reasonable doubt as to that individual's independence from Wexner's (D) will. The shareholders (P) have thus met their burden to demonstrate the futility of making a demand on the Board (D).

(2) Yes. The stockholders have stated an actionable claim for breach of the duty of loyalty because six out of

Continued on next page.

twelve directors (D) who approved the transactions were interested. Because the challenged transactions were not approved by a majority of independent and disinterested directors, the complaint states a loyalty claim.

(3) Yes. The stockholders (P) have failed to state an actionable claim for corporate waste. To constitute waste, the transactions must be shown to have served no corporate purpose. Since the stocks under the Agreement couldn't have been sold until seven years after The Limited's (D) announcement of rescinding the Agreement, it is unknown whether The Limited's (D) stock would have continued to rise in value, and it is mere speculation to say what benefit the Company (D) may have enjoyed. Furthermore, freeing up $350 million, in light of the market's volatility, was well within the realm of reason. Therefore, the stockholders (P) have failed to allege facts supporting a claim that rescission of the Agreement served no corporate purpose. The stockholders (P) have also failed to allege that the self-tender was waste because it was not so one-sided that no business person of ordinary, sound judgment could conclude that the Corporation had not received adequate consideration. It is not enough for the complaint to give alternatives to the tender offer. The stockholders (P) have thus failed to demonstrate that The Limited (D) received no benefit in exchange from these two transactions. Wexner (D) didn't take part in the tender offer, the Company (D) had $350 million in cash to use, and it protected itself from having to fulfill its promise under the Agreement in case the stock prices fell. Furthermore, there is no breach of the duty of care because the complaint does not allege gross negligence. Motions to dismiss denied in part and granted in part.

▌ *ANALYSIS*

This is another case demonstrating the court's unwillingness to substitute its judgment for that of a board, unless there is clear, egregious conduct in the board's decision.

■■■

Quicknotes

BREACH OF FIDUCIARY DUTY The failure of a fiduciary to observe the standard of care exercised by professionals of similar education and experience.

DUTY OF CARE Duty that an officer or director owes to the corporation, by virtue of his fiduciary relationship, to act for the benefit of the corporation.

DUTY OF LOYALTY A director's duty to refrain from self-dealing or to take a position that is adverse to the corporation's best interests.

MOTION TO DISMISS Motion to terminate a trial based on the adequacy of the pleadings.

STOCKHOLDER'S DERIVATIVE SUIT Action asserted by a shareholder in order to enforce a cause of action on behalf of the corporation.

TENDER OFFER An offer made by one corporation to the shareholders of a target corporation to purchase their shares subject to number, time, and price specifications.

■■■

Ryan v. Gifford

Shareholder (P) v. Directors (D)

Del. Ch. Ct., 918 A.2d 341 (2007).

NATURE OF CASE: Action for breach of the duty of loyalty and the duty of care.

FACT SUMMARY: Ryan (P), a shareholder of Maxim Integrated Products, Inc. (Maxim), alleged that Maxim's directors (D) and members of the board's compensation committee breached their duties of loyalty and care by approving or accepting backdated options.

🏛 **RULE OF LAW**
(1) A complaint that alleges the deliberate violation of a shareholder approved stock option plan, coupled with fraudulent disclosures, sufficiently alleges bad faith to rebut the business judgment rule presumption and survive dismissal.
(2) A shareholder does not have standing to bring a breach of fiduciary action based on the backdating of options that occurred while he was not a shareholder.

FACTS: Ryan (P), a shareholder of Maxim Integrated Products, Inc. (Maxim) since 2001, who became a shareholder via a merger, alleged that Maxim's directors (D) and compensation committee members breached their duties of loyalty and care by approving or accepting backdated options for millions of shares of Maxim stock between 1998 and 2002. The practice known as backdating options involves a company issuing stock options to an executive on one date while providing fraudulent documentation asserting that the options were actually issued earlier. Ryan (P) challenged nine options grants, all of which seemed to be backdated; they were all dated on unusually low (if not the lowest) trading days, or on days immediately before sharp increases in Maxim's stock price. The plans pursuant to which the grants were made required that the exercise price of the options granted would be no less than the fair market value of the company's stock. The board or a compensation committee designated by the board was identified as the plans' administrators. As a result of the backdating, Ryan (P) asserted that Maxim received lower payments upon exercise of the option than it would have received in the absence of backdating, and that Maxim suffered adverse effects from tax and accounting rules that would require restatement of the company's financial statements and tax returns. The directors (D) moved to dismiss for failure to state a claim on the grounds that Ryan (P) failed to rebut the business judgment rule, since the directors (D) did not act intentionally, in bad faith, or for personal gain. The directors (D) also asserted that

Ryan (P) lacked standing to challenge the grants that occurred before he was a shareholder.

ISSUE:
(1) Does a complaint that alleges the deliberate violation of a shareholder approved stock option plan, coupled with fraudulent disclosures, sufficiently allege bad faith to rebut the business judgment rule presumption and survive dismissal?
(2) Does a shareholder have standing to bring a breach of fiduciary action based on the backdating of options that occurred while he was not a shareholder?

HOLDING AND DECISION: (Chandler, Chan.)
(1) Yes. A complaint that alleges the deliberate violation of a shareholder approved stock option plan, coupled with fraudulent disclosures, sufficiently alleges bad faith to rebut the business judgment rule presumption and survive dismissal. The business judgment rule is a presumption that in making business decisions, directors act on an informed basis, in good faith, and in the honest belief that the action taken was in the best interest of the company. However, a showing that the board breached either its fiduciary duty of care or of loyalty in connection with its decision may rebut this presumption. Acts taken in bad faith breach the duty of loyalty. The allegations here state a claim for bad faith, because if true, they involve disloyalty to the company's best interests. There would not be an instance where the deliberate violation of a shareholder approved stock option plan and false disclosures, intended to mislead shareholders, would be anything but an act of bad faith. Therefore, well-pleaded allegations of such conduct are sufficient to survive dismissal.
(2) No. A shareholder does not have standing to bring a breach of fiduciary action based on the backdating of options that occurred while he was not a shareholder. Only two of the nine challenged grants occurred while Ryan (P) was a shareholder. The corporate law of the state (DGCL § 327) clearly provides that a shareholder seeking to bring a derivative action must have been a shareholder at the time of the complained-of transaction or acquired his shares by operation of law. Ryan (P) satisfies these requirements as to only two of the grants. Therefore, his claims must be dismissed as to the other seven grants that occurred when he was not a shareholder.

Continued on next page.

▶ *ANALYSIS*

The backdating of option grants is a novel area for the courts, and has arisen primarily based on newspaper articles and some reports that have shed light on backdating of grants as pervading the corporate landscape. As the court points out, it was a March 18, 2006 Wall Street Journal article that sparked controversy throughout the investment community about backdating. The article had published an academic's statistical analysis of option grants that revealed that backdating was likely occurring in many instances. Afterward, Merrill Lynch issued a report demonstrating that officers of numerous companies, including Maxim, had benefited from so many fortuitously timed stock option grants that backdating seemed the only logical explanation. It was the article and report that caused Ryan (P) to file suit.

■▬■

Quicknotes

BAD FAITH   Conduct that is intentionally misleading or deceptive.

BUSINESS JUDGMENT RULE   Doctrine relieving corporate directors and/or officers from liability for decisions honestly and rationally made in the corporation's best interests.

DUTY OF CARE   Duty that an officer or director owes to the corporation, by virtue of his fiduciary relationship, to act for the benefit of the corporation.

DUTY OF LOYALTY   A director's duty to refrain from self-dealing or to take a position that is adverse to the corporation's best interests.

SHAREHOLDERS' DERIVATIVE ACTION   An action asserted by a shareholder in order to enforce a cause of action on behalf of the corporation.

STOCK OPTIONS   The right to purchase or sell a particular stock at a specified price within a certain time period.

■▬■

Stone v. Ritter

Shareholder (P) v. Corporate directors (D)

Del. Sup. Ct., 911 A.2d 362 (2006).

NATURE OF CASE: Appeal from judgment dismissing derivative action.

FACT SUMMARY: Shareholders (P) bringing a derivative action against AmSouth Bancorporation (AmSouth) directors (D) contended that demand was excused because the directors (D) breached their oversight duty and utterly failed to act in good faith regarding compliance with various banking regulations, thus facing a likelihood of personal liability that would render them incapable of exercising independent and disinterested judgment in response to a demand request.

🏛 **RULE OF LAW**

A derivative action will be dismissed for failure to make demand where alleged particularized facts do not create a reasonable doubt that the corporation's directors acted in good faith in exercising their oversight responsibilities.

FACTS: AmSouth Bancorporation (AmSouth) was a holding company whose wholly-owned subsidiary, AmSouth Bank, operated hundreds of banking branches. In 2004, AmSouth and AmSouth Bank paid $40 million in fines and $10 million in civil penalties to resolve government and regulatory investigations pertaining principally to the failure by bank employees to file "Suspicious Activity Reports" (SARs), as required by the federal Bank Secrecy Act (BSA) and various federal anti-money-laundering (AML) regulations. These violations were discovered after a "Ponzi" scheme, which was unwittingly aided by AmSouth branch employees, was uncovered. Although the corporation had in place an extensive, information and reporting system, in its investigation, the government concluded that "AmSouth's compliance program lacked adequate board and management oversight." AmSouth shareholders (P) brought a derivative action against the corporation's present and former directors (D) based on these events, without first making demand on the board. AmSouth's Certificate of Incorporation contained a provision that would exculpate its directors for breaches of their duty of care, provided they acted in good faith. The directors (D) moved to dismiss for lack of demand, and the Chancery Court held that the shareholders (P) had failed to adequately plead that such a demand would have been futile, finding that the directors (D) had not been alerted by any "red flags" that violations of law were occurring. The state's highest court granted review.

ISSUE: Will a derivative action be dismissed for failure to make demand where alleged particularized facts do not create a reasonable doubt that the corporation's directors

acted in good faith in exercising their oversight responsibilities?

HOLDING AND DECISION: (Holland, J.) Yes. A derivative action will be dismissed for failure to make demand where alleged particularized facts do not create a reasonable doubt that the corporation's directors acted in good faith in exercising their oversight responsibilities. The allegations made by the shareholders (P) are a classic "*Caremark*" claim (named after *In re Caremark Int'l Deriv. Litig.* 698 A.2d 959 (Del. Ch. 1996)). Such a claim of directorial liability is premised on the directors' ignorance of liability-creating activities (such as criminal conduct or failure to follow regulations) within the corporation. In *Caremark*, the court ruled that directors will face personal liability only where there has been a sustained or systematic failure of the board to exercise oversight, as where there is an utter failure to even attempt to implement or monitor a reasonable information and reporting system. Here, the shareholders (P) asserted that because it was likely the directors would face such personal liability, they could not be reasonably expected to exercise independent and disinterested judgment when faced with a pre-suit demand. However, AmSouth's Certificate of Incorporation's exculpatory provision will shield the directors (D) from liability as long as they acted in good faith—so if they acted in good faith, demand would not be excused. Thus, it must be determined whether the directors (D) acted in good faith. The standard for this determination has evolved. The standard in cases such as this is that the board must assure itself that information and reporting systems exist in the corporation that are reasonably designed to provide to senior management and to the board itself timely, accurate information to permit the board, as well as management, to reach informed decisions about the corporation's compliance with law and its business performance. As the *Caremark* court observed, "the duty to act in good faith cannot be thought to require directors to possess detailed information about all aspects of the operation of the enterprise." Thus, only where there is a sustained or systematic failure to ensure an adequate information and reporting system is in place, or, if such a system is in place, where the board consciously fails to monitor it or oversee its operations, will there be a showing of lack of good faith. Additionally, there must be a showing that the directors knew they were not discharging their fiduciary duties. In fact, recent decisions show that this formulation is consistent with examples of bad faith. The Chancery Court applied this standard and was, therefore, correct in doing so. When this standard is applied to the

Continued on next page.

facts pleaded by the shareholders (P), it becomes clear that the directors (P) did not fail to act in good faith. The facts showed that the directors (D) had established a reasonable information and reporting system and had set up numerous departments and committees to oversee AmSouth's compliance with federal banking regulations. This system also permitted the board to periodically monitor such compliance. Here, while it is clear with hindsight, that the organization's internal controls were inadequate there were also no "red flags" to put the board on notice of any wrongdoing. The directors (D) took the steps they needed to ensure a reasonable information and reporting system existed. Therefore, although there ultimately may have been failures by employees to report deficiencies to the board, there is no basis for an oversight claim seeking to hold the directors personally liable for such failures by the employees; a bad (and very costly) outcome does not per se equate to bad faith. Affirmed.

▌ ANALYSIS

The court in this case makes a point of clarifying doctrinal issues related to the duty of good faith. First, the court emphasizes that the failure to act in good faith is a condition to finding a breach of the fiduciary duty of loyalty and imposing fiduciary liability. The court explains that "a failure to act in good faith is not conduct that results, ipso facto, in the direct imposition of fiduciary liability. The failure to act in good faith may result in liability because the requirement to act in good faith 'is a subsidiary element[,]' i.e., a condition, 'of the fundamental duty of loyalty.' It follows that because a showing of bad faith conduct . . . is essential to establish director oversight liability, the fiduciary duty violated by that conduct is the duty of loyalty." Second, and as a corollary, the duty to act in good faith does not establish an independent fiduciary duty that stands on the same footing as the duty of care and loyalty. A failure to act in good faith gives rise to liability only indirectly. Further, as a corollary, the fiduciary duty of loyalty is not limited to financial or similar conflicts of interest, but also encompasses cases where a director has failed to act in good faith.

■═■

Quicknotes

DEMAND REQUIREMENT Requirement that a shareholder make a demand for corrective action by the board of directors before commencing a derivative suit.

DERIVATIVE SUIT An action asserted by a shareholder in order to enforce a cause of action on behalf of the corporation.

DUTY OF CARE Duty that an officer or director owes to the corporation, by virtue of his fiduciary relationship, to act for the benefit of the corporation.

DUTY OF LOYALTY A director's duty to refrain from self-dealing or to take a position that is adverse to the corporation's best interests.

FIDUCIARY DUTY A legal obligation to act for the benefit of another, including subordinating one's personal interests to that of the other person.

GOOD FAITH An honest intention to abstain from taking advantage of another.

■═■

Zapata Corp. v. Maldonado

Corporation (D) v. Stockholder (P)

Del. Sup. Ct., 430 A.2d 779 (1981).

NATURE OF CASE: Interlocutory appeal in a stockholder's derivative suit.

FACT SUMMARY: Maldonado (P) had initiated a derivative suit charging officers and directors of Zapata (D) with breaches of fiduciary duty, but four years later an "Independent Investigation Committee" of two disinterested directors recommended dismissing the action.

🏛 RULE OF LAW
Where the making of a prior demand upon the directors of a corporation to sue is excused and a stockholder initiates a derivative suit on behalf of the corporation, the board of directors or an independent committee appointed by the board can move to dismiss the derivative suit as detrimental to the corporation's best interests and the court should apply a two-step test to the motion: (1) Has the corporation proved independence, good faith, and a reasonable investigation? (2) Does the court feel, applying its own independent business judgment, that the motion should be granted?

FACTS: At the time Maldonado (P) instituted a derivative suit against Zapata (D), he was excused from making a prior demand on the board of directors because they were all defendants (Maldonado [P] asserting a breach of fiduciary duty on the part of officers and directors of Zapata [D]). The board had changed membership when, four years later, it appointed an "Independent Investigation Committee," composed of two new directors, to investigate the litigation. The committee recommended dismissing the action, calling its continued maintenance "inimical to the Company's best interests . . ." In an interlocutory appeal before the Supreme Court of Delaware, the primary focus was on whether or not the aforementioned committee had the power to dismiss the action.

ISSUE: In a case in which a stockholder acted properly in instituting a derivative suit on behalf of the corporation without first making a demand on the board of directors to sue, can the board of directors or an independent committee they appoint move to dismiss the suit as detrimental to the best interests of the corporation?

HOLDING AND DECISION: (Quillen, J.) Yes. Where, as in this case, a stockholder acted properly in bringing a derivative suit without first demanding the directors file suit (i.e., where such a demand is "excused"), the board of directors or an independent committee they appoint has the power to choose not to pursue the litigation because such would not be in the best interests of the corporation. The fact that a majority of the board may have been tainted by self-interest is not per se a legal bar to the delegation of the board's power to an independent committee composed of disinterested board members. Thus, a committee, such as that involved in this case, can properly act for the corporation to move to dismiss derivative litigation that is believed to be detrimental to the corporation's best interests. When faced with such a motion, the court should give each side an opportunity to make a record on the motion. The moving party should be prepared to meet the normal burden of showing that there is no genuine issue as to any material fact and that it is entitled to dismiss as a matter of law. The court should apply a two-step test to the motion. First, it should inquire into the independence and good faith of the committee and the bases supporting its conclusions. To aid in such inquiries, limited discovery may be ordered. If the court determines either that the committee is not independent or has not shown reasonable bases for its conclusions, or if the court is not satisfied for other reasons relating to the process, including but not limited to the good faith of the committee, the court shall deny the corporation's motion. It must be remembered that the corporation has the burden of proving independence, good faith, and reasonableness. If the court is satisfied that the committee was independent and showed reasonable bases for good-faith findings and recommendations, the court may proceed, in its discretion, to the second step. This second step provides the essential key in striking the balance between legitimate corporate claims as expressed in a derivative stockholder suit and a corporation's best interests as expressed by an independent investigating committee. The court should determine, applying its own independent business judgment, whether the motion should be granted. This second step is intended to thwart instances where corporation actions meet the criteria of step one, but the result does not appear to satisfy the spirit or where corporate actions would simply prematurely terminate a stockholder grievance deserving of further consideration in the corporation's interest. Of course, the court must carefully consider and weigh how compelling the corporate interest in dismissal is when faced with a nonfrivolous lawsuit. It should, when appropriate, give special consideration to matters of law and public policy in addition to the corporation's best interests. If, after all of this, the court's independent business judgment is satisfied, it may proceed to grant the motion, subject, of course, to any equitable terms or conditions it finds necessary or desirable. Reversed and remanded for further proceedings.

Continued on next page.

▶ *ANALYSIS*

Other courts have chosen to treat this type of situation as one where the business judgment rule is applicable. They look to see if the committee to whom the board of directors delegated the responsibility of determining if the litigation at issue should be continued was composed of independent and disinterested members and if it conducted a proper review of the matters before it to reach a good-faith business judgment concerning whether or not to continue the litigation. If it did, the committee's decision stands. This court found that approach too one-sided, as tending to wrest bona fide derivative actions away from well-meaning derivative plaintiffs and robbing the shareholders of an effective intracorporate means of policing boards of directors.

■≡■

Quicknotes

BREACH OF FIDUCIARY DUTY The failure of a fiduciary to observe the standard of care exercised by professionals of similar education and experience.

BUSINESS JUDGMENT RULE Doctrine relieving corporate directors and/or officers from liability for decisions honestly and rationally made in the corporation's best interests.

■≡■

Owens Corning v. National Union Fire Insurance Co.

Corporation (P) v. Insurer (D)

257 F.3d 484 (6th Cir. 2001).

NATURE OF CASE: Appeal from declaratory judgment in diversity insurance coverage action.

FACT SUMMARY: Owens Corning (P) maintained that indemnification of its officers and directors for litigation costs they incurred in defending and settling asbestos-related shareholder class action claims was covered under an insurance policy issued by National Union Insurance (National Union) (D).

🏛 RULE OF LAW
Where a directors and officers (D & O) insurance policy requires that indemnification of directors and officers be made "pursuant to law," the insurer must reimburse an insured corporation that has indemnified its directors and officers pursuant to a bylaw that presumes the directors and officers acted in good faith, and where that good-faith presumption is unrebutted by the insurer.

FACTS: National Union Insurance (National Union) (D) issued a directors and officers (D & O) insurance policy that insured Owens Corning (P) for expenses it incurred in indemnifying its directors and officers against certain liabilities arising from losses or claims made against directors or officers in the respective capacities as directors and officers, "but only when and to the extent that [Owens Corning (P)] indemnified the Directors or Officers for such Loss pursuant to law, common or statutory, or contract . . ." Owens Corning (P) and several of its directors and officers were named as defendants in an asbestos-related class-action lawsuit brought by Owens Corning (P) shareholders. Owens Corning (P) settled the suit for about $10 million. National Union (D) was kept fully apprised of the ongoing negotiations, but did not participate in the defense of settlement of the action. After indemnifying its directors and officers for their defense and settlement costs which it was required by its bylaws to do, Owens Corning (P) requested reimbursement from National Union (D), which denied coverage. Owens Corning (P) then brought a diversity action in federal district court for a declaratory judgment that National Union (D) was obligated to pay under the policy all sums that Owens Corning (P) had incurred in the defense and settlement of the lawsuit, less the applicable deductible. The district court determined that Owens Corning's (P) indemnification of its directors and officers comported with indemnification law and entered judgment for Owens Corning (P), and the court of appeals granted review.

ISSUE: Where a directors and officers (D & O) insurance policy requires that indemnification of directors and officers be made "pursuant to law," must the insurer reimburse an insured corporation that has indemnified its directors and officers pursuant to a bylaw that presumes the directors and officers acted in good faith, and where that good-faith presumption is unrebutted by the insurer?

HOLDING AND DECISION: (Boggs, J.) Yes. Where a directors and officers (D & O) insurance policy requires that indemnification of directors and officers be made "pursuant to law," the insurer must reimburse an insured corporation that has indemnified its directors and officers pursuant to a bylaw that presumes the directors and officers acted in good faith, and where that good-faith presumption is unrebutted by the insurer. The law requires that directors or officers have acted in good faith before they may be indemnified, even where a corporation's bylaws require that the corporation indemnify directors or officers for their costs. This good-faith requirement is statutory and cannot be waived. National Union (D) contends that Owens Corning (P) failed to comply with the default method for the determination of good faith, and, therefore, the indemnification was not "pursuant to law" as required by the insurance policy. Owens Corning (P) argues that its bylaws provide an independent basis for indemnification without reference to good faith, or, in the alternative, that its indemnification was statutorily mandated and that the settlement constituted "success on the merits or otherwise." Although the indemnification did not violate law, neither of Owens Corning's (P) arguments is persuasive. First, the corporation cannot avoid the good-faith requirement through the provision of an alternative basis for indemnification. Second, it is dubious that the settlement payout (almost $10 million) constituted "success" under the applicable law. Equating compromise of such a degree with success would create considerable tension with the mandatory nature of statutory indemnification, since indemnification arising from such a success could presumably be challenged for lack of directorial good faith. Nonetheless, corporations do have significant flexibility regarding their procedures, as long as they remain consistent with public policy and controlling corporate law. Additionally, it is not impermissible for a corporation to accord a director seeking indemnification a rebuttable presumption of good faith. Therefore, where a corporation has extended indemnification to the maximum permissible extent, as Owens Corning (P) has done, such a presumption may be applied. Thus, good faith may be presumed under the expansive bylaws of Owens Corning (P), even if the relevant determination is not specifically made. On this basis, National Union (D) could have challenged whether the directors and officers were acting in good faith, but it

Continued on next page.

did not. Because the indemnification occurred in relation to a settlement, in which good faith was required, and because such good faith was made subject to a presumption through the corporate bylaws that remains unrebutted, the indemnification proceeded "according to law," and was not made in breach of the policy. Affirmed.

▶ *ANALYSIS*

The law applied in this case was Delaware law. Under Delaware statutory law, there are two types of indemnification. One kind is mandatory indemnification, where the indemnified officer or director has been "successful on the merits or otherwise." The second type is permissive indemnification, which may occur, if the corporation so chooses, where the directors or officers are deemed to have acted in good faith. As the court pointed out, some courts of appeals have been willing to extend the meaning of "success" to payment of a substantial monetary settlement, provided the defendant has not conceded liability. The court in this case saw potential for abuse under such an interpretation, whereby directors would be allowed to structure a settlement to shift costs to the insurer.

■═■

Quicknotes

CLASS ACTION A suit commenced by a representative on behalf of an ascertainable group that is too large to appear in court, who shares a commonality of interests and who will benefit from a successful result.

DECLARATORY JUDGMENT A judgment of the rights between opposing parties that is binding, but does not impose coercive relief (i.e., damages.)

DIVERSITY ACTION An action commenced by a citizen of one state against a citizen of another state or against an alien, involving an amount in controversy of $10,000 or more, over which the federal court has jurisdiction.

DUTY OF GOOD FAITH AND FAIR DEALING An implied duty in a contract that the parties will deal honestly in the satisfaction of their obligations and without intent to defraud.

INDEMNIFICATION The payment by a corporation of expenses incurred by its officers or directors as a result of litigation involving the corporation.

■═■

CHAPTER 5

Protecting Participants' Expectations in Corporations and LLCs

Quick Reference Rules of Law

Zion v. Kurtz

Minority shareholder (P) v. Principal shareholder (D)

N.Y. Ct. App., 50 N.Y.2d 92, 405 N.E.2d 681 (1980).

NATURE OF CASE: Appeal from entry of summary judgment granting enforcement of shareholder's agreement.

FACT SUMMARY: Zion (P) sought enforcement of a shareholder's agreement which prohibited the corporation from entering into any business transaction without his consent.

🏛 RULE OF LAW
A shareholder's agreement requiring minority shareholder approval of corporate activities is enforceable between the original parties to it.

FACTS: Kurtz (D) was the principal shareholder of a corporation in which Zion (P) was a minority shareholder. They executed an agreement which precluded the corporation from entering into any business transaction without Zion's (P) consent. The corporation subsequently breached the agreement, and Zion (P) sued to enforce it. The trial court granted summary judgment for Zion (P), and Kurtz (D) appealed, contending the agreement violated state law by delegating the control over corporate actions from the board of directors to a minority shareholder. The appellate court reversed, and the court of appeals granted certiorari.

ISSUE: Is a shareholder's agreement requiring minority shareholder approval of corporate activities enforceable between the original parties to it?

HOLDING AND DECISION: (Meyer, J.) Yes. A shareholder's agreement requiring minority shareholder approval of corporate activities is enforceable between the original parties to it. Reasonable restrictions on director discretion are not against public policy and are not precluded by statute. Since all stockholders assented to the agreement and it is not prohibited by statute or public policy, it is enforceable. Reversed.

DISSENT: (Gabrielli, J.) A shareholder's agreement of this type illegally transfers control of the corporation from the board of directors to a minority shareholder.

▌ANALYSIS

Agreements of the type discussed in this case are usually found in closely held corporations. Although the corporation in this case was not formed as a close corporation, the court found this inconsequential. It reasoned that because the articles of incorporation granted the board power to take all steps necessary to enforce the terms of the articles, the corporation could easily gain close status in order to render the shareholder's agreement valid.

Quicknotes

CERTIORARI A discretionary writ issued by a superior court to an inferior court in order to review the lower court's decisions; the Supreme Court's writ ordering such review.

CLOSELY HELD CORPORATION A corporation whose shares (or at least voting shares) are held by a closely knit group of shareholders or a single person.

SHAREHOLDER AGREEMENT An agreement establishing a trust whereby shareholders transfer their title to shares to a trustee who is authorized to exercise their voting powers.

SUMMARY JUDGMENT Judgment rendered by a court in response to a motion by one of the parties, claiming that the lack of a question of material fact in respect to an issue warrants disposition of the issue without consideration by the jury.

Blount v. Taft

Stockholder (P) v. Stockholder (D)

N.C. Sup. Ct., 295 N.C. 472, 246 S.E.2d 763 (1978).

NATURE OF CASE: Appeal from reversal of judgment in an action by minority stockholders to specifically enforce a stockholders' agreement.

FACT SUMMARY: When a majority of the shareholders in a close corporation amended bylaws which had been unanimously adopted, the minority shareholders brought this action to enforce the prior bylaws.

🏛 RULE OF LAW

If a shareholders' agreement is made a part of the charter or bylaws, it will be subject to amendment as provided therein or, in the absence of such a provision, as provided by the statutory norms.

FACTS: In a 1971 directors' meeting, the shareholders of a close corporation unanimously adopted bylaws containing a provision, § 7, for the creation of an executive committee composed of one member from each of the families holding stock, Blount (P), Taft (D), and McGowan (D). Section 4, providing for amendment or repeal of the bylaws and adoption of new bylaws by the affirmative vote of a majority of the directors then holding office, was also unanimously adopted. After new bylaws were proposed and adopted in 1974 by a vote of six to three, the minority shareholders, represented by Blount (P), brought this action to enforce the 1971 bylaws. The trial court held that the 1971 bylaws were binding upon the shareholders for a period not to exceed ten years, unless repealed or amended by the unanimous consent of all the shareholders. The court of appeals reversed, and Blount (P) appealed.

ISSUE: If a shareholders' agreement is made a part of the charter or bylaws, will it be subject to amendment as provided therein or, in the absence of such a provision, as provided by the statutory norms?

HOLDING AND DECISION: (Sharp, C.J.) Yes. If a shareholders' agreement is made a part of the charter or bylaws, it will be subject to amendment as provided therein or, in the absence of such a provision, as provided by the statutory norms. Had § 4 been omitted from the bylaws, the directors would have been precluded from amending § 7. Sections 7 and 4 were unanimously incorporated into the bylaws at the same time. Since there was no internal provision in § 7 or elsewhere in the bylaws prohibiting its amendment except by unanimous consent of the shareholders, the parties must have intended § 7 to be subject to amendment by the directors or shareholders according to the procedures applicable to the other bylaws. The reversal by the court of appeals is affirmed.

▶ ANALYSIS

The court declared that § 4 would be enforced, unless enforcement would contravene some principle of equity or public policy. The court recognized that its decision would expose the Blount (P) family, as minority shareholders in a close corporation, to a risk from which § 7 for a while protected them. However, the court admonished minority shareholders who desired greater protection than that afforded by the general statutes or judicial doctrines prohibiting breach of a fiduciary relationship to secure it themselves in the form of "a well-drawn" shareholders' agreement.

Quicknotes

BYLAWS Rules promulgated by a corporation regulating its governance.

EQUITY Fairness; justice; the determination of a matter consistent with principles of fairness and not in strict compliance with rules of law.

PUBLIC POLICY Policy administered by the state with respect to the health, safety and morals of its people in accordance with common notions of fairness and decency.

SHAREHOLDER AGREEMENT An agreement establishing a trust, whereby shareholders transfer their title to shares to a trustee who is authorized to exercise their voting powers.

Ramos v. Estrada

Shareholder (P) v. Shareholder (D)

Cal. Ct. App., 8 Cal. App. 4th 1070, 10 Cal. Rptr. 2d 833 (1992).

NATURE OF CASE: Appeal of judgment finding breach of written corporate shareholder agreement.

FACT SUMMARY: The Estradas (D) signed a shareholder voting agreement and later contended that because the corporation was not a close corporation the agreement was unenforceable.

🏛 RULE OF LAW
A corporate shareholder voting agreement may be valid even though the corporation is not technically a close corporation.

FACTS: Two broadcasting companies, the Broadcast Corp. and Ventura 41 Television Associates (Ventura 41), merged to form Costa del Oro Television, Inc. Upon merger of the two corporations, the shareholders of each company signed a written corporate shareholder agreement, known as the June Broadcast Agreement, which stated that the shareholders agreed to vote the stock under their control with the majority of shareholders of each respective group, and that failure to do so would result in the sale of their stock. Both the Ramoses (P) and the Estradas (D) were members of the Broadcast Corp. group. At the next shareholder meeting, the Estradas (D) voted their shares with the Ventura 41 group to remove Ramos (P), even though the majority of stockholders in the Broadcast Corp. group voted with Ramos (P). The Estradas (D) sought to have the vote of the majority declared null and void and to classify the voting agreement they signed as a proxy agreement that they had revoked. The Ramoses (P) sought and was awarded judgment that the Estradas (D) had breached the voting agreement and must sell their stock. The Estradas (D) appealed.

ISSUE: May a corporate shareholder voting agreement be valid even though the corporation is not technically a close corporation?

HOLDING AND DECISION: (Gilbert, J.) Yes. A corporate shareholder voting agreement may be valid even though the corporation is not technically a close corporation. Proxies were not created by the June Broadcast Agreement. The Agreement closely resembles a shareholder voting agreement, which is expressly authorized by statute for close corporations and others similarly situated. The Estradas (D) breached the agreement by their written repudiation of it. Affirmed.

▶ *ANALYSIS*

Agreements to vote shares as a block are commonly called shareholder vote pooling agreements. As this case indicates, the validity of these agreements is usually a matter of statutory interpretation, and the statutes vary by jurisdiction. The Model Close Corporation Supplement § 20(a)(b)(2) requires that all the shareholders of a statutory close corporation participate in the vote pooling agreement and also requires that the agreement be in writing.

■■■■

Quicknotes

CLOSE CORPORATION A corporation whose shares (or at least voting shares) are held by a closely knit group of shareholders or a single person.

SHAREHOLDER AGREEMENT An agreement establishing a trust, whereby shareholders transfer their title to shares to a trustee who is authorized to exercise their voting powers.

■■■■

Zidell v. Zidell

Shareholder (P) v. Shareholder (D)

Or. Sup. Ct., 277 Or. 413, 560 P.2d 1086 (1977).

NATURE OF CASE: Appeal from a declaration of dividends in a minority shareholder's suit.

FACT SUMMARY: After Emery Zidell (D) and his son acquired a majority interest in the family business, Arnold Zidell (P), Emery's brother, resigned and filed this suit to compel the business to declare reasonable dividends.

🏛 RULE OF LAW
Those in control of corporate affairs have fiduciary duties of good faith and fair dealing toward the minority shareholders.

FACTS: Four closely held, affiliated corporations were all operated as divisions of the Zidell family business. Brothers Emery Zidell (D) and Arnold Zidell (P) held equal shares in the business amounting to 75%, with the other 25% held by Rosenfeld. Rosenfeld later sold a major portion of his shares to Emery's (D) son, effectively giving Emery (D) and his son a majority interest in the business. After his request for a salary increase was denied, Arnold (P) resigned and demanded that the corporations declare reasonable dividends. All earnings were customarily retained in the business. After a dividend was declared, Arnold (P) brought suit, contending the dividends were unreasonably small and were not set in good faith. He noted that at about the same time, corporate salaries and bonuses were increased substantially. The trial court ordered the declaration of a much larger dividend, and Emery (D) appealed.

ISSUE: Do those in control of corporate affairs have fiduciary duties of good faith and fair dealing toward the minority shareholders?

HOLDING AND DECISION: (Howell, J.) Yes. Those in control of corporate affairs have fiduciary duties of good faith and fair dealing toward the minority shareholders. Where dividend policy is concerned, however, those duties are discharged if the decision is made in good faith and reflects legitimate business purposes rather than the private interests of those in control. Arnold (P) has shown the existence of factors which are often present in cases of oppression or attempted squeeze-out by majority shareholders: hostility toward him, an ability to pay additional dividends, and generous salaries and bonuses. However, Arnold (P) left his position voluntarily, and he has not shown that he was being forced to sell his stock at an unreasonably low price. Moreover, Emery (D) has credibly explained the conservative dividend policy, in part, as based on saving for the future needs of the company. Arnold (P) has failed to carry his burden of proving a lack of good faith. Thus, the trial court erred in decreeing the distribution of additional dividends. Reversed.

▶ ANALYSIS

The court considered the following facts relevant to the issue of bad faith: (1) intense hostility of the majority against the minority; (2) exclusion of the minority from employment by the corporation; (3) high salaries, bonuses, or corporate loans made to the majority; (4) the fact that the majority may be subject to high personal income taxes if substantial dividends are paid; and (5) a desire by the majority to acquire the minority stock interests as cheaply as possible. However, unless these facts are motivating causes, they will not constitute bad faith as a matter of law.

Quicknotes

DIVIDEND The payment of earnings to a corporation's shareholders in proportion to the amount of shares held.

FIDUCIARY DUTY A legal obligation to act for the benefit of another, including subordinating one's personal interests to that of the other person.

IMPLIED COVENANT OF GOOD FAITH AND FAIR DEALING An implied warranty, the parties will deal honestly in the satisfaction of their obligations, and without intent to defraud.

Donahue v. Rodd Electrotype Co.

Minority stockholder (P) v. Close corporation (D)

Mass. Sup. Jud. Ct., 367 Mass. 578, 328 N.E.2d 505 (1975).

NATURE OF CASE: Action to rescind a corporate purchase of shares and recover the purchase price.

FACT SUMMARY: Donahue (P), a minority stockholder in a close corporation, sought to rescind a corporate purchase of shares of the controlling shareholder.

🏛 RULE OF LAW
A controlling stockholder (or group) in a close corporation who causes the corporation to purchase his stock breaches his fiduciary duty to the minority stockholders if he does not cause the corporation to offer each stockholder an equal opportunity to sell a ratable number of shares to the corporation at an identical price.

FACTS: As a controlling stockholder of Rodd Electrotype (D), a close corporation, Harry Rodd (D) caused the corporation to reacquire 45 of his shares for $800 each ($36,000 total). He then divested the rest of his holding by making gifts and sales to his children. Donahue (P), a minority stockholder who had refused to ratify this action, offered to sell her shares on the same terms but was refused. A suit followed in which Donahue (P) sought to rescind the purchase of Harry Rodd's (D) stock and make him repay to Rodd Electrotype (D) the $36,000 purchase price with interest. Finding the purchase had been without prejudice to Donahue (P), the trial court dismissed the bill, and the appellate court affirmed.

ISSUE: Must a controlling stockholder in a close corporation who has caused the corporation to purchase some of his shares see to it that an equal offer is made to the other stockholders?

HOLDING AND DECISION: (Tauro, C.J.) Yes. Stemming from the fiduciary duty owed by a controlling stockholder of a close corporation to the minority stockholders, a controlling stockholder who causes such a corporation to purchase some of his shares must cause the corporation to offer each stockholder an equal opportunity to sell a ratable number of shares to the corporation at an identical price. Close corporations are somewhat different in that they are very much like partnerships and require the utmost trust, confidence, and loyalty among the members for success. This means a partnership-type fiduciary duty arises between stockholders. It is the basis for the rule herein announced, under which Donahue (P) must be given an equal opportunity to sell her shares. Reversed and remanded.

▶ ANALYSIS

A problem which exists with close corporations is that there is no ready market to which a minority stockholder can turn when he wishes to liquidate his holdings. Knowing that fact the controlling stockholder has a very powerful weapon which he would not have in a regular corporate setup. This is one of the reasons he is held to a higher degree of fiduciary duty in this case.

Quicknotes

CLOSE CORPORATION A corporation whose shares (or at least voting shares) are held by a closely knit group of shareholders or a single person.

FIDUCIARY DUTY A legal obligation to act for the benefit of another, including subordinating one's personal interests to that of the other person.

Wilkes v. Springside Nursing Home, Inc.

Director/shareholder (P) v. Close corporation (D)

Mass. Sup. Jud. Ct., 370 Mass. 842, 353 N.E.2d 657 (1976).

NATURE OF CASE: Appeal from a ruling dismissing the complaint in an action for declaratory judgment.

FACT SUMMARY: Wilkes (P) was a director, employee, and shareholder in Springside Nursing Home, Inc., a close corporation. The other directors attempted to freeze him out of the corporation.

🏛 RULE OF LAW
Stockholders in a close corporation are in a fiduciary relationship with each other.

FACTS: Wilkes (P), Quinn, Richie, and Conner formed a corporation to establish and operate a nursing home in 1951. Each of the men invested $1,000 and subscribed to ten shares of $100 par value stock. Over the years the parties each bought more stock. At the time of incorporation, it was understood that each would be a director of the corporation and participate in the management and operation thereof. It was further understood that each of the parties would receive money from the corporation in equal amounts for as long as they participated in the operation of the corporation. By 1955, each party was receiving $100 a week. In 1965, the relationship between the parties began to deteriorate. In February 1967, a directors' meeting was held, and a schedule of payments was set up in which Wilkes (P) was not included. In March 1967, the annual meeting was held. Wilkes (P) was not reelected a director and was not reemployed. Wilkes (P) brought suit, arguing that the agreement of the parties was breached when he was forced out of the corporation. A master dismissed the complaint. Wilkes (P) appealed, contending that he was entitled to damages for breach of contract or breach of fiduciary duties owed to him.

ISSUE: May shareholders in a close corporation act, without a business purpose, to the detriment of other shareholders?

HOLDING AND DECISION: (Hennessey, C.J.) No. Stockholders in a close corporation are in a fiduciary relationship with each other. The standard of duty owed is one of utmost good faith and loyalty. The standard, however, cannot be used to impose limitations on legitimate action by a controlling group. The majority has certain rights which must be balanced against the fiduciary obligation owed to the minority. Thus, where there is a legitimate business purpose for the action, it may be valid. Here, it is apparent that the majority had no legitimate purpose for their action. There is no evidence of misconduct on the part of Wilkes (P) for the performance of his duties as a director or employee. The inescapable conclusion from this is that the action was designed to freeze Wilkes (P) out of the corporation in violation of the parties' original agreement. Reversed and remanded for further proceedings on the issue of damages.

▶ ANALYSIS

Controlling shareholders are given a large amount of discretion in establishing corporate policy. It is only where their actions cannot be justified by a business purpose and do injury to others that the court will interfere. *Schwartz v. Marien*, 37 N.Y. 2d 487 (1975). In many older cases and in some jurisdictions, no business purpose is required so long as the majority acts within the permissible limits imposed by statute and their bylaws.

■=■

Quicknotes

BREACH OF CONTRACT The unlawful failure by a party to perform its obligations pursuant to contract.

BYLAWS Rules promulgated by a corporation regulating its governance.

DECLARATORY JUDGMENT An adjudication by the courts which grants not relief but is binding over the legal status of the parties involved in the dispute.

FIDUCIARY DUTY A legal obligation to act for the benefit of another, including subordinating one's personal interests to that of the other person.

■=■

Nixon v. Blackwell

Company (D) v. Shareholders (P)

Del. Sup. Ct., 626 A.2d 1366 (1993).

NATURE OF CASE: Review of decision holding that directors of a closely held corporation breached their fiduciary duties.

FACT SUMMARY: Minority shareholders (P) sued the corporate directors (D) of E.C. Barton & Co. (D) for not providing equal liquidity rights.

🏛 RULE OF LAW
The fairness doctrine requires directors in closely held corporations to treat minority shareholders fairly but not necessarily equally.

FACTS: The founder of E.C. Barton & Co. (the Company) (D), a closely held corporation, bequeathed substantially all of the Company's (D) stock to two groups: employees received Class A voting stock and relatives received Class B non-voting stock. The directors (D) also established an Employee Stock Ownership Plan (ESOP) that allowed employees to trade their Class A voting stock for Class B stock or a cash payment to be determined by an annual independent appraisal. No repurchase plan existed for Class B shareholders, although the Company (D) offered to repurchase the Class B stock. Additionally, the Company (D) purchased key man life insurance policies for executives and directors (D), and some of the proceeds were distributed to survivors. Distributions from the insurance policies exceeded the Company's (D) declared dividends over a five-year period. Class B shareholders (P) sued the corporate directors (D) and the Company (D) for maintaining a discriminatory policy that unfairly favored the majority Class A stockholders. The trial court held that the Company directors (D) unfairly discriminated against Class B (P) stockholders by providing liquidity for Class A stockholders that was not offered to Class B stockholders. The directors (D) appealed.

ISSUE: Must directors of a closely held corporations, treat minority shareholders equally?

HOLDING AND DECISION: (Veasey, C.J.) No. The fairness doctrine requires directors in a closely held corporation to treat minority shareholders fairly but not necessarily equally. The fairness doctrine requires fair price and fair dealing. Fair dealing requires judicial scrutiny of the actions in question. Equal liquidity rights for all stockholders, is not required to satisfy the fairness doctrine. The trial court failed to establish whether the Company (D) had valid business reasons for excluding the minority shareholders from the ESOP and key man insurance policies. Reversed and remanded.

▶ ANALYSIS

The fiduciary duty owed by the majority shareholders to the minority shareholders in a close corporation depends upon which rule the jurisdiction follows. The "Delaware Rule" requires majority shareholders to treat minority shareholders fairly; however, the "Massachusetts Rule" requires majority shareholders to treat minority shareholders equally.

■=■

Quicknotes

CLOSE CORPORATION A corporation whose shares (or at least voting shares) are held by a closely knit group of shareholders or a single person.

DIVIDEND The payment of earnings to a corporation's shareholders in proportion to the amount of shares held.

FIDUCIARY DUTY A legal obligation to act for the benefit of another, including subordinating one's personal interests to that of the other person.

LIQUIDITY RIGHTS The right to convert an asset to cash.

■=■

In re Kemp & Beatley, Inc.

Close corporation (D) v. Minority stockholders (P)

N.Y. Ct. App., 64 N.Y.2d 63, 473 N.E.2d 1173 (1984).

NATURE OF CASE: Appeal from an order dissolving a corporation.

FACT SUMMARY: Gardstein (P) contended the corporation's refusal to make distributions to him in contrast to prior policy constituted oppressiveness justifying dissolution.

🏛 RULE OF LAW
Actions by majority shareholders to restrict distributions to the prejudice of minority shareholders may constitute oppression and justify dissolution.

FACTS: Gardstein (P) and Dissin (P), two longtime employees of Kemp and Beatley (D), owned approximately 20% of the corporation's outstanding stock. While employed by the close corporation, they regularly received distributions as shareholders, yet after leaving the corporation's employ on less than friendly terms, they stopped receiving such distributions, while the other shareholders still did. They sued to dissolve the corporation, contending such action constituted oppression. The trial court ordered the dissolution, and Kemp and Beatley (D) appealed.

ISSUE: May actions by majority shareholders in close corporations to restrict distributions to minority shareholders constitute oppression and justify dissolution?

HOLDING AND DECISION: (Cooke, C.J.) Yes. Actions by majority shareholders of a close corporation to restrict distributions to the prejudice of minority shareholders may constitute oppression and justify dissolution. The action of the majority in this case defeated the expectation of the minority concerning the worth of their stock. Because this was a close corporation, there was little hope of establishing a market for the stock. Thus, dissolution was the only viable remedy. Affirmed.

▶ ANALYSIS

Dissolution is an extraordinary remedy which is granted in very selective cases. Only where the actions constitute fraud, illegality, or oppression will dissolution be ordered. Oppression contemplates action significantly infringing on minority shareholder rights.

■■■

Quicknotes

CLOSE CORPORATION A corporation whose shares (or at least voting shares) are held by a closely knit group of shareholders or a single person.

DISSOLUTION Annulment or termination of a formal or legal bond, tie or contract.

OPPRESSION The abuse of one's authority resulting in the infliction of injury on another.

■■■

Gimpel v. Bolstein

Shareholder (P) v. Corporation (D)

N.Y. Sup. Ct., 125 Misc. 2d 45, 477 N.Y.S.2d 1014 (1984).

NATURE OF CASE: Shareholder's derivative action for dissolution of a corporation.

FACT SUMMARY: After Gimpel (P) was discharged from the family business for embezzlement, the majority shareholders excluded Gimpel (P) from any participation in the business or profits of the corporation.

🏛 RULE OF LAW

A corporation may be subject to dissolution if the majority fails to act with probity and fair dealing and their conduct becomes burdensome, harsh, and wrongful, amounting to oppression of the minority.

FACTS: After Gimpel (P) was discharged from employment in the family business for embezzling a large sum of money, he received no benefits from his ownership position, although the company was profitable. Rather than pay dividends, the company distributed profits in the form of substantial salaries, benefits, and perquisites. Gimpel (P) filed this action for dissolution, alleging "oppressive" conduct by the majority. Namely, he had been excluded from corporate participation; since no dividends were declared, he received no benefit from his ownership interest; and he had been excluded from examination of the corporate books and records.

ISSUE: May the corporation be subject to dissolution if the majority fails to act with probity and fair dealing and their conduct becomes burdensome, harsh, and wrongful, amounting to oppression of the minority?

HOLDING AND DECISION: (Lonschein, J.) Yes. The corporation may be subject to dissolution if the majority fails to act with probity and fair dealing and their conduct becomes burdensome, harsh, and wrongful, amounting to oppression of the minority. Dissolution is a drastic remedy, and, under the Business Corporation Law, it is discretionary with the court. Gimpel's (P) allegations do not constitute oppressive conduct such as would justify dissolution. However, while the other shareholders need not allow him to return to employment with the corporation, they must by some means allow him to share in the profits. The corporation must immediately allow Gimpel (P) full access to corporate records. The majority must also elect to alter the corporate financial structure and begin payment of dividends or to make a reasonable, substantial, and good-faith offer to buy Gimpel's (P) interest.

▶ ANALYSIS

The court phrased its order as a mandatory injunction, with dissolution being one of the remedies for contempt. Noting

that oppression was also defined as a violation by the majority of the reasonable expectations of the minority, the court elected not to apply the "reasonable expectations" definition since the only expectations Gimpel (P) could reasonably entertain were those of a discovered thief: ostracism and prosecution. To the extent that the majority refrained from prosecuting Gimpel (P), they dealt with him more kindly than he had reason to expect.

■=■

Quicknotes

DERIVATIVE SUIT An action asserted by a shareholder in order to enforce a cause of action on behalf of the corporation.

DISSOLUTION Annulment or termination of a formal or legal bond, tie or contract.

OPPRESSION The abuse of one's authority resulting in the infliction of injury on another.

■=■

Concord Auto Auction, Inc. v. Rustin

Close corporation (P) v. Administrator of estate (D)

627 F. Supp. 1526 (D. Mass. 1986).

NATURE OF CASE: Action for specific performance of a stock purchase and restriction agreement.

FACT SUMMARY: When Rustin (D) failed to abide by an agreement requiring him to tender a deceased shareholder's shares in two close corporations for repurchase, this action for specific performance followed.

🏛 RULE OF LAW
Absent ambiguity, contracts must be interpreted and enforced exactly as written.

FACTS: Three siblings, Cox, Powell, and Thomas, each owned one-third of the issued and outstanding stock of two close corporations, Concord Auto Auction, Inc. (Concord) (P) and E.L. Cox Associates, Inc. (Associates) (P). To protect their interests, the three shareholders entered into a stock purchase and restriction agreement, providing that all shares owned by a shareholder at the time of his or her death be acquired by the two corporations. After Cox's death, Rustin (D), the administrator of Cox's estate, failed to effect the repurchase of Cox's shares. Rustin (D) asserted that because the agreement's explicit requirement of a yearly price review clashed with the provision that the price shall remain in effect until changed, a trial was required to determine the intent of the parties. Concord (P) and Associates (P) brought this action for specific performance of the repurchase provision in the agreement.

ISSUE: Absent ambiguity, must contracts be interpreted and enforced exactly as written?

HOLDING AND DECISION: (Young, J.) Yes. Absent ambiguity, contracts must be interpreted and enforced exactly as written. There is no ambiguity and certainly no "clash" between the dual requirements that there be an annual review of share price and that, absent such review, the existing price prevails. Further, under the agreement, raising the share price was discretionary and consensual. The purchase prices were carefully set and fair when established, as evidenced by an agreement binding all parties equally to the same terms without any indication that one sibling would reap a windfall. Moreover, the agreement unambiguously obligated Rustin (D), as administrator of Cox's estate, to tender Cox's shares for repurchase by Concord (P) and Associates (P). The agreement shall be specifically enforced.

▶ ANALYSIS

The court declared it would specifically enforce a consensual bargain, but it would not order the revision of the share price. Moreover, specific performance of an agreement to convey will not be refused merely because the price is inadequate or excessive. The validity of such agreements among shareholders of closely held corporations will be upheld absent any fraud, overreaching, undue influence, duress, or mistake at the time the deceased entered into the agreement.

■══■

Quicknotes

CLOSE CORPORATION A corporation whose shares (or at least voting shares) are held by a closely knit group of shareholders or a single person.

SPECIFIC PERFORMANCE An equitable remedy whereby the court requires the parties to perform their obligations pursuant to a contract.

SUMMARY JUDGMENT Judgment rendered by a court in response to a motion by one of the parties, claiming that the lack of a question of material fact in respect to an issue warrants disposition of the issue without consideration by the jury.

■══■

Gallagher v. Lambert

Employee/shareholder (P) v. Close corporation (D)

N.Y. Ct. App., 74 N.Y.2d 562, 549 N.E.2d 136 (1989).

NATURE OF CASE: Appeal from summary judgment in action for breach of fiduciary duty.

FACT SUMMARY: After Gallagher (P) was fired by the close corporation which employed him on an at-will basis, he refused to abide by the price terms of a negotiated agreement for a mandatory buy-back of the shares he held as a minority stockholder in the corporation.

🏛 RULE OF LAW
An at-will employee of a close corporation who becomes a minority stockholder in that corporation and who contractually agrees to the repurchase of his shares upon termination of his employment for any reason is bound by the terms of that agreement.

FACTS: During his employment by Eastdil Realty (Eastdil) (D), Gallagher (P) was at all times an employee at will. Gallagher (P) accepted an offer to purchase stock of the close corporation subject to a mandatory buy-back provision at book value if his employment was terminated voluntarily or otherwise prior to January 31, 1985. After that date, the buy-back price would be keyed to the company's earnings. When he was fired by Eastdil (D) on January 10, 1985, Gallagher (P) demanded payment for his shares based on Eastdil's (D) earnings. Eastdil (D) refused, and Gallagher (P) filed this action. The trial court denied Eastdil's (D) motion for summary judgment; the appellate division reversed and certified to the court of appeals the question of whether the appellate division's order was proper.

ISSUE: Is an at-will employee of a close corporation who becomes a minority stockholder in that corporation and who contractually agrees to the repurchase of his shares upon termination of his employment for any reason bound by the terms of that agreement?

HOLDING AND DECISION: (Bellacosa, J.) Yes. An at-will employee of a close corporation who becomes a minority stockholder in that corporation and who contractually agrees to the repurchase of his shares upon termination of his employment for any reason is bound by the terms of that agreement. Gallagher (P) not only agreed to the particular buy-back formula, but he helped write it, and he reviewed it with his attorney during the negotiation process. The buy-back price formula was designed for the benefit of both parties precisely so that they would know their respective rights on certain dates and avoid costly and lengthy litigation on the fair value issue. The order of the appellate division should be affirmed.

DISSENT: (Kaye, J.) This case is significantly different from *Ingle v. Glamore Motor Sales*, 73 N.Y.2d 183 (1989), where this court reached only the corporation's duty to plaintiff as an employee. Here, Gallagher (P) questions only the duty Eastdil (D) owes him as a shareholder, the question left open in *Ingle*. However, the majority finds that the same rationale applied in *Ingle* is wholly dispositive here, with no analysis of the fiduciary duty owed to Gallagher (P).

▶ ANALYSIS

The court noted that provisions like the one discussed in the instant case are designed to ensure that ownership of all of the stock of a close corporation stays within the control of the remaining corporate owners-employees. They should not be undone simply upon an allegation of unfairness. The question of the fiduciary duty of fair dealing here cannot be considered separately from the employment issue because the buy-back provision links them together as to timing and consequences.

◼▬◼

Quicknotes

AT-WILL EMPLOYEE An employee who is subject to termination at any time, or for any cause, by an employer, or who may terminate his own employment at any time or for any cause, in the absence of a specific agreement otherwise.

BUY-BACK PROVISION An agreement between partners or shareholders of a closely held corporation that surviving partners or shareholders will purchase the shares of deceased or withdrawing partners or shareholders.

CLOSE CORPORATION A corporation whose shares (or at least voting shares) are held by a closely knit group of shareholders or a single person.

FIDUCIARY DUTY A legal obligation to act for the benefit of another, including subordinating one's personal interests to that of the other person.

SUMMARY JUDGMENT Judgment rendered by a court in response to a motion by one of the parties, claiming that the lack of a question of material fact in respect to an issue warrants disposition of the issue without consideration by the jury.

◼▬◼

Pedro v. Pedro

Shareholder/brother (P) v. Shareholders/brothers (D)

Minn. Ct. App., 489 N.W.2d 798 (1992).

NATURE OF CASE: Appeal from award of damages for breach of fiduciary duty and wrongful termination.

FACT SUMMARY: Alfred Pedro (P) was forced out of his family business by his two brothers (D).

🏛 **RULE OF LAW**
A shareholder of a close corporation may recover damages for breach of fiduciary duty and for wrongful termination.

FACTS: Alfred Pedro (P) owned a one-third interest in The Pedro Companies (TPC), a family-owned close corporation. Alfred's brothers, Carl Pedro (D) and Eugene Pedro (D), owned the other two-thirds interest in TPC. Each brother expected to work at TPC until his death, as their father had done. TPC had a Stock Retirement Agreement (SRA) that allowed for each brother to trade his stock for cash upon death or election to sell the stock. After Alfred (P) discovered an accounting discrepancy, initially believed to be $330,000, relations deteriorated among the brothers. Alfred's (P) authority at TPC was undermined by Eugene (D). Alfred (P) was placed on a mandatory leave of absence and was subsequently fired from TPC. Workers at TPC were told that Alfred (P) had had a nervous breakdown. Eugene (D) and Carl (D) failed to honor the SRA. Alfred (P) sued Eugene (D) and Carl (D) to dissolve the company, and Eugene (D) and Carl (D) moved to buy out Alfred (P). The jury awarded Alfred (P) damages, which were held to be merely advisory. The trial court made findings that Alfred (P) was entitled to damages for breach of fiduciary duty and wrongful termination. Carl (D) and Eugene (D) appealed.

ISSUE: May a shareholder of a close corporation recover damages for breach of fiduciary duty and for wrongful termination?

HOLDING AND DECISION: (Norton, J.) Yes. A shareholder of a close corporation may recover damages for breach of fiduciary duty and for wrongful termination. A minority shareholder of a close corporation may maintain separate interests as an owner and an employee. Thus, allowing recovery for each interest is not double recovery. Shareholders of a close corporation owe one another a fiduciary duty to deal openly, honestly, and fairly with each other. Breach of shareholder fiduciary duty may occur even if the value of the stock has not diminished, if a shareholder has been forced to resign. The trial court's finding that Alfred (P) had an agreement with TPC for lifetime employment is supported by the facts, and recovery for lost wages until age seventy-two is appropriate. Affirmed.

▶ **ANALYSIS**

Modern courts often analogize to partnerships and partners when discussing fiduciary duties of shareholders in a close corporation. As this case indicates, a shareholder may hold several roles within a close corporation. Each role may represent a different interest for purposes of damages.

Quicknotes

BREACH OF FIDUCIARY DUTY The failure of a fiduciary to observe the standard of care exercised by professionals of similar education and experience.

CLOSE CORPORATION A corporation whose shares (or at least voting shares) are held by a closely knit group of shareholders or a single person.

The Limited Liability Company

Quick Reference Rules of Law

Elf Atochem North America, Inc. v. Jaffari

Joint venturer (P) v. Other joint venturer (D)

Del. Sup. Ct., 727 A.2d 286 (1999).

NATURE OF CASE: Appeal from dismissal for lack of jurisdiction under terms of a limited liability company (LLC) agreement.

FACT SUMMARY: Elf Atochem North America, Inc.'s (P) allegations of breach of contract, tortious interference with prospective business relations, and fraud were dismissed because, under the terms of the LLC agreement, all disputes were to be settled in California.

🏛 RULE OF LAW
(1) Because the policy of the Delaware Limited Liability Company Act (Act) is to give maximum effect to the principle of freedom of contract and to the enforceability of LLC agreements, the parties to such agreements may contract to avoid the applicability of those provisions of the Act that are not prohibited from being altered.
(2) An LLC agreement is binding on an LLC where only its members have signed the agreement.

FACTS: Elf Atochem North America, Inc. (Elf) (P), a manufacturer of solvent-based maskants to the aerospace industry, and Jaffari (D), who had developed an innovative, environmentally friendly alternative to the solvent-base maskants recently classified as hazardous by the Environmental Protection Agency (EPA), agreed to undertake a joint venture that would be carried out using a limited liability company (LLC) as the vehicle. Malek LLC (Malek) (D) was formed in Delaware, and the parties entered into several agreements. However, Malek (D) was not a signatory to the agreement detailing the governance of the new company. The agreement contained an arbitration clause and a forum selection clause providing California courts would have jurisdiction over any claims arising out of, under, or in connection with, the agreement. Elf (P) later sued Jaffari (D) for breach of fiduciary duty when he withdrew funds for personal use, interfered with business opportunities, failed to make disclosures and threatened to violate environmental regulations. Elf (P) also alleged breach of contract, tortious interference, and fraud. The Court of Chancery dismissed for lack of subject matter jurisdiction, holding that Elf's (P) claims arose under the agreement and were subject to the provision mandating that all claims be settled in California. Elf (P) appealed, contending that Malek (D) was not a signatory and not a party to the agreement and therefore was not bound to its terms, and that the dispute resolution clauses were invalid because they violated the Act. The Delaware Supreme Court granted review.

ISSUE:
(1) Because the policy of the Delaware Limited Liability Company Act (Act) is to give maximum effect to the principle of freedom of contract and to the enforceability of LLC agreements, may the parties to such agreements contract to avoid the applicability of those provisions of the Act that are not prohibited from being altered?
(2) Is an LLC agreement binding on an LLC where only its members have signed the agreement?

HOLDING AND DECISION: (Veasey, C.J.)
(1) Yes. Because the policy of the Delaware Limited Liability Company Act (Act) is to give maximum effect to the principle of freedom of contract and to the enforceability of LLC agreements, the parties to such agreements may contract to avoid the applicability of those provisions of the Act that are not prohibited from being altered. The Act is designed to permit members maximum flexibility in entering into an agreement to govern their relationship. Only where the agreement is inconsistent with mandatory statutory provisions will the members' agreement be invalidated. Such statutory provisions are likely to be those intended to protect third parties, not necessarily the contracting members. Here, the parties specifically agreed that no action could be brought, except in California, and then, only to enforce arbitration in California. This provision is consistent with Delaware's policy of encouraging alternate dispute resolution mechanisms, including arbitration, and does not otherwise violate a mandatory provision of the Act. Thus, there is no reason why the parties could not alter the Act's default jurisdictional provisions and contract away their right to file suit in Delaware. Specifically, while the Act grants Delaware courts jurisdiction to hear derivative actions, and actions involving breaches of fiduciary duties and the removal of managers, there is no reason why these default jurisdictional provisions may not be altered. In other words, there is no "special" jurisdiction conferred on the Delaware courts in these areas, and parties may contractually alter such default provisions, especially where doing so promotes the state's policy interests, as in promoting arbitration and other alternate dispute resolution mechanisms. Additionally, even though § 18-109(d) of the Act does not expressly provide that parties may agree to the exclusive jurisdiction of a foreign jurisdiction, because that section is otherwise permissive and does not expressly prohibit such action, the parties may contractually agree to such jurisdiction. Affirmed as to this issue.

Continued on next page.

(2) Yes. An LLC agreement is binding on an LLC where only its members have signed the agreement. Again, the Act is designed to permit members maximum flexibility in entering into an agreement to govern their relationship, and it is the members who are the real parties in interest. Here Malek (D) was simply the parties' joint business vehicle, so that Malek's (D) failure to sign the agreement does not affect the members' rights thereunder or the agreement's validity.

▶ *ANALYSIS*

After this decision was rendered, the Delaware legislature amended § 18-109(d) to limit the impact of the decision by limiting LLC members' and managers' ability to contract for exclusive jurisdiction in foreign jurisdictions. It also limited the ability of non-manager members to waive their rights to maintain suits in Delaware regarding an LLC's organization or internal affairs. The amended provision reads as follows:

> In a written limited liability company agreement or other writing, a manager or member may consent to be subject to the nonexclusive jurisdiction of the courts of, or arbitration in, a specified jurisdiction, or the exclusive jurisdiction of the courts of the State of Delaware, or the exclusivity of arbitration in a specified jurisdiction or the State of Delaware, and to be served with legal process in the manner prescribed in such limited liability company agreement or other writing. Except by agreeing to arbitrate any arbitrable matter in a specified jurisdiction or in the State of Delaware, a member who is not a manager may not waive its right to maintain a legal action or proceeding in the courts of the State of Delaware with respect to matters relating to the organization or internal affairs of a limited liability company.

■═■

Quicknotes

ARBITRATION An agreement to have a dispute heard and decided by a neutral third party, rather than through legal proceedings.

FIDUCIARY DUTY A legal obligation to act for the benefit of another, including subordinating one's personal interests to that of the other person.

JURISDICTION The authority of a court to hear and declare judgment in respect to a particular matter.

LIMITED LIABILITY COMPANY A business entity combining the features of both a corporation and a general partnership; the LLC provides its shareholders and officers with limited liability, but it is treated as a partnership for taxation purposes.

■═■

Olson v. Halvorsen

LLC cofounder (P) v. LLC cofounder (D)

Del. Ct. Ch., 2009 WL 1317148 (2009).

NATURE OF CASE: Action for, inter alia, breach of contract and payment of fair value.

FACT SUMMARY: After he was terminated, Olson (P), a cofounder and manager of Viking Global (Viking) and various entities through which Viking operated, contended that he was entitled to the fair value of his interest, rather than his accrued compensation and the balance of his capital account ("cap and comp") as per an oral agreement between the cofounders.

🏛 **RULE OF LAW**
An oral LLC operating agreement will be enforced where it has not been superseded and there is no evidence that the parties have intended to depart from the agreement.

FACTS: Olson (P), Halvorsen (D) and Ott (D) cofounded Viking Global (Viking), an investment management firm and hedge fund, and various limited partnerships and LLCs through which Viking operated. Before operations began, the cofounders reached an oral agreement that all earnings were to be paid out annually, with no deferral of compensation, and that a departing member was to receive only his accrued compensation and the balance of his capital account ("cap and comp" agreement). Written but unexecuted long-form agreements for some of the operating entities reflected this arrangement, as did executed written short-form agreements. Subsequently, Olson (P) raised a new compensation concept with Halvorsen (D) and Ott (D), proposing that upon departure from Viking a founding member (or his estate) would be paid an earnout, through a new entity to be called Founders. Although Olson (P) worked with outside counsel on a draft operating agreement for Founders, Halvorsen (D) and Ott (D) never agreed to its terms or made any promises to Olson (P) about an earnout payment. At Olson's (P) direction, Founders was incorporated and made a member of one of the existing entities, and, also at his direction, certain amounts of the founders' residual earnings were run through Founders for bookkeeping purposes only. Although, after Olson (P) threatened to leave, the founders renegotiated their equity interest percentages, they did not discuss the affect of this renegotiation on departure payouts. Several years later, the founders confirmed that they had never reached agreement on Olson's (P) proposed earnout plan. Even though the earnout concept was on the management committee's agenda for quite some time, issues surrounding it were never resolved. Olson (P) then left on a sabbatical. During this time, it was decided that there was no place for him at Viking. He was terminated and paid his "cap and comp" in each entity. Olson (P) brought suit against Halvorsen (D) and Ott (D), claiming, inter alia, that he was entitled to the fair value of his interests in those entities. However, he presented no evidence that the parties had reached any superseding agreement that countered their understanding under the "cap and comp" agreement.

ISSUE: Will an oral LLC operating agreement be enforced where it has not been superseded and there is no evidence that the parties have intended to depart from the agreement?

HOLDING AND DECISION: (Lamb, V. Chan.) Yes. An oral LLC operating agreement will be enforced where it has not been superseded and there is no evidence that the parties have intended to depart from the agreement. First, the oral agreement here takes precedence over any conflicting provisions in the state's fair value statute, because that statute provides that its terms will govern only if there is no enforceable agreement to the contrary. Thus, any conflict between a valid LLC agreement and the fair value statute is resolved in favor of the agreement. The "cap and comp" agreement was entered into before Viking was founded, and applied to all its entities, including Founders. While written agreements reflected the "cap and comp" term for some of the entities, no other agreements superseded this agreement. Halvorsen (D) and Ott (D) never agreed to change this agreement for Founders or any other entity, and no alternative operating agreement was ever entered into. Accordingly, the "cap and comp" agreement is enforceable and Olson (P) is not entitled to the fair value of his ownership interests.

▌ *ANALYSIS*

As with other oral agreements, oral LLC agreements are subject to the statute of frauds, and will not be enforced unless they can be completed within a year. In a prior opinion, the court found that it was possible that the "cap and comp" agreement could be performed within a year, so that it was not barred by the statute of frauds. In that decision, the court, addressing what was then an issue of first impression, reasoned that since the statute of frauds applies to agreements the terms of which cannot be performed within one year from the making thereof, and since few oral LLC operating agreements would likely contain any term or provision that could not possibly be performed within one year, to that extent, the statute of frauds would not limit the enforcement of any such agreement. The court also held that if an LLC agreement contains a provision or

Continued on next page.

multiple provisions that cannot possibly be performed within one year, such provision or provisions are unenforceable. In rendering its decision, the court observed that its decision balanced the policy considerations underlying the statute of frauds while giving effect to the legislative intent behind the LLC statute to promote flexibility. *Olson v. Halvorsen*, 2008 Del. Ch. LEXIS 156 (Del. Ct. Ch. 2008).

■■■

Quicknotes

INTER ALIA Among other things.

LIMITED LIABILITY COMPANY A business entity combining the features of both a corporation and a general partnership; the LLC provides its shareholders and officers with limited liability, but it is treated as a partnership for taxation purposes.

STATUTE OF FRAUDS A statute that requires specified types of contracts to be in writing in order to be binding.

■■■

Bay Center Apartments Owner, LLC v. Emery Bay PKI, LLC

Member (P) v. Managing member (D)

Del. Ct. Ch., 2009 WL 1124451 (2009).

NATURE OF CASE: Action asserting claims for, inter alia, breach of contract, breach of the contractually implied covenant of good faith and fair dealing, and breach of fiduciary duty.

FACT SUMMARY: Bay Center LLC (P), which formed, for the purpose of developing real estate, Emery Bay Member, LLC (Emery Bay) (D) with Emery Bay PKI, LLC (PKI) (D), which was owned and managed by Nevis (D), contended that even though PKI (D) and Nevis (D) had not signed the management agreement or a note in favor of Bay Center (P), they were nonetheless liable under Emery Bay's (D) LLC Agreement for breach of the contractually implied covenant of good faith and fair dealing, and breach of fiduciary duty.

🏛 RULE OF LAW

(1) A duty of good faith and fair dealing may be implied from an LLC operating agreement and imposed on the LLC's managing member and its owner for the benefit of the LLC's members where the operating agreement provides the managing member with broad authority to manage the LLC.

(2) On a motion to dismiss, an LLC agreement, which provides for traditional fiduciary duties as well as for no duties among members unless expressly included, will be interpreted as providing for traditional fiduciary duties.

(3) The owner or an affiliate of an LLC's managing member may be held liable for breaches of fiduciary duties where the owner or affiliate controls the LLC's assets and uses that control for personal gain.

FACTS: Bay Center LLC (P) formed Emery Bay Member, LLC (Emery Bay) (D) with Emery Bay PKI, LLC (PKI) (D), which was owned and managed by Nevis (D), for the purpose of developing real estate. Bay Center (P) contributed the property and looked to PKI (D) to manage the joint venture ("the Project"). PKI (D) was Emery Bay's (D) managing member. Emery Bay's (D) LLC Agreement gave PKI (D) considerable power and authority to manage the affairs of Emery Bay and also contemplated that PKI (D) would be responsible for managing the Project, but the parties defined those responsibilities through a separate agreement, the "Development Management Agreement." PKI (D) did not sign the Development Management Agreement, but had one of its affiliates, Emery Bay ETI, LLC (ETI) (D) sign it, and ETI's (D) only counterparty in the Development Management Agreement was a wholly owned subsidiary of Emery

Bay (D). The Project encountered numerous problems, and Emery Bay (D) defaulted on a construction loan (the "Loan") that Nevis (D) had personally guaranteed (the "Personal Guarantee"). Allegedly, this loan was secretly renegotiated, resulting in the diversion of cash flow from the Project that was earmarked to repay an unsecured note from Emery Bay (D) held by Bay Center (P) (the "Bay Center Note"). By renegotiating the Loan in this way, Nevis (D) avoided triggering his Personal Guarantee, and PKI (D) avoided capital calls. Eventually, the Project failed and went into receivership. Bay Center (P) brought suit against Nevis (D) and all the entities he controlled (PKI (D), ETI (D), and Emery Bay (D)), asserting numerous claims, including breach of contract (Count I), breach of the contractually implied covenant of good faith and fair dealing (Count III), and breach of fiduciary duty (Count IV), among others. Bay Center (P) argued that even though PKI (D) had not signed the Development Management Agreement or Bay Center Note (collectively the "Supporting Documents"), it was secondarily liable under these agreements through the implied covenant of good faith and fair dealing because PKI (D) agreed in the LLC Agreement to ensure that the Supporting Agreements would be performed by causing ETI (D) to perform its obligations competently under the Development Management Agreement and to cause Emery Bay (D) to perform its obligations under the Bay Center Note. This theory was based on the fact that the LLC Agreement gave PKI (D) broad authority to run Emery Bay (D), and to take actions to "[c]ause the Development Manager to perform its obligations under the Development Management Agreement . . . or, if the Development Manager fails to perform such obligations, performing or causing such services to be performed, at no additional cost"; (2) "[p]erform, or cause to be performed, all of [Emery Bay's] obligations under any agreement to which [Emery Bay] is a party; and relatedly (3) "take all proper and necessary actions reasonably required to cause [Emery Bay] . . . to perform and comply with the provisions . . . of any loan commitment . . . or other contract, instrument or agreement to which [Emery Bay] is a party. . . ." Bay Center (P) reasoned that because PKI (D) had these powers, it also had the obligation to use them for the Project's success and that this obligation could be implied from the LLC Agreement. Bay Center (P) also asserted that PKI (D) and Nevis (D) had breached their fiduciary duties. In support of its claim, it referenced § 6.1 of the LLC Agreement, which provided that the members would have the same duties and obligations to each other that members of a limited liability company formed under the Delaware LLC Act have to each other, unless otherwise expressly noted in

Continued on next page.

the LLC Agreement. To counter this argument, PKI (D) and Nevis (D) invoked § 6.2 of the LLC Agreement, which provided that except for any duties imposed by the LLC Agreement, the members would owe each other no duty of any kind. As to Nevis's (D) breach of fiduciary duties, Bay Center (P) argued that even though he was not a member or officer of Emery Bay (D), he owed a fiduciary duty by virtue of being in a position of control over Emery Bay (D) and benefiting personally from that position. The defendants moved to dismiss all the claims.

ISSUE:

(1) May a duty of good faith and fair dealing be implied from an LLC operating agreement and imposed on the LLC's managing member and its owner for the benefit of the LLC's members where the operating agreement provides the managing member with broad authority to manage the LLC?

(2) On a motion to dismiss, will an LLC agreement, which provides for traditional fiduciary duties as well as for no duties among members unless expressly included, be interpreted as providing for traditional fiduciary duties?

(3) May the owner or an affiliate of an LLC's managing member be held liable for breaches of fiduciary duties where the owner or affiliate controls the LLC's assets and uses that control for personal gain?

HOLDING AND DECISION: (Strine, V. Chan.)

(1) Yes. A duty of good faith and fair dealing may be implied from an LLC operating agreement and imposed on the LLC's managing member and its owner for the benefit of the LLC's members where the operating agreement provides the managing member with broad authority to manage the LLC. To understand this claim (Count III) for the breach of an implied covenant of good faith and fair dealing, it is helpful to understand the breach of contract claims (Count I). In the breach of contract claim, Bay Center (P) argues that PKI (D) was required to cause ETI (D) to perform its obligations under the Development Management Agreement and to cause Emery Bay (D) to perform its obligations under the loan documents. As Bay Center (P) correctly asserts, PKI's (D) duty to manage the affairs of the Project can reasonably be read to mean that PKI (D) had the obligation to exercise its authority on behalf of the members for the success of the Project and so that the parties' expectations would be met. To ensure that the reasonable expectations of the parties were fulfilled, PKI (D) was required to carry out its managerial functions in good faith, meaning PKI (D) could not engage in "arbitrary or unreasonable conduct" that had the effect of preventing Bay Center (P) from "receiving the fruits of its bargain." Bay Center (P) has pled sufficient facts from which it can be inferred that PKI (D) did not exercise its broad powers and discretion in good faith: Emery Bay's (D) alleged breaches of the Bay Center Note benefited PKI (P) by diverting cash that

Emery Bay (D) was supposed to use to repay the Note to fund the depleted Loan reserves, which PKI (D) would have otherwise had to fund through capital calls; and PKI's (D) decision not to pursue claims against ETI (D) under the Development Management Agreement was a conflicted one because Nevis (D), as the controller of both Emery Bay (D) and ETI (D), stood on both sides of it. For these reasons, the motion to dismiss is denied as to this claim.

(2) Yes. On a motion to dismiss, an LLC agreement, which provides for traditional fiduciary duties as well as for no duties among members unless expressly included, will be interpreted as providing for traditional fiduciary duties. In the absence of a contrary provision in an LLC agreement, the manager of an LLC owes the traditional fiduciary duties of loyalty and care to the members of the LLC. Here, the parties take diametrically opposed positions in their interpretation of the LLC Agreement in this regard. However, in the context of a Rule 12(b)(6) motion, a court may not choose between reasonable interpretations of ambiguous contract provisions. Here there are two such reasonable interpretations. The first is that no duties are provided for. The second, propounded by Bay Center (P), is that § 6.1 expressly imposes the default fiduciary duties on PKI (D), so the default fiduciary duties are carved out of § 6.2's elimination of duties by the "except for any duties imposed by this Agreement" language in that provision. Thus, the duties eliminated by § 6.2 are those that are not traditional fiduciary duties or are otherwise not expressly included. It is a maxim of contract interpretation that, given ambiguity between potentially conflicting terms, a contract should be read so as not to render any term meaningless. Because § 6.1 can be read as providing for traditional fiduciary duties, the defendants' argument that there are no duties whatsoever, unless expressly provided for, would render § 6.1 meaningless, and therefore this latter interpretation is not reasonable. Finally, the interpretive scales also tip in favor of preserving fiduciary duties under the rule that the drafters of chartering documents must make their intent to eliminate fiduciary duties plain and unambiguous. For these reasons, Emery Bay's (D) members must act in accord with traditional fiduciary duties, and PKI (D), as a member, is bound by such duties. Therefore, PKI's (D) motion to dismiss the breach of fiduciary count is denied.

(3) Yes. The owner or an affiliate of an LLC's managing member may be held liable for breaches of fiduciary duties where the owner or affiliate controls the LLC's assets and uses that control for personal gain. Here, Nevis (D) was not a member or officer of Emery Bay (D). Thus, he is beyond the normal scope of those who owe fiduciary duties in the corporate context. Bay Center's (P) theory of liability instead rests on a line

Continued on next page.

of cases holding that "those affiliates of a general partner who exercise control over the partnership's property may find themselves owing fiduciary duties to both the partnership and its limited partners." The applicability of that doctrine in the LLC context is not contested. Thus, to prevail, Bay Center (P) must plead that Nevis (D) benefited himself at the expense of Emery Bay (D). Here, it has done so by alleging that Nevis (D) used his control over the assets of Emery Bay (D) to stave off personal liability, thus benefiting himself at the expense of Emery Bay (D), by causing Emery Bay (D) to make cash sweeps to satisfy the renegotiated Loan, which avoided a default on the Loan, and in turn, the triggering of Nevis' (D) substantial Personal Guarantee. Motion to dismiss this claim is denied.

ANALYSIS

The Delaware LLC Act is silent on what fiduciary duties members of an LLC owe each other, leaving the matter to be developed by the common law. Delaware's LLC cases have generally, in the absence of provisions in the LLC agreement explicitly disclaiming the applicability of default principles of fiduciary duty, treated LLC members as owing each other the traditional fiduciary duties that directors owe a corporation. Moreover, when addressing an LLC case and lacking authority interpreting the LLC Act, the Delaware courts often look for help by analogy to the law of limited partnerships. In the limited partnership context, it has been established that "[a]bsent a contrary provision in the partnership agreement, the general partner of a Delaware limited partnership owes the traditional fiduciary duties of loyalty and care to the Partnership and its partners."

Quicknotes

BREACH OF FIDUCIARY DUTY The failure of a fiduciary to observe the standard of care exercised by professionals of similar education and experience.

DUTY OF LOYALTY A director's duty to refrain from self-dealing or to take a position that is adverse to the corporation's best interests.

IMPLIED COVENANT OF GOOD FAITH AND FAIR DEALING An implied warranty that the parties will deal honestly in the satisfaction of their obligations and without intent to defraud.

Kahn v. Portnoy

Shareholder (P) v. Director (D)

Del. Ct. Ch., 2008 WL 5197164 (2008).

NATURE OF CASE: Derivative action for breach of fiduciary duties.

FACT SUMMARY: Kahn (P), a shareholder of TravelCenters of America, LLC (TA), brought suit against TA's directors (D), alleging that they had breached their fiduciary duties by approving a real estate lease transaction that would allegedly primarily benefit one of the directors, Portnoy (D), and entities owned by him, at the expense of TA. TA's LLC Agreement established the contours of the fiduciary duties owed by the directors (D).

🏛 RULE OF LAW
Where an LLC agreement purports to modify common law fiduciary duties, but creates ambiguity in doing so, an action will not be dismissed for failure to state a claim where the court would be forced to choose between reasonable interpretations of ambiguous provisions in the LLC agreement.

FACTS: Kahn (P), a shareholder of TravelCenters of America, LLC (TA), brought suit against TA's directors (D), alleging that they had breached their fiduciary duties by approving a real estate lease transaction that would allegedly primarily benefit one of the directors, Portnoy (D), and entities owned by him, at the expense of TA. TA's LLC Agreement provided that the "authority, powers, functions and duties (including fiduciary duties)" of the board of directors would be identical to those of a board of directors of a business corporation organized under the Delaware General Corporation Law (DGCL), unless otherwise specifically provided for in the LLC Agreement. Some of the LLC Agreement's sections modified the duties owed by the directors of a Delaware corporation. One interpretation of one of those sections, § 7.5 (a), which was espoused by the directors (D), was that it altered the pleading standard by creating a presumption that the board of directors acted in accordance with their duties, notwithstanding that the board's decision may have been interested. Accordingly, they argued that Kahn (P) had to present clear and convincing evidence that this presumption had been rebutted. This provision could also be interpreted to apply only to board decisions that involved a conflict between a shareholder and the board or a shareholder and the company. Under the latter interpretation, the modification would not apply to the decision of the board to approve the challenged lease transaction because the conflicts of interest were not between a shareholder and a director or a shareholder and the company. The LLC Agreement also contained exculpatory provisions in § 10.2 that exculpated directors from personal liability for certain types of conduct, but not others. Section 10.2(a)

contained an exception for "acts or omissions not in good faith," and § 10.2(b) contained an exception for directors who "acted in bad faith." The directors (D) also had strong and extensive relationships to Portnoy (D) and Portnoy-related entities, and contributed to Portnoy's (D) wife's non-profit organization.

ISSUE: Where an LLC agreement purports to modify common law fiduciary duties, but creates ambiguity in doing so, will an action be dismissed for failure to state a claim where the court would be forced to choose between reasonable interpretations of ambiguous provisions in the LLC agreement?

HOLDING AND DECISION: (Chandler, Chan.) No. Where an LLC agreement purports to modify common law fiduciary duties, but creates ambiguity in doing so, an action will not be dismissed for failure to state a claim where the court would be forced to choose between reasonable interpretations of ambiguous provisions in the LLC agreement. Here, there are two reasonable interpretations of § 7.5(a) of the LLC Agreement. The first, as propounded by the directors (D), is that it creates a rebuttable presumption that the directors (D) acted in accordance with their duties regarding all decisions they make. However, another reasonable interpretation, given the sections location in the LLC Agreement, is that this rebuttable presumption applies only to decisions that involve a conflict between a shareholder and the board or a shareholder and the company. Under the former interpretation, the presumption would apply to the lease transaction, but under the latter, it would not, since the challenged lease transaction involved a board decision in the face of a conflict between a single director (Portnoy (D)) and TA. Kahn (P) alleges that Portnoy (D) stood on both sides of the transaction and stood to benefit personally from it. The other directors (D) allegedly acted in Portnoy's (D) best interest at TA's expense. Because the application of § 7.5(a) is ambiguous, the reasonable interpretation that favors the nonmoving party (Kahn (P)) must be adopted; under that interpretation, § 7.5(a) would not apply. Even assuming, arguendo, that it did apply, this would not change the outcome at this stage, since the court does not apply a standard of proof at the motion to dismiss stage of the proceedings; rather, it only determines whether a plaintiff would be entitled to relief under any reasonable interpretation of the facts alleged, and the plaintiff is not subject to a heightened evidentiary standard at this stage. Because § 7.5(a) may be interpreted to be inapplicable to the case at bar, the issue becomes which fiduciary duties the directors (D) are subject to. The LLC

Continued on next page.

Agreement expressly incorporates corporate fiduciary duties, and those are the ones, therefore, to which the directors (D) are subject, including the duty of loyalty. Whether they can be personally liable for a breach of those duties is governed by the exculpatory provisions in § 10.2. Those provisions do not exculpate decisions made in bad faith. A director does not act in good faith if the director acts with a subjective belief that her actions are not in the best interest of the corporation, such as when she is acting for the benefit of a related person at the expense of the company. This is "classic, quintessential bad faith." Here, Kahn (P) has alleged sufficient facts that create a reasonable doubt that Portnoy (D) acted in good faith, since it is alleged Portnoy (D) stood on both sides of the transaction and had divided loyalties. These allegations create a reasonable doubt as to whether he was acting in the best interest of TA. It was also alleged that Portnoy (D) stood to benefit personally from the transaction; intentionally acting to benefit oneself at the expense of a company is a quintessential example of failing to act in good faith. Accordingly, there are sufficient allegations of bad faith to survive a motion to dismiss as to Portnoy (D). As to the other directors, Kahn (P) has pled sufficient facts alleging that they were beholden to Portnoy (D) through their extensive relationships with him and his entities, by serving as directors and officers on those entities, and receiving significant compensation from such service. Additionally, there was not a single director on TA's board that was free of the influence of being otherwise involved in the web of Portnoy-related entities that could question whether the board was acting to benefit TA and not Portnoy (D) individually. Because at this stage all reasonable inferences must be drawn in Kahn's (P) favor, his well pleaded factual allegations are sufficient to survive the motion to dismiss, since it is not possible to conclude with reasonable certainty that there is no set of facts that can be inferred from these allegations upon which Kahn (P) could show that the directors (D) acted in bad faith. Motion to dismiss is denied.

▶ ANALYSIS

This case illustrates the risk that when fiduciary duties are modified in an LLC agreement, modification of such duties will be insufficiently clear to enable the court to choose one reasonable interpretation over another at the summary judgment stage. Another risk is that one will not be able to avail oneself of the multitude of cases in the common law relating to a particular duty. Thus, it is crucial when drafting such modifications to be as clear as possible as to the intended results and to ensure that the modifications are clear in the context of the entire agreement.

■=■

Quicknotes

AMBIGUITY Language that is capable of being understood to have more than one interpretation.

BAD FAITH Conduct that is intentionally misleading or deceptive.

BREACH OF FIDUCIARY DUTY The failure of a fiduciary to observe the standard of care exercised by professionals of similar education and experience.

DUTY OF LOYALTY A director's duty to refrain from self-dealing or to take a position that is adverse to the corporation's best interests.

GOOD FAITH An honest intention to abstain from taking advantage of another.

■=■

Fisk Ventures, LLC v. Segal

LLC managing member (P) v. LLC managing member (D)

Del. Ct. Ch., 2009 WL 73957 (2009).

NATURE OF CASE: Action for judicial dissolution of a limited liability company.

FACT SUMMARY: Fisk Ventures, LLC (Fisk Ventures) (P), a managing member of Genitrix, LLC, sought dissolution of Genitrix because the company was in financial dire straits, the board was effectively deadlocked, the LLC Agreement did not provide a way to break the deadlock, and the company had no office and no prospects of equity or debt infusion. Segal (D), the other managing member, opposed dissolution.

⚖ RULE OF LAW
Where an LLC has no office, no employees, no operating revenue, no prospects of equity or debt infusion, and when the company's board has a long history of deadlock as a result of its governance structure, it is not "reasonably practicable" for it to continue to operate and it may be dissolved.

FACTS: Genitrix, LLC, a limited liability company (LLC), was initially successful, but its financial condition subsequently deteriorated to the point where it was in critical financial straits. Its members included Segal (D) and Fisk Ventures, LLC (Fisk Ventures) (P) (through its owner, Johnson), with each appointing two members to Genitrix's five-member board. To continue operating, Genitrix relied on equity and debt investments and grants from institutions to provide capital, and as its financial condition deteriorated, both Segal (D) and Fisk Ventures (P) paid for certain company expenses. Segal (D) and his appointees declined to attend board meetings for the last two years, requesting instead that the board conduct business by e-mail. Genitrix's LLC Agreement provided that the board could only act pursuant to approval of 75% of its members, whether by vote or by written consent, and provided that dissolution could be effected only by written consent of members holding at least 75% of the membership interests or by judicial decree as provided for by Delaware statute. Under the Agreement, Fisk Ventures (P) had a put option that would permit it to exit Genitrix and obtain fair value for its interest. The company's board had a long history of deadlock as a result of this governance structure. The company also had no office, no employees, no operating revenue, and no prospects of equity or debt infusion. Fisk Ventures (P) brought suit for judicial dissolution, which Segal (D) opposed.

ISSUE: Where an LLC has no office, no employees, no operating revenue, no prospects of equity or debt infusion, and when the company's board has a long history of deadlock as a result of its governance structure, is it "reasonably

practicable" for it to continue to operate and it may be dissolved?

HOLDING AND DECISION: (Chandler, Chan.) No. Where an LLC has no office, no employees, no operating revenue, no prospects of equity or debt infusion, and when the company's board has a long history of deadlock as a result of its governance structure, it is not "reasonably practicable" for it to continue to operate and it may be dissolved. Because the managing members have been hopelessly deadlocked to the extent that 75% of the membership interest in Genitrix would not be voted in favor of dissolution, the only other opportunity for members seeking dissolution would be through a decree of judicial dissolution in accordance with the LLC agreement, and thus, under Del. 6 Del. C. § 18-802. The standard for dissolution under that statute is that the judicial dissolution may be decreed "whenever it is not reasonably practicable to carry on the business in conformity with a limited liability company agreement." In interpreting this statute, the dissolution statute for limited partnerships provides useful guidance. It provides that the test is whether it is "reasonably practicable" to carry on the business, not whether it is "impossible." Therefore, there is no need to show that the LLC's purpose has been completely frustrated. Instead, several circumstances, either together or separately, may be used to satisfy the standard: (1) the members' vote is deadlocked at the board level; (2) the operating agreement gives no means of navigating around the deadlock; and (3) due to the financial condition of the company, there is effectively no business to operate. These factual circumstances are not individually dispositive; nor must they all exist for a court to find it no longer reasonably practicable for a business to continue operating. Here, there is ample evidence of each of these circumstances. First, given the board's history of discord and disagreement, the parties will never be able to harmoniously resolve their differences, and, therefore, the Genitrix's board is deadlocked and unable to resolve any issue, including the issue of dissolution, facing Genitrix. Second, after examining the four corners of the LLC agreement, it appears there is no provision therein that would enable the board to circumvent the deadlock stalemate. Segal's (D) argument that Fisk Venture's (P) put option can be exercised to break the deadlock must be rejected because the put option may be exercised only at the holder's will, and Fisk Ventures (P) may not be forced to exercise it. Finally, given that the company has no sources of funding, and no realistic expectations of additional capital infusions, and because it lacks an office and operating revenue, Genitrix is left with no reasonably

Continued on next page.

practical means to operate. Segal's (D) argument that Fisk Venture's (P) comes to the court with unclean hands is unsupported, since there is no evidence that Fisk Ventures (P) desires dissolution only so it can obtain Genitrix's assets at fire sale prices. Accordingly, dissolution must be ordered.

▶ *ANALYSIS*

Even in the corporate context, with more liberal involuntary dissolution standards designed to protect minority interests, courts have rejected dissolution petitions where even though the parties are at odds, the company continues to be profitable. Here, in contrast, although the parties were at odds with each other, the company itself was failing as a business, with no hopes of resuscitation.

■═■

Quicknotes

DISSOLUTION Annulment or termination of a formal or legal bond, tie or contract.

■═■

R&R Capital, LLC v. Buck & Doe Run Valley Farms, LLC

Member (P) v. Limited liability company (D)

Del. Ct. Ch., 2008 WL 3846318 (2008).

NATURE OF CASE: Motion to dismiss a petition for the judicial dissolution of, or the appointment of a receiver for, several limited liability companies.

FACT SUMMARY: Two New York LLCs (petitioners) (P) sought dissolution of, or the appointment of a receiver for, nine separate Delaware LLCs (respondents) (D). The respondents (D) moved to dismiss, asserting that the petitioners (P) lacked standing to seek dissolution with respect to two of the respondents (D), since the petitioners (P) were neither members nor managers of those entities, and had waived their rights to seek dissolution or the appointment of a receiver with respect to the other respondent (D) entities in those entities' LLC Agreements.

> **RULE OF LAW**
> (1) A member of an LLC which is itself a member of another LLC may not seek dissolution or the winding up of the latter LLC.
> (2) A member of an LLC which is itself a member of another LLC may seek the appointment of a receiver for the latter LLC.
> (3) A member of an LLC may contractually waive the statutory right to seek dissolution of, or the appointment of a receiver for, the LLC.

FACTS: Two New York LLCs (petitioners) (P) sought dissolution of, or the appointment of a receiver for, nine separate Delaware LLCs (respondents) (D) pursuant to 6 Del C. §§ 18-802 (judicial dissolution), 18-803 (winding up), and 18-805 (appointment of a receiver). The petitioners (P) were neither members nor managers of two of those respondent (D) entities (the "Pandora Entities" (D)), but were members of the other seven respondent (D) LLCs. The petitioners (P) alleged that most of the respondent (D) entities had their certificates of formation canceled for failing to designate a registered agent, for failing to pay annual taxes, or for both. They further alleged that the manager, Merritt, could not revive the canceled certificates as a matter of law, that Merritt refused to provide an accounting of the canceled entities, and that Merritt had defrauded the entities and orchestrated self-dealing transactions with her boyfriend. Merritt was not named as a party to the action, however. The respondents (D) moved to dismiss, arguing that the petitioners (P) lacked standing to bring an action for dissolution of the Pandora Entities (D), since the petitioners (P) were neither members nor managers of those entities, and that with respect to the other respondent (D) entities, the petitioners (P) had waived their rights to seek dissolution in those entities' (the

"Waiver Entities'" (D)) LLC Agreements. The seven Waiver Entities (D) had, identical LLC Agreements and each one addressed dissolution explicitly. Specifically, the Agreements limited the events that could cause dissolution to five events, but also provided that the entities' members had waived their rights to seek judicial dissolution or the appointment of a liquidator.

ISSUE:
(1) May a member of an LLC which is itself a member of another LLC seek dissolution or the winding up of the latter LLC?
(2) May a member of an LLC which is itself a member of another LLC seek the appointment of a receiver for the latter LLC?
(3) May a member of an LLC contractually waive the statutory right to seek dissolution of, or the appointment of a receiver for, the LLC?

HOLDING AND DECISION: (Chandler, Chan.)
(1) No. A member of an LLC which is itself a member of another LLC may not seek dissolution or the winding up of the latter LLC. Under § 18-802, "[o]n application by or for a member or manager, the Court of Chancery may decree dissolution of a limited liability company whenever it is not reasonably practicable to carry on the business in conformity with a limited liability company agreement." Similarly, under § 18-803, only managers or members have standing to wind up a limited liability company's affairs. Because the petitioners (P) are neither members nor managers of the Pandora Entities (D), under the plain language of §§ 18-802 and 18-803, the petitioners (P) do not have standing to seek dissolution or winding up of the Pandora Entities (D). Therefore, their petition to dissolve or wind up the Pandora Entities (D) must be dismissed.
(2) Yes. A member of an LLC which is itself a member of another LLC may seek the appointment of a receiver for the latter LLC. Under § 18-805, any "creditor, member or manager of the Limited liability company, or any other person who shows good cause" may present an application for the appointment of a receiver. Here, the Pandora Entities (D) do not challenge, the petitioners' (P) ability to seek relief pursuant to § 18-805 and therefore, that claim survives the motion to dismiss.
(3) Yes. A member of an LLC may contractually waive the statutory right to seek dissolution of, or the appointment of a receiver for, the LLC. Neither the state's LLC Act nor its policy precludes such contractual waiver, and the waiver of such rights will not leave an LLC

Continued on next page.

member inequitably remediless. LLCs are "creatures of contract" that are designed to maximize contractual freedom and flexibility. The petitioners' (P) argument that statutory provisions that do not contain the qualification "unless otherwise provided in a limited liability company agreement" (or a variation thereof) are mandatory and may not be waived is unavailing. The petitioners (P) adduce no support for this broad proposition, and, in fact, the state's Supreme Court has indicated that the language referenced by petitioners (P) is permissive. Generally, the mandatory provisions of the Act are "those intended to protect third parties, not necessarily the contracting members." Sections 18-802, 18-803, and 18-805 are not mandatory provisions of the LLC Act, and therefore they may be modified. Those provisions employ permissive rather than mandatory language, and the rights of third parties would not be affected by waiver of these provisions in an LLC Agreement. Accordingly, the waiver is valid and enforceable under the statute. In addition, because Delaware's LLC Act prohibits the waiver of the implied contractual covenant of good faith and fair dealing, members would be protected even upon waiver of their right to dissolution. In fact, the petitioners (P) made sufficient allegations that would have supported a claim based on the implied covenant of good faith and fair dealing, but had simply failed to bring such a claim. Moreover, there would be no threat to equity in allowing members to waive their right to seek dissolution, because there would be no chance that some members would be trapped in an LLC at the mercy of others acting unfairly and in bad faith. Here, instead, the members were sophisticated in business, and voluntarily and unambiguously waived their rights to petition the court for dissolution. The motion to dismiss is granted as to the petitions relating to the Waiver Entities (D).

▶ ANALYSIS

In this opinion, the court emphasizes repeatedly that the core policy with respect to LLCs is freedom of contract and flexibility. The court says, "The allure of the limited liability company . . . would be eviscerated if the parties could simply petition this court to renegotiate their agreements when relationships sour." Similarly, Professor Larry Ribstein, an LLC scholar, has emphasized that it is the rigor with which Delaware courts apply the contractual language of LLC Agreements that makes limited liability companies successful. Accordingly, the Delaware courts attempt to assiduously guard the freedom of contract principle so that the main attraction of the LLC form is not eroded.

Quicknotes

LIMITED LIABILITY COMPANY A business entity combining the features of both a corporation and a general partnership; the LLC provides its shareholders and officers with limited liability, but it is treated as a partnership for taxation purposes.

RECEIVER An individual who is appointed by the court to maintain the holdings of a corporation, individual or other entity involved in a legal proceeding.

STANDING The right to commence suit against another party because of a personal stake in the resolution of the controversy.

■▬■

VGS, Inc. v. Castiel

LLC manager/shareholders (D) v. LLC originator/manager/shareholder (P)

Del. Ct. Ch., 2000 WL 1277372, *aff'd*, 781 A.2d 696 (2001).

NATURE OF CASE: Equity suit by a manager/shareholder of a limited liability company (LLC) to set aside a reorganization and merger of the LLC by fellow managers.

FACT SUMMARY: David Castiel (P) formed VGS, Inc. (D) as a one-member limited liability company (LLC). The one member was Virtual Geosatellite Holdings. Two other entities, Sahagen Satellite and Ellipso, Inc., later become member/shareholders of the LLC. Castiel named himself and Tom Quinn to the board of managers, and Sahagan named himself as the third member. Sahagen and Quinn subsequently decided to restructure VGS (D) in such a manner that Castiel (P) would become a minority shareholder. They effectuated the restructuring without giving notice to Castiel (P).

> ## 🏛 RULE OF LAW
> Managers under a limited liability corporation agreement must exercise a duty of loyalty by acting in good faith to one another.

FACTS: VGS, Inc. (D) was controlled by David Castiel (P), a single individual who formed VGS (D) as a one-member limited liability company (LLC). Subsequently, two other entities, Sahagen Satellite and Ellipso, Inc., became members of the LLC. The LLC agreement created a three-member board of managers with sweeping authority to govern the LLC. Castiel (P), the individual owning the original member, had the authority to name and remove, two of the three managers and also acted as CEO. Castiel named himself and Tom Quinn to the board of managers, and Sahagan named himself as the third member. Sahagen and Quinn became disenchanted with Castiel's (P) leadership. Ultimately Sahagen convinced Quinn to join him in a clandestine strategic move to merge the LLC into a Delaware corporation. The appointed manager, Quinn, and the disaffected third member, Sahagen, did not give Castiel (P), still a member of the LLC's board of managers, notice of their strategic move. After the merger, Castiel (P) found himself relegated to a minority position in the surviving corporation. Castiel brought suit in equity to set aside the merger, arguing that, although a majority of the board acted by written consent, if Castiel had received notice beforehand that his appointed manager contemplated action against his interests, he would have promptly attempted to remove him. Castiel (P) contended that because his two fellow managers (Sahagen and Quinn) acted without notice to Castiel (P) under circumstances where they knew that with notice he could have acted to protect his majority interest, they breached their duty of loyalty to him by failing to act in good faith.

ISSUE: Must the managers under a limited liability corporation agreement exercise a duty of loyalty by acting in good faith to one another?

HOLDING AND DECISION: (Steele, V. Chan.) Yes. The managers under a limited liability corporation (LLC) agreement must exercise a duty of loyalty by acting in good faith to one another. Here, by failing to give Castiel (P) notice of their proposed action, Sahagen and Quinn (hence VGS, Inc.) (D) failed to discharge their duty of loyalty to Castiel and to exercise their duty of good faith toward him. Section 18-404(d) of the LLC Act states, in part, that the managers of a LLC company may take actions without a vote if a consent in writing, setting forth the action taken, is signed by the managers having not less than the minimum number of votes that would be necessary to authorize such action at a meeting. Therefore, the LLC Act, read literally, did not require notice to Castiel (P) before Sahagen and Quinn could act by written consent. However, this observation does not complete the analysis of Sahagen's and Quinn's actions. Sahagen and Quinn knew what would happen if they notified Castiel (P) of their intention to act by written consent to merge the LLC into VGS, Inc. Castiel (P) would have attempted to remove Quinn and block the planned action. The purpose of permitting action by written consent without notice is to enable LLC managers to take quick, efficient action in situations when a minority of managers could not block or adversely affect the course set by the majority, even if the minority were notified of the proposed action and objected to it. The legislators never intended to enable two managers to deprive, clandestinely and surreptitiously, a third manager representing the majority interest in the LLC of an opportunity to protect that interest by taking an action that the third manager's member would surely have opposed if he had knowledge of it. Equity looks to the intent rather than to the form. Here, in this hopefully unique situation, this application of the maxim requires construction of the statute to allow action without notice only by a constant or fixed majority. It can not apply to an illusory, will-of-the-wisp majority which would implode should notice be given. Nothing in the statute suggests that a court of equity should blind its eyes to a shallow, too clever by half, manipulative attempt to restructure an enterprise through an action taken by a "majority" that existed only so long as it could act in secrecy. Although a majority vote of the LLC's board of managers could properly effect a merger, nevertheless, Sahagen and Quinn failed to discharge their duty of loyalty to Castiel (P) in good faith by failing to give him advance notice of their merger plans under the unique

Continued on next page.

circumstances of this case and the structure of this LLC agreement. Accordingly, the acts taken to merge the LLC into VGS, Inc. were invalid, and the merger is ordered rescinded.

▶ ANALYSIS

In the *VGS* case, Sahagen and Quinn each owed a duty of loyalty to the LLC, its investors, and Castiel (P), their fellow manager. Castiel (P) owned a majority interest in the LLC, and he sat as a member of the board. The majority investor protected his equity interest in the LLC through the mechanism of appointment to the board rather than by the statutorily sanctioned mechanism of approval by members owning a majority of the LLC's equity interests. The agreement allowed the action to merge, dissolve or change to corporate status to be taken by a simple majority vote of the board of managers rather than by reliance upon the default position of the statute which requires a majority vote of the equity interest. Instead, the drafters made the critical assumption that the holder of the majority equity interest had the right to appoint and remove two managers, ostensibly guaranteeing control over a three-member board. When Sahagen and Quinn, fully recognizing that these rights were Castiel's (P) protection against actions adverse to his majority interest, acted in secret and without notice, they failed to discharge their duty of loyalty to him in good faith. The Chancery Court here took the position that the managers owed Castiel (P) a duty to give him prior notice, even if he would have interfered with a plan that they conscientiously believed to be in the best interest of the LLC. Instead, the managers launched a preemptive strike that furtively converted Castiel's (P) controlling interest in the LLC to a minority interest in VGS (D), without affording Castiel (P) a level playing field on which to defend his interest. A traditional maxim of equity holds that equity regards and treats that as done which in good conscience ought to be done. Accordingly, under these circumstances, the court held Sahagen and Quinn should have given Castiel (P) prior notice.

■═■

Quicknotes

ACTION IN EQUITY Lawsuit in which a plaintiff seeks equitable remedies.

DUTY OF GOOD FAITH AND FAIR DEALING An implied duty in a contract that the parties will deal honestly in the satisfaction of their obligations and without an intent to defraud.

DUTY OF LOYALTY A director's duty to refrain from self-dealing or to take a position that is adverse to the corporation's best interests.

EQUITY Fairness; justice; the determination of a matter consistent with principles of fairness and not in strict compliance with rules of law.

LIMITED LIABILITY An advantage of doing business in the corporate form by safeguarding shareholders from liability for the debts or obligations of the corporation.

■═■

The Corporation as a Device to Allocate Risk

Quick Reference Rules of Law

Klang v. Smith's Food & Drug Centers, Inc.

Shareholders (P) v. Corporation (D)

Del. Sup. Ct., 702 A.2d 150 (1997).

NATURE OF CASE: Appeal from dismissal of a purported class action to have certain transactions in a corporate merger and repurchase rescinded.

FACT SUMMARY: Klang (P) filed a class action complaint against Smith's Food & Drug (D) to rescind a merger transaction, arguing that repurchase of shares resulted in impairment of capital and the methodology used in its solvency opinion was inappropriate.

> 🏛 **RULE OF LAW**
> A corporation's balance sheets are not conclusive of whether the Delaware statute forbidding impairment of capital has been violated.

FACTS: Smith's Food & Drug Centers, Inc. (SFD) (D) entered into an agreement with Yucaipa Companies for a merger under which SFD (D) was to repurchase up to 50% of its shares. SFD (D) hired an investment firm to examine these transactions and issue a report with a solvency opinion. The firm determined that the merger could occur without risking SFD's (D) solvency or impairing SFD's (D) capital. Accordingly, the transactions closed, and SFD (D) repurchased 50% of its shares. Klang (P) filed a class action complaint with a motion to rescind the transactions, arguing that the stock repurchase violated 8 Del. C. § 160 by impairing SFD's (D) capital, as evidenced by SFD's (D) books showing a negative net worth following its transactions with Yucaipa. The lower court dismissed Klang's (P) claims in full, and he appealed.

ISSUE: Is the balance sheet method of determining surplus conclusive in finding whether the Delaware statute forbidding impairment of capital has been violated?

HOLDING AND DECISION: (Veasey, C.J.) No. The balance sheet method is not conclusive in determining whether the Delaware statute forbidding impairment of capital has been violated. Section 160 provides that a corporation may not repurchase its shares if doing so would result in an impairment of capital; a corporation may only repurchase shares if using "surplus." In showing surplus, a corporation may revalue its assets and liabilities to thereby comply with the statute. The statute defining surplus through "net assets" does not set forth a particular method in determining surplus; as long as the evaluation is based on good faith, acceptable data, and reasonable methods to render a surplus that is not so unrealistic that is would constitute actual or constructive fraud, a board may deviate from the balance sheet method. Affirmed.

⬤ *ANALYSIS*

Balance sheet tests have been used to determine if a dividend would impair capital. This case allows a board to reasonably diverge from the balance sheet method if calculations are completed in good faith and with reasonable techniques. The court noted that restricting the calculation of surplus to a balance sheet method would not only be unrealistic in that elements such as unrealized appreciation and depreciation might not be reflected on the sheet, but also potentially frustrate the purpose of statutes against impairment of capital (namely, to prevent draining of corporate assets and to maintain healthy corporations).

▄▀▄

Quicknotes

CLASS ACTION A suit commenced by a representative on behalf of an ascertainable group that is too large to appear in court, who shares a commonality of interests and who will benefit from a successful result.

IMPAIRMENT OF CAPITAL When the capital surplus account of a corporation is negative.

▄▀▄

Consumer's Co-op v. Olsen

Corporation (P) v. Stockholder (D)

Wis. Sup. Ct., 142 Wis. 2d 465, 419 N.W.2d 211 (1988).

NATURE OF CASE: Appeal from judgment in a contract action to pierce the corporate veil.

FACT SUMMARY: After Olsen's (D) corporation, ECO, filed for reorganization under Chapter 11, Consumer's Co-op (P) brought this action to pierce the corporate veil to recover the amount owing on ECO's corporate account.

🏛 RULE OF LAW
Both inadequate capitalization and disregard of corporate formalities must be considered in determining whether a corporation has a separate existence shielding shareholders from liability for corporate debts.

FACTS: Olsen (D) and his parents were the sole stockholders, directors, and corporate officers of ECO. Consumer's Co-op (Consumer's) (P) extended credit to ECO through a corporate account established by Olsen (D). The board of directors met and conferred four or five times a week, but the only formal record of their meetings concerned the meeting to elect the corporate officers and the meeting to authorize Chapter 11 Bankruptcy reorganization. Despite ECO's financial difficulties and its failure to pay its account on time, Consumer's (P) continued to extend credit to ECO. Consumer's (P) then brought this action, seeking to pierce the corporate veil. The trial court entered judgment in favor of Consumer's (P), and Olsen (D) appealed.

ISSUE: Must both inadequate capitalization and disregard of corporate formalities be considered in determining whether a corporation has a separate existence shielding shareholders from liability for corporate debts?

HOLDING AND DECISION: (Ceci, J.) Yes. Both inadequate capitalization and disregard of corporate formalities must be considered in determining whether a corporation has a separate existence shielding shareholders from liability for corporate debts. The adequacy of capital must be measured at the time of incorporation. An adequately capitalized corporation will not subsequently be rendered undercapitalized merely because the business suffers losses. Here, the initial capitalization of ECO was not obviously inadequate when measured by the smallness of the initial undertaking. By continuing to extend credit to ECO, Consumer's (P) waived the right to claim inadequacy of capitalization as a basis to pierce the corporate veil. Further, the failure of a statutory close corporation to observe usual corporate formalities is not grounds for imposing personal liability on the shareholders for corporate debts. Reversed.

▌ANALYSIS

The "instrumentality" or "alter ego" doctrine, which allows the corporate veil to be pierced, requires proof of three elements. First, control of the corporation by the defendant, amounting to complete domination; second, use of that control to commit fraud or wrong or to breach a duty; and, third, the control and breach of duty must proximately cause the injury or unjust loss. A combination of these factors may show that the corporate entity had no will of its own, making it a "mere instrumentality or tool" of the shareholder.

■▬■

Quicknotes

ALTER-EGO DOCTRINE The court disregards the corporate entity and holds the individual shareholders liable for acts done knowingly and intentionally in the corporation's name.

CORPORATE VEIL Refers to the shielding from personal liability of a corporation's officers, directors, or shareholders for unlawful conduct engaged in by the corporation.

■▬■

K.C. Roofing Center v. On Top Roofing, Inc.

Creditor (P) v. Debtor (D)

Mo. Ct. App., 807 S.W.2d 545 (1991).

NATURE OF CASE: Appeal from order holding shareholder personally liable for a corporation's debts.

FACT SUMMARY: Creditors of On Top Roofing, Inc. (D) sought to hold shareholder Nugent (D) personally liable for the corporation's debts.

🏛 RULE OF LAW
A shareholder may be held personally liable for a corporation's debts.

FACTS: On Top Roofing, Inc. (D) had as sole shareholders Nugent (D) and his wife Carol (D). They were the corporation's directors and officers as well. From 1977 to 1989, the Nugents (D) were roofing contractors who went through several corporations. On Top Roofing, Inc. (D) ceased business, and the Nugents (D) started RNR, Inc., which itself later ceased business and was replaced by RLN Construction, Inc. This in turn was replaced by Russell Nugent, Inc. Although On Top Roofing, Inc. (D) went out of business in 1987, the other corporations continued to use On Top Roofing (D) as a DBA. During this time, several unsecured creditors of On Top Roofing, Inc. (D) were not paid. K.C. Roofing Center (KCR) (P) and Lumberman's Mutual Wholesale (P), unpaid creditors, obtained judgments against On Top Roofing, Inc. (D), which had no assets. In a consolidated action, both KCR (P) and Lumberman's (P) sought to hold the Nugents (D) personally liable. The trial court held Russell Nugent (D) personally liable, and he appealed.

ISSUE: May a shareholder be held personally liable for a corporation's debts?

HOLDING AND DECISION: (Kennedy, J.) Yes. A shareholder may be held personally liable for a corporation's debts. In order for a court to "pierce the corporate veil" and hold a shareholder personally liable for a corporate debt, the following criteria must be met: (1) complete control of the corporation, so that the corporation has no real existence separate from the individual; (2) the use of such control to perpetrate a wrong or fraud; and (3) proximate cause. Here, it appears that Nugent (D) was in the practice of using successive corporations to incur debts and then leaving lifeless corporate shells to absorb the debts he incurred. This is precisely the sort of activity for which the doctrine of piercing the corporate veil was developed, and it was properly applied here. Affirmed.

▶ ANALYSIS

There is no single type of activity that will invariably lead to piercing the corporate veil, but some readily lend themselves to use of the doctrine. Actual fraud or misrepresentation is an obvious example. Undercapitalization or underinsurance is another. These situations tend to enrich the shareholder at the expense of the creditor and thus invite judicial scrutiny.

Quicknotes

CORPORATE VEIL Refers to the shielding from personal liability of a corporation's officers, directors, or shareholders for unlawful conduct engaged in by the corporation.

FRAUD A false representation of facts with the intent that another will rely on the misrepresentation to his detriment.

MISREPRESENTATION A statement or conduct by one party to another that constitutes a false representation of fact.

Western Rock Co. v. Davis

Corporation (D) v. Landowner (P)

Tex. Ct. Civ. App., 432 S.W.2d 555 (1968).

NATURE OF CASE: Appeal from judgment awarding damages for injury to property.

FACT SUMMARY: Fuller (D) and Stroud (D), directors of shell corporation Western Rock Co. (D), were held personally liable for its torts.

🏛 RULE OF LAW
A director of a shell corporation may be personally liable for its torts.

FACTS: Fuller (D) and Stroud (D) were shareholders of Western Rock Co. (D). Fuller (D) provided almost all of the capital, and Stroud (D) provided expertise. For a period of months, Western Rock (D) had been carrying on blasting operations. Nearby landowners began to complain about damage to their buildings caused by the blasting. An insurance agent told Fuller (D) and Stroud (D) that their insurance would not cover tort claims based on the blasting. Western Rock (D) ceased blasting when it ran out of money. Its tangible assets were transferred to Fuller's (D) personal corporation. Several landowners filed tort claims against Western Rock (D), Fuller (D), and Stroud (D). The latter two demurred, contending that they could not be liable for the corporation's acts. The demurrers were overruled, and Fuller (D) and Stroud (D) appealed.

ISSUE: May a director of a shell corporation be personally liable for its torts?

HOLDING AND DECISION: (Langdon, J.) Yes. A director of a shell corporation may be personally liable for its torts. When a corporation serves as a device by which those in control of it can work a tort against innocent third parties, those controlling individuals will not be permitted to hide behind the corporate shell; personal liability will be imposed. Here, there is no question but that Stroud (D) and Fuller (D) controlled Western Rock Co. (D). They conducted blasting operations to the detriment of neighbors and then left an empty corporation. Such a situation demands personal liability on the part of Fuller (D) and Stroud (D). Affirmed.

▶ ANALYSIS

The usual situation triggering personal liability on the part of corporate directors is the "shell" corporation. A shell corporation, basically, is one that is so undercapitalized or underinsured that it is clear from the beginning that it will not be able to pay its probable debts. Such a situation facilitates perpetration of fraud upon the corporation's creditors.

■═■

Quicknotes

DEMURRER The assertion that the opposing party's pleadings are insufficient and that the demurring party should not be made to answer.

FRAUD A false representation of facts with the intent that another will rely on the misrepresentation to his detriment.

■═■

Baatz v. Arrow Bar

Injured party (P) v. Corporation owners (D)

S.D. Sup. Ct., 452 N.W.2d 138 (1990).

NATURE OF CASE: Appeal from summary judgment dismissing personal injury action.

FACT SUMMARY: The Baatzes (P) sought to hold the Neuroths (D) personally liable for the alleged tort of their corporation.

🏛 RULE OF LAW
Controlling shareholders will not be liable for a corporation's torts absent use of the corporation to effect a wrong.

FACTS: The Neuroths (D) owned Arrow Bar, Inc. (D), which operated a tavern called Arrow Bar. The business was started with a $5,000 loan. The Neuroths (D) personally guaranteed several loans made to purchase equipment. At one point, McBride (D), who had been drinking at the bar, crashed into the Baatzes (P), who were riding a motorcycle, seriously injuring them. The Baatzes (P) sued Arrow Bar, Inc. (D) and the Neuroths (D) for negligently serving alcohol to McBride (D). Prior to trial, the Neuroths (D) successfully moved for summary judgment on the basis that they had not been personally negligent. The Baatzes (P) appealed, contending that the Neuroths (D) should be personally liable for the corporation's (D) debts.

ISSUE: Will controlling shareholders be liable for a corporation's torts absent use of the corporation to effect a wrong?

HOLDING AND DECISION: (Sabers, J.) No. Controlling shareholders will not be liable for a corporation's torts absent use of the corporation to effect a wrong. As a general rule, a corporation's shareholders, even controlling shareholders, will not be personally liable for corporate debts. Exceptions to this rule are only made when it is shown that the shareholders used their status as controllers to effect a wrong. While no one factor automatically leads to personal liability, some of the "red flags" include: fraudulent representation; undercapitalization; failure to observe corporate formalities; absence of corporate records; payment by the corporation of personal debts; and use of the corporation to promote fraud. Here, none of these has been shown. The corporation was started with a loan, but this is far from unusual. Also, the personal guarantee of contract debt by the Neuroths (D) is a standard practice and does not demonstrate fraud. Consequently, the Baatzes (P) have made no showing sufficient to pierce the corporate veil. Affirmed.

DISSENT: (Henderson, J.) Arrow Bar, Inc. (D) was undercapitalized and was nothing more than a front for the Neuroths (D) to escape dramshop liability.

▶ ANALYSIS

The extent to which a corporation must be capitalized so as to not raise the specter of piercing the corporate veil varies greatly. Probably the most important factor, besides size, is riskiness of the venture. The more risky the venture, the more it must be capitalized (or insured).

■■■

Quicknotes

CORPORATE VEIL Refers to the shielding from personal liability of a corporation's officers, directors, or shareholders for unlawful conduct engaged in by the corporation.

SUMMARY JUDGMENT Judgment rendered by a court in response to a motion by one of the parties, claiming that the lack of a question of material fact in respect to an issue warrants disposition of the issue without consideration by the jury.

■■■

Craig v. Lake Asbestos

Injured party (P) v. Corporation (D)

843 F.2d 145 (3d Cir. 1988).

NATURE OF CASE: Appeal from judgment awarding damages for personal injury.

FACT SUMMARY: A district court held a parent corporation liable for a subsidiary's torts on the basis of potential control.

🏛 RULE OF LAW
Potential control is insufficient to hold a parent corporation liable for a subsidiary's torts.

FACTS: North American Asbestos Corp. (NAAC) sold asbestos for 25 years prior to 1978, when it was dissolved. Its parent corporation was Cape Industries (D), a British corporation, of which a majority of shares was owned by Charter Consolidated, P.L.C. (D), also a British corporation. Cape (D) and Charter (D) kept separate books, used different financial professionals, and did not consult with each other on a daily basis. Cape's (D) board consisted of ten to 14 directors, of which three were Charter (D) executives. At one point, Craig (P) filed a lawsuit for injuries related to asbestos exposure. Cape (D) defaulted. The district court, finding that Charter (D) had a high degree of potential control over Cape (D), held it liable for Cape's (D) role as NAAC's alter ego. Judgment in favor of Craig (P) in the amount of $40,000 was entered, and Charter (D) appealed.

ISSUE: Is potential control sufficient for a parent corporation to be liable for a subsidiary's torts?

HOLDING AND DECISION: (Sloviter, J.) No. Potential control is insufficient for a parent corporation to be liable for a subsidiary's torts. The general rule is that corporate separateness will be respected by courts because the limitation of liability inherent in the corporate form is one of the major reasons for its use. Only when a certain set of conditions are met will the corporate form be disregarded. One condition is that, for a parent to be responsible for a subsidiary's debts, the parent must exercise such a level of control over that subsidiary that the subsidiary can be said to have no life of its own. The district court in this case did not make this finding but rather held that Charter (D) had such a potential for control that actual control was unnecessary. This was in error. There must be sufficient facts in the record to indicate complete control, not merely a potential for control. Such facts are not present here. Reversed and remanded.

▶ ANALYSIS

The requirements for piercing the corporate veil vary, but two basic sets of conditions are usually required. The first is a high level of control, although the level necessary does vary from state to state. The other set of conditions relates to some sort of fraud or wrong perpetrated through use of the corporate form.

∎══∎

Quicknotes

ALTER-EGO DOCTRINE The court disregards the corporate entity and holds the individual shareholders liable for acts done knowingly and intentionally in the corporation's name.

CORPORATE VEIL Refers to the shielding from personal liability of a corporation's officers, directors, or shareholders for unlawful conduct engaged in by the corporation.

SUBSIDIARY A company a majority of whose shares are owned by another corporation and which is subject to that corporation's control.

∎══∎

United States v. Bestfoods

Federal government (P) v. Corporate polluters (D)

524 U.S. 51 (1998).

NATURE OF CASE: Review of judgment for defendant in action against parent company of corporate polluter.

FACT SUMMARY: The United States (P) brought this action for the costs of cleaning up industrial waste generated by a chemical plant against Bestfoods (D), the parent company of a subsidiary which operated the facility.

RULE OF LAW
The corporate veil may be pierced to find a corporate parent that actively participated in, and exercised control over, the operations of a polluting facility directly liable in its own right as an operator of the facility.

FACTS: The Ott Chemical Company (Ott I) intentionally and unintentionally dumped hazardous substances which significantly polluted the soil and ground water at a plant near Muskegon, Michigan. CPC International, which has since changed its name to Bestfoods (D), incorporated a wholly owned subsidiary to buy Ott I's assets. The new company (Ott II) continued chemical manufacturing at the site and continued polluting until it was sold to Story Chemical Company, which operated the plant until its bankruptcy in 1977. The Michigan Department of Natural Resources discovered the pollution and sought a buyer for the property who would be willing to contribute toward its cleanup. Aerojet-General Corporation arranged for a transfer of the site from the Story bankruptcy trustee and created a wholly owned California subsidiary to purchase the property (Cordova/California) which in turn created a wholly owned Michigan subsidiary (Cordova/Michigan) which manufactured chemicals at the site until 1986. To recover some of the money necessary for the Environmental Protection Agency to clean up the site, the Government (P) brought an action under the Comprehensive Environmental Response Compensation and Liability Act of 1980 (CERCLA) naming five defendants: CPC (D), Aerojet, Cordova/California, Cordova/Michigan, and Arnold Ott. The district court held both CPC (D) and Aerojet directly liable as an operator (as opposed to indirect liability under veil-piercing) using an "actual control" test focusing on if the parent exerted power or influence over the subsidiary's business during a period of disposal of hazardous waste. The Sixth Circuit (en banc and divided seven to six) limited operator liability based on parental control of the subsidiary to situations where state law piercing requirements are met, and reversed. The Government (P) appealed. The Supreme Court granted certiorari.

ISSUE: May the corporate veil be pierced to find a corporate parent that actively participated in, and exercised control over, the operations of a polluting facility be held directly liable in its own right as an operator of the facility?

HOLDING AND DECISION: (Souter, J.) Yes. The corporate veil may be pierced to find a corporate parent that actively participated in, and exercised control over, the operations of a polluting facility directly liable in its own right as an operator of the facility. The court of appeals was correct in holding that only when the corporate veil may be pierced may a parent corporation be charged with derivative CERCLA liability. But under the plain language of the statute, any person who operates a polluting facility is directly liable for the costs of cleaning up the pollution. This is so regardless of whether that person is the facility's owner, the owner's parent corporation or a business partner. The existence of the parent-subsidiary relationship under state corporate law is simply irrelevant to the issue of direct liability. The court of appeals indicated that a corporate parent can be held liable when the parent operates the facility in the stead of its subsidiary or alongside the subsidiary in some sort of joint venture. Yet another possibility, suggested by the facts of this case, is that an agent of the parent with no hat to wear but the parent's hat might manage or direct activities at the facility. There is some evidence that CPC (D) engaged in just this type and degree of activity at the Muskegon plant. The district court's opinion speaks of an agent of CPC (D) who played a conspicuous part in dealing with the toxic risks emanating from the operation of the plant. Williams worked only for CPC (D), he was not an officer, employee or director of Ott II, and thus, his actions were of necessity taken on behalf of CPC (D). Prudence counsels us to remand for reevaluation of Williams's role, and of the role of any other CPC (D) agent who might be said to have had a part in operating the Muskegon facility. Reversed and remanded.

ANALYSIS

CERCLA was enacted in response to the serious environmental and health risks posed by industrial pollution. CERCLA is a comprehensive statute that grants the president broad power to command government agencies and private parties to clean up hazardous waste sites. The United States may use the "Hazardous Substance Superfund" to finance cleanup efforts which it may then replenish by suits such as this one.

■▬■

Continued on next page.

Quicknotes

AGENT An individual who has the authority to act on behalf of another.

CERCLA—42 U.S.C. § 9601 Et Seq. Gives the government broad powers to command the cleanup of hazardous waste sites.

CERTIORARI A discretionary writ issued by a superior court to an inferior court in order to review the lower court's decisions; the Supreme Court's writ ordering such review.

CORPORATE VEIL Refers to the shielding from personal liability of a corporation's officers, directors, or share-holders for unlawful conduct engaged in by the corporation.

■=■

Kaycee Land and Livestock v. Flahive

Landowner (P) v. Limited liability company (D)

Wyo. Sup. Ct., 46 P.3d 323 (2002).

NATURE OF CASE: Landowner's action for damages against a limited liability company (LLC), alleging that the LLC caused environmental damage to the land when exercising its contractual right to use the surface of the land.

FACT SUMMARY: Kaycee Land and Livestock (Kaycee) (P) contracted with Flahive Oil & Gas LLC allowing the company to use the surface of Kaycee's (P) real property. Roger Flahive (D) was the LLC's managing member. When environmental contamination occurred, Kaycee (P) sued Roger Flahive (D) individually, seeking to pierce the LLC veil and disregard the LLC entity.

🏛 RULE OF LAW
The equitable remedy of piercing the veil is an available remedy under the Limited Liability Company Act.

FACTS: Flahive Oil & Gas (Flahive) was a Wyoming limited liability company (LLC) with no assets at the time of suit. Kaycee Land and Livestock (Kaycee) (P) entered into a contract with Flahive allowing the company to use the surface of Kaycee's (P) real property. Roger Flahive (D) was the managing member of Flahive Oil & Gas at all relevant times. Kaycee (P) brought suit in the district court against Flahive (D) alleging that Flahive (D) caused environmental contamination to its real property. Kaycee (P) sought to pierce the LLC veil, disregard the LLC entity of Flahive Oil & Gas LLC, and hold Roger Flahive (D) individually liable for the contamination. There was no allegation of fraud. The district court certified to the Wyoming Supreme Court the question whether, in the absence of fraud, the entity veil of a limited liability company can be pierced in the same manner as that of a corporation.

ISSUE: Is the equitable remedy of piercing the veil an available remedy under the Limited Liability Company (LLC) Act?

HOLDING AND DECISION: (Kite, J.) Yes. The equitable remedy of piercing the veil is an available remedy under the Limited Liability Company (LLC) Act. While as a general rule a corporation is a separate entity distinct from the individuals comprising it, a corporation's legal entity will be disregarded whenever the recognition of corporate status will lead to injustice. No reason exists in law or equity for treating an LLC differently from a corporation when considering whether to disregard the legal entity. The LLC statute simply states the underlying principle of limited liability for individual members and managers by providing that neither the members of an

LLC nor the managers of an LLC managed by a manager are liable for liabilities of the limited liability company. It is difficult to read this statutory provision as precluding courts from disregarding the veil of an improperly used LLC. Lack of explicit statutory language should not indicate the legislature's desire to make LLC members impermeable. Every state that has enacted LLC piercing legislation has chosen to follow corporate law standards and not develop a separate LLC standard. Statutes which create corporations and LLCs have the same basic purpose of limiting individual investor liability while benefiting economic development. Statutes created the legal fiction of the corporation as a separate entity independent from individuals. If the corporation were created and operated in conformance with the statutory requirements, the law would treat it as a separate entity and shelter the individual shareholders from any liability caused by corporate action, thereby encouraging investment. However, courts have consistently recognized that unjust circumstances can arise if immunity from liability shelters those who have failed to operate a corporation as a separate entity. Consequently, when corporations fail to follow statutorily mandated formalities, co-mingle funds, or ignore the restrictions in their articles of incorporation regarding separate treatment of corporate property, the courts disregard the separate identity and do not permit shareholders to be sheltered from liability to third parties for damages caused by the corporations' acts. There is no reason in law or policy to treat LLCs differently, although the factors justifying piercing an LLC veil would not be identical to those in the corporate situation because many organizational formalities applicable to corporations do not apply to LLCs. Remanded to district court to complete a fact intensive inquiry and exercise equitable powers to determine whether piercing the LLC veil is appropriate under the circumstances presented in this case.

▶ ANALYSIS

In *Kaycee*, the court noted that among the possible factors to be considered in determining whether the interests of justice require piercing the corporate veil are the following: the commingling of funds and other assets, failure to segregate funds of the separate entities, and unauthorized diversion of corporate funds or assets to other than corporate uses; treatment by an individual of assets of the corporation as his or her own; failure to obtain authority to issue or subscribe to stock; the holding out by an individual that he or she is personally liable for the debts

Continued on next page.

of the corporation; failure to maintain minutes or adequate corporate records and the confusion of the records of the separate entities; identical equitable ownership in the two entities; identification of the directors and officers of the two entities in the responsible supervision and management; failure to adequately capitalize a corporation; absence of corporate assets and undercapitalization; use of a corporation as a mere shell, instrumentality or conduit for a single venture or the business of an individual or another corporation; concealment and misrepresentation of the identity of the responsible ownership, management, and financial interest or concealment of personal business activities; disregard of legal formalities and the failure to maintain arm's-length relationships among related entities; use of corporate entity to procure labor, services, or merchandise for another person or entity; diversion of assets from a corporation by or to a stockholder or other person or entity, to the detriment of creditors, or the manipulation of assets and liabilities between entities so as to concentrate the assets in one and the liabilities in another; contracting with another with intent to avoid performance by use of a corporation as a subterfuge of illegal transactions; and formation and use of a corporation to transfer to it the existing liability of another person or entity.

■═■

Quicknotes

LIMITED LIABILITY An advantage of doing business in the corporate form by safeguarding shareholders from liability for the debts or obligations of the corporation.

■═■

RKO-Stanley Warner Theatres, Inc. v. Graziano

Seller (P) v. Promoters (D)

Pa. Sup. Ct., 467 Pa. 220, 355 A.2d 830 (1976).

NATURE OF CASE: Appeal from an equitable decree directing enforcement of a sale agreement.

FACT SUMMARY: Graziano (D) argued that a paragraph in the contract for the purchase of a theater owned by RKO-Stanley Warner (P) relieved the corporate promoters, including himself, from liability upon the mere formation of the proposed corporation, Kent Enterprises, Inc.

🏛 **RULE OF LAW**
A promoter is personally liable on contracts made by him for the benefit of a corporation he intends to organize, and his personal liability continues even after the corporation is formed unless there is a novation or other agreement to release liability.

FACTS: Graziano (D) and Jenofsky (D) were acting as promoters of an intended corporation, Kent Enterprises, Inc., when they signed to purchase a theater from RKO-Stanley Warner (RKO) (P). A paragraph therein provided: "It is understood . . . that it is the intention of the Purchaser to incorporate. Upon condition that such incorporation be completed by closing, all agreements, covenants, and warranties contained herein shall be construed to have been made between Seller and the resultant corporation and all documents shall reflect same." When Jenofsky (D) and Graziano (D) failed to complete settlement on the last scheduled date, RKO (P) sought and obtained an equitable decree ordering the two promoters to complete the transaction. On appeal, they argued that the aforementioned paragraph had relieved them of individual liability for performance of the agreement once the corporation was formed, as it had been.

ISSUE: In general, are promoters of the corporation liable for pre-incorporation contracts they made for its benefit, and does their liability continue even after the corporation is formed?

HOLDING AND DECISION: (Eagen, J.) Yes. The general rule is that corporate promoters are personally liable on contracts they make for the benefit of the intended corporation, and that liability continues even after the corporation is formed unless there is a novation or other agreement to release liability. The paragraph at issue here is ambiguous and susceptible to two interpretations. If it did release the promoters from liability upon mere formation of the corporation, RKO (P) would be left with no accountable party should the corporation then fail to ratify the agreement. Absent a clear expression that this

was the intent of the parties, it is more logical to assume the parties intended to absolve the promoters of liability once the corporation was formed and had ratified the agreement, thus binding the corporation thereto. Affirmed.

DISSENT: (Manderino, J.) The paragraph at issue here indicates clearly on its face the parties' intention to release the promoters from personal liability upon the mere formation of the proposed corporation, provided the incorporation was completed prior to the scheduled closing date.

▶ **ANALYSIS**

A promoter cannot bind the prospective corporation to any pre-incorporation agreement he makes for it. He has three possible avenues open to him: (1) to take on the corporation's behalf an offer which would become a contract once the corporation is formed and it accepts the offer; (2) to make a contract which binds him with the stipulation or understanding that if the company is formed it will take his place and he will then be relieved of all responsibility or liability; or (3) to simply bind himself personally and look to the proposed corporation for indemnity when it is formed.

■=■

Quicknotes

EQUITABLE DECREE A decree that is based upon principles of fairness as opposed to rules of law.

NOVATION The substitution of a new debt, contract or obligation for one that already exists between parties.

■=■

Timberline Equipment Co. v. Davenport

Lessor (P) v. Lessee (D)

Or. Sup. Ct., 267 Or. 64, 514 P.2d 1109 (1973).

NATURE OF CASE: Action to recover moneys due on equipment rentals.

FACT SUMMARY: Timberline Equipment Co. (P) sued the individuals involved in Aero-Fabb Corp., including Davenport (D), to recover for equipment rentals it made before Aero-Fabb's certificate of incorporation issued.

🏛 RULE OF LAW
Those persons who have an investment in and who actively participate in the policy and operational decisions of an organization and who assume to act as a corporation without the authority of a certificate of incorporation are jointly and severally liable for all debts and liabilities incurred or arising as a result thereof.

FACTS: Davenport (D), Bennett (D), and Gorman (D) signed articles of incorporation for Aero-Fabb Corp., which they hoped to involve in selling airplanes, reconditioning planes, and giving flying lessons. Land was leased for this purpose and equipment rented from Timberline Equipment Co. (Timberline) (P) to level and clear for access and for other construction. At that time, no certificate of incorporation had issued because the original articles were not in accord with the statutes. However, subsequently, new articles were filed, and a certificate of incorporation was issued. Timberline (P) eventually sued Bennett (D) et al. individually for the moneys due for equipment rentals. They alleged as a defense that the rentals were to a de facto corporation and that Timberline (P) was estopped from denying the corporate character of the organization to which it had rented the equipment. The trial court held for Timberline (P), apparently finding that the contradictory evidence did not prove Timberline (P) had believed it was contracting with a corporate entity.

ISSUE: Can individuals who assume to act as a corporation without a certificate of incorporation be held jointly and severally liable for debts incurred as a result thereof?

HOLDING AND DECISION: (Denecke, J.) Yes. Under Oregon law, which follows the Model Business Corporation Act, those persons who have an investment in and who actively participate in the policy and operational decisions of an organization and who assume to act as a corporation without the authority of a certificate of incorporation are jointly and severally liable for all debts and liabilities incurred or arising as a result thereof. Thus, Bennett (D) et al. are liable here unless Timberline (P) is estopped from denying the corporate existence of Aero-Fabb or the

doctrine of de facto incorporation applies. As to the doctrine of de facto incorporation, Oregon law makes issuance of the articles of incorporation a conclusive presumption of incorporation except as to quo warranto proceedings. Similar provisions, all based on the Model Business Corporation Act, have been held to do away with the doctrine of a de facto corporation, and that is the proper interpretation. As to the contention that Timberline (P) is estopped from denying Aero-Fabb's corporate existence, the doctrine of corporation by estoppel would be of no use since one element necessary for its application is missing. The lower court did not find that Timberline (P) believed it was contracting with a corporate entity. Furthermore, it would be inequitable to apply the doctrine. Therefore, Bennett (D) et al. are individually and severally liable in this case. Affirmed.

▶ ANALYSIS

This case clearly held that various provisions akin to those in the Model Business Corporation Act had in fact abolished the de facto corporation defense, but it avoided making a determination of the same kind as to the defense of corporation by estoppel. Other courts have held that the corporation by estoppel defense has been similarly abolished.

■■■

Quicknotes

CERTIFICATE OF INCORPORATION The written instrument that gives rise to the existence of a corporation when filed with the appropriate governmental agency.

CORPORATION BY ESTOPPEL Arises when parties are estopped from denying the existence of the corporation as a result of their agreements or conduct.

DE FACTO CORPORATION A corporation arising from the good-faith attempt to comply with the statutory requirements of establishing a corporation.

QUO WARRANTO PROCEEDINGS A proceeding brought in order to determine whether an officer legally holds office or a corporation legally holds a franchise.

■■■

General Overseas Films, Ltd. v. Robin International, Inc.

Lender (P) v. Borrower (D)

542 F. Supp. 684 (S.D.N.Y. 1982).

NATURE OF CASE: Action seeking to collect on a loan guarantee.

FACT SUMMARY: General Overseas Films, Ltd. (P) contended that Kraft, treasurer of Anaconda Company (D), could bind that company to an unauthorized loan guarantee on the basis of apparent authority.

🏛 RULE OF LAW
A corporate officer cannot, through apparent authority, bind the corporation to a loan guarantee outside its normal type of business.

FACTS: Reisini approached Haggiag (P), president of General Overseas Films, Ltd. (P), for a loan. Haggiag (P) agreed to loan him $500,000 in exchange for a $1,000,000 note from Reisini. In addition, Kraft, a vice president and treasurer of Anaconda Company (D), agreed on behalf of Anaconda Company (D) to guarantee the note. Kraft, however, had no authority to provide a guarantee in Anaconda's (D) name. Anaconda's (D) regular course of business did not include loan guarantees. With $300,000 remaining to be paid on the loan, Reisini and Kraft were indicted for fraud. Haggiag (P) sought to collect on the guarantee from Anaconda (D).

ISSUE: Can a corporate officer, through apparent authority, bind the corporation to a loan guarantee outside its normal type of business?

HOLDING AND DECISION: (Sofaer, J.) No. A corporate officer cannot, through apparent authority, bind the corporation to a loan guarantee outside its normal type of business. The general rule is that one who deals with an agent does so at his peril. However, the law, recognizing that third parties will sometimes have a reasonable belief that a corporate agent has the power to bind a corporation even if he does not, has evolved the doctrine of apparent authority. As the name implies, in some situations, when a corporate agent would seem to have the power to bind the corporation even when he does not, the corporation will be estopped from denying such authority. The reasoning is that a loss occasioned by a corporate agent should fall on the corporation that put the agent in place, not a duped third party. In any situation, whether apparent authority existed depends upon the type of transaction. Normally a corporate treasurer has broad authority to bind a corporation in financial matters. However, when he engages in a transaction far removed from the corporation's line of business, the party with whom he transacts must be on notice of authority problems. Here, Anaconda (D) was not a financial institution, and guaranteeing a debt was not part of its regular line of business. For this reason, Haggiag (P) should have made inquiries into Kraft's authority to bind Anaconda (D). Judgment for Anaconda (D).

▶ ANALYSIS

It is elemental that a corporation can act only through its agents. This situation presents the inherent problem involved in determining when an agent acts personally and when he acts on behalf of the corporation. Apparent authority is one of the legal doctrines that have been developed to deal with possible injustices arising out of problems with corporate agency.

■■■

Quicknotes

APPARENT AUTHORITY The authority granted to an agent to act on behalf of the principal in order to effectuate the principal's objective, which is not expressly granted but which is inferred from the principal's conduct.

FRAUD A false representation of facts with the intent that another will rely on the misrepresentation to his detriment.

■■■

Menard, Inc. v. Dage-MTI, Inc.

Purchaser (P) v. Corporation (D)

Ind. Sup. Ct., 726 N.E.2d 1206 (2000).

NATURE OF CASE: Appeal of an adverse judgment by a land purchaser in his specific performance suit against a corporation.

FACT SUMMARY: Arthur Sterling, the president of Dage-MTI, Inc. (Dage) (D), accepted an offer by Menard, Inc. (P) to purchase land, in a written agreement in which Sterling represented that he had the requisite authority to bind Dage (D) to the sale. Sterling had not, in fact, been given such authority. When the Dage (D) board of directors refused to honor the agreement, Menard (P) sued Dage (D) contending that Sterling, as an agent, had the inherent authority to bind Dage (D) as the principal.

RULE OF LAW

An agent's inherent authority subjects the principal to liability for acts on his account which (1) usually accompany or are incidental to transactions which the agent is authorized to conduct if, although they are forbidden by the principal, (2) the other party reasonably believes that the agent is authorized to do, and (3) the other party has no notice that the agent is not so authorized.

FACTS: Menard, Inc. (P) offered to purchase 30 acres of land from Dage-MTI, Inc. (Dage) (D). Arthur Sterling, Dage's (D) president, accepted the offer in a written agreement in which he represented that he had the requisite authority to bind Dage (D) to the sale. Sterling had not, in fact, been given such authority. The Dage (D) board of directors did not approve the sale and refused to complete the transaction. In addition to being a Dage (D) board member, Sterling had served as president of Dage (D) for at least 20 years. For many years, Sterling had operated Dage (D) without significant input or oversight by the board. No one at Dage (D) had informed Menard (P) that Sterling's authority with respect to the sale of the 30-acre parcel had been limited to only the solicitation of offers. Upon learning of the signed agreement with Menard (P), the board instructed Sterling to extricate Dage (D) from the agreement. Menard (P) ultimately filed suit to require Dage (D) to specifically perform the agreement and to secure the payment of damages. Menard (P) initially filed a motion for partial summary judgment, which motion was denied. Following a bench trial, the trial court ruled in favor of Dage (D). The intermediate appellate court affirmed, finding that Sterling did not have the express or apparent authority to bind Dage (D) in this land transaction. Menard (P) appealed.

ISSUE: Does an agent's inherent authority subject the principal to liability for acts on his account which

(1) usually accompany, or are incidental to, transactions which the agent is authorized to conduct if, although they are forbidden by the principal, (2) the other party reasonably believes that the agent is authorized to do, and (3) the other party has no notice that the agent is not so authorized?

HOLDING AND DECISION: (Sullivan, J.) Yes. An agent's inherent authority subjects the principal to liability for acts on his account which (1) usually accompany, or are incidental to, transactions which the agent is authorized to conduct if, although they are forbidden by the principal, (2) the other party reasonably believes that the agent is authorized to do, and (3) the other party has no notice that the agent is not so authorized. Here, the concept of inherent authority, rather than actual or apparent authority, was applicable to Menard's (P) dealings with Dage's (D) president regarding the sale of Dage's (D) land. Menard (P) did not negotiate and ultimately contract with a lower-tiered employee or prototypical "general" or "special" agent, but instead dealt directly with a person whom the law recognized as one of the officers who was the means by which corporations normally act. Arthur Sterling, the president of Dage (D), a closely held corporation, acted within the usual and ordinary scope of his authority as president when he negotiated and ultimately contracted for the sale of Dage's (D) real estate, even though Dage's (D) board had not authorized Sterling to sell the particular parcel without its prior approval. Sterling had managed Dage's (D) affairs for an extended period of time with little or no board oversight and had purchased real estate for Dage (D) in the past without board approval. Menard (P) reasonably believed that Sterling was authorized to contract for the sale of Dage's (D) real property, notwithstanding that Sterling had informed him early in negotiations that the sale required the approval of Dage's (D) board of directors. Sterling had been the sole negotiator with Menard (P), and Sterling later "confirmed" that he had authority from the board to proceed. Furthermore, Menard (P) did not have notice that Sterling was unauthorized to sell the specific parcel without board approval. Menard (P) was unaware of the existence of the board's consent resolution limiting Sterling's authority to the solicitation of offers, and Sterling personally acknowledged that he had signed sales agreements by authority of the board of which he was a member. An agent's inherent authority is derived from the status of the office that he or she holds. A third party is not required to scrutinize too carefully a knowledge or awareness that the officer's authority has possibly been limited. Finally, if one of two innocent parties, the principal or the

Continued on next page.

third party, must suffer due to a betrayal of trust by the agent, the loss should fall on the party who is most at fault. Because the principal puts the agent in a position of trust, the principal should bear the loss. Judgment reversed in favor of the purchaser Menard (P).

DISSENT: (Shepard, J.) This decision will leave most corporate lawyers wondering what the law actually is and how to advise their clients. When all parties to a corporate transaction understand that board approval is required and that it may or may not be forthcoming, today's opinion points toward a conclusion that the buyer's offer was not accepted by the seller. While I agree with the general legal principles laid out by the majority, those principles seem undercut by the resolution of this case.

▌ *ANALYSIS*

The *Menard* court noted that the scope of an agency must be measured not solely by the words in which it is created but by the whole context in which those words are used, including the customary powers of such agents. Thus, a contract may be enforceable because the customary implication would seem to be that the agent's authority was without limitation of the kind actually imposed. A principal benefits from the existence of inherent authority because the very purpose of delegated authority is to avoid constant recourse by third persons to the principal, which would be a corollary of denying the agent any latitude beyond his or her exact instructions.

■═■

Quicknotes

PARTIAL SUMMARY JUDGMENT Judgment rendered by a court in response to a motion by one of the parties, claiming that the lack of a question of marital fact in respect to one of the issues warrants disposition of that issue without going to the jury.

SPECIFIC PERFORMANCE An equitable remedy whereby the court requires the parties to perform their obligations pursuant to a contract.

■═■

Mergers

Quick Reference Rules of Law

Hewlett v. Hewlett-Packard Co.

Director of corporation (P) v. Corporation (D)

Del. Ct. Ch., 2002 WL 818091 (2002).

NATURE OF CASE: Challenge by a corporate director to a shareholder vote in connection with a proposed corporate merger.

FACT SUMMARY: After a hotly contested proxy battle between Walter B. Hewlett (Hewlett) (P) and Hewlett-Packard Corp. (HP) (D), HP's (D) shareholders approved the issuance of shares in connection with a merger with Compaq Computer Corp. at a special meeting by a very slim margin. Hewlett (P) brought suit against HP (D), challenging the validity of that vote on the grounds, among others, that the HP (D) board of directors had knowingly misrepresented facts to the shareholders about the proposed merger (integration).

> ## 🏛 RULE OF LAW
> To set aside a corporate merger (integration) on nondisclosure grounds, the challenger has the burden of proving the knowing misrepresentation of material facts.

FACTS: Hewlett-Packard Corp. (HP) (D) proposed a merger (integration) with Compaq Computer Corp. Walter B. Hewlett (Hewlett) (P), who had been a director of HP (D) for 15 years, strongly objected. As HP (D) management was receiving e-mails and value capture updates (VCUs) regarding the merger, Hewlett (P) and HP (D) were actively engaged in a proxy contest. Each was trying to secure as many votes as possible. An independent consultant issued a report to its subscribers recommending that HP (D) shareholders vote in favor of the merger. The report noted that both sides had made various claims about the financial benefits of the merger. After a hotly contested battle, HP's (D) shareholders ultimately approved the issuance of shares in connection with the merger. Hewlett (P) brought suit to set aside the merger, arguing essentially that HP (D) management knowingly and intentionally made material misrepresentations about the progress of the integration process. To support that claim, he relied on various VCUs and e-mails generated by HP (D). Hewlett (P) contended that these documents demonstrated that the integration process was going poorly, contrary to the public statements by HP (D) management and that the newly combined company could not meet the revenue projections which HP (D) had communicated to its shareholders to obtain their votes.

ISSUE: To set aside a corporate merger (integration) on nondisclosure grounds, does the challenger have the burden of proving the knowing misrepresentation of material facts?

HOLDING AND DECISION: (Chandler, Chan.) Yes. To set aside a corporate merger (integration) on nondisclosure grounds, the challenger has the burden of proving a knowing misrepresentation of material facts. Here, the evidence supported the conclusion that management had done everything it could to maximize the chance that integration would be a success. HP (D) management focused on integration even before the merger was announced. HP's (D) board believed from the beginning that successful integration of the two companies would be critical to the success of the merger. HP (D) acted accordingly by planning its integration efforts carefully and thoroughly, selecting hundreds of its "best" and "brightest" managers for the integration teams, and involving key senior executives in an Integration Steering Committee, actively involved in weekly integration meetings. The public statements made by HP (D) management about the progress of the integration were supported by the facts when they were made and were neither false nor misleading. HP (D) had entered an advanced phase of its integration planning, and detailed business plans were being created. Information available to management also indicated that the company was overachieving on both its cost-reduction and revenue targets. HP (D) management continued to be aware of revenue synergies and other cost upsides that were not included in the external projections. Nothing in the record indicated that HP (D) lied to or deliberately misled its shareholders or others about its integration efforts. The crux of Hewlett's (P) argument was that HP (D) learned that the top-line revenue projections—implied in its materials and used illustratively in its filings—were unattainable. This argument proceeded from two faulty premises: first, that the revenue numbers generated in the value capture process represented realistic projections of expected future results; and second, that the estimated revenue and profit filings represented firm commitments by HP (D) management. On the contrary, it was reasonable for HP (D) to believe that it would achieve even better results than those contained in the filings. The projections contained in the materials and filings were clearly labeled as "forward-looking estimates." More importantly, however, the numbers were purely illustrative and, indeed, were only one set of several presented by HP (D). The important numbers discussed repeatedly by HP (D) management were the merger-related numbers of $2.5 billion in cost synergies and not more than 4.9% revenue loss. Hewlett (D) has been unable to prove that HP (D)

Continued on next page.

misrepresented or omitted material facts about integration in the proxy contest. Instead, the evidence demonstrated that HP's (D) statements concerning the merger were true, complete, and made in good faith. During the trial, members of HP's (D) senior management testified credibly, in accordance with the evidence and without exception, that throughout the proxy contest they believed that the cost synergy and revenue loss targets were realistic and, in fact, would be exceeded. Finally, there is no legal requirement that companies disclose all documents generated in a budgeting process. Hewlett (P) has failed to prove that HP (D) disseminated materially false information about its integration efforts or about the financial data provided to its shareholders. Finding is entered in favor of HP (D) on the disclosure claim.

▶ *ANALYSIS*

In the *Hewlett-Packard* case, Walter Hewlett (P), failing to prove that HP (D) affirmatively and knowingly misrepresented facts about integration, fell back on the argument that HP (D) should have disclosed the negative information contained in some of the VCUs and some e-mails because that information would have been material to shareholders. The court noted that omitted facts are material if there is a "substantial likelihood that the disclosure of the omitted fact would have been viewed by the reasonable investor as having significantly altered the 'total mix' of information made available." The court, however, did not agree with Hewlett (P) that the VCUs and e-mails were in fact material. While this information clearly would be material if presented in final reports or projections, which was not the case here.

Quicknotes

BURDEN OF PROOF The duty of a party to introduce evidence to support a fact that is in dispute in an action.

INTEGRATION An agreement between two parties to a contract that the document represents the total and final expression of their agreement.

MERGER The acquisition of one company by another, after which the acquired company ceases to exist as an independent entity.

NONDISCLOSURE The failure to communicate certain facts to another person.

PROXY A person authorized to act for another.

Applestein v. United Board & Carton Corp.

Corporate shareholders (P) v. Corporation (D)

N.J. Super. Ct., Ch. Div., 159 A.2d 146 (1960).

NATURE OF CASE: Motions by stockholders, submitted on stipulation, as to whether a combination of two corporations constituted a valid merger.

FACT SUMMARY: Saul Epstein exchanged his Interstate Container Corporation (Interstate) stock for stock in United Board & Carton Corp. (United) (D) under an agreement between Interstate and United (D). Under the so-called "exchange of stock" agreement, United (D) would wholly own Interstate and its subsidiaries. Although the agreement did not use the word "merger," Applestein (P) and other United stockholders brought suit against United (D) to have what they contended was a corporate merger declared invalid for failure to follow statutory requirements.

🏛 RULE OF LAW
When there is a de jure merger of corporations, formally expressed and clearly intended, the dissenting stockholders of any of the merged or consolidated corporations are given statutory appraisal rights, and it matters not whether they are stockholders of the absorbed or absorbing corporation.

FACTS: Two corporations, United Board & Carbon Corp. (United) (P) and Interstate Container Corporation (Interstate), entered into a written agreement that was not designated or referred to as a merger agreement and did not contain the word "merger." On the contrary, the agreement stated that it was an "exchange of Interstate stock for United Stock." By the agreement, Saul Epstein agreed to assign and deliver to United (D) his 1,250 shares of Interstate common stock in exchange solely for 160,000 as yet unissued shares of voting common stock (par value $10) of United (D). Thus, by this so-called "exchange of stock," United (D) would wholly own Interstate and its subsidiaries, and Epstein would thereupon own a 40% stock interest in United (D). The agreement did not contemplate the continued operation of Interstate as a subsidiary of United (D). Rather, it provided that United (D) would take over all the outstanding stock of Interstate, that all of Interstate's "assets and liabilities will be recorded on the books of the Company (United)," and that Interstate would be dissolved. Subsequently, the notice of the stockholders' meeting for United (D) did not indicate that the purpose of the meeting was to effect a merger of United (D) and Interstate and failed to give notice to the shareholders of their right to dissent to the plan of merger. Applestein (P) and other United stockholders brought suit against United (D) to have the merger declared invalid. By stipulation, the parties submitted the issue of whether the agreement between United and Interstate constituted a

corporate merger, bringing into operation a statutory obligation to notify stockholders prior to such action being taken so that the shareholders could voice an objection to the plan and obtain an appraisal of shares.

ISSUE: When there is a de jure merger of corporations, formally expressed and clearly intended, are the dissenting stockholders of all of the merged or consolidated corporations given statutory appraisal rights so that it matters not whether they are stockholders of the absorbed or absorbing corporation?

HOLDING AND DECISION: (Kilkenny, J.) Yes. When there is a de jure merger of corporations, formally expressed and clearly intended, the dissenting stockholders of any of the merged or consolidated corporations are given statutory appraisal rights, and it matters not whether they are stockholders of the absorbed or absorbing corporation. Here, the corporate combination of United (D) and Interstate was a practical or de facto "merger of corporations" in substance and in legal effect so that the shareholders of the first corporation were entitled to be notified and advised of their statutory rights of dissent and appraisal. There was a proposed transfer of all shares and all assets of Interstate to United (D), the assumption by United (D) of Interstate's liabilities, and a pooling of interests of both corporations. Furthermore, there was an absorption of Interstate by United (D) and the dissolution of United (D), joinder of officers and directors from both corporations on an enlarged board of directors, retention of executive and operating personnel of Interstate in the employ of United (D), and a surrender by Interstate's sole stockholder of his shares in Interstate for newly issued shares in United (D). Accordingly, the shareholders of United (D) were entitled to be notified and advised of their statutory rights of dissent and appraisal. The failure of the corporate officers of United (D) to take these steps and to obtain stockholder approval of the agreement by the statutory two-thirds vote at a properly convened meeting of the stockholders rendered the proposed corporate action invalid.

▶ ANALYSIS

As noted in the *Applestein* case, whether a corporate merger is de jure or de facto, the reason for protecting the dissenting stockholders will apply equally to stockholders of the acquired or the acquiring corporation. The reason for statutory protection is that stockholders should

Continued on next page.

not be forced against their will into something fundamentally different from that for which they bargained when they acquired their shares. If such protection were not afforded to the shareholders, then by the simple device of labeling one of the corporations the acquiring corporation and the other the acquired corporation, the substantial rights of appraisal would be arbitrarily taken away.

■≡■

Quicknotes

DE FACTO MERGER   The acquisition of one company by another without compliance with the requirements of a statutory merger but treated by the courts as such.

DE JURE CORPORATION   A corporation that results from the incorporator(s) full satisfaction of the statutory requirements of establishing a corporation.

MERGER   The acquisition of one company by another, after which the acquired company ceases to exist as an independent entity.

■≡■

Hariton v. Arco Electronics, Inc.

Shareholder (P) v. Corporation (D)

Del. Sup. Ct., 188 A.2d 123 (1963).

NATURE OF CASE: Action to declare sale of corporate assets void.

FACT SUMMARY: Arco (D) sold all of its assets to Loral Corporation in exchange for Loral common stock. Hariton (P), a shareholder in Arco Electronics, Inc. (D), challenged the transaction as a de facto merger.

🏛 RULE OF LAW
A corporation may sell its assets to another corporation even if the result is the same as a merger without following the statutory merger requirements.

FACTS: Arco Electronics, Inc. (Acro) (D) was an electronics distributor; Loral Corporation (Loral) was an electronics producer. The two corporations entered into an agreement under which Arco's (D) assets would be sold to Loral in exchange for Loral stock, after which the Loral stock would be distributed to Arco (D) shareholders and Arco (D) would dissolve. Arco (D) called a special meeting, at which the shareholders present voted unanimously in favor of the sale. After the transaction was carried out, Hariton (P), an Arco (D) shareholder, challenged the action as a de facto merger and sued to have it set aside since the statutory merger provisions were not complied with. Arco (D) argued that it had engaged in a legal sale of corporate assets and had complied with all the applicable provisions.

ISSUE: If a transaction is in the form of a sale of corporate assets but has the same effect as if a merger had been undertaken, must the formalities of a merger be followed?

HOLDING AND DECISION: (Southerland, C.J.) No. The statutes dealing with merger and sale of corporate assets may be overlapping in the sense that they may be used to achieve similar results, but the two procedures are subject to equal dignity. If all of the applicable provisions are complied with, a corporation may achieve a result in a manner which would be illegal under another statute. In other words, there is no interaction between these statutes, and since the sale of corporate assets statute was followed correctly, the provisions of the merger statute are of no relevance. The theory of de facto merger can only be introduced by the legislature, not the courts. Also, it is impossible to differentiate this transaction from one in which no dissolution of the selling corporation is required by the agreement since Arco (D) continued in existence after the sale, even though only to distribute the Loral stock to its shareholders. Therefore, Arco (D) didn't immediately cease to exist as it would have in an actual merger. Finally, the rationale of de facto merger which is based upon the theory that a shareholder shouldn't be forced to accept a new investment in a different corporation fails in this case. In Delaware, there is no right of appraisal for a sale of corporate assets, so Hariton (P) knew when he purchased the Arco (D) stock that Arco (D) might at any time sell all of its assets for stock in another corporation. Affirmed.

▶ ANALYSIS

The *Hariton* decision rejects the de facto merger doctrine set forth in *Farris*. The reason for the *Hariton* holding is a desire to give corporations greater freedom of reorganization than is given under the restrictive merger statutes. The court mentions that the fact that no appraisal right is given for a sale of corporate assets is a possible indication of legislative sympathy for corporate freedom. The *Hariton* result is the minority rule and has been criticized for its emphasis on the form rather than the substance of the transaction in question. Since the merger procedure is authorized to achieve the result sought by Arco (D), it seems unfair to allow the use of another device to obtain the same result indirectly in order to deny the protections given to minority shareholders under the more direct approach.

◼━◼

Quicknotes

DE FACTO MERGER The acquisition of one company by another without compliance with the requirements of a statutory merger but treated by the courts as such.

DISSOLUTION Annulment or termination of a formal or legal bond, tie or contract.

◼━◼

Coggins v. New England Patriots Football Club, Inc.

Shareholder (P) v. Corporation (D)

Mass. Sup. Jud. Ct., 492 N.E.2d 1112 (1986).

NATURE OF CASE: Appeal of order awarding rescissory damages subsequent to a freeze-out merger.

FACT SUMMARY: Coggins (P), minority shareholder of New England Patriots Football Club, Inc. (D), contended that a freeze-out merger was undertaken expressly for the financial benefit of the majority owner.

 RULE OF LAW
A majority owner of a corporation cannot effect a freeze-out merger purely for his own benefit.

FACTS: Sullivan (D) had been controlling owner of New England Patriots Football Club, Inc. (the Patriots) (D), which operated an American Football League (AFL) franchise. In 1974 he was ousted as corporate president, but by the following year he had accumulated 100% of the voting stock and had regained control. He instituted a freeze-out merger wherein a new corporation would be formed with him owning all the shares. Unlike the old corporation, the new corporation would have no class of nonvoting stock. The merger was effected. Coggins (P), a former owner of several shares of nonvoting stock, sued to rescind the merger, contending that it had been illegal. The trial court found that the merger had been illegal in that it had been undertaken solely for Sullivan's (D) financial benefit but declined to order rescission of the merger, instead awarding rescissory damages. Both sides appealed.

ISSUE: Can a majority owner of a corporation effect a freeze-out merger purely for his own benefit?

HOLDING AND DECISION: (Liacos, J.) No. A majority owner of a corporation cannot effect a freeze-out merger purely for his own benefit. The dangers of self-dealing and abuse of fiduciary duty are greatest in freeze-out situations like the Patriots (D) merger, where a controlling director chooses to eliminate public ownership. Because of such potential abuse, judicial scrutiny of such transactions is at its highest. Such a merger must be done as part of the legitimate course of the corporation's business; it cannot be done solely to benefit the owner, even if the owner performs all the acts necessary to effect the merger in a legal manner. Here, the trial court found the merger to have been undertaken purely for Sullivan's (D) benefit, not for any legitimate corporate purpose, and properly held it illegal. The usual remedy in such a situation would be rescission of the merger, but the court elected to award damages because passage of time had made return to the status quo ante impractical. This was within the court's discretion. Affirmed in part, reversed in part, and remanded.

ANALYSIS

In most cases, courts do not require a lack of self-interest on the part of controlling owners. Such an owner does have a right, in most cases, to deal for his benefit. However, when the specter of self-dealing looms too large, as in a freeze-out merger, the owner's fiduciary duties take over.

Quicknotes

FIDUCIARY DUTY A legal obligation to act for the benefit of another, including subordinating one's personal interests to that of the other person.

FREEZE-OUT MERGER Merger whereby the majority shareholder forces minority shareholders into the sale of their securities.

RESCISSION The canceling of an agreement and the return of the parties to their positions prior to the formation of the contract.

Weinberger v. UOP, Inc.

Minority shareholder (P) v. Corporation (D)

Del. Sup. Ct., 457 A.2d 701 (1983).

NATURE OF CASE: Appeal of class action to rescind a merger.

FACT SUMMARY: Claiming that a cash-out merger between UOP, Inc. (D) and Signal (D) was unfair, Weinberger (P), a former minority shareholder of UOP (D), brought a class action to have the merger rescinded.

🏛 RULE OF LAW
When seeking to secure minority shareholder approval for a proposed cash-out merger, the corporations involved must comply with the fairness test, which has two basic interrelated aspects: (1) fair dealings, which imposes a duty on the corporations to completely disclose to the shareholders all information germane to the merger, and (2) fair price, which requires that the price being offered for the outstanding stock be equivalent to a price determined by an appraisal where "all relevant nonspeculative factors," were considered.

FACTS: Signal, Inc. (D) owned 50.5% of UOP, Inc. (D) stock. Seven of UOP's (D) 13 directors, including the president, were also directors of or employees of Signal (D). Arledge and Chitiea, who were directors of UOP (D) and Signal (D), prepared a feasibility study for Signal (D). The study reported that it would be a good investment for Signal (D) to acquire the remaining 49.5% of UOP (D) shares through a cash-out merger at any price up to $24 per share. The study was given to all the Signal (D) directors, including those who also served as directors on UOP's (D) board. However, the evidence indicates that the study was never disclosed to UOP's (D) six non-Signal (D), i.e., outside, directors. Nor was it disclosed to the minority shareholders who owned the remaining 49.5% of UOP (D) stock. On February 28, Signal (D) offered UOP (D) a cash-out merger price of $21 per share. Four business days later, on March 6, the six non-Signal (D) UOP (D) directors (the seven common Signal-UOP (D) directors abstained from the voting) voted to approve the merger at $21 per share. The vote was largely due to the fact that at the time, UOP's (D) market price was only $14.50 per share, and also there was a "fairness opinion letter" from UOP's (D) investment banker stating that the $21 per share was a fair price. The merger was then approved by a majority (51.9%) of the minority, i.e., the remaining 49.5%, of UOP (D) shareholders. Weinberger (P), a former minority shareholder of UOP (D), then brought a class action to have the merger rescinded, claiming it was unfair to UOP's (D) former shareholders. The Court of Chancery held for UOP (D) and Signal (D). Weinberger (P) appealed.

ISSUE: May a minority shareholder successfully challenge the approval of a cash-out merger that was approved by the majority of the minority shareholders?

HOLDING AND DECISION: (Moore, J.) Yes. A minority shareholder may successfully challenge the approval of a cash-out merger that was approved by the majority of the minority shareholders if he can demonstrate that the corporations involved failed to comply with the fairness test in securing the approval. The fairness test consists of two basic interrelated aspects. The first aspect is "fair dealings," which imposes a duty on the corporations involved to completely disclose to the minority shareholders all information germane to the merger. Here, Signal (D) failed to disclose to the non-Signal (D) UOP (D) directors and the minority shareholders of UOP (D) the Arledge-Chitiea feasibility study that reported it would be a "good investment" for Signal (D) to acquire the minority shares up to a price of $24 per share. In addition, UOP's (D) minority was given the impression that the "fairness opinion letter" from UOP's (D) investment banker had been drafted only after the banker had made a careful study, when, in fact, the investment banker had drafted the letter in three days with the price left blank. Consequently, Signal (D) did not meet the "fair dealings" aspect of the test. The second aspect of the fairness test is "fair price," which requires that the price being offered for the outstanding stock be equivalent to an appraisal where "all relevant nonspeculative factors" were considered. In this case, the Court of Chancery tested the fairness of Signal's (D) $21 per-share price against the Delaware weighted average method of valuation. That method shall no longer exclusively control the determination of "fair price." Rather, a new method which considers "all relevant nonspeculative factors" shall now be used for determining fair price. This new method is consistent with the method used in determining a shareholder's appraisal remedy. Here, the Court of Chancery did not consider the $24 per-share price determined by the Arledge-Chitiea study. Nor did the court consider Weinberger's (P) discounted cash flow analysis, which concluded that the UOP (D) stock was worth $26 per share on the date of merger. Therefore, since these factors were not considered, it cannot be said that the $21 per-share price paid by Signal (D) meets the new method of determining fair price. Finally, in view of the new, more liberal test for determining fair price, together with the Chancery Court's broad remedial discretion, it is concluded that the business purpose requirement for mergers, as required by *Singer v. Magnavox Co.*, 380

Continued on next page.

A.2d 969 (1977), *Tanzer v. International General Industries, Inc.*, 379 A.2d 1121 (1977), and *Roland International Corp. v. Najjar*, 407 A.2d 1032 (1979), adds no further protection to minority shareholders. Accordingly, the business purpose requirement is no longer law. Reversed.

▮ *ANALYSIS*

This case demonstrates the use of a cash-out merger to eliminate or "freeze out" the minority interest. A footnote in the case suggests that Signal's (D) freeze-out of UOP's (D) minority interest would have met the court's fairness test if UOP (D) had appointed an independent negotiating committee of its non-Signal (D) directors to deal with Signal (D) at arm's length.

■══■

Quicknotes

CASH-OUT MERGER Occurs when a merging company prematurely redeems the securities of a holder as part of the merger.

CLASS ACTION A suit commenced by a representative on behalf of an ascertainable group that is too large to appear in court, who shares a commonality of interests and who will benefit from a successful result.

RESCISSION The canceling of an agreement and the return of the parties to their positions prior to the formation of the contract.

■══■

Cede & Co. v. Technicolor, Inc.

Shareholders (P) v. Corporation (D)

Del. Sup. Ct., 684 A.2d 289 (1996).

NATURE OF CASE: Appeal from a final judgment in an appraisal action.

FACT SUMMARY: When the value of Technicolor's (D) shares was determined by the Court of Chancery, the value added as a result of the merger was excluded, and Cede & Co. (P) appealed, alleging that the court had erred as a matter of law.

RULE OF LAW

Value added to the going concern by the majority acquiror during the transient period of a two-step merger accrues to the benefit of all shareholders and must be included in the appraisal process on the date of the merger.

FACTS: MacAndrews & Forbes Group Incorporated (MAF) commenced an all-cash tender offer to the shareholders of Technicolor (D). The tender offer was accepted and shortly after becoming Technicolor's (D) controlling shareholder, MAF began liquidating Technicolor's (D) assets. The merger was completed when Technicolor (D) shareholders voted in favor of the merger. Cede & Co. (P), the record-owner of shares of Technicolor (D) common stock, requested that the Court of Chancery appraise the fair value of its shares during the cash-out merger. The Court of Chancery concluded that future value that would not exist but for the merger was irrelevant in a Delaware statutory appraisal proceeding, and excluded the value added to Technicolor (D) by the implementation or the expectation of the implementation of Perelman's new business plan. Cede (P) appealed, arguing that the court had erred in that it had not valued the corporation as an operating entity, and that the Court of Chancery should have valued Technicolor (D) as it existed on the date of the merger and with due regard for the strategies that had been conceived and implemented following the merger agreement by MAF's controlling shareholder, the "Perelman Plan," Technicolor (D) argued that the Court of Chancery properly considered Technicolor (D) without regard to the Perelman Plan.

ISSUE: Does value added to the going concern by the majority acquiror during the transient period of a two-step merger, accrue to the benefit of all shareholders and must it be included in the appraisal process on the date of the merger?

HOLDING AND DECISION: (Holland, J.) Yes. Value added to the going concern by the majority acquiror during the transient period of a two-step merger, accrues to the benefit of all shareholders and must be included in the appraisal process on the date of the merger. The Court of Chancery erred, as a matter of law, by determining the fair value of Technicolor (D) on the date of the merger "but for" the Perelman Plan. By failing to accord Cede (P) the full proportionate value of its shares in the going concern on the date of the merger, the court imposed a penalty upon Cede (P) for lack of control. Only the speculative elements of value that may arise from the accomplishment or expectation of the merger should have been excluded from the court's calculation of fair value on the date of the merger. Elements of future value which are known or susceptible of proof as of the date of the merger and not the product of speculation, may be considered in a statutory appraisal proceeding. This appraisal action will be remanded to the Court of Chancery for a recalculation of Technicolor's (D) fair value on the date of the merger. Reversed and remanded.

ANALYSIS

The court in this case explained that known elements of value, including those which exist on the date of the merger because of a majority acquiror's interim action in a two-step cash-out transaction should not be excluded from the valuation. The "accomplishment or expectation" of the merger exception to the appraisal statute is very narrow. It was designed to eliminate the use of pro forma data and projections of a speculative variety relating to the completion of a merger.

Quicknotes

APPRAISAL RIGHTS A statutory remedy whereby minority shareholders, objecting to extraordinary transactions entered into by the corporation may require the corporation to repurchase their shares at a price equal to its value immediately prior to the action.

CASH-OUT MERGER The acquisition of one company by another by exchanging cash for the shares of the target corporation, after which the acquired company ceases to exist as an independent entity.

DELAWARE GENERAL CORPORATION LAW § 262 The appraisal remedy states that any stockholder of a corporation of the state of Delaware who has not voted in favor of the merger shall be entitled to an appraisal of the fair value of his stock.

MERGER The acquisition of one company by another, after which the acquired company ceases to exist as an independent entity.

Glassman v. Unocal Exploration Corp.

Minority shareholders of subsidiary (P) v. Parent corporation (D)

Del. Sup. Ct., 777 A.2d 242 (2001) (*en banc*).

NATURE OF CASE: Appeal of an adverse decision against a subsidiary's minority shareholders in their class action alleging that the parent and its directors breached their fiduciary duties of entire fairness and full disclosure.

FACT SUMMARY: The boards of Unocal Exploration Corporation (UXC) (D) and Unocal Corp. effected a corporate merger pursuant to the Delaware statute which authorized "short-form" mergers. Glassman (P) and others filed a class action against UXC (D) asserting that UXC (D) and its directors breached their fiduciary duties of entire fairness and full disclosure. UXC (D) argued that in a statutory "short-form" merger, a parent corporation did not have to establish entire fairness, and that, absent fraud or illegality, the only recourse for minority stockholders who were dissatisfied with the consideration resulting from a "short-form" merger was appraisal.

> 🏛 **RULE OF LAW**
> Absent fraud or illegality, appraisal is the exclusive remedy available to a minority stockholder who objects to a "short-form" merger.

FACTS: Unocal Corp. is an earth-resources company engaged in exploration for, and production of, oil and gas. Unocal owned approximately 96% of the stock of Unocal Exploration Corporation (UXC) (D), an oil and gas company operating around the Gulf of Mexico. After a drop in both companies' revenues and earnings, Unocal decided that by eliminating the UXC (D) minority, it would reduce taxes and overhead expenses. The boards of Unocal and UXC (D) appointed committees to consider merger. The UXC (D) committee consisted of three directors who, although also directors of Unocal, were not officers or employees of the parent Unocal. The UXC (D) committee retained financial and legal advisors and met four times before agreeing to a merger exchange ratio of .54 shares of Unocal stock for each share of UXC (D). Unocal and UXC (D) announced the merger, and it was effected pursuant to a Delaware statute which authorized "short-form" mergers. The "short-form" merger statute essentially authorized a parent corporation to merge with its wholly owned subsidiary by filing and recording a certificate evidencing the parent's ownership and its merger resolution. The notice of merger and prospectus stated the terms of the merger and advised the former UXC (D) stockholders of their appraisal rights. Glassman (P) and others filed a class action against UXC (D), asserting that Unocal and its directors breached their fiduciary duties of entire fairness and full disclosure. The Court of Chancery found for UXC (D), holding that the entire fairness standard

did not control in a "short-form" merger and that the exclusive remedy of members of the class in this case was appraisal. Glassman (P) and the class appealed.

ISSUE: Absent fraud or illegality, is appraisal the exclusive remedy available to a minority stockholder who objects to a "short-form" merger?

HOLDING AND DECISION: (Berger, J.) Yes. Absent fraud or illegality, appraisal is the exclusive remedy available to a minority stockholder who objects to a "short-form" merger. Under settled principles, a parent corporation and its directors undertaking a "short-form" merger are self-dealing fiduciaries who should be required to establish entire fairness, including fair dealing and fair price. The problem is that a Delaware statute authorizes a summary procedure that is inconsistent with any reasonable notion of fair dealing. In a "short-form" merger, there is no agreement of merger negotiated by two companies. There is only a unilateral act: a decision by the parent company that its subsidiary shall no longer exist as a separate entity. The minority stockholders receive no advance notice of the merger; their directors do not consider or approve it; and there is no vote. Those who object are given the right to obtain fair value for their shares through appraisal. The equitable claim plainly conflicts with the statute. If a corporate fiduciary follows the truncated process authorized by the statute, it will not be able to establish the fair dealing prong of entire fairness. If instead, the corporate fiduciary sets up negotiating committees and hires independent financial and legal experts, then it will have lost the very benefit provided by the statute: a simple, fast, and inexpensive process for accomplishing a merger. Effect is to be given to the legislative intent; hence here to serve its purpose, the statute must be construed to obviate the requirement of establishing entire fairness. The determination of fair value must be based on all relevant factors, including damages and elements of future value, when appropriate. So, for example, if the merger were timed to take advantage of a depressed market or a low point in the company's cyclical earnings, or to precede an anticipated positive development, the appraised value may be adjusted to account for those factors. These are the types of issues frequently raised in entire fairness claims, and claims for unfair dealing cannot be litigated in an appraisal. However, equitable claims may not be engrafted onto a statutory appraisal proceeding. Stockholders may not receive rescissionary relief in an appraisal. Those decisions should not be read to restrict the elements of value that properly may be considered in an appraisal. Affirmed.

Continued on next page.

▶ *ANALYSIS*

In *Glassman*, the court noted that although fiduciaries are not required to establish entire fairness in a "short-form" merger, the duty of full disclosure remains in the context of their request for stockholder action. When the only choice for the minority stockholders is whether to accept the merger consideration or seek appraisal, the stockholders must be given all the factual information that is material to that decision.

■═■

Quicknotes

BREACH OF FIDUCIARY DUTY The failure of a fiduciary to observe the standard of care exercised by professionals of similar education and experience.

CLASS ACTION A suit commenced by a representative on behalf of an ascertainable group that is too large to appear in court, who shares a commonality of interests and who will benefit from a successful result.

MERGER The acquisition of one company by another, after which the acquired company ceases to exist as an independent entity.

■═■

Stringer v. Car Data Systems, Inc.

Minority shareholders (P) v. Corporation and other shareholders (D)

Or. Sup. Ct., 841 P.2d 1183 (1992).

NATURE OF CASE: Appeal from an adverse judgment in a suit by minority shareholders against other shareholders and corporate directors claiming violation of various rights incident to a cash-out merger.

FACT SUMMARY: When Stringer (P) and other minority shareholders in Consumer Data Systems, Inc. (CDS) filed suit against CDS and Car Data Systems, Inc. (Car Data) (D) claiming a violation of various rights incident to a cash-out merger, Car Data (D) argued that Stringer's (P) sole remedy was a statutory appraisal.

RULE OF LAW
Appraisal is the exclusive remedy for minority shareholders who allege only a disagreement as to majority's valuation of their shares in a cash-out merger and that payment by corporation was unreasonably low, with no allegations of self-dealing, fraud, deliberate waste of corporate assets, misrepresentation, or other unlawful conduct.

FACTS: Stringer (P) and others were minority shareholders in Consumer Data Systems, Inc. (CDS). They filed suit, claiming a violation of various rights incident to a cash-out merger involving CDS and another corporation, Car Data Systems, Inc. (Car Data) (D). Stringer (P), Schubert, and two other minority shareholders owned 43% of the shares of CDS. According to the complaint, the CDS directors and the larger CDS shareholders decided to squeeze the minority shareholders out of their ownership in CDS and to offer them a nominal sum for their stock, which sum was significantly below the fair market value of the stock. The directors and larger shareholders formed a new company that subsequently became Car Data (D), transferred their shares in CDS to Car Data (D) in exchange for its stock, and solicited all the remaining shareholders, except for the four minority shareholders, to participate in their plan. A total of 32 CDS shareholders transferred their stock to Car Data (D), amounting to 57% of the CDS shares. Car Data shareholders then voted for a merger between Car Data (D) and CDS. Pursuant to the merger proposal, each CDS shareholder would receive $0.02 per share. As owner of 57% of CDS, Car Data (D) voted for the merger. The merger was approved over the objections of Stringer (P) and two other minority shareholders. Stringer (P) argued that his shares were worth at least $0.10 per share and refused to accept the $0.02 which was offered. Car Data rejected the demand for $0.10 per share and instituted a statutory appraisal proceeding. Stringer (P) sued Car Data (D), CDS, the 32 individual former shareholders of CDS, the present shareholders of

Car Data (the shareholder defendants), and the lawyers who represented both CDS and Car Data (D) during the merger process. The trial court granted Car Data's (D) motion to dismiss on the grounds that Stringer's (P) sole remedy was under the statutory appraisal procedure. The intermediate appellate court affirmed, and Stringer (P) appealed.

ISSUE: Is appraisal the exclusive remedy for minority shareholders who allege only a disagreement as to majority's valuation of their shares in a cash-out merger and that payment by corporation was unreasonably low, with no allegations of self-dealing, fraud, deliberate waste of corporate assets, misrepresentation, or other unlawful conduct?

HOLDING AND DECISION: (Peterson, J.) Yes. Appraisal is the exclusive remedy for minority shareholders who allege only a disagreement as to majority's valuation of their shares in a cash-out merger and that payment by corporation was unreasonably low, with no allegations of self-dealing, fraud, deliberate waste of corporate assets, misrepresentation, or other unlawful conduct. Here, the complaint alleged neither fraud nor misleading representations that were relied upon. From the complaint, one can infer only that the amount paid by CDS was unfair and unreasonably low in an attempt to avoid paying fair value to Stringer (P) and others for their shares. Cases such as this are the very kind addressed by the statutory scheme. Here, with the exception of punitive damages, every element of damages that Stringer (P) seeks is recoverable under the statute. The complaint contains no allegations of fact that, if proved, would support a punitive damages award. The legislative plan expressly provides for recovery of attorney fees and expenses and of expert fees and expenses for arbitrary or vexatious action or actions "not in good faith" in connection with a cash-out merger. This provision suggests that the legislature intended that, even if the corporation offers too little money to the dissenters for their shares arbitrarily, vexatiously, or not in good faith, and the disagreement is solely as to the value of the shares, statutory appraisal is the exclusive remedy. To the extent, if any, that Stringer (P) seeks damages for any appreciation or depreciation in anticipation of the corporate action, those damages can be considered if exclusion would be inequitable. There is, therefore, a legislative intent to fully compensate shareholders for whatever their loss may be, subject only to the narrow limitation that one cannot take speculative effects of the merger into account. It may be that the $0.02 offer was insulting to Stringer (P), and it may even have been motivated by bad faith. However,

Continued on next page.

because the facts alleged in the complaint, if established, support no claim for damages apart from the fair value of the shares, it is clear that the legislature intended that dissenting shareholders in the position of Stringer (P) be limited to their remedies under the appraisal statutes. Affirmed.

▶ *ANALYSIS*

As noted in *Stringer*, the statutory scheme as a whole was designed to benefit both minority shareholders and controlling shareholders. Minority shareholders benefit because the assertion of their rights is made easier, and penalties are introduced for vexatious obstruction by corporate management. Controlling shareholders benefit directly and indirectly. They benefit directly by the added incentives for dissenters to settle without a judicial appraisal. They benefit indirectly because the provision of an adequate appraisal right diminishes the justification for courts to enjoin or set aside corporate changes because of the absence of an adequate remedy at law or because the corporate action would operate as a fraud.

■═■

Quicknotes

CASH-OUT MERGER The acquisition of one company by another by exchanging cash for the shares of the target corporation, after which the acquired company ceases to exist as an independent entity.

CONTROLLING SHAREHOLDER A person who has power to vote a majority of the outstanding shares of a corporation, or who is able to direct the management of the corporation with a smaller block of stock because the remaining shares are scattered among small, disorganized holdings.

PUNITIVE DAMAGES Damages exceeding the actual injury suffered for the purposes of punishment, deterrence and comfort to plaintiff.

■═■

In re Emerging Communications, Inc. Shareholders Litigation

[Parties not identified.]

Del. Ct. Ch., 2004 WL 1305745 (2004).

NATURE OF CASE: Consolidated statutory appraisal and class actions for breach of fiduciary duty.

FACT SUMMARY: Minority shareholders of Emerging Communications, Inc. (ECM) contended that the board of directors and a majority shareholder of ECM undervalued the company when its majority owner, Prosser, took it private, and that, therefore, they were paid an unfair price as a result of unfair dealing.

🏛 RULE OF LAW
(1) A going-private transaction is not the product of fair dealing where the majority shareholder stands on both sides of the transaction, where the minority shareholders are frozen out, where a majority of the board and of a special committee are not independent of the majority shareholder, where material financial information is withheld, and where board and shareholder approvals of the transaction are uninformed.
(2) Directors breach their fiduciary duties of loyalty and/or good faith where they receive an improper personal benefit from a transaction, aid another director in improperly benefiting from a transaction, or approve a transaction that improperly benefits another director even though they know or should know that the transaction is unfair.

FACTS: In a two-step going-private transaction, the publicly owned shares of Emerging Communications, Inc. (ECM) were acquired by Innovative Communications Corp., LLC (Innovative), ECM's majority shareholder, for $10.25 per share. At the time, 52% of the outstanding shares of ECM, and 100% of the outstanding shares of Innovative, were owned by Innovative Communication Company, LLC (ICC). ICC, in turn, was wholly owned by ECM's Chairman and CEO, Prosser. Thus, Prosser had voting control of both of the parties to the privatization transaction. Originally, Prosser had intended to merge Innovative into ECM, so that the legal advisor (Cahill) and financial advisor (Prudential) would be working to advance the interests of ECM and its minority stockholders. As a result of low interest in ECM, however, Prosser changed course, and instead of attempting to sell ECM shares, he decided ECM was undervalued and decided to purchase its shares in the going-private transaction. However, he retained the same advisors for this purpose. Thus, the advisors would now be working against the interests of ECM and its minority shareholders. The ECM board did not object either to the change of course or to Prosser's co-opting of the advisors. A special committee was formed to review the fairness of the proposed

privatization. The members on that committee were Ramphal, Vondras, and Goodwin. They were each located on separate continents and never met face-to-face. Goodwin, based in the United States, effectively led the committee. The advisors to that committee were Paul Hastings, legal, and Houlihan, financial. Houlihan was not provided with the latest financial projections, which forecasted substantially higher growth than prior projections. Prosser did, however, share those more favorable projections with his own advisors and lender. In addition, Prosser misled the committee by falsely representing that $10.25 was straining the limits of financing available to him. Finally, the committee routed all of its communications through Prosser's secretary. Prosser initially offered $9.125 per share. The special committee, without the benefit of the latest financial projections, rejected this and other offers and finally accepted and recommended an offer of $10.25, which Houlihan opined was fair. The entire board approved this price, along with a "majority of the minority" provision (i.e., a majority of the minority shareholders would have to approve the transaction), and Prosser agreed to this non-waivable minimum tender condition. The board members, in addition to Prosser and the members on the special committee, were Raynor—who had just negotiated a $2.4 million compensation deal with Prosser but failed to disclose this deal to the rest of the board—Todman, and Muoio. Muoio was a financial expert. The shareholders approved the transaction, and the merger was consummated. Minority shareholders brought actions for statutory appraisal, as well as class actions for breach of fiduciary duties. These actions were consolidated by the Chancery Court, which held that for statutory appraisal purposes, ECM's fair value on the merger date was $38.05 per share, and therefore, the transaction price of $10.25 was not a "fair price" within the meaning of fiduciary duty case law.

ISSUE:
(1) Is a going-private transaction the product of fair dealing where the majority shareholder stands on both sides of the transaction, where the minority shareholders are frozen out, where a majority of the board and of a special committee are not independent of the majority shareholder, where material financial information is withheld, and where board and shareholder approvals of the transaction are uninformed?
(2) Do directors breach their fiduciary duties of loyalty and/or good faith where they receive an improper personal benefit from a transaction, aid another director in improperly benefiting from a transaction, or approve a transaction that improperly benefits another director

Continued on next page.

even though they know or should know that the transaction is unfair?

HOLDING AND DECISION: (Jacobs, J.)

(1) No. A going-private transaction is not the product of fair dealing where the majority shareholder stands on both sides of the transaction, where the minority shareholders are frozen out, where a majority of the board and of a special committee are not independent of the majority shareholder, where material financial information is withheld, and where board and shareholder approvals of the transaction are uninformed. An initial threshold issue is whether a fair dealing analysis must be conducted, even though the court has determined that the merger price was not fair. Such an analysis is necessary because ECM has an exculpatory provision and the court must identify the basis for the defendants' liability for exculpation purposes. A second threshold issue is which side has the burden of proof. The applicable standard is entire fairness. Because the merger was not approved by a committee of independent directors who were properly informed, and the shareholder vote was not informed, the burden of proof rests on the defendants. A fair dealing analysis requires the court to address issues of when the transaction was timed, how it was initiated, structured, negotiated, and disclosed to the board, and how director and shareholder approval was obtained. Where, as here, the freeze-out merger is initiated by the majority stockholder, that fact, even though not dispositive, is evidence of unfair dealing. Here, too, the timing of the privatization was disadvantageous to the minority and correspondingly beneficial to Prosser, who structured the deal to take advantage of the temporarily and artificially depressed ECM stock price. That stock price then became the "floor" for the equally depressed and unfair privatization price. The transaction was also unfairly structured, in that Prudential and Cahill, the firms that had been retained as advisors to ECM in the initially proposed (but later abandoned) merger, were co-opted by Prosser to serve as his advisors. That switch was unfair to ECM, because during ECM's entire existence, Prudential and Cahill had been its advisors and they possessed material nonpublic information about ECM's values, business and prospects. As such, Prudential and Cahill were in the best position to represent the interests of the ECM minority. Those same advisors were now switching sides to represent interests that were adverse to that same minority. At a minimum, the board or special committee should have insisted that the advisors remain ECM advisors, or that they recuse themselves from the negotiations. Here, too, the majority of the directors on the board, and on the special committee, had disabling conflicts. They were not independent because they were economically beholden to Prosser, either because their livelihoods depended on Prosser to a great extent and/or because they received extremely generous compensation for sitting on the board and counted on continuing to receive such compensation. For these reasons, neither the board nor the committee adequately represented the minority shareholders' interests. Furthermore, the committee did not have access to the latest financial projections, was falsely under the impression that $10.25 was the most Prosser's financing would let him offer, and channeled all its communications through Prosser's secretary. These factors placed the committee in a position to not negotiate vigorously for a substantial increase in Prosser's opening offer, and gave Prosser access to the committee's confidential deliberations and strategy, thus placing a significant information imbalance in place that favored Prosser. For all these reasons, the committee could not effectively represent the minority shareholders' interests. Finally, neither the board nor the shareholder approvals were informed. Therefore, they were of no legal consequence. First, the board was ignorant of the final financial projections, and, therefore, of the inadequacy of Houlihan's valuation that was based on prior, less favorable, projections. Second, Raynor did not disclose a special $2.4 million compensation deal he had just made with Prosser. Such a nondisclosure was material and violated the fiduciary duty of disclosure. Third, the approval of the transaction by a majority of the minority shareholders was also legally ineffective, because the misdisclosures and omissions in the disclosure documents sent to shareholders in connection with the privatization rendered that vote uninformed. Those misdisclosures and omissions also violated the fiduciary duty of disclosure owed by ECM's majority stockholder and by the ECM directors who were responsible for the accuracy of those documents. These highly material disclosure failures included: the failure to disclose the latest financial projections, or the fact that they had been disclosed to Prudential but not to the special committee and its advisors; the failure to disclose dependent board members' consulting relationships or retainer agreements with Prosser entities; the failure to disclose Raynor's $2.4 million compensation deal; and other similar omissions. For all these reasons, the privatization transaction and the $10.25 merger price were the product of unfair dealing.

(2) Yes. Directors breach their fiduciary duties of loyalty and/or good faith where they receive an improper personal benefit from a transaction, aid another director in improperly benefiting from a transaction, or approve a transaction that improperly benefits another director even though they know or should know that the transaction is unfair. Here, the determination of whether the directors breached their fiduciary duties must be made on a director-by-director basis. This is because ECM's charter exculpates those directors who have only breached their fiduciary duty of care. Prosser breached

Continued on next page.

his duty of loyalty by deriving an improper personal benefit from the privatization transaction. Raynor breached his fiduciary duty of loyalty by actively assisting Prosser in carrying out the transaction and acting to further Prosser's interests in that transaction. Although Raynor did not benefit directly from the transactions, his loyalties ran solely to Prosser because Raynor's economic interests were tied solely to Prosser and he acted to further those economic interests. Muoio, as a financial expert and principal of an investment advising firm, is similarly liable because he voted to approve the transaction even though he knew, or at the very least had strong reasons to believe, that the $10.25 per share merger price was unfair. Because he had specialized expertise that would have enabled him to know ECM's intrinsic value, it was incumbent upon him to advocate that the board reject the merger price. The only reasons for him to not oppose that price was that he either decided to further his own personal business interests, or consciously and intentionally disregarded his duty to safeguard the minority stockholders from the transaction's unfairness. As to the other directors, there is insufficient evidence to indicate that they acted in bad faith or out of disloyalty. Goodwin's conduct, although violative of the duty of care, did not act volitionally to aid Prosser in his scheme to freeze out the minority at an unfair price. Although there was no justification for Goodwin to communicate with the other committee members through Prosser's secretary, that misstep constituted a violation of Goodwin's duty of care and resulted in critical information being leaked to the other side. But, that fiduciary breach was of no actionable consequence, because Goodwin had all along been deprived of material information that both he and Houlihan needed to negotiate a fair price. And the wholesale abdication to Goodwin by Ramphal and Vondras of their responsibility to take an active and direct role as committee members also bespeaks of their breach of the duty of care. But negligent or even gross negligent conduct, however misguided, does not automatically equate to disloyalty or bad faith. There is no evidence that Goodwin, Ramphal and Vondras intentionally conspired with Prosser to engage in a process that would create the illusion, but avoid the reality, of arm's length bargaining to obscure the true purpose of benefiting Prosser at the expense of the minority stockholders. Here, too, there is no evidence that these directors acted with conscious and intentional disregard of their responsibilities, or made decisions with knowledge that they lacked material information. The same is true for Todman, who played no role in the negotiations, but only voted for the transaction. For these reasons, Innovative, ICC, Prosser, Raynor, and Muoio are jointly and severally liable to the plaintiffs in the amount equal to $27.80 per share.

▶ ANALYSIS

One of the most controversial aspects of this case was the court's ruling that director Muoio was liable for a breach of the duty of good faith and/or loyalty from his professional background rather than from his behavior. The case supports the view that a director, in defending a decision as being taken in good faith, may not rely upon an expert's fairness opinion if the director knows, or reasonably should know, the transaction is unfair. This case was settled and, therefore, there will not be an appeal to establish a firm precedent or provide further guidance with respect to this particular fact pattern. However, despite the settlement, this decision is noteworthy because the author, Justice Jacobs, now serves on the Delaware Supreme Court.

■═■

Quicknotes

BREACH OF FIDUCIARY DUTY The failure of a fiduciary to observe the standard of care exercised by professionals of similar education and experience.

BURDEN OF PROOF The duty of a party to introduce evidence to support a fact that is in dispute in an action.

EXCULPATORY CLAUSE A clause in a contract relieving one party from liability for certain unlawful conduct.

FIDUCIARY DUTY A legal obligation to act for the benefit of another, including subordinating one's personal interests to that of the other person.

■═■

In re Cox Communications, Inc. Shareholders Litigation

[Parties not identified.]

Del. Ct. Ch., 879 A.2d 604 (2005).

NATURE OF CASE: Objection to a request for attorneys' fees in a shareholder action challenging a going private transaction involving a controlling shareholder.

FACT SUMMARY: Shareholders objected to the attorneys' fees requested by plaintiffs' counsel after settlement of a shareholder action that had been filed prematurely and hastily, and that attacked a fully negotiable proposal by the controlling shareholder group of Cox Communications, Inc. (Cox), the Cox Family (the Family), to take the corporation private; the objectors argued that the attorneys had played no role in achieving the final price increase from the Family's initial offer that had been obtained by the board's Special Committee.

🏛 RULE OF LAW
In a going-private transaction involving a controlling shareholder, where premature and hastily drafted shareholder actions are filed, and an independent special committee of the board negotiates a price increase, the plaintiffs' attorneys are entitled to attorneys' fees to the extent that the attorneys' involvement played a role in achieving the price increase negotiated by the special committee.

FACTS: The Cox Family (the Family) was the controlling shareholder (74%) of Cox Communications, Inc. (Cox), a public company. The Family decided it would be in its best interest to acquire the remaining shares of Cox that it did not own, and to take Cox private. At a Cox board meeting, the Family proposed paying $32 per share as an initial bid. The Family made clear that it expected that Cox would form an independent special committee (the Special Committee) to respond to and negotiate this proposal. In fact, the Family's proposal was specifically conditioned on agreement to final merger terms by the Special Committee. A few hours after the proposal was announced, various shareholders filed premature, hastily-drafted, makeweight complaints attacking the Family's fully negotiable proposal. Abbey was selected as lead counsel. The Special Committee was then formed, and the committee selected its legal and financial advisors. After vigorous negotiations, the Family and the Special Committee reached a tentative agreement on a merger at $34.75 per share that would be subject to approval by a majority of the minority stockholders. The tentative agreement was conditioned on settlement of the outstanding lawsuits, receipt of a final fairness opinion from the Special Committee's financial advisor, and agreement on the terms of a final merger agreement. After the tentative agreement with the Special Committee, the Family's litigation counsel gave the plaintiffs, through Abbey, the $34.75 per share and minority approval condition

as a "best and absolutely final offer." The plaintiffs settled with the Family, agreeing in a Memorandum of Understanding (MOU) that the pendency of the litigation had contributed to their decision to increase their bid to the final price it reached. Although no objections to the settlement itself were filed, an objection was made to the request by plaintiffs' counsel for attorneys' fees, which the Family had agreed not to oppose up to $4.95 million. The objections essentially challenged the common law rules that govern mergers with controlling shareholders as creating inefficient incentives for plaintiffs' lawyers and corporate defense counsel, leading to lawsuits that exist almost entirely as a vehicle for the payment of attorneys' fees and the entry of a judgment of the court providing the defendants with a broad release from any future lawsuits relating to the underlying transactions. Thus, the objections were not driven by anything unusual about the Cox merger, but were being used to challenge the perpetuation of a pattern of settlements and fee requests similar to the one in the Cox merger.

ISSUE: In a going-private transaction involving a controlling shareholder, where premature and hastily drafted shareholder actions are filed, and an independent special committee of the board negotiates a price increase, are the plaintiffs' attorneys entitled to attorneys' fees to the extent that the attorneys' involvement played a role in achieving the price increase negotiated by the special committee?

HOLDING AND DECISION: (Strine, V. Chan.) Yes. In a going-private transaction involving a controlling shareholder, where premature and hastily drafted shareholder actions are filed, and an independent special committee of the board negotiates a price increase, the plaintiffs' attorneys are entitled to attorneys' fees to the extent that the attorneys' involvement played a role in achieving the price increase negotiated by the special committee. Regardless of the procedural protections employed, such as a special committee, or approval by a majority of the minority, a merger with a controlling stockholder is subject to the entire fairness standard. *Kahn v. Lynch Communications, Inc.*, 638 A.2d 1110 (Del. 1994). However, to encourage use of such procedural protections, the burden of persuasion shifts on the ultimate issue of fairness to the plaintiffs as long as the procedural devices are shown to have operated with integrity. This system of incentives created by *Lynch* led to a pattern of which this case is an example. This pattern involves the plaintiffs' lawyers, the special committee, and the controlling shareholder(s). However, there has never been an instance in this pattern of cases where the plaintiffs' lawyers have refused to settle

Continued on next page.

once the special committee has agreed on a price with a controlling shareholder. In this "ritual" it is relatively easy for the plaintiffs' lawyers to achieve "success," which is a prerequisite for the granting of an attorneys' fee request. By suing on the proposal, the plaintiffs' lawyers can claim that they are responsible, in part, for price increases in a deal context in which price increases are overwhelmingly likely to occur. Added to this incentive is the fact that the plaintiffs' lawyers know that the *Lynch* standard gives them the ability, procedurally, to defeat a motion to dismiss addressed to any complaint challenging an actual merger agreement with a special committee, even one conditioned on approval by a majority of the minority. Because of this ability, the plaintiffs' claims always have settlement value because of the costs of discovery and time to the defendants. Also, once a special committee has negotiated a material price increase with the aid of well-regarded financial and legal advisors, the plaintiffs' lawyers can contend with a straight face that it was better to help get the price up to where it ended than to risk that the controller would abandon the deal. Abandonment of the deal, the plaintiffs' lawyers will say with accuracy, will result in the company's stock price falling back to its pre-proposal level, which is always materially lower as it does not reflect the anticipation of a premium-generating going-private transaction. Having vigorously aided the special committee to get into the range of fairness and having no reason to suspect that the special committee was disloyal to its mission, the plaintiffs' lawyers can say, in plausible good faith, that it was better for the class to take this improved bid, which is now well within the range of fairness, rather than to risk abandonment of the transaction. Moreover, for those stockholders who wish to challenge the price, appraisal still remains an option. Another facet to the juridical landscape is that under the doctrine of independent legal significance, corporations may take, if statutory law permits, a variety of routes to achieve the same end. Thus, another route to going private was established, involving less negotiation and litigation, whereby the controller would use a front tender offer to obtain 90% of the shares, coupled with a back-end short form merger. This method of transaction has come to be known as the *Siliconix* method, named after the first case to address it: *In re Siliconix Inc. Shareholders Litigation*, 808 A.2d 421 (Del. Ch. 2002). Here, the objectors and the plaintiffs have presented conflicting scholarship as to whether the kind of litigation brought in this case achieves a material benefit for minority shareholders. Some scholars conclude that the *Lynch* form of transaction results, on average, in a higher premium in comparison to the pre-announcement market price than *Siliconix* deals. Some scholars also have found that controlling shareholders increase their opening bids more in a *Lynch* deal. These scholars conclude that these differences between *Lynch* and *Siliconix* deals result from the stronger bargaining hand given to the special committee in the *Lynch* context by watchdog plaintiffs. Although the record supports the proposition that *Lynch* deals tend

to generate higher final premiums than *Siliconix* deals, one awkward fact nonetheless strongly suggests that the threat of bare knuckles litigation over fairness is not as important as the special committee's role as an negotiating force. This fact is the absence of evidence that "traditional" plaintiffs' lawyers, who attacked going-private proposals by controllers, have ever refused to settle once they have received the signal that the defendants have put on the table their best and final offer—i.e., an offer that is acceptable to the special committee. What can be most charitably said is that the pendency of litigation and the theoretical threat that the plaintiffs will press on provides special committee members with additional clout that they wield to get good results. Another observation is that litigation under *Lynch* never seems to involve actual litigation conflict if the lawsuit begins with a suit attacking a negotiable proposal. These cases almost invariably settle or are dismissed voluntarily by the plaintiffs. Where the transaction itself is challenged, usually plaintiffs with a large stake will hire non-traditional law firms to actually litigate the matter. And finally, under both *Lynch* and *Siliconix* deals, minority shareholders seem to be getting significant premiums to market. Here, because the attorneys' involvement likely played at least a small role in achieving the price increase negotiated by the Special Committee, they are entitled to attorneys' fees commensurate with the role they played—here, substantially less than requested.

CODA: The common law should be adjusted to account for the consequences flowing from the current standard of review governing going private mergers. A relatively modest alteration of *Lynch* would ensure continued integrity while providing important, as well as enhanced, protections for minority stockholders. That alteration would permit the invocation of the business judgment rule for a going-private merger that involved procedural protections that mirrored what is contemplated in an arm's-length merger—independent, disinterested director and stockholder approval. Put simply, if a controller proposed a merger, subject from inception to negotiation and approval of the merger by an independent special committee and a majority of the minority approval condition, the business judgment rule should presumptively apply. With such a modification, complaints would be dismissed unless (1) the plaintiffs plead particularized facts that the special committee was not independent or was not effective because of its own breach of fiduciary duty or wrongdoing by the controller (e.g., fraud on the committee); or (2) the approval of the minority stockholders was tainted by misdisclosure, or actual or structural coercion. Such a modified *Lynch* standard would encourage the filing of claims only by plaintiffs and plaintiffs' lawyers who genuinely believed that a wrong had been committed. The chance to free ride on

Continued on next page.

the expected increase in the controller's original proposal would be eliminated and therefore litigation would only be filed by those who believed that they possessed legal claims with value. Similarly, *Siliconix* deals could be strengthened by equitable review. In such deals, the controller would be relieved of the burden of proving entire fairness if: (1) the tender offer was recommended by an independent special committee; (2) the tender offer was structurally non-coercive; and (3) there was a disclosure of all material facts. In that case, the transaction should be immune from challenge in a breach of fiduciary duty action unless the plaintiffs pled particularized facts from which it could be inferred that the special committee's recommendation was tainted by a breach of fiduciary duty or that there was a failure in disclosure.

▶ *ANALYSIS*

This case is practically a primer on the two current routes for going private: the *Lynch* route and the *Siliconix* route. As would be expected, *Lynch* deals tend to generate higher premiums for the cashed out minority shareholders than do *Siliconix* deals. Some of the reasons for this are: (1) the greater leverage that the form of transaction gives to special committees; (2) the fact that the governing standard of review always gives the plaintiffs settlement value; (3) the reality that signing up a merger when the votes are locked up results in the greatest certainty for a controller; and (4) signing up a merger with a special committee and a settlement with plaintiffs' lawyers provides not only deal certainty, but a broad release and the most effective discouragement of appraisal claims. Additionally, factors determining which route a controlling shareholder will choose include: the controller's ownership stake, the extent of the public float, the presence of big holders, the desire for certainty and closure, and which route might yield the best price for it. For example, the further a controller was from 90% to begin with, the more attractive the merger route might be, and vice versa, simply for efficiency reasons in both cases.

■══■

Quicknotes

BREACH OF FIDUCIARY DUTY The failure of a fiduciary to observe the standard of care exercised by professionals of similar education and experience.

BURDEN OF PROOF The duty of a party to introduce evidence to support a fact that is in dispute in an action.

BUSINESS JUDGMENT RULE Doctrine relieving corporate directors and/or officers from liability for decisions honestly and rationally made in the corporation's best interests.

MEMORANDUM A brief written note outlining the terms of a transaction or an agreement.

MOTION TO DISMISS Motion to terminate a trial based on the adequacy of the pleadings.

■══■

Tryon v. Smith

Minority shareholder (P) v. Majority shareholder (D)

Or. Sup. Ct., 229 P.2d 251 (1951).

NATURE OF CASE: Appeal from damages awarded for breach of fiduciary duty.

FACT SUMMARY: Various minority shareholders of First National Bank contended that majority shareholder Smith (D) breached a fiduciary duty in obtaining, upon sale of his stock, a price substantially higher than that offered to the minority shareholders.

🏛 RULE OF LAW
A majority shareholder violates no duty to minority shareholders by obtaining a higher price for his shares than that obtained by the minority shareholders.

FACTS: Smith (D) and his family owned approximately 70% of the shares of First National Bank. Transamerica, Inc. (Transamerica) approached Smith (D) about selling the corporation. Smith (D) informed Transamerica that he wouldn't sell his shares unless minority shareholders received at least $220 per share and he received substantially more as a premium for control. The book value of shares was $200 at that time. Transamerica eventually bought all of Smith's (D) shares for $460 per share and purchased minority shares at $220. Various minority shareholders, upon learning of this, sued Smith (D) for breach of fiduciary duty. The trial court held in favor of the minority shareholders and awarded $500,000 against Smith (D), who appealed.

ISSUE: Does a majority shareholder violate a duty to minority shareholders by obtaining, upon sale of his stock, a price substantially higher than that offered to minority shareholders?

HOLDING AND DECISION: (Latourette, J.) No. A majority shareholder violates no duty to minority shareholders by obtaining a higher price for his shares than that obtained by the minority shareholders. Majority shareholders may sell their stock at any time and for any price they can obtain, provided they act in good faith. Good faith here means not driving down the price of minority shares or in some other fashion exploiting his controlling position at the expense of smaller shareholders. Merely selling control for a premium in no way does this. It is generally recognized that the stock of majority shareholders is of more value than that of the minority. Here, there is no evidence that Smith (D) did anything to drive down the price of minority shares. In fact, he may have done the opposite. All he did was obtain a higher price for his shares without so informing the minority shareholders, which was fully within his rights. Affirmed.

▶ ANALYSIS

A majority shareholder will often be a director and officer. These three elements of control present an obvious opportunity for overreaching. Consequently, one in such a position does have fiduciary duties to minority shareholders. Mere sale of control, however, does not in itself violate that duty.

■=■

Quicknotes

FIDUCIARY DUTY A legal obligation to act for the benefit of another, including subordinating one's personal interests to that of the other person.

■=■

Essex Universal Corp. v. Yates

Buyer (P) v. Seller (D)

305 F.2d 572 (2d Cir. 1962).

NATURE OF CASE: Action for breach of contract.

FACT SUMMARY: Yates (D) contracted to sell shares in and control of Republic Pictures Corp. to Essex Universal (P), but then reneged.

🏛 RULE OF LAW
A seller of corporate control may not, as a general rule, profit by facilitating actions of the purchasers which operate to the detriment of the corporation or remaining shareholders; but where the facts do not indicate the existence of any such detriment, there is no question of the right of a controlling shareholder to derive a premium from the sale of a controlling block of stock.

FACTS: Essex Universal (Essex) (P) contracted with Yates (D) to purchase his controlling interest in Essex (P). One provision of the contract provided that Yates (D) was to arrange for a special meeting of the Republic Board of Directors to be called at which Yates's (D) directors were to resign one at a time (seriatim) and Essex (P) directors were to be elected in their place. The purpose of this special meeting clearly was to effect immediate transfer of control. Had Essex (P) been forced to wait until the next annual meeting to elect any directors and until the meeting after that to gain control (directors were elected for three-year terms, one-third elected at each annual meeting), it would have taken 18 months. When Yates (D) refused to close the deal, however, Essex (P) sued for breach of contract, claiming damages of $2.7 million. As a defense, Yates (D) set up illegality of the contract, claiming that a contract for the sale of control of a corporation should be deemed invalid as against public policy. From summary judgment for Yates (D), Essex (P) appealed.

ISSUE: Is a contract for sale of corporate stock invalid as against public policy solely because it includes a provision guaranteeing a takeover of control (by replacement of the board of directors)?

HOLDING AND DECISION: (Lumbard, C.J.) No. A seller of corporate control may not, as a general rule, profit by facilitating actions of the purchasers which operate to the detriment of the corporation or remaining shareholders; but, where the facts do not indicate the existence of any such detriment, there is no question of the right of a controlling shareholder (under New York law) to contract to sell or derive a profit from the sale of controlling stock. It is, of course, illegal to sell corporate office or management control by itself (i.e., separate from sale of stock). Such control of a corporation is held by fiduciaries

on behalf of all stockholders. Directors, as such fiduciaries, hold control for all the stockholders, as their representatives. So, while sale of a controlling block of stock is not illegal, sale of the board of directors would be. Here, the summary judgment below does not indicate whether or not a determination of fact was made as to whether the contract involved merely a sale of stock or, in fact, a sale of the board. As such, the judgment is reversed and remanded for determination of whether the clause accelerating takeover constituted an illegal sale of corporate control. In dicta, Chief Judge Lumbard answers the remand question in the negative. It would be unreasonable to prohibit a group who has bought a controlling block of stock from taking control of the corporation. With no evidence of detriment here to the other stockholders, the contract should be upheld.

CONCURRENCE: (Clark, J.) Summary judgment was clearly improper. On remand, however, any restraining instruction to the trial court should be avoided. In light of the complexity of corporate transfers and the court's limited knowledge of such matters, the general determination of illegality should be left to the trier of fact, as a question of fact.

CONCURRENCE: (Friendly, J.) The contract here is violative of public policy. A seriatim resignation procedure such as this would be valid if the stock involved were over 50% of voting stock, since in that case all stockholders would be, as a matter of "practical certainty," know that such transfer would mean transfer of control. But where, as here, only 28% of the stock was to be sold, circumventing the normal stockholder elections does constitute a detriment to the stockholders and corporation which must be violative of public policy. The contract should be held invalid.

▶ ANALYSIS

This case points up both the general standards for measuring the legality of transfer of control clauses in stock sale contracts and three differing applications of those standards. The proper application (in New York) was determined two years later in *Matter of Caplan v. Lionel Corp.,* 246 N.Y.S.2d 913 (N.Y.A.D. 1964), in which the New York court stated, "Where there has been a transfer of a majority of the stock, or even such a percentage as gives working control, a change of directors by resignation and filling of vacancies is proper." As such, the view of Chief Judge Lumbard that forcing controlling shareholders to wait for board control is unreasonable was adopted. Note that under SEC Act § 14(f), when a corporation comes within SEC Act jurisdiction, information about the nominees for

Continued on next page.

election (in transfer of control such as here) must be sent to all stockholders at least 10 days prior to the election unless (1) less than a majority of the board, or (2) less than 10% of outstanding stock, was involved.

■═■

Quicknotes

MINORITY SHAREHOLDER A stockholder in a corporation controlling such a small portion of those shares which are outstanding that its votes have no influence in the management of the corporation.

PROXY A person authorized to act for another.

SERIATIM In order; successively.

■═■

Harris v. Carter

Minority shareholder (P) v. Majority shareholder (D)

Del. Ct. Ch., 582 A.2d 222 (1990).

NATURE OF CASE: Motion to dismiss action seeking damages for breach of fiduciary duties.

FACT SUMMARY: Harris (P) and other minority shareholders of Atlas Energy Corp. contended that Carter (D) and his associates committed a breach of fiduciary duty by negligently selling control of the corporation to a group who looted it.

RULE OF LAW
A majority shareholder may be liable if he negligently sells control and such sale damages the corporation.

FACTS: Carter (D) and his associates owned 52% of the stock of Atlas Energy Corp. The Carter group (D) sold control of the corporation to Mascolo (D) and his associates, receiving in exchange shares of stock in a Mascolo corporation, Insuranshares of America. The Mascolo group (D) then took control of Atlas and, in a series of transactions, allegedly looted the corporation. Harris (P) and other minority shareholders of Atlas sued not only the Mascolo group (D) but also the Carter group (D). The gist of their allegations against Carter (D) was that facts were present which should have put him and his associates on notice of Mascolo's (D) intentions and that their failure to investigate constituted a fiduciary breach. The Carter group (D) moved to dismiss for failure to state a claim.

ISSUE: May a majority shareholder be liable if he negligently sells control and such sales damages the corporation?

HOLDING AND DECISION: (Allen, Chan.) Yes. A majority shareholder may be liable if he negligently sells control and such sale damages the corporation. It is an established legal doctrine that, unless privileged, each person owes a duty to those who may foreseeably be harmed by his failure to take reasonable steps to prevent such harm. While this doctrine is usually cited in the context of tort law, it also applies to fiduciary obligations. When a corporate fiduciary's action may forseeably harm the corporation, his negligent acts causing such harm are compensable. In the context of this case, the Carter group (D) controlled the corporation as majority shareholders and officers and were thus fiduciaries. Harris's (P) complaint states a claim for breach of a duty of care owed by the Carter group (D). Motion to dismiss denied.

▶ ANALYSIS

Most authority on the issue here is consistent with the approach taken here: a negligent sale of control may lead to liability. The main contrary authority is *Levy v.*

American Beverage, 38 N.Y.S.2d 517 (1942). In that case, actual knowledge of the buyer's wrongful intentions was required for liability. This is the minority view.

Quicknotes

FIDUCIARY DUTY A legal obligation to act for the benefit of another, including subordinating one's personal interests to that of the other person.

Perlman v. Feldmann

Minority stockholder (P) v. Director/dominant stockholder (D)

219 F.2d 173 (2d Cir. 1955).

NATURE OF CASE: Stockholder derivative action for an accounting.

FACT SUMMARY: Feldmann (D), a director and dominant stockholder of Newport Steel Corp., sold, along with others, the controlling interest of that steel manufacturer to steel users, along with the right to control distribution.

🏛 RULE OF LAW
A corporate director who is also a dominant shareholder stands, in both situations, in a fiduciary relationship to both the corporation and the minority stockholders (as beneficiaries of the fiduciary relationship), and where such a director-shareholder sells controlling interest in the corporation, he is accountable to it (and the minority shareholders) to the extent that the sales price represents payment for the right to control.

FACTS: Feldmann (D) was director and dominant stockholder (he and his family owned controlling interest) of Newport Steel Corp. (Newport), a small steel-producing company. Though actually too small to compete with other steel suppliers, Newport was able to survive and thrive because of a severe steel shortage which existed at the time of this case and because of the so-called Feldmann Plan. Under this plan, Newport was able to exact from buyers (who were desperate for steel) interest-free advances which permitted it to expand and finance operations without incurring normal financing costs (allowing it to compete with other steel suppliers). To avoid this, and to assure themselves of a higher percentage of Newport's steel, several independent steel users formed the Wilport Company. Though Newport stock had never been worth more than $12 per share, Wilport paid Feldmann (D) and his family $20 per share for controlling interest in Newport, which included control over distribution of steel (since Feldmann (D), directors, and officers quickly resigned and were replaced by Wilport nominees). Perlman (P), a minority stockholder in Newport, sued Feldman (D) for an accounting for all profits gained from his sale of the controlling interest, charging a breach of fiduciary duty in depriving Newport of future Feldmann Plan benefits by selling to someone whose purpose in buying was to circumvent the Feldmann Plan pressures. From judgment for Feldmann (D), Perlman (P) appealed.

ISSUE: May a controlling shareholder or corporate director be held accountable for profits from sale of controlling interest?

HOLDING AND DECISION: (Clark, C.J.) Yes. A corporate director, who is also a dominant shareholder, stands, in both situations, in a fiduciary relationship to both the corporation and the minority stockholders (as beneficiaries of the fiduciary relationship), and where such a director-shareholder sells controlling interest in the corporation, he is accountable to it and the minority shareholders, thereby, to the extent that the sales price represents payment for the right to control. Directors of a corporation act in a strictly fiduciary capacity. Their office is a trust. They must not in any degree allow their official conduct to be determined by their private interests. This same rule should apply to controlling stockholders as well. In both cases, their actions are subject to strict scrutiny by the courts. The burden is upon them to justify their actions and establish their undivided loyalty to the corporation. Here, Feldmann (D) quite obviously acted in self-interest and to the detriment of the corporation and the minority shareholders. His actions in siphoning off, for personal gain, the value of market advantages sold to Wilport, to the detriment of Newport (they lose Feldmann Plan advantages), violate his trust relationship with Newport. The decision below is reversed and remanded to the trial court for determination of damages, i.e., the exact increment in the sales price attributable to control.

DISSENT: (Swan, J.) The majority does not clearly delineate what fiduciary duties are owed as directors and what duties are owed as controlling stockholders. Further, ignoring the loss of Feldmann Plan benefits, he sees no detriment to the minority here in permitting the sale to Wilport.

▶ ANALYSIS

This case points up the clear trend of authority which attributes liability to controlling stockholders for sale of corporate control. Note the manner of proof here. The fact that "control" was the object of Wilport is to be inferred from the fact that they obviously bought so as to avoid the Feldmann Plan. Minority shareholders, of course, feared worse. Even though it had not yet occurred, it is obvious that minority stockholders feared a situation similar to *Gerdes v. Reynolds*, N.Y. Sup. Ct., 28 N.Y.S.2d 622 (1941) in which control is purchased in order to permit waste of corporate assets. To be sure, Wilport companies had little reason to care about Newport progress and every reason during the steel shortage to take Newport for all it was worth, forcing it to operate at little or no profit. As such, this case may be viewed as a further step in protecting minority stockholder interests from abuse.

▬▬■

Continued on next page.

Quicknotes

ACCOUNTING The evaluation of assets for the purpose of assigning relative interests.

FIDUCIARY DUTY A legal obligation to act for the benefit of another, including subordinating one's personal interests to that of the other person.

SHAREHOLDER'S DERIVATIVE ACTION An action asserted by a shareholder in order to enforce a cause of action on behalf of the corporation.

STRICT SCRUTINY The method by which courts determine the constitutionality of a law, when a law affects a fundamental right. Under the test, the legislature must have a compelling interest to enact the law and measures prescribed by the law must be the least restrictive means possible to accomplish its goal.

■▬■

Thorpe v. CERBCO, Inc.

Shareholder (P) v. Corporate directors (D)

Del. Sup. Ct., 676 A.2d 436 (1996).

NATURE OF CASE: Appeal from denial of plaintiff damages in shareholder's derivative action.

FACT SUMMARY: Thorpe (P), a shareholder, alleged that the directors (D) of CERBCO had usurped an opportunity which belonged to the corporation, and sued for damages.

🏛 RULE OF LAW

It is a breach of fiduciary duty for a director to profit personally from the use of information secured through a confidential relationship with the corporation, even if such profit or advantage is not gained at the expense of the shareholders.

FACTS: The Erikson (D) brothers constituted CERBCO's controlling group of shareholders and were also officers and directors with fiduciary duties owing to CERBCO. Thorpe (P), a shareholder, alleged that the Eriksons (D) had usurped an opportunity that belonged to the corporation. That opportunity was the potential sale of control of one of CERBCO's subsidiaries. The Eriksons (D) did not inform CERBCO's outside directors that INA had approached them with the intention of buying one of CERBCO's subsidiaries. At a meeting with INA, the Eriksons (D) suggested that INA purchase their controlling interest in CERBCO, rather than the subsidiary itself. The Eriksons (D) later denied that INA had ever been interested in buying the subsidiary. The chancellor held that the Eriksons (D) breached their duty of loyalty by failing to make complete disclosure to CERBCO of this corporate opportunity and by not removing themselves from consideration of the matter. The court concluded, however, that as controlling shareholders, the Eriksons (D) had the right to veto any transaction for the sale of all or substantially all of the assets of the corporation. Thus, since the Eriksons' (D) conduct had caused no injury to CERBCO, they would not be liable for any damages. Thorpe (P) appealed.

ISSUE: Is it a breach of fiduciary duty for a director to profit personally from the use of information secured through a confidential relationship with the corporation, even if such profit or advantage is not gained at the expense of the shareholders?

HOLDING AND DECISION: (Walsh, J.) Yes. It is a breach of fiduciary duty for a director to profit personally from the use of information secured through a confidential relationship with the corporation, even if such profit or advantage is not gained at the expense of the shareholders. While there are no transactional damages in this case, the Eriksons (D) are liable for damages incidental

to their breach of duty. In addition, they must reimburse CERBCO (D) for any expenses, including legal and due diligence costs, which the corporation incurred to accommodate the Eriksons' pursuit of their own interests prior to the deal being abandoned by the Eriksons and INA. Affirmed in part, reversed in part, and remanded to the Court of Chancery for a further determination of damages.

▶ ANALYSIS

The court in this case decided that as a matter of law damages should have been awarded. The Eriksons (D) profited from their dealings with INA, and CERBCO incurred certain expenses in connection with those negotiations which it would not have otherwise incurred had the Eriksons not attempted to expropriate the INA sale opportunity. The court also awarded plaintiff's counsel fees.

■■■

Quicknotes

CORPORATE OPPORTUNITY DOCTRINE Prohibits fiduciaries from usurping business opportunities that rightly belong to the corporation.

DERIVATIVE SUIT An action asserted by a shareholder in order to enforce a cause of action on behalf of the corporation.

DUTY OF LOYALTY A director's duty to refrain from self-dealing or to take a position that is adverse to the corporation's best interests.

FIDUCIARY DUTY A legal obligation to act for the benefit of another, including subordinating one's personal interests to that of the other person.

■■■

CHAPTER 9

Hostile Acquisitions

Quick Reference Rules of Law

Cheff v. Mathes

Officer of corporation (D) v. Shareholder (P)

Del. Sup. Ct., 199 A.2d 548 (1964).

NATURE OF CASE: Derivative suit to rescind purchase of stock and accounting for damages.

FACT SUMMARY: Holland Furnace Corp. used corporate funds to buy up its own stock to prevent a threatened takeover of the corporation by Maremont. Mathes (P) filed a derivative suit alleging that the true purpose of the purchase was to insure perpetuation of control by the present board of directors.

🏛 RULE OF LAW
The board of directors may use corporate funds to acquire stock in the corporation if motivated by a proper business purpose but not to perpetuate its own control of the corporation.

FACTS: Holland Furnace Corp. (Holland) was approached by Maremont about the possibility of a merger of his corporation with Holland. Holland rejected the offer. Maremont subsequently purchased a sizable block of Holland stock and demanded to join Holland's board of directors. At the same time, he informed the Holland board that he considered Holland's distribution system obsolete and in need of reorganization. The Holland board voted to investigate Maremont's business history and found that he had been involved in the takeover and liquidation of a number of companies and also that Maremont's current corporation had lost money the preceding year. At this time, there was also unrest among Holland's employees, with some employees quitting because of the fear of a Maremont takeover and subsequent reorganization of the corporation. When informed of the investigation and Maremont's demand for board membership, the board authorized purchase of Holland stock with corporate funds, ostensibly for use in a stock option plan. Holland began purchasing its own shares, driving up the market price. Maremont then made a buy/sell offer to Holland which Holland accepted, purchasing Maremont's shares at a price greater than market price. Mathes (P), a Holland shareholder, brought a derivative suit against Holland, Chaff (D), the executive officer of Holland, and the individual members of the Holland board, alleging that the purchase of stock with corporate funds was to insure perpetuation of control by the current directors rather than for a proper business purpose.

ISSUE: Was the purchase of stock undertaken to insure perpetuation of control by the directors and, therefore, an improper use of corporate funds?

HOLDING AND DECISION: (Carey, J.) No. The evidence presented does not prove that the purchase of the stock was accomplished in order to perpetuate control by the current board. By statute, a corporation is authorized to purchase its own shares, but, here, the shareholders allege that the purchase was for an improper motive. There is an inherent conflict of interest in a corporation's purchase of its own stock in order to revoke a threat to the control of the corporation, so the board has the burden of proof of showing its good faith in authorizing the purchase. Here, they met that burden. First, the shareholders allege the purchase was unfair because Holland paid more than market price for the stock. This argument fails because a block of stock, as opposed to small amounts of stock, always sells at a greater price because of its "control premium." The remaining question is whether the board proved that it had reasonable grounds to believe that there was a danger to corporate policy. If there was good-faith action based on reasonable investigation, the purchase will be upheld. Here, there was evidence of employee unrest from Maremont's threatened takeover, reports on Maremont's history of liquidation of corporations, and Maremont's own statements that he wanted to reorganize the corporation, which was sufficient to justify the board's belief of a reasonable threat to the continued existence of Holland in its present form. Since the motivation for the purchase was a proper business motive, the purchase will be upheld. Reversed and remanded.

▶ ANALYSIS

In reacquiring outstanding shares, the board of directors stands in a fiduciary relationship to the corporation. This means that a board can use corporate funds to prevent a takeover and thereby stay in control but only if justified by a valid business purpose. The transaction will be evaluated by the "business judgment rule"—it will be upheld if within the power of the corporation, done in good faith, as a result of an independent exercise of discretion, if the board acts in what it believes to be the best interest of the corporation, and without being influenced by any improper considerations. The court in *Cheff* felt that this rule was met, and even though Maremont's plan to reorganize might have been beneficial to the corporation, its desire to prevent Maremont's takeover was justifiable.

■=■

Quicknotes

BUSINESS JUDGMENT RULE Doctrine relieving corporate directors and/or officers from liability for decisions honestly and rationally made in the corporation's best interests.

DERIVATIVE SUIT An action asserted by a shareholder in order to enforce a cause of action on behalf of the corporation.

Continued on next page.

FIDUCIARY DUTY   A legal obligation to act for the benefit of another, including subordinating one's personal interests to that of the other person.

RESCISSION   The canceling of an agreement and the return of the parties to their positions prior to the formation of the contract.

Unocal Corp. v. Mesa Petroleum Co.

Corporation (D) v. Shareholder company (P)

Del. Sup. Ct., 493 A.2d 946 (1985).

NATURE OF CASE: Interlocutory appeal from a temporary restraining order.

FACT SUMMARY: Mesa (P), which was a stockholder in Unocal Corp. (D), was attempting a takeover that Unocal's (D) directors tried to fight by making an exchange offer from which Mesa (P) was excluded.

🏛 RULE OF LAW
Unless it is shown by a preponderance of the evidence that the directors' decision in fighting a takeover by one of the shareholders in the corporation was primarily based on perpetuating themselves in office or some other breach of fiduciary duty, a court will not substitute its judgment for that of the board.

FACTS: In response to a takeover attempt by Mesa (P), one of the shareholders in Unocal (D), the board of directors of Unocal (D) determined that the takeover was not in the best interests of the corporation and should be fought. To do so, Unocal (D) made its own exchange offer, from which Mesa (P) was excluded. Mesa (P) sought and obtained a preliminary injunction from proceeding with the exchange offer unless it included Mesa (P). One of the main issues when the matter was heard via an interlocutory appeal was whether or not the action taken by the board was covered by the business judgment rule.

ISSUE: Will a court substitute its own judgment for that of the board of directors of a corporation that has decided to fight a takeover attempt by one of the shareholders in the absence of a showing that the decision was primarily based on some breach of the directors' duty?

HOLDING AND DECISION: (Moore, J.) No. There is no duty owed to a stockholder in a corporation that would preclude the directors from fighting a takeover bid by the stockholder if the board determines that the takeover is not in the best interests of the corporation. If such a decision is made, the court will not substitute its judgment for that of the board unless it is shown by a preponderance of the evidence that the directors' decision was primarily based on perpetuating themselves in office or some other breach of fiduciary duty, such as fraud, overreaching, lack of good faith, or being uninformed. No such showing was made here. Reversed.

▶ ANALYSIS

The business judgment rule protects only those actions by directors that are reasonable in relation to the threat posed. Among the considerations the courts have held are appropriate concerns of the board of directors in taking "defensive" actions are the impact on "constituencies" other than shareholders (such as creditors, customers, employees, and maybe even the community generally) and, also, the risk of nonconsummation.

■▬■

Quicknotes

BREACH OF FIDUCIARY DUTY The failure of a fiduciary to observe the standard of care exercised by professionals of similar education and experience.

BUSINESS JUDGMENT RULE Doctrine relieving corporate directors and/or officers from liability for decisions honestly and rationally made in the corporation's best interests.

INTERLOCUTORY APPEAL The appeal of an issue that does not resolve the disposition of the case, but is essential to a determination of the parties' legal rights.

■▬■

Moran v. Household International, Inc.

Board member (P) v. Holding company (D)

Del. Sup. Ct., 500 A.2d 1346 (1985).

NATURE OF CASE: Appeal from judgment permitting corporate antitakeover provisions.

FACT SUMMARY: Household International, Inc. (D) adopted a poison pill to discourage takeovers generally, rather than a specific takeover threat.

🏛 RULE OF LAW
A corporation may adopt a poison pill as a general antitakeover device, as opposed to a response to a particular threat.

FACTS: Moran (P) was a board member of Household International, Inc. (Household) (D), a diversified holding company. He was also the largest shareholder. Concerned with the general takeover climate of the times, Household's (D) board adopted a poison pill. Moran (P), who had made vague overtures about acquisition but had stated nothing specific, sued to enjoin enforcement of the poison-pill provisions. The Chancery Court upheld the provisions, and Moran (P) appealed.

ISSUE: May a corporation adopt a poison pill as a general antitakeover device, as opposed to a response to a particular threat?

HOLDING AND DECISION: (McNeilly, J.) Yes. A corporation may adopt a poison pill as a general antitakeover device, as opposed to a response to a particular threat. When corporate directors prove that they had reasonable grounds for believing that a danger to corporate policy and effectiveness existed, and that a defensive mechanism adopted was reasonable in relation to the threat posed, the deferential business judgment rule will be applied as the level of scrutiny to the directors' decision. Whether the response is to a particular threat or a general threat is of no great relevance. Here, the Chancery Court found that the majority of Household's (D) board was concerned about a two-tier tender offer takeover and that the defensive measures taken were reasonable. Based on these findings, the court's application of the business judgment rule was correct. Affirmed.

▷ ANALYSIS

The two-tier tender offer is a device calculated to intimidate shareholders into selling. Essentially, it consists of an offer at a high price until a controlling block of shares is acquired, with a lower price to be paid to late sellers. The idea is to force shareholders to sell under a threat of realizing smaller gains if they don't sell quickly.

Quicknotes

BUSINESS JUDGMENT RULE Doctrine relieving corporate directors and/or officers from liability for decisions honestly and rationally made in the corporation's best interests.

POISON PILL A tactic employed by a company, which is the target of a takeover attempt, to make the purchase of its shares less attractive to a potential buyer by requiring the issuance of a new series of shares to be redeemed at a substantial premium over their stated value if a party purchases a specified percentage of voting shares of the corporation.

Revlon, Inc. v. MacAndrews & Forbes Holdings, Inc.

Takeover target (D) v. Suitor (P)

Del. Sup. Ct., 506 A.2d 173 (1986).

NATURE OF CASE: Appeal of injunction prohibiting exercise of certain options.

FACT SUMMARY: Solely to prevent a hostile takeover, the board of Revlon, Inc. (D) granted Forstmann (D) certain lock-up options.

🏛 RULE OF LAW
A board of directors cannot grant lock-up options solely to prevent competitive bidding for a corporation.

FACTS: Pantry Pride (P) instituted a tender offer for Revlon, Inc. (D) stock at a price of $47.50. Revlon's (D) board took certain defensive measures. Pantry Pride (P) upped its offer to $53. At this point, Revlon's (D) directorate negotiated a leveraged buyout by Forstmann Little, Inc. (Forstmann) (D). When Pantry Pride's (P) offer had increased to $56.25 and Forstmann's (D) offer increased to $57.25, Revlon's (D) directors executed certain "lock-up" options, granting financial favors to Forstmann (D) if its buyout did not occur and effectively making acquisition by Pantry Pride (P) financially impracticable. Pantry Pride (P) brought an action seeking to enjoin the lock-ups. The Chancery Court issued such an injunction, and Revlon (D) appealed.

ISSUE: Can a board of directors grant lock-up options solely to prevent competitive bidding for a corporation?

HOLDING AND DECISION: (Moore, J.) No. A board of directors cannot grant lock-up options solely to prevent competitive bidding for a corporation. When it appears that an active bidding contest for a corporation is underway, the board of directors, whose primary duty is to the shareholders, is under an obligation to do what it can to maximize the sale price for the benefit of the stockholders. A lock-up is not necessarily illegal, and when it is done to prevent a takeover which would be detrimental to shareholders, it may be employed. Where, however, the lock-up has no effect other than to prevent competitive bidding, thus depressing the stock's price, the lock-up works not to benefit the shareholders, but rather it burdens them. Here, it has not been shown that the lock-ups were designed to do anything other than stifle competition, and this was improper. Affirmed.

▶ ANALYSIS

Pantry Pride's (P) original tender offer, $47.50, was considered by the board to be too low. This was verifiable, based on expert opinion. The court did not argue with the board's early defensive measures. These measures drove up the price of the stock. In doing this, the court felt, the board properly discharged its duties.

■═■

Quicknotes

INJUNCTION A court order requiring a person to do or prohibiting that person from doing a specific act.

LEVERAGED BUYOUT A transaction whereby corporate outsiders purchase the outstanding shares of a publicly held corporation mostly with borrowed funds.

LOCK-UP OPTION A defensive strategy to a takeover attempt whereby a target corporation sets aside a specified portion of the company's shares for purchase by a friendly investor.

■═■

Paramount Communications, Inc. v. Time, Inc.

Corporation (P) v. Corporation (D)

Del. Sup. Ct., 571 A.2d 1140 (1990).

NATURE OF CASE: Appeal from judgment upholding corporate antitakeover actions.

FACT SUMMARY: Paramount Communications (P) contended that antitakeover measures enacted by Time's (D) directors in response to its tender offer were invalid because Paramount's (P) per-share offer amount was fair market value.

🏛 RULE OF LAW
A board of directors' efforts to prevent a takeover via tender offer will not be invalid merely because the takeover offer constituted fair market value.

FACTS: Time, Inc.'s (D) board was considering an acquisition-merger with Warner Communications, Inc. (Warner). Time's (D) board had been considering a merger with an entertainment company for some time and decided that a merger with Warner presented the best prospects for long-term enrichment, as well as preservation of Time's (D) corporate climate. A deal was struck with Warner's management wherein Time (D) would acquire Warner, Warner's shareholders would receive 62% of the new company, and the two company's directorates would share control. A proxy statement urging shareholder approval was sent to Time's (D) shareholders. However, before the vote, Paramount Communications, Inc. (Paramount) (P) announced a $175 per-share tender offer for Time (D) stock, which was then selling for $126 per share. Time's (D) board concluded that: (1) the $48 per-share premium was insufficient consideration for control and (2) the Warner deal presented a better long-term opportunity for preservation of corporate climate than did Paramount's (P) proposed acquisition. Time (D) instituted certain antitakeover measures. Paramount (P) sued to enjoin the measures. The Chancery Court upheld the measures. Paramount (P) appealed.

ISSUE: Will a board of directors' efforts to prevent a takeover via tender offer be invalid merely because the offer constituted fair market value?

HOLDING AND DECISION: (Horsey, J.) No. A board of directors' efforts to prevent a takeover via tender offer will not be invalid merely because the offer constituted fair market value. A directorate is under a duty to maximize shareholder prices only when it is clear that a corporation is "on the block," that is, when a sale is a foregone conclusion. This was not the case here; Warner was not a suitor, even though its shareholders would eventually own a majority of the new corporation's stock. Consequently, Time (D) was not the object of a bidding war, which would have triggered a duty on the part of Time's (D) directors to maximize per-share value. This being so, the rule is that a directorate may

oppose a takeover if: (1) there are reasonable grounds for believing that a danger to corporate effectiveness and policy exist and (2) the defensive measures adopted are reasonable. Paramount (P) argues that since its tender offer was more valuable to shareholders than shares in the new corporation would have been, no danger to Time (D) existed. However, short-term dollar value is not the only factor here. Time's (D) board had decided, after long deliberation, that the Warner deal was in the best long-term interests of the corporation. The Chancery Court held that the Time (D) board had properly exercised its discretion in this regard. For these reasons, its defensive measures, which frustrated Paramount's (P) tender offer, were reasonable. Affirmed.

▶ ANALYSIS

When a corporation becomes a target in a bidding war, the discretion of the target's directorate becomes severely limited. All it can do is try to get the shareholders the best deal possible. Ironically, Paramount (P) itself became the subject of such a bidding war in its highly publicized 1994 takeover by Viacom, Inc., after a long bidding war with QVC.

■═■

Quicknotes

TENDER OFFER An offer made by one corporation to the shareholders of a target corporation to purchase their shares subject to number, time, and price specifications.

■═■

Paramount Communications, Inc. v. QVC Network, Inc.

Corporation (D) v. Corporation (P)

Del. Sup. Ct., 637 A.2d 34 (1994).

NATURE OF CASE: Appellate review of preliminary injunction.

FACT SUMMARY: The board of Paramount Communications, Inc. (Paramount) (D) approved unusually restrictive contractual provisions to prevent unsolicited tender offers from interfering with their intention to transfer control of Paramount (D) to Viacom, Inc.

🏛 RULE OF LAW

(1) A change of corporate control or a breakup of the corporation subjects directors to enhanced scrutiny and requires them to pursue a transaction that will produce the best value for stockholders.

(2) A board of directors breaches its fiduciary duty if it contractually restricts its right to consider competing merger bids.

FACTS: Paramount Communications, Inc. (Paramount) (D) is a Delaware corporation that had over 100 million shares outstanding as of early 1993. Viacom is a Delaware corporation that is controlled by Sumner Redstone. QVC (P) is a Delaware corporation with several large stockholders. In the late 1980s, Paramount (D) began exploring acquisition of or merger with, companies in the entertainment industry. In April, 1993, Paramount (D) met with Viacom to discuss a merger. The discussions broke down, but reopened when Davis, chairman of Paramount (D), learned of QVC's (P) possible interest in Paramount. On September 12, 1993, the Paramount (D) board unanimously approved the original merger agreement whereby Paramount (D) would merge into Viacom. The Paramount (D) shareholders were to receive primarily nonvoting shares in the new company. Additionally, the merger agreement included numerous provisions pertaining to Paramount's (D) activities with other potential bidders. First, under the no-shop provision, the Paramount (D) board would not engage in any way with a competing transaction unless: (1) a third party makes an unsolicited proposal not subject to any material financing contingencies; and (2) the Paramount (D) board determines that negotiations with the third party are necessary for the Paramount (D) board to comply with its fiduciary duties. Second, under the termination fee provision, Viacom would receive a $100 million fee if a competing transaction was responsible for a termination of the original merger agreement, a recommendation by the board of Paramount (D) of a competing transaction ended the negotiations, or the stockholders of Paramount (D) did not approve the merger. The third, and most significant provision, was the stock option agreement. The provision gave Viacom the option to purchase

19.9% of Paramount's (D) outstanding common stock for $69.14 per share if any of the termination fee triggering events occurred. The payment clause was not capped at a maximum dollar value. On September 20, 1993, QVC (P) sent a merger proposal letter to Davis at Paramount (D), offering $80 per share and later publicly announced an $80 cash tender offer. On November 6, 1993, Viacom unilaterally raised its tender offer price to $85 per share. QVC (P) responded by upping its offer to $90 per share. At its November 15 meeting, the Paramount (D) board determined that the QVC (P) offer was not in the best interest of the shareholders. QVC (P) filed suit to preliminarily enjoin the defensive measures of the original and amended agreements promulgated by the Paramount (D) board. The Court of Chancery's preliminary injunction was then heard in an expedited interlocutory appeal.

ISSUE:

(1) Are both a change of corporate control and a breakup of the corporation required before directors are subject to enhanced scrutiny and required to pursue a transaction that will produce the best value for stockholders?

(2) Has a board of directors breached its fiduciary duty if it contractually restricts its right to consider competing merger bids?

HOLDING AND DECISION: (Veasey, C.J.)

(1) No. Either a change of corporate control or a breakup of the corporation will subject directors to enhanced scrutiny and require them to pursue a transaction that will produce the best value for stockholders. In general, the board of directors in a corporation is given broad discretion to run the corporation. However, when the board undertakes actions that strike at the heart of the corporate entity, certain safeguards to protect the shareholders are activated. In situations where the shareholders' power is substantially changed, such as a sale of control of the corporation to another entity, or a threatened loss of majority status of existing shareholders, board action is subject to enhanced scrutiny. A judicial determination must be made as to whether the board's decision-making process was reasonable, and whether the board's actions were reasonable given the existing circumstances. By selling a controlling interest in Paramount (D) to Viacom, the majority shareholders in Paramount (D) would lose the ability to guide the corporation through the selection of directors. The very contemplation of a change in corporate control is a significant action. Therefore, the fiduciary duties of the directors require that they endeavor to assure that the shareholders receive the greatest possible value for their

Continued on next page.

interests. Enhanced judicial review is appropriate when either a change of corporate control or a corporate break-up is contemplated.

(2) Yes. A board of directors has breached its fiduciary duty if it contractually restricts its right to consider competing merger bids. In this case, the board of Paramount (D) is subject to enhanced judicial scrutiny by its consideration of a change in corporate control. Solicitation of competing bids for the corporation is a reasonable method to ensure that shareholder interests are properly valued. In this case, the Paramount (D) board entered into highly restrictive contracts which prevented it from considering other offers. The board had several meetings at which the value of the QVC (P) offers could have been explored in detail. Although the board of Paramount (D) suggested that the merger with Viacom met their long-term strategic plans more effectively, this argument overlooks the fact that the board was essentially giving control of the corporation to one individual. Thus, after the merger, the strategic goals of the Paramount (D) board would become highly moot. The disparity between the competing offers could have given the board tremendous negotiation leverage had it permitted itself to consider it. The board was under a duty to inform itself of all realistic options that might maximize the position of the shareholders. The Paramount (D) board failed in its fiduciary duties. Affirmed and remanded for further proceedings.

▶ *ANALYSIS*

After *Paramount Communications, Inc. v. QVC Network, Inc.*, stock option lockups are seen as being legally too risky. Termination fees are still considered acceptable as a price for canceling a major negotiation. The reasonableness of different termination fee sizes has not yet been tested clearly.

■■■

Quicknotes

FIDUCIARY DUTY A legal obligation to act for the benefit of another, including subordinating one's personal interests to that of the other person.

INTERLOCUTORY APPEAL The appeal of an issue that does not resolve the disposition of the case, but is essential to a determination of the parties' legal rights.

PRELIMINARY INJUNCTION A judicial mandate issued to require or restrain a party from certain conduct; used to preserve a trial's subject matter or to prevent threatened injury.

TENDER OFFER An offer made by one corporation to the shareholders of a target corporation to purchase their shares subject to number, time, and price specifications.

■■■

Schnell v. Chris-Craft Industries, Inc.

Shareholder (P) v. Corporation (D)

Del. Sup. Ct., 285 A.2d 437 (1971).

NATURE OF CASE: Appeal from denial of injunctive relief to prevent change in date of annual meeting.

FACT SUMMARY: Chris-Craft (D) directors advanced the annual stockholder meeting date to thwart shareholder efforts to change management.

RULE OF LAW
Advancement of an annual stockholder meeting date by directors for improper purposes is voidable.

FACTS: Schnell (P) served on a stockholder committee that sought to elect new directors for Chris-Craft Industries, Inc. (Chris-Craft) (D) because of the company's poor financial performance. On October 18, 1971, the Chris-Craft (D) board of directors advanced the annual stockholder meeting date from the second Tuesday of January, 1972, to December 8, 1971, by changing the corporate bylaws. Chris-Craft (D) asserted that the advanced annual meeting date was for valid business purposes as a pre-Christmas meeting date allowed for better mail delivery of proxies. Schnell (P) contended that Chris-Craft (D) directors changed the meeting date to impede his efforts to elect new directors as evidenced by Chris-Craft's (D) failure to provide shareholder lists. Schnell (P) sought injunctive relief to reinstate the original meeting date. The trial court found that Chris-Craft (D) directors were using the law for improper purposes, but denied Schnell's (P) request for injunctive relief due to laches. Schnell (P) appealed.

ISSUE: Is advancement of an annual meeting date by directors for improper purposes voidable?

HOLDING AND DECISION: (Herrmann, J.) Yes. Advancement of an annual meeting date by directors for improper purposes is voidable. Corporate directors may not improperly utilize the Delaware law and the corporate machinery to perpetuate themselves in office. When bylaws designate an annual meeting date, it is expected that those mounting a proxy contest will gear their campaign for that date. Accordingly, the original annual shareholder meeting date is reinstated. Reversed and remanded.

DISSENT: (Wolcott, C.J.) The application for injunctive relief came too late and should be denied.

ANALYSIS

The Model Business Corporations Act § 7.01 provides directors with flexibility to hold an annual meeting at a stated time or fixed in accordance with the bylaws. Directors violate the duty of loyalty when they utilize corporate processes or legal procedures to maintain their management team without regard to the best interests of shareholders.

Quicknotes

DUTY OF LOYALTY A director's duty to refrain from self-dealing or to take a position that is adverse to the corporation's best interests.

INJUNCTION A court order requiring a person to do or prohibiting that person from doing a specific act.

LACHES An equitable defense against the enforcement of rights that have been neglected for a long period of time.

MM Companies, Inc. v. Liquid Audio, Inc.

Shareholders (P) v. Corporation (D)

Del. Sup. Ct., 813 A.2d 1118 (2003).

NATURE OF CASE: Appeal by shareholders from the denial of their request for injunctive relief after corporation's incumbent board of directors took a defensive action to expand the board.

FACT SUMMARY: The incumbent board of directors of Liquid Audio, Inc. (D) took a defensive action to expand the board from five members to seven. The shareholders of MM Companies, Inc. (P) sought injunctive relief to set aside the expansion, contending that the purpose of Liquid Audio's (D) board's expansion was to impede the shareholders in electing successor directors.

🏛 RULE OF LAW
A corporation's incumbent board of directors has the burden of demonstrating a compelling justification for expanding the size of its membership when the expansion is a defensive action taken for the primary purposes of interfering with, and impeding, the effectiveness of the shareholder franchise in electing successor directors.

FACTS: For over a year, MM Companies, Inc. (MM) (P) had sought control of Liquid Audio, Inc. (Liquid Audio) (D). MM (P) sent a letter to the Liquid Audio board of directors indicating its willingness to acquire the company at approximately $3 per share. Liquid Audio's (D) board rejected MM's (P) offer as inadequate. Liquid Audio's (D) bylaws provided for a staggered board of directors that was divided into three classes. Only one class of directors was up for election in any given year. The effect was to prevent an insurgent from obtaining control of the company in under two years. MM (P) sought injunctive relief against the defensive action taken by the board of directors of Liquid Audio (D) to expand from five to seven members and the purported effects that expansion might have on Liquid Audio's (D) forthcoming 2002 annual meeting. MM (P) argued that the decision of Liquid Audio's (D) directors to expand the board violated established legal principles. The Chancery Court denied the injunctive relief, permitting the incumbent board of directors to adopt the defensive measures which changed the size and composition of the board's membership. MM (P) appealed.

ISSUE: Does a corporation's incumbent board of directors have the burden of demonstrating a compelling justification for expanding the size of its membership when the expansion is a defensive action taken for the primary purposes of interfering with, and impeding, the effectiveness of the shareholder franchise in electing successor directors?

HOLDING AND DECISION: (Holland, J.) Yes. A corporation's incumbent board of directors has the burden of demonstrating a compelling justification for expanding the size of its membership when the expansion is a defensive action taken for the primary purposes of interfering with, and impeding, the effectiveness of the shareholder franchise in electing successor directors. Furthermore, the defensive actions need not actually prevent the shareholders from attaining success in seating one or more nominees in a contested election for directors, and the election contest need not involve a challenge for outright control of the board to place the burden of demonstrating a compelling justification for the action on the board. Rather, the defensive actions need only be taken for the primary purpose of interfering with, or impeding, the effectiveness of the stockholder vote in a contested election for directors. Here, the board of directors of Liquid Audio (D) did not meet its burden. The defensive measure taken by Liquid Audio's (D) incumbent board to expand its membership from five to seven was not proportionate and reasonable in relation to the threat posed by the shareholder franchise, who sought to place two members on the board. The board utilized its otherwise valid powers to expand the size and composition of the board for the primary purpose of impeding, and interfering with, the efforts of the shareholders' power to effectively exercise their voting rights in a contested election for directors. Such action compromised the essential role of corporate democracy in maintaining the proper allocation of power between the shareholders and the board. Inequitable action by a board of directors does not become permissible simply because it is legally possible. Reversed.

▶ ANALYSIS

In the *MM Companies* case, the court noted that maintaining a proper balance in the allocation of power between the stockholders' right to elect directors and the board of directors' right to manage the corporation is dependent upon the stockholders' unimpeded right to vote effectively in an election of directors. If the stockholders are not satisfied with the management or actions of their elected representatives on the board of directors, the power of corporate democracy is available to the stockholders to replace the incumbent directors when they stand for re-election. Consequently, courts will not allow the wrongful subversion of corporate democracy by manipulation of the corporate machinery or by machinations under the cloak of law. Accordingly, careful

Continued on next page.

judicial scrutiny will be given a situation in which the right to vote for the election of successor directors has been effectively frustrated and denied, as it was in the *MM Companies* case.

■══■

Quicknotes

INJUNCTIVE RELIEF A court order issued as a remedy, requiring a person to do, or prohibiting that person from doing, a specific act.

■══■

Carmody v. Toll Brothers, Inc.

Shareholder (P) v. Corporation (D)

Del. Ct. Ch., 723 A.2d 1180 (1998).

NATURE OF CASE: Pending defendant's motion to dismiss suit alleging that a "dead hand" provision in a poison pill rights plan is invalid.

FACT SUMMARY: Carmody (P) alleged that the dead hand provision in a poison pill rights plan was invalid as ultra vires or as a breach of fiduciary duty.

🏛 RULE OF LAW

A defensive measure is unreasonable if it is either coercive or preclusive and therefore unreasonable in relation to the threat posed.

FACTS: Toll Brothers (D), a Delaware corporation that designed and marketed homes in thirteen states, adopted a rights plan to protect its shareholders from coercive or unfair tactics to gain control of the company by placing them in a position of having to accept or reject an unsolicited offer without adequate time to consider the offer. The rights plan would become exercisable when a tender offer was commenced to obtain 15% or more of Toll Brothers (D) stock. The dilutive mechanism of the rights plan would be triggered and remain in effect until 2007. The "flip in" feature of the rights plan would massively dilute the value of the holdings of the unwanted acquiror. In effect the dead hand provision prevented any directors of Toll Brothers (D), except those that were in office as of the date of the rights plan adoption, from redeeming the rights until they expired in 2007. The complaint alleged that the rights plan provision made an unsolicited offer for the company more unlikely and also deprived the shareholders of any practical choice except to vote for the incumbent directors. Carmody (P), a shareholder, alleged that the dead hand provision of a poison pill rights plan designed to prevent unwanted takeover attempts was invalid as ultra vires, or as a breach of fiduciary duty, or both.

ISSUE: Is a defensive measure unreasonable if it is either coercive or preclusive, and therefore unreasonable in relation to the threat posed?

HOLDING AND DECISION: (Jacobs, V. Chan.) Yes. A defensive measure is unreasonable if it is either coercive or preclusive, and therefore unreasonable in relation to the threat posed. The board has the burden to satisfy the court that it had reasonable grounds for believing that a danger to corporate policy and effectiveness existed. A defensive measure is preclusive if it makes bidder's ability to wage a successful proxy contest and gain control either mathematically impossible or realistically unattainable. The complaint alleged that the dead hand provision disenfranchised shareholders by coercively influencing them to vote for incumbent directors or their designees if shareholders wanted to be represented by a board entitled to exercise its full statutory prerogatives. That was sufficient to satisfy the claim that the dead hand provision was coercive. The complaint stated claims under Delaware law upon which relief could be granted. Toll Brothers' (D) motion to dismiss is denied.

▶ ANALYSIS

The court in this case also found that the rights plan violated Delaware corporate law. The rights plan conferred the power to redeem the pill only upon some, but not all, of the directors. The state statute clearly states that if one category or group of directors is given distinctive voting rights not shared by the other directors, those distinctive rights must be set forth in the certificate of incorporation. In this case they were not so set forth, nor was the rights plan's allocation of voting rights found anywhere in the Toll Brothers (D) certificate of incorporation. Hence the dead hand feature of the rights plan was ultra vires and also statutorily invalid under Delaware law.

■■■

Quicknotes

FIDUCIARY DUTY A legal obligation to act for the benefit of another, including subordinating one's personal interests to that of the other person.

POISON PILL A tactic employed by a company, which is the target of a takeover attempt, to make the purchase of its shares less attractive to a potential buyer by requiring the issuance of a new series of shares to be redeemed at a substantial premium over their stated value if a party purchases a specified percentage of voting shares of the corporation.

ULTRA VIRES An act undertaken by a corporation that is beyond the scope of its authority pursuant to law or its articles of incorporation.

■■■

Omnicare, Inc. v. NCS Healthcare, Inc.

Acquiring corporation (P) v. Target corporation (D)

Del. Sup. Ct., 818 A.2d 914 (2003) (*en banc*).

NATURE OF CASE: Appeal from decision holding that lockup deal protection measures were reasonable.

FACT SUMMARY: Omnicare, Inc. (Omnicare) (P) sought to acquire NCS Healthcare, Inc. (NCS) (D). Genesis Health Ventures, Inc. (Genesis) had made a competing bid for NCS (D) that the NCS board had originally recommended, but the NCS board withdrew its recommendation and instead recommended that stockholders accept the Omnicare (P) offer, which was worth more than twice the Genesis offer. However, the agreement between Genesis and NCS (D) contained a provision that the agreement be placed before the NCS (D) shareholders for a vote, even if the board no longer recommended it. There was also no fiduciary out clause in the agreement. Pursuant to voting agreements, two NCS shareholders who held a majority of the voting power agreed unconditionally to vote all their shares in favor of the Genesis merger, thus assuring that the Genesis transaction would prevail. Omnicare (P) challenged the defensive measures that were part of the Genesis transaction.

⚖ RULE OF LAW
Lock-up deal protection devices, that when operating in concert, are coercive and preclusive, invalid and unenforceable in the absence of a fiduciary out clause.

FACTS: In late 1999, NCS Healthcare, Inc. (NCS) (D) began to experience serious liquidity problems that led to a precipitous decline in the market value of its stock. As a result, it began to explore strategic alternatives to address its situation. In the summer of 2001, Omnicare, Inc. (Omnicare) (P), a NCS (D) competitor, made a series of offers to acquire NCS's (D) assets in a bankruptcy sale—at less than face value of NCS's (D) outstanding debts, and with no recovery for NCS stockholders. NCS (D) rejected Omnicare's (P) offers. By early 2002, NCS's (D) financial condition was improving, and the NCS board began to believe it might be able to realize some value for its shareholders. An Ad Hoc Committee of NCS (D) creditors contacted Genesis Health Ventures, Inc. (Genesis), an Omnicare (P) competitor, and Genesis expressed interest in bidding on NCS (D). Genesis made it clear that it did not want to be a "stalking horse" for NCS (D) and demanded an exclusivity agreement. After Genesis steadily increased its offers, NCS (D) granted Genesis the exclusivity it sought. The NCS board consisted of Outcalt and Shaw, who together controlled more than 65% of voting power in NCS (D), and Sells and Osborne, both of whom were disinterested, outside directors. In its negotiations, Genesis sought an agreement that would require, as permitted by Delaware General Corporation Law (DGCL) § 251(c), NCS (D) to submit the merger to NCS stockholders regardless of whether the NCS Board recommended the merger; an

agreement by Outcalt and Shaw to vote their NCS stock in favor of the merger; and omission of any effective fiduciary out clause from the agreement. Meanwhile, Omnicare (P) learned that NCS (D) was negotiating with Genesis and made a proposed bid for a transaction in which all of NCS's (D) debt would be paid off and NCS stockholders would receive greater value than offered by Genesis. This offer was conditioned on satisfactory completion of due diligence. Fearing that Genesis might abandon its offer, NCS (D) refused to negotiate with Omnicare (P), but used Omnicare's (P) proposal to negotiate for improved terms with Genesis, which Genesis provided. However, in exchange, Genesis conditioned its offer on approval the next day. The NCS board gave such approval to the merger, in which NCS stockholders would receive Genesis stock and all NCS (D) debt would be paid off. The merger transaction included the provisions that Genesis had sought during negotiations, as well as the voting agreements with Outcalt and Shaw. Thus, the combined terms of the merger agreement and voting agreement guaranteed that the transaction proposed by Genesis would be approved by the NCS stockholders. Omnicare (P) filed suit to enjoin the merger and then launched a tender offer for all NCS (D) stock at a value of more than twice the then current market value of the shares to be received in the Genesis transaction. Otherwise, its offer equaled that of Genesis. Several months later, but before the NCS stockholders were to vote on the Genesis merger, as a result of Omnicare (P) irrevocably committing itself to its offer, the NCS board withdrew its recommendation of the Genesis merger and recommended, instead, that NCS shareholders vote for the Omnicare (P) merger because it was a superior proposal. The Chancery Court ruled that the voting agreements with Outcalt and Shaw, combined with the provision requiring a stockholder vote regardless of board recommendation, constituted defensive measures, but found that, under the enhanced judicial scrutiny standard of *Unocal Corp. v. Mesa Petroleum Co.*, 493 A.2d 946 (Del. 1985), these measures were reasonable. The Delaware Supreme Court granted review.

ISSUE: Are lock-up deal protection devices, that when operating in concert, coercive and preclusive, invalid and unenforceable in the absence of a fiduciary out clause?

HOLDING AND DECISION: (Holland, J.) Yes. Lock-up deal protection devices, that when operating in concert, are coercive and preclusive, invalid and unenforceable in the absence of a fiduciary out clause. The Chancery Court concluded that because the Genesis transaction did not result in a change of control, the transaction would be reviewed under the business judgment rule standard. Under this standard, the Chancery Court concluded that the NCS

Continued on next page.

board had not breached its duty of care in approving the transaction. The Chancery Court's decision to use the business judgment rule standard, rather than enhanced scrutiny, is not outcome-determinative and this court will assume that the NCS board exercised due care when it approved the Genesis transaction. However, as to the defensive measures, enhanced scrutiny is required because of the inherent potential conflict of interest between a board's interest in protecting a merger transaction it has approved and the shareholders' statutory right to make the final decision to either approve or not approve a merger. This requires a threshold determination that the board approved defensive measures comport with the directors' fiduciary duties. In applying enhanced judicial scrutiny to defensive measures designed to protect a merger agreement, a court must first determine that those measures are not preclusive or coercive before its focus shifts to a "range of reasonableness" proportionality determination. When the focus shifts to the range of reasonableness, *Unocal* requires that any devices must be proportionate to the perceived threat to the corporation and its stockholders if the merger transaction is not consummated. Here, the voting agreements were inextricably intertwined with the defensive aspects of the Genesis merger agreement, and, under *Unocal*, the defensive measures require special scrutiny. Under such scrutiny, these measures were neither reasonable nor proportionate to the threat NCS (D) perceived from the potential loss of the Genesis transaction. The threat identified by NCS (D) was the possibility of losing the Genesis offer and being left with no comparable alternative transaction. The second part of the *Unocal* analysis requires the NCS directors to demonstrate that their defensive response was reasonable in response to the threat posed. This inquiry itself involves a two-step analysis. The NCS directors must first establish that the deal protection devices adopted in response to the threat were not "coercive" or "preclusive," and then must demonstrate that their response was within a "range of reasonable responses" to the threat perceived. Here, the defensive measures were both preclusive and coercive, and, therefore, draconian and impermissible. That is because any stockholder vote would be "robbed of its effectiveness" by the impermissible coercion that predetermined the outcome of the merger without regard to the merits of the Genesis transaction at the time the vote was scheduled to take place. They were also preclusive because they accomplished a fait accompli. Accordingly, the defensive measures are unenforceable. They are alternatively unenforceable because the merger agreement completely prevented the board from discharging its fiduciary responsibilities to the minority stockholders when Omnicare (P) presented its superior transaction. Here, the NCS board could not abdicate its fiduciary duties to the minority by leaving it to the stockholders alone to approve or disapprove the merger because Outcalt and Shaw had combined to establish a majority of the voting power that made the outcome of the stockholder vote a foregone conclusion. Thus, the NCS board did not have authority to accede to the Genesis demand for an absolute "lock-up." Instead, it was required to

negotiate a fiduciary out clause to protect the NCS shareholders if the Genesis transaction became an inferior offer. Therefore, the defensive measures—the voting agreements and the provision requiring a shareholder vote regardless of board recommendation—when combined to operate in concert in the absence of an effective fiduciary out clause are invalid and unenforceable.

DISSENT: (Veasey, C.J.) The NCS board's actions should have been evaluated based on the circumstances present at the time the Genesis merger agreement was entered into—before the emergence of a subsequent transaction offering greater value to the stockholders. The lock-ups were reached at the conclusion of a lengthy search and intense negotiation process in the context of insolvency, at a time when Genesis was the only viable bidder. Under these facts, the NCS board's action before the emergence of the Omnicare (P) offer reflected the actions of "a quintessential, disinterested, and informed board" made in good faith, and was within the bounds of its fiduciary duties and should be upheld. Moreover, situations arise where business realities demand a lock-up so that wealth enhancing transactions may go forward. Accordingly, any bright-line rule prohibiting lock-ups, such as the one put forth by the majority, could, in circumstances such as those faced by the NCS board, chill otherwise permissible conduct. Here, the deal protection measures were not preclusive or coercive in the context of what they were intended for. They were not adopted to fend off a hostile takeover, but were adopted so that Genesis—the "only game in town"—would save NCS (D), its creditors, and stockholders. Still, here there was no meaningful minority stockholder vote to coerce, given Outcalt and Shaw's majority position, so that the "preclusive" label has no application. Thus, giving Genesis an absolute lock-up under the circumstances, by agreeing to omit a fiduciary out clause, was not a per se violation of fiduciary duty. Hopefully, the rule announced by the majority will be interpreted narrowly and will be seen as sui generis.

▶ ANALYSIS

One of the primary troubling aspects of the majority opinion, as voiced by the dissent, is the majority's suggestion that it can make a *Unocal* determination after-the-fact with a view to the superiority of a competing proposal that may subsequently emerge. Many commentators agree with the dissent that the lock-ups in this case should not have been reviewed in a vacuum. In a separate dissent, Justice Steele argued that when a board agrees rationally, in good faith, without conflict and with reasonable care to include provisions in a contract to preserve a deal in the absence of a better one, their business judgment should not be second-guessed in order to invalidate or declare unenforceable an otherwise valid merger agreement. Given the tension between the majority's and

Continued on next page.

dissenters' positions, the full impact of the court's decision will need to await further judicial development.

■▬■

Quicknotes

FIDUCIARY DUTY   A legal obligation to act for the benefit of another, including subordinating one's personal interests to that of the other person.

LOCK-UP OPTION   A defensive strategy to a takeover attempt whereby a target corporation sets aside a specified portion of the company's shares for purchase by a friendly investor.

SUI GENERIS   Peculiar to its own type or class.

■▬■

Amanda Acquisition Corp. v. Universal Foods Corp.

Suitor (P) v. Target corporation (D)

877 F.2d 496 (7th Cir.), *cert. denied* 493 U.S. 955 (1989).

NATURE OF CASE: Appeal from judicial declaration as to the validity of a state antitakeover statute.

FACT SUMMARY: Amanda Acquisition Corp.'s (P) tender offer for Universal Foods Corp.'s (D) stock was conditional on a judicial declaration that Wisconsin's antitakeover statute was invalid since it required a three-year wait for any merger to occur.

🏛 RULE OF LAW
Skepticism about the wisdom of a state's law does not lead to the conclusion that the law is beyond the state's power.

FACTS: Amanda Acquisition Corp. (Amanda) (P) made a tender offer for the stock of Universal Food Corp (Universal) (D). However, Wisconsin had a moratorium law that required a three-year wait for any merger to occur, unless the target's board consented to the takeover before the bidder obtained 10% of the target's stock. Even when the time was up, the bidder needed the approval of a majority of the remaining investors, without any provision disqualifying shares still held by the managers who resisted the transaction. Amanda's (P) financing was contingent on a prompt merger with Universal (D), so the offer was conditioned on a judicial declaration that Wisconsin's law was invalid. The district court found that the statute effectively eliminated hostile leveraged buyouts. This appeal followed.

ISSUE: Does skepticism about the wisdom of a state's law lead to the conclusion that the law is beyond the state's power?

HOLDING AND DECISION: (Easterbrook, J.) No. Skepticism about the wisdom of a state's law does not lead to the conclusion that the law is beyond the state's power. A law like Wisconsin's does not add options to firms that would like to give more discretion to their managers but instead destroys the possibility of divergent choices. Wisconsin's law applies even when the investors prefer to leave their managers under the gun, to allow the market full sway. This court believes that such antitakeover legislation injures shareholders. However, though it may be economically unwise, it is nevertheless within the state's power to enact.

▶ ANALYSIS

If managers are not maximizing a firm's value, a bidder that believes it can realize more of the firm's value will make investors a higher offer. The prospect of monitoring by would-be bidders, and an occasional bid at a premium, induces managers to run corporations more efficiently and

replaces them if they will not. The court declared that a statute that precludes investors from receiving or accepting a premium offer makes them worse off and makes the economy worse off too because the higher bid reflects the better use to which the bidder can put the target's assets.

■■■

Quicknotes

LEVERAGED BUYOUT A transaction whereby corporate outsiders purchase the outstanding shares of a publicly held corporation mostly with borrowed funds.

MORATORIUM LAW Law suspending legal remedies or proceedings.

TENDER OFFER An offer made by one corporation to the shareholders of a target corporation to purchase their shares subject to number, time, and price specifications.

■■■

Disclosure and Corporate Governance

Quick Reference Rules of Law

In the Matter of Informix Corp.

Securities and Exchange Commission

Exchange Act Release #34-42326, January 11, 2000.
http://www.sec.gov/litigation/admin/34-42326.htm

NATURE OF CASE: Offer of settlement to the SEC.

FACT SUMMARY: Following the failure by Informix Corporation (D) to maintain a system of internal accounting to enable it to prepare proper financial statements, thus violating federal securities laws, Informix (D) submitted an Offer of Settlement that the Securities and Exchange Commission (SEC) accepted.

🏛 RULE OF LAW
A company violates SEC requirements if it fails to maintain a system of internal accounting controls that is sufficient to enable it to prepare financial statements in conformity with generally accepted accounting practices.

FACTS: In November 1997, Informix Corporation (Informix) (D) restated its financial statements for fiscal years 1994 through 1996 and the fiscal quarter ended March 30, 1997. During the period covered by the restatements, former employees of Informix (D), including salespersons, members of management, and others engaged in a variety of fraudulent and other practices that inflated annual and quarterly revenues and earnings in violation of generally accepted accounting principles (GAAP). These practices included: (1) backdating license sale agreements; (2) entering into side agreements granting rights to refunds and other concessions to customers; (3) recognizing revenue on transactions with reseller customers that were not creditworthy; (4) recognizing amounts due under software maintenance agreements as software license revenues; and (5) recognizing revenue on disputed claims against customers. Revenue was recognized improperly. No disclosure of the fraudulent or other improper practices appeared in the Informix (D) filings with the Securities and Exchange Commission (SEC). The filings also omitted or misrepresented information concerning the extent to which revenues were derived from nonmonetary exchanges and the extent to which revenues were derived from transactions with resellers that had not yet resold software licenses to end-users. In a subsequent restatement process, Informix (D) and its auditors identified $114 million of accounting irregularities in 1995 and 1996 involving more than a hundred transactions. In anticipation of the institution of SEC enforcement proceedings, Informix (D) submitted an Offer of Settlement which the SEC accepted. The SEC then issued a cease and desist order.

ISSUE: Does a company violate SEC requirements if it fails to maintain a system of internal accounting controls

that is sufficient to enable it to prepare financial statements in conformity with generally accepted accounting practices?

HOLDING AND DECISION: [Judge not stated in casebook excerpt.] Yes. A company violates SEC requirements if it fails to maintain a system of internal accounting controls that is sufficient to enable it to prepare financial statements in conformity with GAAP. In this matter, through former members of management and others, Informix (D) engaged in an accounting fraud that lasted more than two years and resulted in the preparation of numerous materially false and misleading financial statements and other disclosures that were included in filings with the SEC and disseminated to investors. As this fraud was being uncovered certain of these individuals engaged in further fraudulent conduct that delayed the restatements of Informix's (D) financial statements. In addition, as a result of the conduct of former management and others, Informix (D) failed to maintain books, records, and accounts which, in reasonable detail, accurately and fairly reflected its transactions and dispositions of assets. It also failed to maintain a system of internal accounting controls sufficient to permit the preparation of financial statements in conformity with GAAP. The type of conduct that occurred, strikes at the heart of the financial reporting system established by the federal securities laws. Based on the foregoing, Informix (D) is ordered to cease and desist from committing or causing any future violations of the Securities Act.

▶ ANALYSIS

In *Informix*, the SEC made clear that complete and accurate financial reporting by public companies is of paramount importance to the disclosure system underlying the stability and efficient operation of capital markets. Investors need reliable financial information when making investment decisions. To achieve the objective of providing investors with complete and accurate financial information, it is essential that public companies maintain accurate books, records, and accounts and establish and maintain internal controls that serve to prevent and to detect fraudulent and other improper conduct. In addition, management, through its own conduct and through the policies and practices that it prescribes for others, must create an environment in which only the highest standards of integrity will be tolerated. The financial information that an issuer discloses should present completely and accurately the issuer's financial condition for the relevant reporting period. Without this information,

Continued on next page.

investors are deprived of the opportunity to make informed investment decisions.

■══■

Quicknotes

CEASE AND DESIST ORDER An order from a court or administrative agency prohibiting a person or business from continuing a particular course of conduct.

SECURITIES EXCHANGE ACT OF 1934 Federal statute regulating stock exchanges and trading and requiring the disclosure of certain information in relation to securities traded.

■══■

J.I. Case Co. v. Borak

Corporation (D) v. Shareholder (P)

377 U.S. 426 (1964).

NATURE OF CASE: Civil action brought by a shareholder against the corporation for violation of prohibitions against false and misleading proxy statements.

FACT SUMMARY: Borak (P) was a shareholder of J.I. Case Co. (D). The shareholders approved a merger of J.I. Case (D) with another corporation, and Borak (P) contended the proxy statements violated federal securities laws and sought private relief.

🏛 RULE OF LAW

Where a federal securities act has been violated, but no private right of action is specifically authorized or prohibited, a private civil action will lie, and the court is free to fashion an appropriate remedy.

FACTS: The management of J.I. Case Co. (D) submitted a proposal of merger to the shareholders for their approval. In connection with this proposal, management solicited shareholder proxies in support of the merger. Borak (P) contended that the proxy solicitations were false and misleading in violation of § 14(a) of the Securities Exchange Act, and he sought rescission of the consummated merger plus damages for himself and all other shareholders similarly situated and any other appropriate equitable relief. The trial court held that the federal statute authorized only declaratory relief, and any other remedies would have to be sought under state law. The applicable Wisconsin statute required the posting of security for expenses, which was set at $75,000 by the court. Borak (P) refused to post security, and all counts of the complaint were dismissed save the portion which would result in a judgment of declaratory relief. Borak (P) appealed, contending that the Securities Exchange Act authorized a private right of action by implication and that he was not limited to the state courts for other than declaratory relief.

ISSUE: May a shareholder seek rescission of a merger or damages for a violation of a federal regulation relating to proxy statements where no private right of action is specifically authorized nor private remedies specified?

HOLDING AND DECISION: (Clark, J.) Yes. The purpose of § 14(a) is to prevent management or others from obtaining authorization for corporate action through the use of false or misleading proxy solicitations. The Act, under which the rule was promulgated, authorized the Securities and Exchange Commission (SEC) to enact whatever rules and regulations are deemed necessary to protect both the public interest and interests of shareholders. The congressional mandate to protect the interests of the investors requires an available judicial remedy to enforce that protection. The SEC states that it is not equipped to probe the accuracy of all proxy statements submitted for registration. If the investors' interests are to be protected in the spirit of the congressional mandate, a private right of action for shareholders who believe they have been wronged must be afforded. Since the statute does not provide for specific types of relief, the court must determine for itself what remedies are appropriate to redress the alleged wrong. In this regard, any remedy which is available to a federal court can be utilized to provide relief for the plaintiff. To hold that the plaintiff is restricted to declaratory relief in federal courts, with any other relief to be pursued in a state court, could conceivably leave the plaintiff without an effective remedy. Once having obtained the federal declaration of his rights, the plaintiff might find that the state does not recognize the defendant's actions as unlawful. This would leave the plaintiff without a means to enforce his judicially declared rights. The case is remanded to the trial court for a hearing on the merits, with relief to be granted abiding the outcome.

▶ ANALYSIS

By completely removing state law from consideration in cases alleging violations of federal securities laws, the court relieved plaintiffs of a tremendous burden in many instances. A large number of jurisdictions have a requirement that the plaintiff post a security for expenses on behalf of the defendant. The posting of such security can be an onerous burden, particularly if the case involves complex issues that would result in prolonged litigation. Had Borak (P) been required to proceed under state law, he would have had to post $75,000. This type of burden might very well stop the plaintiff from proceeding with his case, no matter how meritorious. Further, the court's ruling greatly expands the remedies available to a plaintiff shareholder. Most state statutes limit a shareholder who dissents from a merger to a right of appraisal for his shares. The federal court could conceivably rescind the merger completely if that action was warranted. This decision greatly expanded the effectiveness of the federal securities regulations by providing a broad range of enforcement techniques.

■═■

Quicknotes

DECLARATORY RELIEF A judgment of the court establishing the rights of the parties.

Continued on next page.

EQUITABLE RELIEF   A remedy that is based upon principles of fairness as opposed to rules of law.

PROXY   A person authorized to act for another.

RESCISSION   The canceling of an agreement and the return of the parties to their positions prior to the formation of the contract.

TSC Industries, Inc. v. Northway, Inc.

Corporation (D) v. Corporation (P)

426 U.S. 438 (1976).

NATURE OF CASE: Appeal from summary judgment in favor of a shareholder challenging a proxy statement.

FACT SUMMARY: Northway, Inc. (P) claimed that a proxy solicitation issued prior to a merger of TSC Industries (D) with National Industries omitted material facts.

🏛 RULE OF LAW
An omitted fact is material if there is a substantial likelihood that a reasonable shareholder would consider it important in deciding how to vote.

FACTS: Prior to an anticipated merger of TSC Industries, Inc. (TSC) (D) with National Industries (National), a proxy statement was issued. After Northway, Inc. (P) approved a plan to liquidate TSC (D), Northway (P) challenged the solicitation which led to shareholder approval of the merger, claiming that it omitted material facts related to National's control over TSC (D) and the attractiveness of the terms of the proposal to TSC (D) stockholders. The district court granted summary judgment in favor of Northway (P), and the court of appeals affirmed, concluding that material facts include "all facts which a reasonable shareholder might consider important." TSC (D) appealed.

ISSUE: Is an omitted fact material if there is a substantial likelihood that a reasonable shareholder would consider it important in deciding how to vote?

HOLDING AND DECISION: (Marshall, J.) Yes. An omitted fact is material if there is a substantial likelihood that a reasonable shareholder would consider it important in deciding how to vote. The purpose of SEC Rule 14a-9 is not merely to ensure by judicial means that the transaction is fair and otherwise adequate but to ensure disclosures by corporate management in order to enable the shareholders to make an informed choice. However, the disclosure policy embodied in the proxy regulations is not without limit. Some information is of such dubious significance that insistence on its disclosure may accomplish more harm than good. Management's fear of exposing itself to substantial liability if the standard governing materiality is unnecessarily low may cause it simply to bury the shareholders in an avalanche of trivial information. Only if the established omissions are so obviously important to an investor that reasonable minds cannot differ on the question of materiality is the ultimate issue of materiality appropriately resolved as a matter of law by summary judgment. Reversed.

▶ **ANALYSIS**

The formulation of the "might" test of materiality applied by the court of appeals has been explicitly rejected by at least two courts as setting too low a threshold for the imposition of liability under SEC Rule 14a-9. See *Gerstle v. Gamble-Skogmo, Inc.*, 478 F.2d 1281 (1973), and *Smallwood v. Pearl Brewing Co.*, 489 F.2d 579 (1974). The Court also noted that doubts as to the critical nature of information misstated or omitted should be resolved in favor of the shareholders whom the statue is designed to protect, particularly in view of the prophylactic purpose of the Rule and the fact that the content of the proxy statement is within management's control.

■▬■

Quicknotes

MATERIAL FACT A fact without the existence of which a contract would not have been entered.

PROXY STATEMENT A statement containing specified information by the Securities and Exchange Commission in order to provide shareholders with adequate information upon which to make an informed decision regarding the solicitation of their proxies.

SUMMARY JUDGMENT Judgment rendered by a court in response to a motion by one of the parties, claiming that the lack of a question of material fact in respect to an issue warrants disposition of the issue without consideration by the jury.

■▬■

Virginia Bankshares, Inc. v. Sandberg

Corporation (D) v. Minority shareholder (P)

501 U.S. 1083 (1991).

NATURE OF CASE: Appeal from affirmance of a jury award of damages in a minority shareholder suit.

FACT SUMMARY: After a freeze-out merger in which minority shareholders lost their interest, Sandberg (P), a minority shareholder, brought suit, alleging that the directors had not believed that the price offered was high or that the terms of the merger were fair but had recommended the merger in order to remain on the board.

🏛 RULE OF LAW
Proof of mere disbelief or belief undisclosed in a proxy solicitation, standing alone, is insufficient to impose liability under federal law.

FACTS: In a freeze-out merger, the First American Bank of Virginia (Bank) eventually merged into Virginia Bankshares, Inc. (VBI) (D). VBI's (D) parent company hired an investment banking firm to give an opinion as to the appropriate price for shares of the Bank's minority holders, who would lose their interest as a result of the merger. The investment banking firm's opinion that $42 a share would be a fair price was based on market quotations and unverified information from VBI's (D) parent company. The merger proposal was approved at that price, and the directors solicited proxies for voting on the proposal. The solicitation stated the plan had been approved because of its opportunity for the minority shareholders to achieve a high value, which the directors also described as a fair price for the minority stock. Sandberg (P) brought this action, alleging that the directors had not believed that the price was high or that the terms of the merger were fair but had recommended the merger because they believed they had to in order to remain on the board. The jury ruled for Sandberg (P) finding that she would have received $60 if her stock had been properly valued. The court of appeals affirmed, and VBI (D) appealed.

ISSUE: Is proof of mere disbelief or belief undisclosed in a proxy solicitation, standing alone, insufficient to impose liability under federal law?

HOLDING AND DECISION: (Souter, J.) Yes. Proof of mere disbelief or belief undisclosed in a proxy solicitation, standing alone, is insufficient to impose liability under federal law. However, proof of mere disbelief or belief undisclosed are sufficient for liability under § 14(a) when they are supported by objective evidence. Here, there was objective evidence of a value in excess of $60 per share of common stock, a fact never disclosed. Such evidence was not subject to Sandberg's (P) control or ready

manufacture, and there was no undue risk of open-ended liability or uncontrollable litigation in allowing her the opportunity for recovery on the allegation that it was misleading to call $42 high.

CONCURRENCE: (Scalia, J.) Sometimes, as in this case, a sentence with the word "opinion" in it actually represents facts as facts rather than opinions; in that event, no more need be done than apply the normal rules for § 14(a) liability.

▌ANALYSIS

The Court declared that directors' statements of reasons, opinion, or beliefs are factual in two senses: as statements that the directors do act for the reasons given or hold the belief stated and as statements about the subject matter of the reason or belief expressed. Reasons for directors' recommendations or statements of belief are, in contrast, characteristically matters of corporate record subject to documentation.

■■■

Quicknotes

FREEZE-OUT MERGER Merger whereby the majority shareholder forces minority shareholders into the sale of their securities.

PROXY SOLICITATION A statement containing specified information by the Securities and Exchange Commission in order to provide shareholders with adequate information upon which to make an informed decision regarding the solicitation of their proxies.

■■■

Mills v. Electric Auto-Lite Co.

Shareholder (P) v. Corporation (D)

396 U.S. 375 (1970).

NATURE OF CASE: Review of reversal of decision finding a violation of proxy statement rules.

FACT SUMMARY: A court of appeals held, in a suit based on an alleged proxy statement rules violation, that fairness of the transaction being voted upon was a defense.

RULE OF LAW
Transactional fairness is not a defense to an action predicated on proxy statement rule violations.

FACTS: The board of directors of Electric Auto-Lite Co. (Auto-Lite) (D), pursuant to a proposed merger into Mergenthaler Linotype Co. (Mergenthaler) (D), solicited proxies from the shareholders of Auto-Lite (D) in order to obtain shareholder approval. Shareholder approval was given, and the merger went forward. Mills (P), a shareholder of Auto-Lite (D), brought an action seeking to nullify the merger, contending that the board had disseminated a misleading proxy statement in violation of § 14 of the 1934 Securities Exchange Act by not disclosing that the board was controlled by Mergenthaler (D), which was a major shareholder. The district court found the omission material and held that a violation had occurred. The court of appeals reversed, holding that the fairness of the transaction cut off causation. The Supreme Court granted certiorari.

ISSUE: Is transactional fairness a defense to an action predicated on proxy statement rule violations?

HOLDING AND DECISION: (Harlan, J.) No. Transactional fairness is not a defense to an action based on proxy statement rule violations. The policy behind § 14 is full corporate suffrage. To permit a defense to a claim based on an allegedly misleading proxy statement would substitute the judgment of a court for that of shareholders, which would seriously contravene this policy. Also, throwing this obstacle in front of aggrieved shareholders would discourage shareholders from attempting to assert their rights. All that should be necessary for a § 14 cause of action to exist should be a find that a misrepresentation or omission was material. This ensures that no liability will occur for trivial defects. Extending the further defense of transactional fairness would only serve to undercut the policies embodied in § 14. Reversed.

▶ ANALYSIS

Private actions under § 14 had existed for some time before the present case was published. However, such actions only became officially recognized in 1964, with *J.I. Case Co. v. Borak*, 377 U.S. 426 (1964). The Court there

held that it was the policy behind § 14 to supplement SEC enforcement by providing a private right of action.

Quicknotes

CERTIORARI A discretionary writ issued by a superior court to an inferior court in order to review the lower court's decisions; the Supreme Court's writ ordering such review.

PROXY STATEMENT A statement containing specified information by the Securities and Exchange Commission in order to provide shareholders with adequate information upon which to make an informed decision regarding the solicitation of their proxies.

Virginia Bankshares, Inc. v. Sandberg

Corporation (D) v. Minority shareholder (D)

501 U.S. 1083 (1991).

NATURE OF CASE: Appeal from affirmance of a jury award of damages in a minority shareholder suit.

FACT SUMMARY: After a freeze-out merger in which minority shareholders lost their interest, Sandberg (P), a minority shareholder, brought suit, alleging violation of § 14(a) and Rule 14a-9 and breach of fiduciary duties.

🏛 RULE OF LAW
Causation of damages compensable under § 14(a) of the Securities Exchange Act cannot be demonstrated by a member of a class of minority shareholders whose votes are not required by law or corporate by-law to authorize the transaction giving rise to the claim.

FACTS: In a freeze-out merger, the First American Bank of Virginia (Bank) eventually merged into Virginia Bankshares, Inc. (VBI) (D). The parent company of VBI (D) hired an investment banking firm to give an opinion as to the appropriate price for shares of the Bank's minority holders, who would lose their interest as a result of the merger. The investment banking firm's opinion that $42 a share would be a fair price was based on market quotations and unverified information from VBI's (D) parent company. The merger proposal was approved at that price, and the directors solicited proxies for voting on the proposal. The solicitation stated the plan had been approved because of its opportunity for the minority shareholders to achieve a high value, which the directors also described as a fair price for the minority stock. Sandberg (P) brought this action, alleging violation of § 14(a) of the Securities Exchange Act and Rule 14a-9 and the breach of fiduciary duties owed to the minority shareholders under state law. The jury ruled for Sandberg (P), finding that she would have received $60 if her stock had been properly valued. The court of appeals affirmed, and VBI (D) appealed.

ISSUE: Can causation of damages compensable under § 14(a) of the Securities Exchange Act be demonstrated by a member of a class of minority shareholders whose votes are not required by law or corporate by-law to authorize the transaction giving rise to the claim?

HOLDING AND DECISION: (Souter, J.) No. Causation of damages compensable under § 14(a) of the Securities Exchange Act cannot be demonstrated by a member of a class of minority shareholders whose votes are not required by law or corporate by-law to authorize the transaction giving rise to the claim. Recognition of any private right of action for violating a federal statute must ultimately rest on congressional intent to provide a private remedy, and the right should not grow beyond the scope Congress intended. Under Sandberg's (P) theory, causation would turn on inferences about what the corporate directors would have thought and done without the minority shareholder approval unneeded to authorize action. Reliable evidence would seldom exist. The issues would be hazy, their litigation protracted, and their resolution unreliable. Any theory of causation that raised such prospects should be rejected. Further, the Virginia statute bars a shareholder from seeking to avoid a transaction tainted by a director's conflict if the minority shareholders ratified the transaction following disclosure of the material facts and the conflict. Here, the minority votes were inadequate to ratify the merger; thus, there was no loss of state remedy to connect the proxy solicitation with harm to minority shareholders. Reversed.

DISSENT: (Kennedy, J.) Causation is established where the proxy statement is an essential link in completing the transaction, even if the minority lacks sufficient votes to defeat a proposal of management. Thus, the judgment of the court of appeals should be affirmed.

▶ ANALYSIS

Sandberg (P) urged the Court to apply the test of causation it had developed in *Mills v. Electric Auto-Lite Co.*, 396 U.S. 375 (1970). In *Mills*, the Court described the causal relationship by calling the proxy solicitation an "essential link in the accomplishment of the transaction." Justice Souter distinguished *Mills*, where the solicitation linked a director's proposal with the votes legally required to authorize the action proposed, from the instant case involving shareholders whose initial authorization of the transaction prompting the proxy solicitation was not required.

■==■

Quicknotes

CAUSATION The aggregate effect of preceding events that bring about a tortious result; the causal connection between the actions of a tortfeasor and the injury that follows.

FIDUCIARY DUTY A legal obligation to act for the benefit of another, including subordinating one's personal interests to that of the other person.

FREEZE-OUT MERGER Merger whereby the majority shareholder forces minority shareholders into the sale of their securities.

PROXY SOLICITATION A statement containing specified information by the Securities and Exchange Commission in order to provide shareholders with adequate information upon which to make an informed decision regarding the solicitation of their proxies.

■==■

Wilson v. Great American Industries, Inc.

Minority shareholder (P) v. Corporation (D)

979 F.2d 924 (2d Cir. 1992).

NATURE OF CASE: Pending an appeal of damages for plaintiff, defendants sought dismissal based upon the holding in *Virginia Bankshares, Inc. v. Sandberg,* 501 U.S. 1083 (1991).

FACT SUMMARY: A misstatement in proxy materials may have induced minority shareholders to approve a merger and thus lose state law appraisal rights.

🏛 RULE OF LAW
If a shareholder, induced by a deceptive proxy, has lost the right of state appraisal proceedings due to a vote in favor of merger, a § 14(a) cause of action exists.

FACTS: Majority shareholders, controlling 73% of Chenango common stock, sought a stock swap, offering new preferred stock in Great American (D) in exchange for the minority shares in Chenango. The 73% interest was more than sufficient to meet New York's requirement that two-thirds approve a merger. However, even though the merger could have proceeded based on majority vote alone, the directors of Chenango mailed out joint proxy and registration statements seeking Chenango minority shareholders' approval. Certain omissions or misrepresentations in the proxy created an unfair stock exchange ratio by overvaluing Great America's (D) stock and undervaluing Chenango's. After voting, minority shareholder's sued, claiming they had been unfairly induced to forego state appraisal rights.

ISSUE: If a shareholder, induced by a deceptive proxy, loses the right to state appraisal proceedings due to a vote in favor of merger, does a § 14(a) cause of action exist?

HOLDING AND DECISION: (Cardamone, J.) Yes. If a shareholder, induced by a deceptive proxy, loses the right to state appraisal proceedings due to a vote in favor of merger, then a § 14(a) cause of action exists. Section 14(a) was written with the purpose of preventing false or misleading statements in proxy materials. Just because a proxy is not required does not excuse the requirement that it be completely factual. Even though there is not a causal link between the proxy and the merger if the minority vote was not necessary does not mean that a causal link between the proxy and some other injury does not exist. Here, the potential harm is that shareholders accepted an unfavorable stock swap ratio rather than recouping a greater value in a state appraisal proceeding. Great American (D) did not have to send out the proxy, but once they did, the burden was upon them to send a truthful statement. Remanded, for the sole purpose of determining whether the minority shareholders did in fact lose state appraisal rights by voting for the merger.

▶ ANALYSIS

Ironically, the holding in this case suggests that if a majority has sufficient votes to force a merger, then it may be better off not sending out a proxy, rather than risking a contest based upon a mistake in the proxy materials. The corporation must balance its particular need to receive shareholder approval through a proxy with the possibility of arriving in an appraisal proceeding if no vote is held.

■══■

Quicknotes

APPRAISAL RIGHTS A statutory remedy whereby minority shareholders, objecting to extraordinary transactions entered into by the corporation, may require the corporation to repurchase their shares at a price equal to its value immediately prior to the action.

PROXY STATEMENT A statement containing specified information by the Securities and Exchange Commission in order to provide shareholders with adequate information upon which to make an informed decision regarding the solicitation of their proxies.

■══■

In re The Topps Company Shareholders Litigation

[Parties not identified.]

Del. Ct. Ch., 926 A.2d 58 (2007).

NATURE OF CASE: Action for preliminary injunction to prevent a merger.

FACT SUMMARY: Shareholders and The Upper Deck Company (Upper Deck) sought to enjoin a going private transaction (the Eisner Merger) of The Topps Company, Inc. (Topps), claiming that the Topps board had failed to adequately disclose material information about the Eisner Merger and Upper Deck's higher bid, and also sought to enjoin the Topps board from using a standstill agreement it had with Upper Deck to silence Upper Deck about its offer.

🏛 RULE OF LAW
(1) A going private transaction will be enjoined where the target's board has failed to fully disclose material information to shareholders.
(2) A target company will be enjoined from using a standstill agreement to prevent a bidder from communicating with the target company's stockholder or presenting a bid that the stockholders could find materially more favorable than offered in a going private transaction.

FACTS: The Topps Company, Inc. (Topps), the well-known maker of trading cards and old-style confections, faced a proxy contest in 2005. Shorin, Topps's Chairman and CEO, ended that threat with a promise to explore strategic options. He also avoided almost certain defeat from insurgents by expanding the company's board so that he was elected with all insurgent nominees. The board was split between Dissident Directors and Incumbent Directors. Shorin also entertained a going private transaction proposal made by Eisner, Walt Disney's former CEO and a current private equity investor. Eisner assured Shorin and the board that existing management would be retained. After the elections, an Ad Hoc Committee was formed, with an equal number of Dissident and Incumbent Directors, to explore strategic options for the company. The two factions split on almost every issue. In particular, the Ad Hoc Committee divided on the issue of whether and how Topps should be sold. The Dissident Directors insisted that if a sale was to occur, it should involve a public auction process, whereas the Incumbents were resistant to the idea that Topps should be in an auction process. Eisner was the only serious bidder to emerge. He bid $9.24 per share in a proposal that envisioned his retention of existing management, including Shorin's son-in-law, Silverstein, who was Topps's President and COO. Eisner was willing to tolerate a post-signing Go Shop process, but not a pre-signing auction. The Ad Hoc

Committee split evenly over whether to negotiate with Eisner. An Incumbent Director nevertheless reached agreement with Eisner on a merger at $9.75 per share. The "Merger Agreement" gave Topps the chance to shop the bid for 40 days after signing, and the right to accept a "Superior Proposal" after that, subject only to Eisner's receipt of a termination fee and his match right. The Topps board approved the Merger Agreement in a divided vote, with the Incumbent Directors all favoring the merger, and the Dissident Directors all dissenting. Shortly before the Merger Agreement was approved, Topps's chief competitor in the sports cards business, The Upper Deck Company, expressed a willingness to make a bid. Notwithstanding this bid, Topps signed the Merger Agreement with Eisner without responding to Upper Deck's overture. In doing so, the board was advised by Lehman Brothers (Lehman), which provided a favorable discounted cash flow (DCF) valuation that supported its fairness opinion. However, only a month earlier, Lehman had prepared a similar analysis, but had used different assumptions. After the Merger Agreement was signed, the Go Shop process began, and by the end of that period, Upper Deck had expressed a willingness to pay $10.75 per share in a friendly merger, subject to its receipt of additional due diligence and other conditions. Although having the option freely to continue negotiations to induce an even more favorable topping bid by finding that Upper Deck's interest was likely to result in a Superior Proposal, the Topps board voted not to make such a finding. After the Go Shop period, Upper Deck again made an unsolicited bid at $10.75 without a financing contingency and with a strong promise to deal with antitrust issues. The bid, however, limited Topps to a remedy for failing to close, limited to a reverse break-up fee in the same amount ($12 million) Eisner secured as the only recourse against him. Without ever seriously articulating why Upper Deck's proposal for addressing the antitrust issue was inadequate and without proposing a specific higher reverse break-up fee, the Incumbent Directors refused to treat Upper Deck as having presented a Superior Proposal, a prerequisite to putting the onus on Eisner to match that price or step aside. Instead, Topps went public with a disclosure about Upper Deck's bid, but in a form that did not accurately represent that expression of interest and that disparaged Upper Deck's seriousness. Topps did that knowing that it had required Upper Deck to agree to a contractual standstill (the "Standstill Agreement") prohibiting Upper Deck from making public any information about its discussions with Topps or proceeding with a tender offer for Topps shares

Continued on next page.

without permission from the Topps board. The Topps board refused Upper Deck's request for relief from the Standstill Agreement to allow Upper Deck to make a tender offer and to tell its side of events. A vote on the Eisner Merger was scheduled to occur within a couple of weeks. A group of Topps stockholders and Upper Deck brought suit for a preliminary injunction, contending that the upcoming Merger vote would be tainted by Topps's failure to disclose in its proxy statement material facts about the process that led to the Merger Agreement and about Topps's subsequent dealings with Upper Deck. They contended that the Incumbent Directors preferred a deal with Eisner that would enable the company's current managers to continue in their positions. More pointedly, they suggested that the Incumbent Directors wanted to help Shorin preserve his influence over the business his family started by perpetuating Silverstein in office. Even more, they argued that Topps was denying its stockholders the chance to decide for themselves whether to forsake the lower-priced Eisner Merger in favor of the chance to accept a tender offer from Upper Deck at a higher price. Regardless of whether the Topps board preferred the Eisner Merger as lower risk, the moving parties contended that the principles animating *Revlon, Inc. v. MacAndrews & Forbes Holdings, Inc.*, 506 A.2d. 173 (Del. 1986) should prevent the board from denying the stockholders the chance to make a mature, uncoerced decision for themselves.

ISSUE:

(1) Will a going private transaction be enjoined where the target's board has failed to fully disclose material information to shareholders?

(2) Will a target company be enjoined from using a standstill agreement to prevent a bidder from communicating with the target company's stockholder or presenting a bid that the stockholders could find materially more favorable than offered in a going private transaction?

HOLDING AND DECISION: (Strine, V. Chan.)

(1) Yes. A going private transaction will be enjoined where the target's board has failed to fully disclose material information to shareholders. The moving parties have shown a likelihood of success on their claim that the proxy statement was materially misleading in its current form. The key proxy statement omissions here were the failure to disclose Eisner's assurances to Topps's management that it would retain them; the failure to disclose a valuation presentation by a leading investment firm (Lehman Brothers) that cast doubt on the fairness of the Merger; and omissions as well as material misstatements of fact bearing on Upper Deck's credibility as a serious bidder. The Topps's board's conduct vis-à-vis Upper Deck indicated clearly that it had abandoned any pretense of trying to secure the highest price reasonably available. Regarding disclosures related to Eisner's retention assurances, it is true—but in a misleading literal sense—that the company's management did not discuss

post-merger employment with Eisner before the Merger Agreement was signed. However, the proxy statement failed to indicate that Eisner explicitly stated that his proposal was "designed to" retain "substantially all of [Topps's] existing senior management and key employees," and that Eisner had continually communicated that intention during negotiations. The proxy statement should have disclosed these facts. With respect to Lehman's valuations, what is concerning is that in the one-month period between Lehman's first presentation to the Topps board and its second presentation, Lehman had significantly changed its analytical approach in an inexplicable way that seemed to be biased toward the Eisner offer. In other words, it seems that Lehman manipulated its analyses to try to make the Eisner offer look more attractive once it was clear Eisner would not budge on price. The proxy statement does not fairly address this issue, since there is no indication that the earlier analysis was flawed or in need of an analytical revision. The first analysis cast the price Eisner was offering to pay in a quite different light than the second analysis, and the proxy statement should have discussed the first valuation. Because it did not, it was materially misleading as to this issue. Finally, as to the alleged mischaracterization of Upper Deck's overtures, Topps had publicly disclosed that it rejected Upper Deck's bid because of Upper Deck's failure to provide a firm debt financing commitment. The proxy statement failed to disclose, however, that Upper Deck's bid was not subject to a financing contingency. It also failed to disclose that in the event of a breach, Upper Deck would be subject to the same liability that Eisner would face in a similar situation. Further, while the proxy statement mentioned potential antitrust problems, it failed to mention that in Upper Deck's revised unsolicited bid that it submitted after the close of the Go Shop Period, Upper Deck agreed to a strong "hell or high water" antitrust provision in which Upper Deck agreed to divest itself of any and all assets necessary to obtain regulatory approval. It also did not note that Upper Deck had received an opinion from a reputable antitrust scholar that no significant antitrust risks would be posed by a merger of Topps and Upper Deck. For these reasons, the proxy statement is materially misleading, and the transaction must be enjoined to permit the board to make corrective disclosures.

(2) Yes. A target company will be enjoined from using a standstill agreement to prevent a bidder from communicating with the target company's stockholder or presenting a bid that the stockholders could find materially more favorable than offered in a going private transaction. The moving parties have established a reasonable probability of success on their claim that the Topps board was breaching its fiduciary duties by misusing the Standstill in order to prevent Upper Deck from communicating with the Topps stockholders

Continued on next page.

and presenting a bid that the Topps stockholders could find materially more favorable than the Eisner Merger. Under the *Revlon* standard, directors proposing to sell a company for cash or engage in a change of control transaction must take reasonable measures to ensure that the stockholders receive the highest value reasonably attainable. While Topps directors do not have to disclose a version of events that they contend never happened, since the shareholders can hear out both sides on most issues where there is a dispute as to how the events transpired, that is not true with respect to matters of contention between the Topps Incumbent Directors and Upper Deck. Topps and Upper Deck have many disagreements about the true course of events, but only Topps has been able to tell its story to the Topps stockholders. For example, the proxy statement indicates Topps had been advised there was no suitable strategic buyer, but Upper Deck claims it had repeatedly indicated its interest in acquiring Topps on several occasions before Topps entered into negotiations with Eisner. Similarly, Upper Deck believes that the proxy statement misrepresents the dynamics of the negotiations between Upper Deck and Topps during the Go Shop Period. Ordinarily, shareholders will be able to get both sides of this kind of "he said, she said" arguing, but here, the Topps Incumbent Directors have refused to release Upper Deck from the Standstill, even for the limited purpose of communicating with the Topps stockholders. Such use of the Standstill furthers a breach of the directors' *Revlon* duty. To help Shorin meet his personal objectives, the Topps board majority supposedly resisted the Dissidents' desire for a public auction of Topps, and signed up a deal with Eisner without any effort to shop the company beforehand. However, there was no unreasonable flaw in the approach that the Topps board took to negotiating the Merger Agreement with Eisner, given that there were no other serious bidders at the time, and the Agreement itself does not contain an unreasonable approach to value maximization. The Go Shop Period, the break up fee, the match, etc. were all reasonable substantive terms under the circumstances. In other words, the deal protections the Topps board agreed to in the Merger Agreement seem to have left reasonable room for an effective post-signing market check. There was also "value" in having the proverbial bird in hand. Thus, the decision to enter into the agreement with Eisner a few days after Topps received Upper Deck's unsolicited bid was also not unreasonable. Notwithstanding the reasonableness of entering the Eisner Merger, the board's response to Upper Deck was arguably less reasonable. The Topps board was certainly less receptive than would be expected to a competitor who had long expressed interest in buying Topps in a friendly deal and who, given the likely synergies involved in a combination of the two businesses, might, if serious about doing a deal, be able to pay a materially higher price than a financial buyer like Eisner. On the other hand, Upper Deck did not move quickly and could reasonably have been interpreted as not being serious. Regardless of this conduct, Upper Deck did make a formal bid at $10.75 two days before the close of the Go Shop Period. Under *Revlon*, the Topps board had a fiduciary obligation to consider that bid in good faith and to determine whether it was a Superior Proposal or reasonably likely to lead to one. Even though Topps had legitimate concerns about Upper Deck's bid, the Topps board's decision not to treat Upper Deck as an "Excluded Party," with which it could continue to negotiate after the close of the Go Shop, is highly questionable. Upper Deck was offering a substantially higher price, and rather than responding to Upper Deck's proposal by raising the legitimate concerns that it had, the Topps board chose to tie its hands by failing to declare Upper Deck an Excluded Party in a situation where it would have cost Topps nothing to do so and would have given the parties an opportunity to address Topps's concerns. In fact, Upper Deck's second, higher bid addressed many of these concerns, but the Topps directors did not pursue the potential for higher value with the diligence and genuineness expected of directors seeking to get the best value for stockholders; it never made reasonable suggestions to Upper Deck about a higher reverse break-up fee, antitrust issues, or price. This is consistent with Shorin's antipathy to Upper Deck and enthusiasm for Eisner. Shorin's and the other directors' claim that they truly desired to get the highest value for shareholders is belied by their apparent failure to undertake diligent good faith efforts at bargaining with Upper Deck, as well as by the misrepresentations of fact about Upper Deck's offer that were contained in Topps's public statements. This raises the related issue of the improper use of the Standstill. The Topps board reserved the right to waive the Standstill if its fiduciary duties required, since it had the duty to use this contractual provision only for proper purposes, but its failure to use the Standstill only to get reasonable concessions from Upper Deck to unlock higher value is an abuse of its power and a violation of its *Revlon* duties. Upper Deck asked for a release from the Standstill to make a tender offer on the terms it offered to Topps and to communicate with Topps's stockholders. The Topps board's refusal to grant the release for this purpose not only keeps the stockholders from having the chance to accept a potentially more attractive higher priced deal, it keeps them in the dark about Upper Deck's version of important events, and it keeps Upper Deck from obtaining antitrust clearance, because it cannot begin the process without either a signed merger agreement or a formal tender offer. Because the Topps board is recommending that the

Continued on next page.

stockholders cash out, its decision to foreclose its stockholders from receiving an offer from Upper Deck seems likely to be found a breach of fiduciary duty. If Upper Deck were to make a tender offer at $10.75 per share on the conditions it outlined, the Topps stockholders would still be free to reject that offer if the Topps board convinced them it was too conditional. For these reasons, an injunction requiring Topps to release Upper Deck from its prior restraint is justified. Not only does the board's use of the Standstill threaten irreparable harm to the stockholders, who might otherwise never have the opportunity to consider Upper Deck's offer, it also forces the stockholders to accept Eisner's bid without hearing the full story and threatens the stockholders with making an important decision on an uninformed basis, a threat that justifies injunctive relief. To address the possible danger that an injunction will reduce the board's leverage in bargaining with Upper Deck, the injunction will provide that the Merger is enjoined so that Upper Deck can make an all shares, non-coercive tender offer of $10.75 cash or more per share, on conditions as to financing and antitrust no less favorable to Topps than contained in Upper Deck's most recent offer; and to communicate with Topps stockholders about its version of relevant events. Although the injunction will not prevent Topps from keeping the Standstill in place, if it chooses to do so, it will not be able to proceed with the Merger vote. Finally, an injunction will not prevent the Topps board from informing its shareholders of its opinion of an Upper Deck tender offer, or require it to enter into a merger with Upper Deck if it believes doing so is not in the shareholders' best interest. However, the shareholders must be permitted to decide between the two competing, non-coercive offers that are on the table. Motion for an injunction is granted.

▶ ANALYSIS

Standstill agreements serve legitimate purposes. When a corporation is running a sale process, it is responsible, if not mandated, for the board to ensure that confidential information is not misused by bidders and advisors whose interests are not aligned with the corporation, to establish rules of the game that promote an orderly auction, and to give the corporation leverage to extract concessions from the parties who seek to make a bid. However, as this case illustrates, standstills can also be abused. Parties like Eisner often, as was done here, insist on a standstill as a deal protection. Furthermore, a standstill can be used by a target improperly to favor one bidder over another, not for reasons consistent with stockholder interest, but because managers prefer one bidder for their own motives.

Quicknotes

ANTITRUST Body of federal law prohibiting business conduct that constitutes a restraint on trade.

BREACH OF FIDUCIARY DUTY The failure of a fiduciary to observe the standard of care exercised by professionals of similar education and experience.

INJUNCTION A court order requiring a person to do, or prohibiting that person from doing, a specific act.

PROXY STATEMENT A statement containing specified information by the Securities and Exchange Commission in order to provide shareholders with adequate information upon which to make an informed decision regarding the solicitation of their proxies.

■■■

Birnbaum v. Newport Steel Corp.

Stockholder (P) v. Corporation (D)

193 F.2d 461 (2d Cir.), *cert. denied*, 343 U.S. 956 (1952).

NATURE OF CASE: Appeal from trial court's dismissal of a complaint alleging fraud and misrepresentation.

FACT SUMMARY: Birnbaum (P) alleged that Feldmann (D), a fellow stockholder, had perpetrated a fraud on the stockholders and the corporation in connection with the sale of his stock, thus violating Security and Exchange Commission (SEC) Rule X-10b-5.

🏛 RULE OF LAW
SEC Rule X-10b-5 protects only against a fraud perpetrated upon a purchaser or seller of securities.

FACTS: Feldmann (D), owner of a controlling interest in Newport Steel Corp. (Newport) (D), was also its president and chairman of the board of directors. After rejecting a merger offer from one corporation, Feldmann (D) sold his stock for twice its market value to Wilport Co. (D). Wilport (D) paid a premium to obtain voting control and to have a captive source of steel during a period of shortage. Birnbaum (P) and other stockholders of Newport (D) brought suit on behalf of the corporation and as representatives of all similarly situated stockholders. Birnbaum (P) claimed that misrepresentations made by both Feldmann (D) and Newport's (D) new president in connection with the sale of Feldmann's (D) stock operated as a fraud upon the corporation and its stockholders, in violation of SEC Rule X-10b-5. The district court granted Newport's (D) motion to dismiss, and Birnbaum (P) appealed.

ISSUE: Does SEC Rule X-10b-5 only protect against a fraud perpetrated upon a purchaser or seller of securities?

HOLDING AND DECISION: (Hand, J.) Yes. SEC Rule X-10b-5 only protects against a fraud perpetrated upon a purchaser or seller of securities, not from mismanagement of corporate affairs resulting in fraud upon stockholders who were not purchasers or sellers. When Congress intended to protect the stockholders of a corporation against a breach of fiduciary duty by corporate insiders, it left no doubt as to its meaning. For example, § 16(b) of the Securities Exchange Act of 1934 expressly gives the corporate issuer or its stockholders a right of action against corporate insiders using their position to profit in the sale or exchange of corporate securities. The absence of a similar provision in § 10(b) of the Act strengthens the conclusion that it applies only to fraud associated with the sale or purchase of securities. SEC Rule X-10b-5 promulgated by the SEC pursuant to the Act, extended protection only to the defrauded purchaser or seller. Since the complaint failed to allege that Birnbaum

(P) or any of the other plaintiffs fell within either class, the judgment of the district court was correct. Affirmed.

▶ ANALYSIS

SEC Rule X-10b-5 was formulated in 1942 by Milton Freeman and Jim Treanor, Director of the Trading and Exchange Division, in response to fraudulent misrepresentations made by the president of a company to the shareholders when he purchased the company's stock from them. A conscious decision was made to put the language "in connection with the purchase or sale" at the end of the rule. The rule was intended to give the SEC the power to deal with such problems. Over time, as the membership of the Supreme Court has changed, the application of the rule has expanded and contracted.

■══■

Quicknotes

FIDUCIARY DUTY A legal obligation to act for the benefit of another, including subordinating one's personal interests to that of the other person.

FRAUD A false representation of facts with the intent that another will rely on the misrepresentation to his detriment.

MISREPRESENTATION A statement or conduct by one party to another that constitutes a false representation of fact.

■══■

Superintendent of Insurance v. Bankers Life & Casualty Co.

State agency (P) v. Corporation (D)

404 U.S. 6 (1971).

NATURE OF CASE: Suit for fraud in securities transaction brought under Rule 10b-5.

FACT SUMMARY: By manipulating the books of an insurance company, an individual used $5 million of the insurance company's own money to purchase all the shares of the insurance company. Suit was brought by the insurance commission to recover the lost funds under § 10b and Rule 10b-5.

🏛 RULE OF LAW
The scope of § 10b and Rule 10b-5 of the Securities Exchange Act of 1934 is not limited to transactions occurring in the organized securities markets (stock exchanges and over-the-counter market) but applies to individual face-to-face transactions as well.

FACTS: There were numerous defendants in this case, among them Begole (D) and Bourne (D), individuals. Also named were lrving Trust Company (D), a bank, and Garvin, Bantel (D), a loan brokerage company, and New England Note (D), another loan broker alleged to have been controlled by Bourne (D). Begole (D) entered into an agreement with Bankers Life and Casualty Co. (D) to purchase all of the stock of Manhattan Casualty Company, which was a wholly owned subsidiary of Bankers Life (D). The purchase price was $5 million to be paid in one installment. Begole (D) arranged to have a check drawn on Irving Trust (D) for the $5 million despite the fact that he had no funds on deposit there. The arrangements were made through Garvin, Bantel (D). This check was used to pay for the shares of Manhattan Casualty, and the sale was consummated. Having controlling interest in Manhattan Casualty, Begole (D) and Bourne (D) immediately installed their own directors, including themselves, and hired a cohort as president. At their direction, Manhattan Casualty sold $4.8 million of U.S. Treasury bonds, and this amount, plus another $.2 million of Manhattan Casualty cash, was deposited in Irving Trust (D) to cover the check previously written. The result of this transaction was that Begole (D) now owned 100% of the stock of Manhattan Casualty by using Manhattan Casualty's own assets for the purchase money. To cover this transaction, further machinations were required to balance Manhattan Casualty's books. Toward that end, a second check for $5 million was drawn on Irving Trust (D). This money was used to buy a certificate of deposit from a European bank which was credited to Manhattan Casualty. To cover the second check, the certificate of deposit was pledged as collateral to the European bank for a $5 million loan. The loan was arranged through New England Note (D). The proceeds of the loan were used to cover the second check. The certificate of deposit was credited to Manhattan Casualty without noting that it was pledged as collateral for the loan, which also was not entered as a liability on Manhattan's books. Acting under proper authority, the Insurance Superintendent of New York (P) put Manhattan Casualty into receivership and instituted this action to recover the funds lost through the gyrations of the various defendants. The suit was brought under § 10b and Rule 10b-5, among other theories of recovery. The action was dismissed by the district court and the dismissal affirmed by the court of appeals. The grounds for affirmation were that § 10b was not applicable since no investor had been injured and there were no improper actions in the trading markets.

ISSUE: Is § 10b intended to apply only to purchases or sales of securities by investors dealing in the open market?

HOLDING AND DECISION: (Douglas, J.) No. Section 10b states, that it is unlawful to use any manipulative, deceptive device or contrivance in connection with the purchase or sale of any security. The term security as defined in other sections of the Act covers Treasury bonds. There is no limitation indicated in the section itself or anywhere else that it was intended to apply only to transactions in the public securities markets. The fact that the Treasury bonds were sold at the current market price does not erase the fact that a fraudulent scheme was connected to that transaction. The inventiveness of schemers is limitless. To protect against their actions, the law cannot be read so narrowly as to permit their actions simply because the legislators didn't outthink the schemers. The fact remains that Manhattan Casualty was the victim of a manipulative scheme in connection with the sale of a security. The Act protects corporations as well as individuals. We read the congressional intent in enacting § 10b in such broad terms to mean that its application should be broad. As such, its application to this case is clearly warranted. Reversed and Remanded.

▶ ANALYSIS

Section 10b has become the section of the securities laws "where the action is." By this decision and others, the Supreme Court has indicated that the broadest possible interpretation is to be given to its terms. A private right of action is impliedly authorized, and class actions are also proper. The term "securities" is not restricted to the traditional concepts of stocks and bonds. While the people bent on fraud and deceptive practices will never be totally

Continued on next page.

deterred by any law, § 10b gives to the government and to the public a powerful tool and weapon to prosecute accused offenders. As this case indicates, the person who desires to take advantage of a complex market can devise some incredibly ingenious devices. While many may suspect the morality of legislators, those who suspect would not also imbue them with the foresight to specifically prohibit so complex a transaction as devised by Begole (D) and Bourne (D). In its place, they have written a flexible law that is adaptable to the ingenuity of manipulators.

■≡■

Quicknotes

CLASS ACTION   A suit commenced by a representative on behalf of an ascertainable group that is too large to appear in court, who shares a commonality of interests and who will benefit from a successful result.

COLLATERAL   Property that secures the payment of a debt.

PRIVATE RIGHT OF ACTION   A fact or set of facts the occurrence of which entitles a party to seek judicial relief.

RULE 10b-5   It is unlawful to defend or make untrue statements in connection with purchase or sale of securities.

SECURITIES   Instruments that reflect ownership rights in a company or a debt owed by the company.

■≡■

Blue Chip Stamps v. Manor Drug Stores

Corporation (D) v. Offeree (P)

421 U.S. 723 (1975).

NATURE OF CASE: Action in damages for violations of Rule 10b-5.

FACT SUMMARY: Blue Chip Stamps (D), under the terms of an antitrust consent decree, filed a prospectus offering users and former users an opportunity to purchase its stock.

> ## 🏛 RULE OF LAW
> No civil action for damages is available under Rule 10b-5 to those who have neither bought nor sold shares in stock.

FACTS: The United States filed an antitrust action against Blue Chip Stamps (Blue Chip) (D). As part of a consent decree, Blue Chip (D) was required to offer its stock to all current and former users of its stamps. A prospectus was filed with the Securities and Exchange Commission (SEC). Approximately 50% of the offered stock was purchased. Manor Drug (Manor) (P) had never owned or traded in Blue Chip's (D) stock. Manor (P) decided not to purchase the proffered offering because the filed prospectus appeared to be pessimistic concerning future earnings potential. Manor (P) subsequently brought class action against Blue Chip (D) for violations of Rule 10b-5 alleging that the prospectus contained inaccuracies and misrepresentation designed to convey an overly pessimistic picture of Blue Chip (D) to discourage purchasers of the proffered offering. The action prayed for $21 million dollars in damages for lost opportunity to purchase stock and $25 million in exemplary damages. The action was dismissed for failure to state an action under Rule 10b-5. The decision was reversed on appeal.

ISSUE: May a party who has never traded in a stock bring a civil action for damages under Rule 10b-5?

HOLDING AND DECISION: (Rehnquist, J.) No. Rule 10b-5 has consistently been limited to purchasers and sellers of stock. It was designed to provide a civil action for actual damages resulting from fraud, misrepresentation, etc. It was never intended to apply to situations involving a potential loss of profits to those not trading in the stock. The Rule allows the purchaser/seller to void transactions. Where there has been no purchase/sale this rationale/remedy is absent. To allow a suit to be maintained for potential losses by those who have suffered no actual injury has too great a potential for abuse and injury to the corporation. The problems of proof would create additional problems. Manor (P) would merely have to advert that it did not purchase due to the overly pessimistic prospectus. No other proof need be adduced. Policy considerations based on the above mentioned factors militate against an extension of the purview of Rule 10b-5. Reversed.

▶ ANALYSIS

A party who is neither a buyer nor a seller may obtain an injunction for violations of Rule 10b-5, *Mutual Shares Corp. v. Genesco, Inc.*, 3843 F.2d 540 (2d Cir. 1967). Occasionally, damages have been allowed under Rule 10b-5 where, because of manipulations, the shareholders have been left with either worthless stock or a mere claim for money even though they have not parted with ownership of their shares, *Dudley v. Southeastern Factor & Finance Co.*, 446 F.2d 303 (5th Cir.).

■==■

Quicknotes

CONSENT DECREE A decree issued by a court of equity ratifying an agreement between the parties to a lawsuit; an agreement by a defendant to cease illegal activity.

■==■

Santa Fe Industries, Inc. v. Green

Corporation (D) v. Shareholder (P)

430 U.S. 462 (1977).

NATURE OF CASE: Action for violation of § 10(b) of the Securities Act of 1934 and Rule 10b-5.

FACT SUMMARY: Santa Fe Industries (D) merged with Kirby Lumber for the sole purpose of eliminating minority shareholders.

🏛 RULE OF LAW
Before a claim of fraud or breach of fiduciary duty may be maintained under 10(b) or Rule 10b-5, there must first be a showing of manipulation or deception.

FACTS: Santa Fe Industries (Santa Fe) (D) owned 90% of Kirby Lumber's Kirby's) stock. Under Delaware law, a parent could merge with a subsidiary without prior notice to minority shareholders and could pay them the fair market value of the stock. Solely to eliminate these minority shareholders, Santa Fe (D) merged with Kirby. A complete audit was run of the business, and shareholders were sent an offer of $150 a share plus the asset appraisal report and an opinion letter that the shares were worth $125. Green (P) and other shareholders did not appeal the price offered them, as provided by state law. Instead, they initiated suit under § 10(b) of the Securities Act of 1934 and Rule 10b-5. Green (P) alleged that the merger had not been made for a business purpose, and no prior notice was given shareholders. Green (P) further alleged that the value of the stock as disclosed in the appraisal should have been $722 per share based on the assets of Kirby divided by the number of shares. The court held that the merger was valid under state law, which did not require a business purpose or prior notice for such mergers. The court held there was no misrepresentation, manipulation, or deception as to the value of the shares since all relevant information appeared in the appraisal report. The court of appeals reversed, finding a breach of fiduciary duty to the minority shareholders and no business purpose or notice.

ISSUE: Is breach of duty alone, without a showing of deception or manipulation, a ground for a § 10(b) or Rule 10b-5 action?

HOLDING AND DECISION: (White, J.) No. Before any action may be brought under § 10(b) or Rule 10b-5, there must be a showing of manipulation or deception. The Act and Rule speak plainly in these terms. Not every act by a corporation or its officers was intended to be actionable under § 10(b) or Rule 10b-5. Here, there was full disclosure. If the minority shareholders were dissatisfied, they could seek a court appraisal under the state statute. Neither notice nor a business purpose is required under state law. If minority shareholders feel aggrieved, they must pursue state remedies since no private right of action has even been granted under § 10(b) or Rule 10b-5 in cases such as this one. Ample state remedies exist for breach of fiduciary duty actions and for appraisals. Reversed.

▶ ANALYSIS

In *Blue Chip Stamps v. Manor Drug Stores*, 421 U.S. 723 (1975), the Court also held that mere negligence is not grounds for an action under § 10(b) and Rule 10b-5. In *Ernst & Ernst v. Hochfelder*, 425 U.S. 185 (1976), the Court held that the SEC could not enact rules which conflicted with plain expressions of congressional intent. Hence, Rule 10b-5 could not be more restrictive in nature than could actions under § 10(b) of the Securities Act of 1934.

Quicknotes

BUSINESS PURPOSE RULE Doctrine relieving corporate directors and/or officers from liability for decisions honestly and rationally made in the corporation's best interests.

FIDUCIARY DUTY A legal obligation to act for the benefit of another, including subordinating one's personal interests to that of the other person.

Basic Inc. v. Levinson

Corporation (D) v. Shareholder (P)

485 U.S. 224 (1988).

NATURE OF CASE: Review of reversal of summary judgment dismissing a class-action suit based on Rule 10b-5.

FACT SUMMARY: When management of Basic Incorporated (D) falsely denied the existence of merger negotiations, the question of this information's materiality arose.

🏛 RULE OF LAW
A misstatement regarding merger negotiations is material if there is a substantial likelihood that a reasonable shareholder would consider it important in deciding whether to buy or sell.

FACTS: Combustion Engineering, Inc. demonstrated an interest in merging Basic Incorporated (D) into it. Management of Basic (D) was approached regarding this. At one point, management issued a release denying the merger rumors that were circulating. Two other such releases were made. The merger was finally agreed upon and announced, driving up Basic's (D) stock prices. A class action suit was brought consisting of shareholders who sold before the official announcement was held, the contention being that the press release violated Securities and Exchange Commission (SEC) Rule 10b-5, which prohibits false information regarding securities sales. The district court granted Basic (D) summary judgment, but the appellate court reversed, holding that a false denial of merger discussions is inherently material. The Supreme Court granted certiorari.

ISSUE: Is a misstatement regarding merger negotiations material if there is a substantial likelihood that a reasonable shareholder would consider it important in deciding whether to buy or sell?

HOLDING AND DECISION: (Blackmun, J.) Yes. A misstatement regarding merger negotiations is material if there is a substantial likelihood that a reasonable shareholder would consider it important in deciding whether to buy or sell. A major purpose behind the 1934 Securities Exchange Act was to prevent market manipulation. The guaranteeing of honest and complete dissemination of information, mandated under § 10 of the Act, was an important vehicle toward that end. However, for a misstatement to be actionable, it must be material. The question thus becomes, when is a misstatement material? To hold that any misstatement is material sets too low a threshold, as it would compel management to bury an investor under an avalanche of trivial information which would hardly facilitate informed investor decisionmaking.

Rather, materiality is best viewed as existing when the information in question, viewed objectively, would tend to influence a shareholder's decision. This requires an investigation into the totality of the facts. Here, the court of appeals held the information to be inherently material. Therefore, the case must be remanded for consideration under the standard enunciated here.

▶ *ANALYSIS*

There had been a conflict in the various circuits prior to this decision. The Sixth Circuit, which the Court reversed here, had adopted the rigorous "inherently material" rule. The Third Circuit had adopted a bright line rule that such information was not material until an "agreement in principle" was reached. The Court steered a middle path.

■≡■

Quicknotes

CERTIORARI A discretionary writ issued by a superior court to an inferior court in order to review the lower court's decisions; the Supreme Court's writ ordering such review.

CLASS ACTION A suit commenced by a representative on behalf of an ascertainable group that is too large to appear in court, who shares a commonality of interests and who will benefit from a successful result.

MATERIAL FACT A fact without the existence of which a contract would not have been entered.

SUMMARY JUDGMENT Judgment rendered by a court in response to a motion by one of the parties, claiming that the lack of a question of material fact in respect to an issue warrants disposition of the issue without consideration by the jury.

■≡■

In re Time Warner, Inc. Securities Litigation

Corporation (D) v. Shareholder (P)

9 F.3d 259 (2d Cir. 1993).

NATURE OF CASE: Appeal of dismissal of a securities fraud complaint.

FACT SUMMARY: Time Warner (D) made overly optimistic statements about the securing of large partners to help with the debt burden remaining after the corporate merger, inducing some stockholders to wait rather than sell their holdings.

🏛 RULE OF LAW

Rule 10b-5 gives rise to a duty to update statements or opinions to avoid misrepresentation when interviewing events have made statements false or misleading.

FACTS: On June 7, 1989, Time, Inc. received a surprise tender offer for its stock from Paramount. Time's directors declined and continued talks with Warner about the possibility of a merger. Eventually, Time acquired all outstanding Warner stock for $70 per share. Purchasing the stock left Time with a $10 billion debt. Time Warner (D), the new entity, was criticized by shareholders for the huge debt burden. The company then went on a highly publicized campaign to find "strategic partners" who could bring billions of dollars into the company. Time Warner (D) was unable to locate a substantial partner, and on July 12, 1991, the Securities and Exchange Commission (SEC) approved a stock issuance which would allow Time Warner (D) to cover the balloon payments on their debt. The announced offering caused stock to fall from $117 to $89.75. Plaintiffs, shareholders during the period of stock price decline, filed suit. The case was dismissed. Plaintiffs then appealed.

ISSUE: Does Rule 10b-5 give rise to a duty to update information once an initial disclosure has been made?

HOLDING AND DECISION: (Newman, C.J.) Yes. If original statements or opinions have become misleading due to intervening events, Rule 10b-5 gives rise to a duty to update statements or opinions to avoid misrepresentation by silence. An omission is actionable under the securities law only when the corporation has a duty to disclose. However, determining when disclosure is required is a difficult issue. Generally, if prior statements are such that a reasonable investor would rely upon them to make decisions, then a material change in circumstance must also be disclosed. But a duty to disclose does not attach just because an investor would like to know the information. Rather, the duty to disclose attaches when reliance would be expected. Here, Time Warner (D) made aggressive statements regarding their positive expectations about finding partners. While a seasoned investor may have taken this to mean that there

was only a hope of solving the debt problem with partners, this is an issue of fact which still must be resolved. There is sufficient question as to whether the statements by Time Warner (D) required updating. Grant of motion to dismiss is reversed and the case remanded.

▶ ANALYSIS

A safe harbor was passed by Congress in 1995 for earnings projections. Unstable industries, particularly in Silicon Valley, were generating instant lawsuits alleging fraud whenever the actual earnings differed substantially from the projections. Statements that are known to be false by the issuer do not fall within the safe harbor.

■■■■

Quicknotes

MISREPRESENTATION A statement or conduct by one party to another that constitutes a false representation of fact.

■■■■

Ernst & Ernst v. Hochfelder

Auditors (D) v. Investor (P)

425 U.S. 185 (1976).

NATURE OF CASE: Appeal from judgment in an action for securities fraud.

FACT SUMMARY: After Hochfelder (P) was fraudulently induced to invest in escrow accounts by an Ernst & Ernst (D) client, Hochfelder (P) brought suit, alleging Ernst & Ernst (D) negligently aided and abetted the fraud.

🏛 RULE OF LAW
A private cause of action will not lie in the absence of scienter, an intent to deceive.

FACTS: A client of Ernst & Ernst (D) had fraudulently induced Hochfelder (P) to invest in escrow accounts. Ernst & Ernst's (D) client owned a small brokerage firm regulated by the SEC, and Ernst & Ernst (D) had audited the client's books. The fraud was discovered after the client committed suicide. Hochfelder (P) filed this action, alleging that Ernst & Ernst (D) had negligently aided and abetted the fraud by failing to discover an irregular procedure advocated by the client which prevented an effective audit. The lower court ruled in favor of Hochfelder (P), and this appeal followed.

ISSUE: Will a private cause of action lie in the absence of scienter, intent to deceive?

HOLDING AND DECISION: (Powell, J.) No. A private cause of action will not lie in the absence of scienter, an intent to deceive. It is unlawful to use or employ any manipulative or deceptive device or contrivance in violation of federal securities rules. The words manipulative or deceptive used in conjunction with device or contrivance strongly suggest that § 10(b) was intended to proscribe knowing or intentional misconduct. Use of the word "manipulative" is especially significant. It is and was virtually a term of art when used in connection with securities markets. It connotes intentional or willful conduct designed to deceive or defraud investors by controlling or artificially affecting the price of securities. Furthermore, a review of the legislative history of § 10(b) of the Securities Exchange Act does not support Hochfelder's (P) contention that the broad remedial goal of the Act embraces negligence as a standard of liability. Here, Ernst and Ernst (D) was merely negligent and therefore cannot be held liable under § 10(b). Reversed.

▶ ANALYSIS

In its amicus brief, the Securities and Exchange Commission (SEC) argued that since the "effect" on the investors of given conduct was the same regardless of whether the conduct was negligent or intentional, Congress must have intended to bar all such practices, not just those done knowingly or intentionally. But the Court declared that this effect-oriented approach would impose liability for wholly faultless conduct where such conduct resulted in harm to investors, a result the SEC would be unlikely to support. In a dissenting opinion, Justice Blackmun also focused on the effect on the investors rather than the wrongful conduct on the part of Ernst & Ernst (D).

■■■

Quicknotes

AMICUS BRIEF A brief submitted by a third party, not a party to the action, which contains information for the court's consideration in conformity with its position.

FRAUD A false representation of facts with the intent that another will rely on the misrepresentation to his detriment.

SCIENTER Knowledge of certain facts; often refers to "guilty knowledge," which implicates liability.

SECURITIES EXCHANGE ACT § 10(b) Prohibits use of any "manipulative or deceptive device or contrivance" in connection with the purchase or sale of a security and in violation of any regulation adopted by the Securities and Exchange Commission.

■■■

Tellabs, Inc. v. Makor Issues & Rights, Ltd.

Corporation (D) v. Shareholder (P)

551 U.S. 308 (2007).

NATURE OF CASE: Appeal from reversal of dismissal of action brought under the Private Securities Litigation Reform Act of 1995 for securities fraud.

FACT SUMMARY: Shareholders (P) of Tellabs, Inc. (Tellabs) (D), who brought suit under the Private Securities Litigation Reform Act of 1995 (PSLRA) claiming that Tellabs (D) and its officers (D) had intentionally deceived investors about the true value of the company's stock, contended that they had pled with particularity facts giving rise to a "strong inference" that Tellabs (D) and the officers (D) had acted with the required scienter.

🏛 **RULE OF LAW**
Under the Private Securities Litigation Reform Act of 1995 (PSLRA), to qualify as "strong" within the intendment of § 21D(b)(2), an inference of scienter must be found by a reasonable person to be cogent and at least as compelling as any opposing inference of nonfraudulent intent.

FACTS: Shareholders (P) of Tellabs, Inc. (Tellabs) (D) who purchased stock over a seven-month period filed a class action under the Private Securities Litigation Reform Act of 1995 (PSLRA) alleging that Tellabs (D) and Notebaert (D), then Tellabs' (D) CEO and president, had engaged in securities fraud in violation of § 10(b) of the Securities Exchange Act of 1934 and SEC Rule 10b-5. Specifically, the shareholders (P) alleged that during the seven-month period, Notebaert (D) (and by imputation Tellabs (D)) falsely reassured public investors, in a series of statements, that Tellabs (D) was continuing to enjoy strong demand for its products and earning record revenues when, in fact, Notebaert (D) knew the opposite was true. When it was finally revealed, after the seven-month class period, that demand for Tellabs' (D) products had dropped significantly, the price of its stock per share plunged from a high of $67 to a low of around $16. The district court dismissed the action without prejudice, and the shareholders (P) amended their complaint to add 27 confidential sources and other new, more specific allegations, some as to Notebaert's (D) mental state, but the district court again dismissed, this time with prejudice, because it found the shareholders (P) had failed to plead scienter with sufficient particularity. The court of appeals reversed, finding that the requirement in PSLRA that plaintiffs must "state with particularity facts giving rise to a strong inference that the defendant acted with the required state of mind" had been met. The court of appeals held that the "strong inference" standard would be met if the complaint, "allege[d] facts from which, if true, a reasonable

person could infer that the defendant acted with the required intent." Tellabs (D) appealed, and the United States Supreme Court granted certiorari.

ISSUE: Under the Private Securities Litigation Reform Act of 1995 (PSLRA), to qualify as "strong" within the intendment of § 21D(b)(2), must an inference of scienter be found by a reasonable person to be cogent and at least as compelling as any opposing inference of nonfraudulent intent?

HOLDING AND DECISION: (Ginsburg, J.) Yes. Under the Private Securities Litigation Reform Act of 1995 (PSLRA), to qualify as "strong" within the intendment of § 21D(b)(2), an inference of scienter must be found by a reasonable person to be cogent and at least as compelling as any opposing inference of nonfraudulent intent. To prevail on a claim under § 10(b) of the Securities Act and Rule 10(b)-5, a plaintiff must prove the defendant acted with scienter, "a mental state embracing intent to deceive, manipulate, or defraud." Setting a uniform pleading standard for § 10(b) actions was among Congress's objectives in enacting the PSLRA. As a check against abusive litigation in private securities fraud actions, PSLRA includes exacting pleading requirements that require plaintiffs to state with particularity both the facts constituting the alleged violation, and the facts evidencing scienter, i.e., the defendant's intention "to deceive, manipulate, or defraud." As set out in § 21D(b)(2), plaintiffs must "state with particularity facts giving rise to a strong inference that the defendant acted with the required state of mind." However, Congress left the key term "strong inference" undefined. The key issue in this case is whether the court of appeals' formulation of that term is adequate; it is not, because it does not capture the stricter demand Congress sought to convey by its use of that term. Congress did not shed much light on what facts would create a strong inference or how courts could determine the existence of the requisite inference. With no clear guide from Congress other than its intention to strengthen existing pleading requirements, courts of appeals have diverged in construing the term "strong inference." Among the uncertainties are whether courts should consider competing inferences in determining whether an inference of scienter is "strong." Thus, the Court's task is to prescribe a workable construction of the "strong inference" standard that promotes the PSLRA's twin goals of curbing frivolous, lawyer-driven litigation, while preserving investors' ability to recover on meritorious claims. The Court establishes the following prescriptions: First, faced with a motion to dismiss a § 10(b) action, courts must, as with

Continued on next page.

any motion to dismiss for failure to plead a claim on which relief can be granted, accept all factual allegations in the complaint as true. Second, courts must consider the complaint in its entirety, as well as other sources courts ordinarily examine when ruling on motions to dismiss. The inquiry is whether all of the facts alleged, taken collectively, give rise to a strong inference of scienter, not whether any individual allegation, scrutinized in isolation, meets that standard. Third, in determining whether the pleaded facts give rise to a "strong" inference of scienter, the court must take into account plausible opposing inferences. The court of appeals expressly declined to engage in such a comparative inquiry, but Congress did not merely require plaintiffs to allege facts from which an inference of scienter rationally could be drawn. Instead, Congress required plaintiffs to plead with particularity facts that give rise to a "strong"—i.e., a powerful or cogent—inference. To determine whether the plaintiff has alleged facts giving rise to the requisite "strong inference," a court must consider plausible, nonculpable explanations for the defendant's conduct, as well as inferences favoring the plaintiff. The inference that the defendant acted with scienter need not be irrefutable, but it must be more than merely "reasonable" or "permissible"—it must be cogent and compelling. In this way, the inference is "strong" in light of other explanations. Tellabs (D) contends that when competing inferences are considered, as per this formulation, Notebaert's (D) evident lack of pecuniary motive will be dispositive. While motive can be a relevant consideration, and personal financial gain may weigh heavily in favor of a scienter inference, the absence of such a motive is not fatal. Because allegations must be considered collectively, the significance that can be ascribed to an allegation of motive, or lack thereof, depends on the entirety of all the facts alleged. Tellabs (D) also maintains that several of the shareholders' (P) allegations are too vague or ambiguous to contribute to a strong inference of scienter. While omissions and ambiguities count against inferring scienter, the Court's job is not to scrutinize each allegation in isolation but to assess all the allegations holistically. Vacated and remanded.

CONCURRENCE: (Scalia, J.) An inference at least as likely as competing inferences is not a "strong inference." The correct test should be whether the inference of scienter (if any) is more plausible than the inference of innocence.

▶ *ANALYSIS*

The majority rejected Tellabs (D) assertion that even applying its "strong inference" formulation, Notebaert's (D) evident lack of pecuniary motive would be dispositive. The Court noted instead that while motive can be a relevant consideration, the absence of such a motive is not dispositive. One motive that courts have found dispositive is where there has been unusual insider trading following

the allegedly fraudulent conduct. On the other hand, the mere assertion that a corporate officer has lied to maximize her compensation or to keep her job is insufficient by itself to create a "strong inference" of fraud.

Quicknotes

INFERENCE A deduction from established facts.

MOTIVE Reason or other impetus inciting one to action.

SCIENTER Knowledge of certain facts; often refers to "guilty knowledge," which implicates liability.

Makor Issues & Rights, Ltd. v. Tellabs, Inc.

Shareholder (P) v. Corporation (D)

513 F.3d 702 (7th Cir. 2008).

NATURE OF CASE: Case on remand to court that had previously reversed dismissal of an action brought under the Private Securities Litigation Reform Act of 1995 for securities fraud.

FACT SUMMARY: Shareholders (P) of Tellabs, Inc. (Tellabs) (D) alleged that Tellabs (D) and its officers (D) violated § 10(b) of the Securities Exchange Act of 1934, and SEC Rule 10b-5, by making materially false statements regarding demand and sales of certain products at a time when the demand and sales were in fact sharply declining. The district court had dismissed the case, and the court of appeals had reversed, but the United States Supreme Court vacated and remanded the case to the court of appeals to decide whether the complaint sufficiently alleged a strong inference of scienter as required by the Private Securities Litigation Reform Act of 1995 (PSLRA).

🏛 RULE OF LAW
An action brought under the Private Securities Litigation Reform Act of 1995 (PSLRA) will not be dismissed where the inference of scienter is much more likely than an inference of innocence.

FACTS: Shareholders (P) of Tellabs, Inc. (Tellabs) (D) who purchased stock over a seven-month period filed a class action under the Private Securities Litigation Reform Act of 1995 (PSLRA) alleging that Tellabs (D) and Notebaert (D), then Tellabs' (D) CEO and president, had engaged in securities fraud in violation of § 10(b) of the Securities Exchange Act of 1934, and SEC Rule 10b-5. Specifically, the shareholders (P) alleged that during the seven-month period, Notebaert (D) (and by imputation Tellabs (D)) falsely reassured public investors, in a series of statements, that Tellabs (D) was continuing to enjoy strong demand for its key products—the TITAN 5500 and TITAN 6500—and earning record revenues when, in fact, Notebaert (D) knew the opposite was true. When it was finally revealed, after the seven-month class period, that demand for the 5500 and 6500 had dropped significantly, the price of its stock per share plunged from a high of $67 to a low of around $16. The complaint relied on 26 confidential sources who were employed at Tellabs (D) and who were in a position to know of the falsity of the statements. The district court dismissed the action, the court of appeals reversed, but the United States Supreme Court vacated and remanded the case to the court of appeals to decide whether the complaint sufficiently alleged a strong inference of scienter as required by the Private Securities Litigation Reform Act of 1995 (PSLRA)—in accord with the Supreme Court's formulation of "strong inference."

ISSUE: Will an action brought under the Private Securities Litigation Reform Act of 1995 (PSLRA) be dismissed where the inference of scienter is much more likely than an inference of innocence?

HOLDING AND DECISION: (Posner, J.) No. An action brought under the Private Securities Litigation Reform Act of 1995 (PSLRA) will not be dismissed where the inference of scienter is much more likely than an inference of innocence. The key question here is the whether it is more likely that the allegedly false statements were the result of merely careless mistakes at the senior management level based on false information fed it from below (i.e., were "innocent"), or were the result of an intent to deceive or a reckless indifference to whether the statements were false and misleading. If the former, even if senior management had been careless in failing to detect the error, there would be no corporate scienter. The key is what was in the minds of the corporate officials making the statements, not the collective knowledge of all corporate employees. It is "exceedingly" unlikely that the allegedly false statements were the result of careless mistakes and errors, given that the 5500 and 6500 were the company's most important products. Given that no plausible story has been presented by Tellabs (D) as to why the statements were the product of mistake, it is most unlikely that the senior officers, including Notebaert (D), who made the allegedly misleading statements, did not know that they were false. Tellabs' (D) argument that the officers did not stand to personally benefit from the statements, and that there was no motive in painting an inaccurate picture of the prospects for the 5500 and 6500 given that the truth was revealed within months, is rejected. Such an argument conflates expected benefits with realized benefits. If Notebaert (D) thought that the situation regarding the 5500 and 6500 would right itself, the benefits of concealment might exceed the costs. It is possible that prompt disclosure would not only have led to a precipitous drop in the company's stock price, but would have prevented recovery to previous levels since the company would be perceived as volatile. In this sense, Notebaert (D) may have been gambling that concealed bad news would be overtaken by good news and prevent such a scenario. Thus, the inference of corporate scienter is not only as likely as its opposite, but much more likely since the theory of mistakes and errors is far less likely than a theory of scienter at the corporate level at which the statements were approved. That is, it is exceedingly unlikely that the company's CEO and president was unaware of the problems with its key products and was

Continued on next page.

merely repeating lies fed to him by other executives. Given that the inference of corporate scienter is much more likely, it is also cogent. Finally, Tellabs (D) argues that the shareholders' (P) reliance on confidential sources weakens the inference. This assertion must also be rejected. The confidential sources are important sources for the allegations not only of falsity but also of scienter. Here, the sources have been kept confidential so that they will not be retaliated against by Tellabs (D)—even though such retaliation is unlawful, it still is a concern of the sources. These sources consist of persons who from the description of their jobs were in a position to know at first hand the facts to which they were prepared to testify. The facts they detail are convincing and, in some instances, are corroborated by multiple sources. Although it would have been better if these sources had been named, the absence of proper names does not invalidate the drawing of a strong inference from their assertions. Because the shareholders (P) have succeeded in pleading scienter in conformity with the PLSRA, the decision to reverse the district court's dismissal is adhered to. Reversed.

▶ ANALYSIS

The idea of drawing a "strong inference" from factual allegations is inconsistent with the prevalent practice of notice pleading. Even when a plaintiff is required by Rule 9(b) of the Federal Rules of Civil Procedure to plead facts (such as the when and where of an alleged fraudulent statement), the court must treat the pleaded facts as true and "draw all reasonable inferences in favor of the plaintiff." To draw a "strong inference" in favor of the plaintiff might seem to imply that the defendant had pleaded facts or presented evidence that would, by comparison with the plaintiff's allegations, enable a conclusion that the plaintiff had the stronger case; and therefore that a judge could not draw a strong inference in the plaintiff's favor before hearing from the defendant. But comparison is not essential, and obviously is not contemplated by the PLSRA, which requires dismissal in advance of the defendant's answer unless the complaint itself gives rise to a strong inference of scienter. A defendant will usually have evidence to present in his defense, so a complaint that on its face, and without reference to the defendant's case, creates only a weak or bare inference of scienter, suggesting that the plaintiff would prevail only if there were no defense case at all, would be quite likely to fail eventually when the defendant had a chance to put on his case, which would normally be after pretrial discovery. Apparently, Congress does not believe that weak complaints should put a defendant to the expense of discovery in a complex securities-fraud case, such as the one at issue in this decision.

Quicknotes

INFERENCE A deduction from established facts.

MOTIVE Reason or other impetus inciting one to action.

SCIENTER Knowledge of certain facts; often refers to "guilty knowledge," which implicates liability.

Basic Inc. v. Levinson

Company directors (D) v. Shareholders (P)

485 U.S. 224 (1988).

NATURE OF CASE: Appeal from circuit court decision in a class action suit.

FACT SUMMARY: Levinson (P) and other shareholders of Basic Incorporated (D) brought a class action against the company (D) and its directors (D), alleging they suffered injuries from selling their shares at depressed prices, in reliance on materially misleading statements issued by Basic (D) in violation of the Securities and Exchange Act of 1934 and Rule 10b-5.

🏛 RULE OF LAW
Reliance on materially misleading statements by a corporation will be presumed for a class action plaintiff asserting a Rule 10b-5 claim where he relied instead on the integrity of the price set by the market in trading.

FACTS: Basic Incorporated (D) was a publicly traded company engaged in the business of manufacturing for the steel industry. Another company, Combustion Engineering, Inc. met with Basic directors (D) concerning the possibility of a merger. Basic (D) made three public statements denying that it was engaged in merger discussions. Levinson (P) and other shareholders (P) sold their stock after these denials. Basic's (D) board subsequently endorsed Combustion's offer and publicly announced its merger approval. Levinson (P) and the shareholders then brought a class action suit, asserting that Basic (D) issued misleading public statements in violation of Rule 10b-5.

ISSUE: Can reliance on materially misleading statements by a corporation be presumed for a class action plaintiff asserting a Rule 10b-5 claim where he relied instead on the integrity of the price set by the market in trading?

HOLDING AND DECISION: (Blackmun, J.) Yes. Reliance on materially misleading statements by a corporation will be presumed for a class action plaintiff asserting a Rule 10b-5 claim where he relied instead on the integrity of the price set by the market in trading. The "fraud-on-the-market" theory is based on the premise that misleading material information in the open market will affect the price of a company's stock, whether or not the individual investor relied on the misrepresentation. The lower courts applied a rebuttable presumption of reliance. Levinson (P) argued that the shareholders sold their stock in Basic (D) based on the depressed price created by Basic's (D) misrepresentation. If a court required proof of each individual shareholder's reliance in a class action, such proof would prevent the case from going forward since the individual issues would overwhelm issues common to

the class. Basic (D) contended that a claim under Rule 10b-5 requires proof of reliance and that, in applying the fraud-on-the-market theory the court effectively eliminated that requirement. While reliance is an element of a Rule 10b-5 cause of action, there are other ways of demonstrating a causal connection between the company's misrepresentations and the shareholder's injury. This Court has held that the causal connection has been demonstrated where a duty to disclose material information was breached or material omissions or misstatements were made in connection with a proxy solicitation. The Court's interpretation on Rule 10b-5 must take into consideration the conditions of modern securities markets, in which millions of shares are traded daily. Presumptions allow the Court to manage such circumstances in which direct proof is difficult to obtain. Here, the lower courts accepted a presumption that the individual shareholders traded in reliance on Basic's depressed price and that because of the company's (D) material misrepresentations that price was fraudulently depressed. Requiring each individual shareholder to demonstrate reliance would impose an unrealistic burden on the shareholder who traded on the open market. The presumption is consistent with Congress's intent in enacting the 1934 Act to facilitate investors' reliance on the integrity of the market and information provided in relation thereto, as well as with common sense. Most courts have held that where misleading statements have been issued, reliance of individual shareholders on the integrity of the market price may be presumed. Since an investor buys or sells stock based on the integrity of that price, it may be presumed for Rule 10b-5 purposes that the investor also relied on the public material misrepresentation as reflected in the market price. The court of appeals found that Basic (D) made public material misrepresentations and sold its shares in the open market. Since the shareholders (P) established their loss, the burden shifted to Basic (D) to rebut the elements giving rise to the presumption. Basic (D) failed to rebut the presumption.

CONCURRENCE IN PART/DISSENT IN PART: (White, J.) Even as the Court attempts to limit the fraud-on-the-market theory it endorses today, the pitfalls in its approach are revealed by previous uses by the lower courts of the broader versions of the theory. Confusion and contradiction in court rulings are inevitable when traditional legal analysis is replaced with economic theorization by the federal courts. While the economists' theories which underpin the fraud-on-the-market presumption may have the appeal of mathematical exactitude and scientific

Continued on next page.

certainty, they are nothing more than theories which may or may not prove accurate upon further consideration. Thus, while the majority states that, for purposes of reaching its result it need only make modest assumptions about the way in which "market professionals generally" do their jobs and about how the conduct of market professionals affects stock prices, I doubt that we are in much of a position to assess which theories aptly describe the functioning of the securities industry. Consequently, I cannot join the Court in its effort to reconfigure the securities laws, based on recent economic theories, to better fit what it perceives to be the new realities of financial markets. I would leave this task to others more equipped for the job than we. While I do not propose that the law retreat from the many protections that § 10(b) and Rule 10b-5, as interpreted in our prior cases, provide to investors, any extension of these laws, to approach something closer to an investor insurance scheme, should come from Congress, and not from the courts.

▶ *ANALYSIS*

Early cases involving Rule 10b-5 involved face-to-face transactions in which plaintiffs were required to demonstrate their reliance on the defendant's misrepresentation and that such reliance caused their losses. The development of the modern securities exchange eliminated this personal interaction, thus making it difficult or impossible to prove the element of reliance in order to establish the causal connection. The fraud-on-the-market theory eliminates the necessity of the plaintiffs' demonstrating reliance on the alleged misstatement or omission, or that the plaintiff was privy to the misleading information.

■═■

Quicknotes

FRAUD A false representation of facts with the intent that another will rely on the misrepresentation to his detriment.

MISREPRESENTATION A statement or conduct by one party to another that constitutes a false representation of fact.

RELIANCE Dependence on a fact that causes a party to act or refrain from acting.

RULE 10b-5 Unlawful to defend or make untrue statements in connection with purchase or sale of securities.

■═■

Dura Pharmaceuticals, Inc. v. Broudo

Public corporation (D) v. Investors (P)

544 U.S. 336 (2005).

NATURE OF CASE: Appeal from reversal of dismissal of private securities fraud action.

FACT SUMMARY: Dura Pharmaceuticals, Inc., and some of its managers and directors (collectively, Dura), argued that investors (P) in Dura who brought a private securities fraud action against Dura (D) could not satisfy the "loss causation" requirement simply by alleging that a security's price at the time of purchase was inflated because of the misrepresentation.

> 🏛 **RULE OF LAW**
> A plaintiff in a private securities fraud action cannot satisfy the "loss causation" requirement simply by alleging that a security's price at the time of purchase was inflated because of the misrepresentation.

FACTS: Investors (P) filed a securities fraud class action, alleging that Dura Pharmaceuticals, Inc., and some of its managers and directors (collectively Dura), made, inter alia, misrepresentations about future Food and Drug Administration approval of a new asthmatic spray device, leading the investors (P) to purchase Dura (D) securities at an artificially inflated price. The federal district court dismissed, finding that the complaint failed adequately to allege "loss causation," i.e., a causal connection between the spray device misrepresentation and the economic loss. The court of appeals reversed, finding that a plaintiff can satisfy the loss causation requirement simply by alleging that a security's price at the time of purchase was inflated because of the misrepresentation. The Supreme Court granted certiorari to resolve a dispute among the circuits on this issue.

ISSUE: Can a plaintiff in a private securities fraud action satisfy the "loss causation" requirement simply by alleging that a security's price at the time of purchase was inflated because of the misrepresentation?

HOLDING AND DECISION: (Breyer, J.) No. A plaintiff in a private securities fraud action cannot satisfy the "loss causation" requirement simply by alleging that a security's price at the time of purchase was inflated because of the misrepresentation. A private plaintiff who claims securities fraud must prove that the defendant's fraud caused an economic loss. First, an inflated purchase price will not by itself constitute or proximately cause the relevant economic loss needed to allege and prove "loss causation." As a matter of pure logic, the moment the transaction takes place, the plaintiff has suffered no loss because the inflated purchase price is offset by ownership of a share that possesses equivalent value at that instant.

Also, the logical link between the inflated purchase price and any later economic loss is not invariably strong, since other factors may affect the price. Thus, the most logic alone permits this Court to say is that the inflated purchase price suggests that misrepresentation "touches upon" a later economic loss. However, to touch upon a loss is not to cause a loss, and it is the latter that the law requires. Moreover, the court of appeals' position is not supported by precedent. The common-law deceit and misrepresentation actions that private securities fraud actions resemble require a plaintiff to show not only that had he known the truth he would not have acted, but also that he suffered actual economic loss. Additionally, the court of appeals' holding cannot be reconciled with the views of other courts of appeals, which have rejected the inflated purchase price approach to showing loss causation. Finally, the court of appeals' approach is inconsistent with an important securities law objective: to maintain public confidence in the marketplace by permitting private securities fraud actions. Such actions, however, are not intended to provide investors with broad insurance against marketplace losses, but to protect investors only against those economic losses that misrepresentations actually cause. Therefore, such actions may proceed only where plaintiffs adequately allege and prove the traditional elements of cause and loss. Contrary to this requirement, the court of appeals' approach would allow recovery where a misrepresentation leads to an inflated purchase price, but does not proximately cause any economic loss. Applying this holding, here the investors' (P) complaint was legally insufficient in respect to its allegation of "loss causation." The complaint's short and plain statement of the claim did not give Dura (D) fair notice of what the investors' (P) claim was and the grounds upon which it rested. The complaint here contained only the investors' (P) allegation that their loss consisted of artificially inflated purchase prices. However, as the Court has concluded here, such a price is not itself a relevant economic loss, and the complaint nowhere else provided Dura (D) with notice of what the relevant loss might be or of what the causal connection might be between that loss and the misrepresentation. Ordinary pleading rules are not meant to impose a great burden on a plaintiff, but it should not prove burdensome for a plaintiff suffering economic loss to provide a defendant with some indication of the loss and the causal connection that the plaintiff has in mind. Allowing a plaintiff to forgo giving any indication of the economic loss and proximate cause would bring about the very sort of harm the securities statutes seek to avoid, namely the abusive practice of filing lawsuits with only a

Continued on next page.

faint hope that discovery might lead to some plausible cause of action. Reversed and remanded.

▶ *ANALYSIS*

The constant flow of new information into securities markets and the inevitable time that occurs between any fraud and its subsequent correction means that there is always a need to separate any change in a stock price due to the fraud from change in the stock price due to the changes in the market. That is a recurring challenge in almost any securities case and the basis for the Court's concern, expressed on two occasions in this case, that the securities laws not become an insurance program against market losses. What this means in a case like this one is that the plaintiff must be able to show not only that the price was inflated because of the fraud, but that also some sort of correction occurred before the plaintiff traded leading to an economic loss for the plaintiff. For example, a plaintiff's claim of inflation and the sharp stock price drop that occurred when the truth became known satisfies this requirement.

Quicknotes

CAUSATION The aggregate effect of preceding events that bring about a tortious result; the causal connection between the actions of a tortfeasor and the injury that follows.

CAUSE OF ACTION A fact or set of facts the occurrence of which entitles a party to seek judicial relief.

CLASS ACTION A suit commenced by a representative on behalf of an ascertainable group that is too large to appear in court, who shares a commonality of interests and who will benefit from a successful result.

INTER ALIA Among other things.

Green v. Occidental Petroleum Corp.

Shareholder (P) v. Corporation (D)

541 F.2d 1335 (9th Cir. 1976).

NATURE OF CASE: Appeal from class certification in an action to recover damages related to securities transactions.

FACT SUMMARY: Alleging damages suffered due to Occidental Petroleum Corp.'s (D) issuance of false information which inflated the market price of its securities, Green (P) and other Occidental (D) shareholders brought a class action to recover their losses.

🏛 RULE OF LAW
[Proposed:] Certification of a class based on an out-of-pocket measure of damages does not constitute an abuse of discretion.

FACTS: Green (P) and other Occidental Petroleum Corp. (Occidental) (D) shareholders brought a class action against Occidental (D) and other defendants, alleging improper accounting practices and overstatement of profits in the quarterly reports issued by Occidental (D). These practices resulted in an inflated price for Occidental's (D) securities. Green (P) alleged that these actions constituted a violation of § 10b-5 of the Securities and Exchange Act of 1934, damaging him and others who traded in Occidental's (D) securities in reliance on that false information. This action sought to recover the damages suffered by Green (P) and all other similarly situated shareholders. The trial court certified the class. On appeal, the Circuit Court held that the class could be certified for actions brought against Occidental (D) and other defendants under Fed. R. Civ. P. 23(b)(3) but not under Fed. R. Civ. P. 23(b)(1). Judge Sneed concurred in part and concurred in the result of the majority opinion.

ISSUE: [Proposed:] Does certification of a class based on an out-of-pocket measure of damages constitute an abuse of discretion?

HOLDING AND DECISION: [Holding and Decision not included in casebook excerpt.]

CONCURRENCE IN PART: (Sneed, J.) No. Certification of a class based on an out-of-pocket measure of damages does not constitute an abuse of discretion. The proper measure of damages is what the purchasers lost as a result of Occidental's (D) wrong, not what Occidental (D) gained. A rescissory measure of damages would not properly measure any loss sustained by Green (P) and the other shareholders. Rescission would permit Green (P) to place on Occidental (D) the burden of any decline in the value of the stock between the date of purchase and the date of disclosure of the fraud, even though only a portion of that decline may have been proximately caused by Occidental's

(D) wrong. The reason is that rescission contemplates a return of the injured party to the position he occupied before he was induced by wrongful conduct to enter the transaction. Here, in an open-market situation, Occidental (D) did not undertake to assume the risk of the stock's decline in value since it never directly sold stock to the plaintiffs. Thus, the use of a rescissory measure of damages would make certification an abuse of discretion. On the other hand, the out-of-pocket measure of damages fixes recovery as the difference between the purchase price and the value of the stock at the date of purchase. This difference is proximately caused by the misrepresentations of Occidental (D). It measures precisely the extent to which the purchaser has been required to invest a greater amount than otherwise would have been necessary, and furthers the purpose of rule 10b-5 without subjecting the wrongdoer to excessive or unpredictable damages. To properly measure the damages for each plaintiff, a price line and a value line must be established for the entire period at issue, and then each plaintiff can determine, based on the difference between the two lines for the date of purchase (at least for those class members who held their shares until disclosure of the misrepresentations), his or her damages. As for plaintiffs who did not hold onto their shares until disclosure was made, the spread between the price and value lines may not remain constant, and, therefore, there may be a conflict of interest between these plaintiffs and those who held the stock until disclosure. While these conflicting interests may require the creation of sub-classes, they do not make class certification an arbitrary or capricious act. Additionally, the out-of-pocket measure of damages will permit a recovery by purchasers who sold for a price greater than they paid for the stock. Thus, purchasers who disposed of their stock after disclosure are entitled to recover the difference between the price and value of the stock on the date of their purchase even though they ultimately sold the stock for more than they paid for it. Thus, for all these reasons, if the trial court's certification of the class was based on intent to properly apply the out-of-pocket measure of damages, the majority's affirmance of that certification was made on the correct basis.

▶ ANALYSIS

As Judge Sneed points out, the rescissory measure of damages (the difference between the purchase price and the value of the stock as of the date of disclosure) works justly when a defrauded seller proceeds after an increase in value of the stock against a fraudulent buyer who is

Continued on next page.

unable to return the stock he fraudulently purchased. His inability to return the stock should not deprive the injured seller of the remedy of restitution. Under these circumstances it is appropriate to require the fraudulent buyer to account for his "ill-gotten profits" derived from an increase in the value of the stock following his acquisition of the stock. Otherwise, the seller will not be put in the position he occupied before the contract was made. Such a remedy should also work when the defrauded purchaser retains the stock until the date of disclosure. The purchaser pursuing a remedy of restitution is entitled to the return of his purchase price upon return of the stock, or an amount equal to the purchase price reduced by the value of the stock at the date of disclosure. This remedy imposes upon the wrongful seller the burden of any loss in the value of the stock between the date of sale and the disclosure date. This is appropriate because the wrongful seller as a direct consequence of his wrong shifted to the purchaser the risks which he would have borne but for the wrongful sale. The seller's obligation to accept the return of the risk he wrongfully shifted is rooted in the contract of sale. That is, it springs from his contractual undertakings. Here, Judge Sneed emphasized that the plaintiffs' damages were not rooted in a contract for sale.

■═■

Quicknotes

CLASS ACTION A suit commenced by a representative on behalf of an ascertainable group that is too large to appear in court, who shares a commonality of interests and who will benefit from a successful result.

RESCISSION The canceling of an agreement and the return of the parties to their positions prior to the formation of the contract.

■═■

Malone v. Brincat

Shareholders (P) v. Corporation (D)

Del. Sup. Ct., 722 A.2d 5 (1998) (*en banc*).

NATURE OF CASE: Appeal by corporate shareholders of a dismissal with prejudice of their complaint against their corporation.

FACT SUMMARY: Malone and other shareholders (P) filed a class action against Mercury Corporation (D) and its directors, alleging that the directors knowingly and intentionally breached their fiduciary duty of disclosure in that the Securities and Exchange Commission (SEC) filings made by the directors (D) and every communication from the company to the shareholders since 1994 were materially false and that as a result of the false disclosures, Mercury (D) lost nearly $2 billion.

🏛 RULE OF LAW
Directors who knowingly disseminate false information that results in corporate injury or damage to an individual stockholder violate their fiduciary duty and may be held accountable in a manner appropriate to the circumstances.

FACTS: Mercury Corporation and its directors (D) disseminated information containing overstatements of Mercury's earnings, financial performance, and shareholders' equity. Mercury's (D) earnings for 1996 were only $56.7 million, rather than the $120.7 million as reported by its directors (D). Mercury's (D) earnings in 1995 were $76.9 million, rather than $98.9 million as reported by its directors (D). Shareholders' equity on December 31, 1996 was disclosed by the directors (D) as $353 million but was actually only $263 million or less. The complaint of Malone (P) and other Mercury shareholders alleged that the foregoing inaccurate information was included or referenced in virtually every filing Mercury (D) made with the SEC and every communication Mercury's directors (D) made to the shareholders during this period of time. The shareholders (P) alleged that as a result of these false disclosures, the company lost virtually all its value (about $2 billion). They sought class action status to pursue damages against Mercury (D) and its directors (D). The individual director defendants (D) filed a motion to dismiss contending that they owed no fiduciary duty of disclosure. The Chancery Court granted the motion to dismiss with prejudice, holding that the directors (D) had no fiduciary duty of disclosure under Delaware law in the absence of a request for shareholder action. The shareholders (P) appealed.

ISSUE: Do directors who knowingly disseminate false information that results in corporate injury or damage to an individual stockholder violate their fiduciary duty with the result that they may be held accountable in a manner appropriate to the circumstances?

HOLDING AND DECISION: (Holland, J.) Yes. Directors who knowingly disseminate false information that results in corporate injury or damage to an individual stockholder violate their fiduciary duty and may be held accountable in a manner appropriate to the circumstances. Since the board of directors has the legal responsibility to manage the business of a corporation for the benefit of its shareholder owners, fiduciary duties are imposed on the directors of corporations to regulate their conduct when they discharge that function. Corporate directors stand in a fiduciary relationship not only to the stockholders but also to the corporations upon whose boards they serve. The directors' fiduciary duty to both the corporation and their shareholders encompasses due care, good faith, and loyalty. The issue is not whether Mercury's directors (D) breached their duty of disclosure. It is whether they breached their more general fiduciary duty of loyalty and good faith by knowingly disseminating to the stockholders false information about the financial condition of the company, given that the directors' fiduciary duties include the duty to deal with their stockholders honestly. Shareholders are entitled to rely upon the truthfulness of all information disseminated to them by the directors they elect to manage the corporate enterprise. Directors disseminate information in at least three contexts: public statements to the market, including shareholders; statements informing shareholders about the affairs of the corporation without a request for shareholder action; and statements to shareholders in conjunction with a request for shareholder action. Inaccurate information in these contexts may be the result of a violation of the fiduciary duties of care, loyalty, or good faith. Here, the complaint alleges an egregious violation of fiduciary duty by Mercury's directors (D) in knowingly disseminating materially false information and in the corporation's loss of about $2 billion in value as a result. Then the complaint merely states that the action is brought on behalf of the named plaintiffs (P) and the putative class. The allegation that the false disclosures resulted in the corporation losing virtually all its equity seems obliquely to claim an injury to the corporation. The shareholders (P), however, never expressly assert a derivative claim on behalf of the corporation or allege compliance with the court rule which requires pre-suit demand or cognizable and particularized allegations that a demand is excused. If the shareholders (P) here intended to assert a derivative claim, they should be permitted to replead to assert such a claim and any damage or equitable remedy sought on behalf of the corporation. Likewise, the shareholders (P) should have the opportunity to replead to assert any individual cause of

Continued on next page.

action and articulate a remedy that is appropriate on behalf of the named share-holders (P) individually or of a properly recognizable class, consistent with court rules. Judgment to dismiss is affirmed. However, the judgment to dismiss with prejudice is reversed.

▶ *ANALYSIS*

In *Malone*, the court made clear that shareholders of a corporation are entitled to rely upon their elected directors to discharge their fiduciary duties at all times. Whenever directors communicate publicly or directly with shareholders about the corporation's affairs, with or without a request for shareholder action, directors have a fiduciary duty to shareholders to exercise due care, good faith, and loyalty. It follows a fortiori that when directors communicate publicly or directly with shareholders about corporate matters the sine qua non of directors' fiduciary duty to shareholders is honesty. The focus of the fiduciary duty of disclosure is to protect shareholders as the "beneficiaries" of all material information disseminated by the directors. The duty of disclosure is, and always has been, a specific application of the general fiduciary duty owed by directors. The duty of disclosure obligates directors to provide the stockholders with accurate and complete information material to a transaction or other corporate event that is being presented to them for action.

■══■

Quicknotes

A FORTIORI A method of reasoning whereby if one fact is true then a lesser fact, which is necessarily encompassed by the greater fact, must also be true.

BREACH OF FIDUCIARY DUTY The failure of a fiduciary to observe the standard of care exercised by professionals of similar education and experience.

CLASS ACTION A suit commenced by a representative on behalf of an ascertainable group that is too large to appear in court, who shares a commonality of interests and who will benefit from a successful result.

DUTY OF CARE Duty that an officer or director owes to the corporation, by virtue of his fiduciary relationship, to act for the benefit of the corporation.

DUTY OF GOOD FAITH AND FAIR DEALING An implied duty in a contract that the parties will deal honestly in the satisfaction of their obligations and without intent to defraud.

DUTY OF LOYALTY A director's duty to refrain from self-dealing or to take a position that is adverse to the corporation's best interests.

FIDUCIARY DUTY A legal obligation to act for the benefit of another, including subordinating one's personal interests to that of the other person.

MOTION TO DISMISS Motion to terminate a trial based on the adequacy of the pleadings.

SECURITIES EXCHANGE ACT OF 1934 Federal statute regulating stock exchanges and trading and requiring the disclosure of certain information in relation to securities traded.

■══■

Federal Regulation of Tender Offers

Quick Reference Rules of Law

Prudent Real Estate Trust v. Johncamp Realty, Inc.

Target company (P) v. Close corporation (D)

599 F.2d 1140 (2d Cir. 1979).

NATURE OF CASE: Appeal from denial of a motion for a temporary injunction against the continuation of a tender offer.

FACT SUMMARY: When Johncamp Realty, Inc. (D) failed to disclose financial information about all the bidders in its tender offer for Prudent Real Estate Trust's (Prudent's) (P) outstanding shares, Prudent (P) sought a temporary injunction against the offer.

🏛 **RULE OF LAW**
An omitted fact is a material fact which must be disclosed where there is a substantial likelihood that disclosure would have assumed actual significance in the deliberations of the reasonable shareholder.

FACTS: Johncamp Realty, Inc. (Johncamp) (D), a close corporation, made a tender offer to purchase any and all outstanding shares of (Prudent Real Estate Trust (Prudent) (P). The purpose of the offer was to acquire all Prudent's (P) shares or, alternatively, to acquire enough shares to exercise control. Prudent (P) brought this action for a temporary injunction against the continuation of the tender offer, alleging that the material filed by Johncamp (D) with the Securities and Exchange Commission (SEC) was insufficient and that, because of certain statements and omissions, the offer violated § 14(e) of the Securities and Exchange Act (Act). The information filed with the SEC disclosed financial information as to some but not all of the bidders. The district court denied Prudent's (P) motion for a temporary injunction, and Prudent (P) appealed. The court of appeals granted the motion until argument of an expedited appeal and then extended the injunction pending decision.

ISSUE: Is an omitted fact a material fact which must be disclosed where there is a substantial likelihood that disclosure would have assumed actual significance in the deliberations of the reasonable shareholder?

HOLDING AND DECISION: (Friendly, J.) Yes. An omitted fact is a material fact which must be disclosed where there is a substantial likelihood that disclosure would have assumed actual significance in the deliberations of the reasonable shareholder. The shareholder of a target company has to determine whether to tender, to sell, or to hold part or all of his securities and should be able to consider the financial condition of all the bidders in making that decision. An important factor here is the impracticability of obtaining the omitted financial information from other sources. A temporary injunction will be sufficient if it extends only until Johncamp (D) makes the necessary corrections and if it allows a reasonable period for withdrawal of stock already tendered. Reversed.

▶ **ANALYSIS**

The test of materiality applied here by the court of appeals was stated in *TSC Industries, Inc. v. Northway, Inc.*, 426 U.S. 438, 449 (1976). Although *TSC* arose under Rule 14a-9 concerning proxy contests, the court of appeals here extended it to a cash tender offer. The court also declared that, from the beginning of litigation under the Williams Act, it had been conscious of its responsibility not to allow management to "resort to the courts on trumped-up or trivial grounds as a means for delaying and thereby defeating tender offers."

━━■

Quicknotes

INJUNCTION A court order requiring a person to do or prohibiting that person from doing a specific act.

MATERIALITY Importance; the degree of relevance or necessity to the particular matter.

SECURITIES & EXCHANGE ACT, RULE 14e Prohibits any fraudulent, deceptive, or manipulative acts or practices in connection with any tender offer.

TENDER OFFER An offer made by one corporation to the shareholders of a target corporation to purchase their shares subject to number, time, and price specifications.

WILLIAMS ACT Regulates the process of tender offers.

━━■

Securities and Exchange Commission v. Amster & Co.

Government agency (P) v. Risk arbitrageur (D)

762 F. Supp. 604 (S.D.N.Y. 1991).

NATURE OF CASE: Action alleging violations of a federal act regulating tender offers.

FACT SUMMARY: When Amster & Co.'s (D) final amendment to their original filing stated an intention to acquire control of Graphic, contrary to their originally stated purpose of a mere investment in Graphic, the Securities and Exchange Commission (SEC) (P) brought this action, alleging violations of the Williams Act.

RULE OF LAW
If the purpose of the purchases of a company's securities is to acquire control of that company, the person holding more than 5% of the shares must disclose any plans to liquidate the company, to sell its assets, or to make any major change in its corporate structure.

FACTS: Amster & Co. (D) and its predecessor, Lafer, Amster & Co. (LACO) (D), were risk arbitrageurs who purchased shares of companies expecting that some anticipated event would drive the price of the shares up. LACO (D) began purchasing shares of Graphic after Graphic publicly announced liquidation. When LACO's (D) purchases of Graphic shares amounted to a 5% interest, LACO (D) complied with the disclosure provisions of the Securities Exchange Act, stating its purpose was to acquire shares of Graphic as an investment. However, when Graphic indicated that the announced liquidation might not take place, LACO (D) amended its original filing, stating an intention to acquire control of Graphic. The SEC (P) brought this action, alleging violations of § 13(d) of the 1934 Securities Exchange Act, a section popularly known as the Williams Act.

ISSUE: If the purpose of the purchases of a company's securities is to acquire control of that company, must the person holding more than 5% of the shares disclose any plans to liquidate the company, to sell its assets, or to make any major change in its corporate structure?

HOLDING AND DECISION: (Haight, J.) Yes. If the purpose of the purchases of a company's securities is to acquire control of that company, the person holding more than 5% of the shares must disclose any plans to liquidate the company, to sell its assets, or to make any major change in its corporate structure. The SEC (P) argues that § 13(d) implies a duty to report a proxy contest before deciding to wage one. Contrary to the SEC's (P) assertion, disclosure only applies to definite plans, and there is no requirement to make predictions of future behavior or to disclose tentative plans. Otherwise, investors might be misled, contrary to the Act's purpose. LACO (D) had not reached a decision to wage a

proxy contest prior to the time they announced that intention in Amendment 7. Therefore, Amster & Co. (D) and LACO (D) are entitled to summary judgment dismissing the SEC's (P) § 13(d) claim.

ANALYSIS

The disclosure provisions of securities laws are intended to protect investors and enable them to receive the facts necessary for informed investment decisions. In *Chromalloy American Corp. v. Sun Chemical Corp.*, 611 F.2d 240, 248 (8th Cir. 1979), the Eighth Circuit explained that the objective of full and fair disclosure can be endangered as much by overstating the definiteness of plans as by understating them. The danger inherent in overstating the definiteness of plans is that the overstatement may cause the offeree or the public investor to rely on them unjustifiably.

Quicknotes

SUMMARY JUDGMENT Judgment rendered by a court in response to a motion by one of the parties, claiming that the lack of a question of material fact in respect to an issue warrants disposition of the issue without consideration by the jury.

TENDER OFFER An offer made by one corporation to the shareholders of a target corporation to purchase their shares subject to number, time, and price specifications.

WILLIAMS ACT Regulates the process of tender offers.

Field v. Trump

Shareholder (P) v. Offeror (D)

850 F.2d 938 (2d Cir. 1988), *cert. denied*, 489 U.S. 1012 (1989).

NATURE OF CASE: Appeal from dismissal of a claim for damages related to withdrawal of a tender offer.

FACT SUMMARY: When the Trumps (D) withdrew their initial tender offer in order to negotiate a higher price and then made another tender offer at the initial price offered, Field (P) brought this action, alleging violation of Rule 14(d)(7).

🏛 **RULE OF LAW**
A tender offer must be extended to all holders of the class of securities which is the subject of the offer, and all such holders must be paid the highest consideration offered under the tender offer.

FACTS: In a leveraged buy-out, the Trumps (D) commenced a tender offer at $22.50 per share for the shares of Pay'n Save Corporation (D). Four days after the announcement of the tender offer, the Trumps (D) "withdrew" the offer in order to arrange a purchase of a bloc of shares from certain dissident directors. When they had acquired an option to purchase the dissidents' shares for a premium which brought the price paid to the dissidents to $25.00 per share, the Trumps immediately announced a new tender offer at $23.50 per share. Field (P), a Pay'n Save (D) shareholder who tendered shares for $23.50, brought this class action for damages, alleging that the $1.50 premium paid to the dissident directors violated the so-called best price rule contained in § 14(d)(7) of the Williams Act. The district court dismissed the claim, and Field (P) appealed.

ISSUE: Must a tender offer be extended to all holders of the class of securities which is the subject of the offer, and must all such holders be paid the highest consideration offered under the tender offer?

HOLDING AND DECISION: (Winter, J.) Yes. A tender offer must be extended to all holders of the class of securities which is the subject of the offer, and all such holders must be paid the highest consideration offered under the tender offer. In dismissing the claim, the district court relied on Rule 14d-2(b), which provides that a tender offer will be deemed not to have commenced if its withdrawal is announced within five business days. However, the mere announcement of a withdrawal may not be effective if followed by purchases of shares and other conduct inconsistent with a genuine intent to withdraw. The complaint here alleged that the Trumps' (D) offer to purchase explicitly stated that the purported withdrawal was intended to allow negotiations with the dissidents. Such negotiations indicate a continuing intent to obtain control of Pay'n Save (D).

Accordingly, Field's (P) claim should not have been dismissed. Reversed.

▶ **ANALYSIS**

The following factors should be considered in determining whether formally separate offers should be "integrated" and considered to be one continuing offer: First, are the offers part of a single plan of acquisition; second, do the offers involve the purchase of the same class of security; and, third, are the offers made at or about the same time? Where the goal of an initial tender offer has not been abandoned, a purported withdrawal followed by a "new" offer must be treated as a single continuing offer for purposes of the "best-price rule."

∎▬∎

Quicknotes

LEVERAGED BUYOUT A transaction whereby corporate outsiders purchase the outstanding shares of a publicly held corporation mostly with borrowed funds.

TENDER OFFER An offer made by one corporation to the shareholders of a target corporation to purchase their shares subject to number, time, and price specifications.

WILLIAMS ACT Regulates the process of tender offers.

∎▬∎

Schreiber v. Burlington Northern, Inc.

Shareholder (P) v. Corporation (D)

472 U.S. 1 (1985).

NATURE OF CASE: Appeal from dismissal of a class action involving securities violations.

FACT SUMMARY: After Burlington Northern (D) withdrew its first tender offer for El Paso Gas Co. (D), substituting a new tender offer in a negotiated agreement with management, shareholder Schreiber (P) brought this action, alleging violation of § 14(e).

RULE OF LAW
A violation of § 14(e) of the 1934 Securities Exchange Act requires misrepresentation or nondisclosure, connoting conduct designed to deceive or defraud investors by controlling or artificially affecting the price of securities.

FACTS: Burlington Northern (D) made a hostile tender offer for El Paso Gas Co. (El Paso) (D) at $24 a share. Burlington (D) later announced terms of a new and friendly takeover agreement after negotiations with El Paso (D) management, rescinded the previous tender offer, made a new tender offer, and executed "golden parachute" contracts for four of El Paso's (D) senior officers. The rescission of the first tender offer caused a diminished payment to those shareholders who had tendered during the first offer. Shareholder Schreiber (P) filed this class action, alleging that Burlington (D) had violated § 14(e), because withdrawal of the first offer and substitution of the second tender offer constituted a "manipulative" distortion of the market for El Paso (D) stock. She also alleged that failing to disclose the golden parachute offer was a deceptive act forbidden by § 14(e). The district court dismissed the suit. The court of appeals affirmed, and this appeal followed.

ISSUE: Does a violation of § 14(e) require, misrepresentation or nondisclosure, connoting conduct designed to deceive or defraud investors by controlling or artificially affecting the price of securities?

HOLDING AND DECISION: (Burger, C.J.) Yes. A violation of § 14(e) requires misrepresentation or nondisclosure, connoting conduct designed to deceive or defraud investors by controlling or artificially affecting the price of securities. This conclusion is supported by the purpose and legislative history of the provision, which was originally added to the Securities Exchange Act as part of the Williams Act. The purpose of the Williams Act is to insure that public shareholders who are confronted by a cash tender offer for their stock will not be required to respond without adequate information. In this case, all activity that could have conceivably affected the price of El Paso (D) shares was done openly. The actions of Burlington (D) were not manipulative, and there was no misrepresentation or nondisclosure. Affirmed.

ANALYSIS

The Court declared that nowhere in the legislative history is there the slightest suggestion that § 14(e) serves any purpose other than disclosure or that the term "manipulative" should be read as an invitation to the courts to oversee the substantive fairness of tender offers. The quality of any offer is a matter for the marketplace. The meaning given to the term "manipulative" by the Court is consistent with its traditional dictionary definition. That is, manipulation is "management with use of unfair, scheming, or underhanded methods."

Quicknotes

CLASS ACTION A suit commenced by a representative on behalf of an ascertainable group that is too large to appear in court, who shares a commonality of interests and who will benefit from a successful result.

GOLDEN PARACHUTE Agreement whereby corporate executives are shielded from changes in the corporation's control.

MISREPRESENTATION A statement or conduct by one party to another that constitutes a false representation of fact.

RESCISSION The canceling of an agreement and the return of the parties to their positions prior to the formation of the contract.

TENDER OFFER An offer made by one corporation to the shareholders of a target corporation to purchase their shares subject to number, time, and price specifications.

WILLIAMS ACT Regulates the process of tender offers.

CTS Corp. v. Dynamics Corp. of America

Corporation (D) v. Corporation (P)

481 U.S. 69 (1987).

NATURE OF CASE: Appeal from invalidation of state corporate antitakeover law.

FACT SUMMARY: Indiana enacted a statutory scheme requiring shareholder approval prior to significant shifts in corporate control.

🏛 RULE OF LAW
A law permitting in-state corporations to require shareholder approval prior to significant shifts in corporate control is constitutional.

FACTS: Indiana enacted a statutory scheme whereby large Indiana public corporations, if they so opted, could require any entity acquiring either a 20%, 33%, or 50% interest to be subjected to a shareholder referendum wherein voting power of those shares could be withheld. Dynamics Corp. of America (Dynamics) (P), holder of 9.6% of CTS Corporation's (D) shares, announced a tender offer that would have brought its control to 27.5%. Dynamics (P) challenged the statute as void on statutory and Commerce Clause grounds. The district court found the statute to violate federal securities laws and the Commerce Clause and invalidated the statute. The court of appeals affirmed. CTS (D) appealed.

ISSUE: Is a law permitting, in-state corporations to require shareholder approval prior to significant shifts in corporate control, constitutional?

HOLDING AND DECISION: (Powell, J.) Yes. A law permitting in-state corporations to require shareholder approval prior to significant shifts in corporate control is constitutional. [The Court first held that the federal securities laws were not violated.] The principal objects of dormant Commerce Clause scrutiny are statutes discriminating against interstate commerce. The law in question here does not so discriminate, as it applies to both Indiana and non-Indiana would-be acquiring entities. Another type of law often struck down is that which would subject interstate commerce to inconsistent regulations. Such is not the case here, as Indiana's laws would be the only regulations applicable here. The court of appeals found the Act unconstitutional because it had great potential to hinder tender offers. This may be, but it is an insufficient reason to invalidate the Act. Corporations are creatures of state law, and states are free to formulate policy regarding the internal operations of corporations, provided they do so in a nondiscriminatory manner, which is the case here. Reversed.

▶ ANALYSIS

The Court implies an acceptance of heavy regulation of the workings of a corporation by the state of its incorporation. States have, according to the Court, a great interest in their corporations, and this justifies the regulations. This analysis is what Justice Scalia thought unnecessary to the Court's decision.

■■■

Quicknotes

COMMERCE CLAUSE Article 1, section 8, clause 3 of the United States Constitution, granting Congress the power to regulate commerce with foreign countries and between the states.

TENDER OFFER An offer made by one corporation to the shareholders of a target corporation to purchase their shares subject to number, time, and price specifications.

■■■

Amanda Acquisition Corp. v. Universal Foods Corp.

Suitor (P) v. Target corporation (D)

877 F.2d 496 (7th Cir.), *cert. denied*, 493 U.S. 955 (1989).

NATURE OF CASE: Appeal from judicial declaration as to the validity of a state antitakeover statute.

FACT SUMMARY: After making a tender offer for Universal Food Corp. (D), Amanda Acquisition Corp. (P) sought a judicial declaration that Wisconsin's anti-takeover statute was invalid, since it required a three-year wait for any merger to occur.

> 🏛 **RULE OF LAW**
> Skepticism about the wisdom of a state's law does not lead to the conclusion that the law is beyond the state's power.

FACTS: Amanda Acquisition Corp. (Amanda) (P) made a tender offer for the stock of Universal Foods Corp. (Universal) (D). However, Wisconsin had a moratorium law which required a three-year wait for any merger to occur, unless the target's board consented to the takeover before the bidder obtained 10% of the target's stock. Even when the time was up, the bidder needed the approval of a majority of the remaining investors, without any provision disqualifying shares still held by the managers who resisted the transaction. Amanda's (P) financing was contingent on a prompt merger with Universal (D), so the offer was conditioned on a judicial declaration that Wisconsin's law was invalid. The district court found that the statute effectively eliminated hostile leveraged buy-outs. This appeal followed.

ISSUE: Does skepticism about the wisdom of a state's law lead to the conclusion that the law is beyond the state's power?

HOLDING AND DECISION: (Easterbrook, J.) No. Skepticism about the wisdom of a state's law does not lead to the conclusion that the law is beyond the state's power. Unless a federal statute or the Constitution bars the way, Wisconsin's choice must be respected. Federal securities laws frequently regulate process, while state corporate law regulates substance. The Williams Act does not create a right to profit from the business of making tender offers. It is not attractive to put bids on the table for Wisconsin corporations, but because Wisconsin leaves the process alone once a bidder appears, its law is not preempted and may coexist with the Williams Act. In addition, the Commerce Clause does not demand that states leave bidders a "meaningful opportunity for success." Wisconsin's law only regulates the internal affairs of firms incorporated there. Investors may buy or sell stock as they please. No interstate transaction is regulated or forbidden. Every rule of corporate law affects investors who live outside the state of incorporation, yet this has never been thought sufficient to authorize a form of cost-benefit inquiry through the medium of the Commerce Clause. The Constitution has room for many economic policies.

▶ ANALYSIS

The court noted that Wisconsin's law makes a potential buyer less willing to buy. However, many other rules of corporate law—supermajority voting requirements, staggered and classified boards, and so on—have similar or greater effects on some persons' willingness to purchase stock. Investors do have recourse, however; they can turn to firms incorporated in states committed to the dominance of market forces, or they can turn on legislators who enact unwise laws.

■▬■

Quicknotes

COMMERCE CLAUSE Article 1, section 8, clause 3 of the United States Constitution, granting Congress the power to regulate commerce with foreign countries and between the states.

LEVERAGED BUYOUT A transaction whereby corporate outsiders purchase the outstanding shares of a publicly held corporation mostly with borrowed funds.

TENDER OFFER An offer made by one corporation to the shareholders of a target corporation to purchase their shares subject to number, time, and price specifications.

WILLIAMS ACT Regulates the process of tender offers.

■▬■

Insider Trading

Quick Reference Rules of Law

Securities and Exchange Commission v. Texas Gulf Sulphur Co.

Federal government agency (P) v. Corporation (D)

401 F.2d 833 (2d Cir. 1968), *(en banc) cert. denied*, 404 U.S. 1005 (1971).

NATURE OF CASE: Appeal from judgment in an action to compel rescission of securities transactions made in violation of federal securities law.

FACT SUMMARY: The Securities and Exchange Commission (SEC) (P) brought this action based on insider trading after certain employees and officers of Texas Gulf Sulphur Co. (TGS) (D) purchased shares and options of TGS (D) stock before knowledge of a rich ore strike became public.

🏛 RULE OF LAW
Anyone in possession of material inside information must either disclose it to the investing public, or, if ordered not to disclose it to protect a corporate confidence, abstain from trading in the securities concerned while such inside information remains undisclosed.

FACTS: Employees of Texas Gulf Sulphur (TGS) (D), doing exploratory drilling in Canada, discovered unusually rich ore deposits. To facilitate purchase of all the land containing those deposits, Stephens, president of TGS (D), instructed the exploratory team not to disclose the results of their drilling. TGS (D) issued a press release downplaying rumors of a major ore strike and stated that the work done to date was not sufficient to reach definite conclusions as to the size and grade of any ore discovered. Four days later, TGS (D) officially announced a major strike. During those four days, certain TGS (D) employees and officers who knew about the strike purchased substantial amounts of TGS (D) stock and call options. The SEC (P) sued, alleging that TGS's (D) conduct constituted insider trading in violation of § 10(b) of the Securities Exchange Act and SEC Rule 10b-5. It sought to compel the rescission of those securities transactions which violated the Act. The trial court concluded that the results of the first drill core were too remote to be deemed material or to have had any significant impact on the market. The SEC (P) appealed.

ISSUE: Must anyone in possession of material inside information either disclose it to the investing public, or, if ordered not to disclose it to protect a corporate confidence, abstain from trading in the securities concerned while such inside information remains undisclosed?

HOLDING AND DECISION: (Waterman, J.) Yes. Anyone in possession of material inside information must either disclose it to the investing public, or, if ordered not to disclose it to protect a corporate confidence, abstain from trading in the securities concerned while such inside information remains undisclosed. Material facts include those that may affect the desire of investors to buy, sell, or hold the company's securities. Here, knowledge of the possible existence of a remarkably rich drill core would certainly have been an important fact to a reasonable investor in deciding whether he should buy, sell, or hold. A survey of the facts found by the trial court conclusively establishes that knowledge of the results of the discovery hole constituted material information. Therefore, all transactions in TGS (D) stock by individuals apprised of the drilling results were made in violation of SEC Rule 10b-5. Reversed.

▶ ANALYSIS

Whether facts are material within SEC Rule 10b-5 will depend upon a balancing of both the indicated probability that an event will occur and the anticipated magnitude of the event in light of the totality of the company activity. The court of appeals' disagreement with the district judge on the issue of materiality did not go to his findings of basic fact but to his understanding of the legal standard applicable to them. One TGS (D) officer was absolved by the trial court because his telephone order was placed shortly after a press release announcing the strike. However, the court of appeals stated that, at the minimum, the officer should have waited until the news could reasonably have been expected to appear over the media of widest circulation, the Dow Jones broad tape.

■═■

Quicknotes

INSIDER TRADING Trading accomplished by any person within a corporation who has access to information not available to the public.

MATERIAL FACT A fact without the existence of which a contract would not have been entered.

RESCISSION The canceling of an agreement and the return of the parties to their positions prior to the formation of the contract.

■═■

Chiarella v. United States

Printer (P) v. Federal government (D)

445 U.S. 222 (1980).

NATURE OF CASE: Appeal from conviction for violating federal securities law.

FACT SUMMARY: While employed as a printer, Chiarella (P) saw information that one corporation was planning to attempt to secure control of another, and he used this information by going out and obtaining stock in the target companies and then selling after the takeover attempt was made public.

🏛 RULE OF LAW
A purchaser of stock who has no duty to a prospective seller because he is neither an insider nor a fiduciary has no obligation to disclose material information he has acquired, and his failure to disclose such information does not, therefore, constitute a violation of § 10(b) of the Securities Exchange Act of 1934.

FACTS: In the course of his job as a printer at Pandick Press, Chiarella (P) was exposed to documents of one corporation revealing its plan to attempt to secure control of a second corporation. Although the identities of the corporations were concealed by blank spaces or false names until the true names were sent over on the night of the final printing, Chiarella (P) had deduced the names of the target companies beforehand from other information contained in the documents. Without revealing any of this information to the prospective sellers, he went about purchasing shares in the target corporations. He sold them after the takeover attempts were made public, thus realizing a gain of more than $30,000 in the course of fourteen months. The Securities and Exchange Commission (SEC) began an investigation, which culminated in Chiarella's (P) entering into a consent decree agreeing to return his profits to the sellers of the shares. He was, that same day, fired by Pandick Press. Eight months later, he was indicted on seventeen counts of violating § 10(b) of the Securities Exchange Act of 1934 and SEC Rule 19b-5. Chiarella (P) argued that his silence about the information he had obtained did not constitute a violation of § 10(b) because he was under no duty to disclose the information to the prospective sellers, inasmuch as he was neither an insider nor a fiduciary. The district court charged the jury that Chiarella (P) should be convicted if it found he had willfully failed to inform sellers of target companies securities that he knew of a forthcoming takeover bid that would make their shares more valuable. In affirming the resulting conviction, the court of appeals held that "[a]nyone— corporate insider or not—who regularly receives material non-public information may not use that information to trade in securities without incurring an affirmative duty to disclose." The Supreme Court granted certiorari.

ISSUE: If a stockholder owed no duty of disclosure to the party from whom he purchased securities, does his failure to disclose to the seller material information he has acquired constitute a violation of § 10(b) of the Securities Exchange Act of 1934?

HOLDING AND DECISION: (Powell, J.) No. If one who purchases stock is neither an insider nor a fiduciary and thus owes no duty to the prospective seller, his failure to disclose inside material information he has acquired does not constitute a fraud in violation of § 10(b) of the Securities Exchange Act of 1934. Administrative and judicial interpretations have established that silence in connection with the purchase or sale of securities may operate as a fraud actionable under § 10(b) despite the absence of statutory language or legislative history specifically addressing the legality of nondisclosures. However, such liability is premised upon a duty to disclose arising from a relationship of trust and confidence between parties to a transaction. In this case, the charges of the lower courts did not reflect this duty requirement adequately. Furthermore, both courts failed to identify a relationship between Chiarella (P) and the sellers that could give rise to a duty and thus provide a basis for his conviction under § 10(b) for failure to disclose the information he had. It may well be that he breached a duty to the acquiring corporation when he acted upon information he obtained by virtue of his position as an employee of the printer employed by the corporation. Whether this breach of duty would support a conviction under § 10(b) for fraud need not be decided, for this theory was not presented to the jury. Reversed.

DISSENT: (Blackmun, J.) Section § 10(b) and Rule 10b-5 mean that a person who has misappropriated non-public information has an absolute duty to disclose that information or to refrain from trading. The broad language of the statute and Congress's intent to use it as an elastic "catchall" provision to protect the uninitiated investor from misbehavior evidences the propriety of such an interpretation.

▶ ANALYSIS

The SEC has not made a practice of challenging trading by noninsiders on the basis of undisclosed market information. In fact, it has generally pointed to some fiduciary duty or special relationship between the purchaser or seller and the outsider trader as a basis for such challenges. For example, in *SEC v. Campbell*, 993 F.2d 878 (3d Cir. 1993), the writer of a financial column engaged in "scalping," i.e., purchasing stocks shortly before recommending them in

Continued on next page.

his column and then selling them when the price rose after the recommendation was published. The SEC went to great lengths to equate his relationship with his readers to that of an adviser's relationship with his clients.

■══■

Quicknotes

CERTIORARI A discretionary writ issued by a superior court to an inferior court in order to review the lower court's decisions; the Supreme Court's writ ordering such review.

DUTY TO DISCLOSE The duty owed by a fiduciary to reveal those facts that have a material effect on the interests of the party that must be informed.

FIDUCIARY DUTY A legal obligation to act for the benefit of another, including subordinating one's personal interests to that of the other person.

INSIDER TRADING Trading accomplished by any person within a corporation who has access to information not available to the public.

■══■

Dirks v. Securities and Exchange Commission

Officer of broker-dealer firm (D) v. Federal government agency (P)

463 U.S. 646 (1983).

NATURE OF CASE: SEC action for violation of § 10(b).

FACT SUMMARY: Dirks (D), based on some nonpublic information he received and a subsequent investigation, aided the Securities and Exchange Commission (SEC) (P) in convicting Equity Funding of America (EFA) for corporate fraud and was then sued by the SEC (P) for violating § 10(b) because he openly disclosed the nonpublic information to investors.

🏛 RULE OF LAW
Before a tippee will be held liable for openly disclosing nonpublic information received from an insider, the tippee must derivatively assume and breach the insider's fiduciary duty to the shareholders of not trading on nonpublic information, and the tippee will be deemed to have derivatively assumed and breached such a duty only when he knows or should know that the insider will benefit in some fashion for disclosing the information to the tippee.

FACTS: Dirks (D), the tippee and officer of a brokerage firm, was told by Secrist, the insider, Equity Funding of America (EFA) was engaging in corporate fraud. Dirks (D) then investigated EFA to verify Secrist's information. Neither Dirks (D) nor his firm owned or traded EFA stock. However, during Dirks's (D) investigation he openly revealed the information to investors and caused many of them to sell their EFA stock. Consequently, the price of EFA stock dropped from $26 to $15. However, largely due to Dirks's (D) investigation, the SEC (P) was able to convict the officers of EFA for corporate fraud. Still, the SEC (P) sued and reprimanded Dirks (D) for his disclosure of the nonpublic information to the investors. The court of appeals affirmed; Dirks (D) then applied for and was granted certiorari by the U.S. Supreme Court.

ISSUE: Will a tippee automatically be held liable for openly disclosing nonpublic information received from an insider?

HOLDING AND DECISION: (Powell, J.) No. Before a tippee will be held liable for openly disclosing nonpublic information received from an insider, the tippee must derivatively assume and breach the insider's fiduciary duty to the shareholders of not trading on nonpublic information. The tippee will be deemed to have derivatively assumed and breached such a duty only when he knows or should know that the insider will benefit in some fashion for disclosing the information to the tippee. Mere receipt for nonpublic information by a tippee from an insider does not automatically carry with it the fiduciary duty of an insider. In

this case, Secrist, the insider, did not receive a benefit for his disclosure. He disclosed the information to Dirks (D), the tippee, solely to help expose the fraud being perpetrated by the officers of EFA. Therefore, since Secrist, the insider, did not receive a benefit for his disclosure of nonpublic information to Dirks (D), the tippee, Secrist, did not breach his fiduciary duty to the shareholders. Consequently, since Secrist, the insider, did not breach his duty to the shareholders, there was no derivative breach by Dirks (D) when he passed on the nonpublic information to investors. Reversed.

DISSENT: (Blackmun, J.) It is not necessary that an insider receive a benefit from his disclosure of nonpublic information before a court can hold that he breached his duty to the shareholders. All that is necessary is that the shareholders suffer an injury. Here, Secrist's disclosure to Dirks (D) resulted in Dirks's (D) clients trading on the information, which in turn resulted in a market loss of $11 per share for the shareholders. Consequently, Secrist, the insider, breached his duty, and therefore Dirks (D), as tippee, derivatively breached. Thus, Dirks (D) violated § 10(b).

▶ ANALYSIS

This case is consistent with the Court's decision in *Chiarella v. U.S.*, 445 U.S. 222 (1980), where the Court found that there is no general duty to disclose before trading on material nonpublic information and held that a duty to disclose under § 10(b) does not arise from mere possession of nonpublic market information. Rather, such a duty, the Court found, arises from the existence of a fiduciary relationship.

■▬■

Quicknotes

CERTIORARI A discretionary writ issued by a superior court to an inferior court in order to review the lower court's decisions; the Supreme Court's writ ordering such review.

FIDUCIARY DUTY A legal obligation to act for the benefit of another, including subordinating one's personal interests to that of the other person.

INSIDER TRADING Trading accomplished by any person within a corporation who has access to information not available to the public.

TIPPEE A person who obtains material nonpublic information from another standing in a fiduciary relationship to the corporation that is the subject of such information.

■▬■

Securities and Exchange Commission v. Siebel Systems, Inc.

Federal government agency (P) v. Corporation (D)

384 F. Supp. 2d 694 (S.D.N.Y. 2005).

NATURE OF CASE: Motion to dismiss for failure to state a claim in SEC action for violation of Regulation FD (Fair Disclosure).

FACT SUMMARY: The Securities and Exchange Commission (SEC) (P) brought suit against Siebel Systems, Inc. (Siebel Systems) (D), and its CFO, Goldman (D), alleging that Goldman (D) had made material nonpublic statements to investors in violation of Regulation FD; the company and Goldman (D) moved to dismiss for failure to state a claim, contending that Goldman's (D) statements were neither material nor nonpublic.

RULE OF LAW

A statement that repeats information, the substance of which has been previously disclosed publicly or that on its own is not "material," does not violate Regulation FD.

FACTS: The Securities and Exchange Commission (SEC) (P) brought suit in federal district court against Siebel Systems, Inc. (Siebel Systems) (D), and its CFO, Goldman (D), claiming that they had violated, or aided and abetted the violation of, Regulation FD, 17 C.F.R. § 243.100, which prohibits a company and its senior officials from privately disclosing any material nonpublic information regarding the company or its securities to certain persons such as analysts and institutional investors. The SEC (P) claimed that Goldman (D) made positive comments about the company's business activity levels and sales transaction pipeline at two private events attended by institutional investors. Specifically, the SEC (P) charged that Goldman (D) stated that the company's activity levels were "good" or "better," that new deals were coming back into the pipeline, that the pipeline was "building" and "growing," and that "there were some $5 million deals in Siebel's pipeline." The SEC (P) also alleged that immediately following the disclosure of this information or soon thereafter, certain attendants of the meetings and their associates made substantial purchases of shares of Siebel Systems' (D) stock. Allegedly, these statements materially contrasted with public statements made by the company's founder, Siebel, on several occasions a few days earlier. Siebel's statements conditioned the company's prospective performance on the economy's performance, whereas Goldman's (D) did not. According to the SEC (P), Goldman's (D) comments gave investors the impression that an increase in second quarter deals was not simply because the deals that had slipped from the first quarter were closing, whereas Siebel's statements indicated that some deals that had been expected to close in the first quarter had slipped into the second quarter. Finally, the SEC (P) maintained that the company

failed to timely disclose what it characterized as the material nonpublic information. However, the SEC (P) did not rely for its assertions on any statements regarding specific earnings or sales figures. The defendants responded by contending that Goldman's (D) statements could not support a conclusory allegation that the statements were either material or nonpublic, and by moving to dismiss for failure to state a claim.

ISSUE: Does a statement that repeats information, the substance of which has been previously disclosed publicly or that on its own is not "material," violate Regulation FD?

HOLDING AND DECISION: (Daniels, J.) No. A statement that repeats information, the substance of which has been previously disclosed publicly or that on its own is not "material," does not violate Regulation FD. Regulation FD does not contain definitions for the terms "material" or "nonpublic." The SEC (P) itself noted its concern that the regulation would have a chilling effect on disclosure of information by issuers, and, accordingly, modified the proposed regulation to include certain safeguards to narrow the regulation's applicability so as not to diminish the flow of information. In addition, the Adopting Release advised that the terms "material" and "nonpublic" were to be defined as those terms had been defined in case law. With regard to the "nonpublic" element, information is nonpublic if it has not been disseminated in a manner sufficient to ensure its availability to the investing public. With regard to the definition of "materiality," "information is material if 'there is a substantial likelihood that a reasonable shareholder would consider it important' in making an investment decision." To satisfy the materiality element, there must be a substantial likelihood that a reasonable investor would have considered the information as having significantly altered the "total mix" of information made available. The "total mix" of information includes all information that is reasonably available to the public. Information that would affect the probable future of the company and which may affect an investor's desire to buy, sell, or hold the company's securities is material. The question of materiality generally presents a mixed question of law and fact as it involves the application of a legal standard to a particular set of facts. A complaint may only be dismissed on the grounds that the alleged private disclosure of information was immaterial if the subject information is "so obviously unimportant to a reasonable investor that reasonable minds could not differ on the question of [its] importance." Applying these principles here, the allegations in the complaint fail to demonstrate that Regulation FD was violated. First, Goldman's (D) private statement regarding the existence of $5 million

Continued on next page.

dollar deals in the company's pipeline for the second quarter was equivalent in substance ("materially") to the information previously disclosed by Siebel. In attempting to distinguish the statements between the two men, the SEC (P) contended that Siebel's statements were forward-looking, whereas Goldman's (D) were made in the present tense. However, there is no support for the SEC's (P) approach, whereby it scrutinizes, at an extremely heightened level, every particular word used in the statement, including the tense of verbs and the general syntax of each sentence. Such an approach places an unreasonable burden on a company's management and spokespersons to become linguistic experts, or otherwise live in fear of violating Regulation FD should the words they use later be interpreted by the SEC as connoting even the slightest variance from the company's public statements. Regulation FD does not require that corporate officials only utter verbatim statements that were previously publicly made. If the regulation were applied in such a manner, the very purpose of the regulation, i.e., to provide the public with a broad flow of relevant investment information, would be thwarted. Here, Goldman's (D) statement did not add, contradict, or significantly alter the material information already available to the public. Similarly unavailing are the SEC's (P) claims that Goldman's (D) private statements regarding new business in the pipeline and that the pipeline was "growing" or "building" was information which was not previously disclosed to the public. Publicly available information indicated that the second quarter pipeline would include new deals and that revenues would be higher for that quarter than the previous quarter, in part based on those in-the-pipeline deals. Based on this information, a reasonable investor would be aware that the sales pipeline was "growing" and "building." Hence Goldman's (D) private wording, to that effect, added nothing to the total mix of information publicly available. The same was true of Goldman's (D) use of "good" or "better" to describe the company's sales or business activity levels. These were merely generalized descriptive labels based on the underlying quantitative information already provided publicly by Siebel Systems (D). Moreover, the information available to the public provided a sufficient factual basis for a reasonable investor to conclude that business was improving. This was consistent with Goldman's (D) overall positive forecast. Although the attendees at Goldman's (D) presentations, or others with whom they communicated, allegedly purchased Siebel System (D) stock almost immediately after the presentations, stock movements, while a relevant factor in determining materiality, are not a sufficient factor alone to establish materiality. The actions taken by those in attendance at Goldman's (D) speaking engagements, although a relevant consideration, do not change the nature or content of his statements. Regulation FD deals exclusively with the disclosure of material information. The regulation does not prohibit persons speaking on behalf of an issuer, from providing mere positive or negative characterizations, or their optimistic or pessimistic subjective general impressions, based upon or drawn from the material infor-

mation available to the public. The mere fact that analysts might have considered Goldman's (D) private statements significant is not, standing alone, a basis to infer that Regulation FD was violated. Despite the SEC's (P) assertion that Goldman's (D) failure to link the company's performance to the economy's performance was a material omission that constituted new information, and even if potential effects of the economy constituted material information, the company had already publicly disclosed such a link. Nonetheless, Regulation FD does not require an individual, speaking privately on behalf of an issuer, to repeat material information which has already been previously publicly proclaimed. In other words, Regulation FD only pertains to the required public disclosure of information, not the failure to repeat a particular public statement in private. Even accepting all the SEC's (P) factual allegations as true, and drawing all reasonable inferences from them in the SEC's (P) favor, Goldman (D) did not make material nonpublic statements in violation of Regulation FD. Complaint dismissed for failure to state a claim.

▶ ANALYSIS

There are seven categories of information that are deemed to have a higher probability of being "material" for Regulation FD purposes. These categories are: (1) earnings information; (2) mergers, acquisitions, tender offers, joint ventures, or changes in assets; (3) new products or discoveries, or developments regarding customers or supplies (e.g., the acquisition or loss of a contract); (4) changes in control or in management; (5) change in auditors or auditor notification that the issuer may no longer rely on an auditor's audit report; (6) events regarding the issuer's securities—e.g., defaults on strict securities, calls of securities for redemption, repurchase plans, stock splits or changes in dividends, changes to rights of security holders, public or private sales of additional securities; and (7) bankruptcies and receiverships. Significant to the court was that none of Goldman's (D) statements fell squarely within any of these categories.

■═■

Quicknotes

BANKRUPTCY A legal proceeding whereby a debtor, who is unable to pay his debts as they become due, is relieved of his obligation to pay his creditors either by liquidation and distribution of his remaining assets or through reorganization and payment from future income.

JOINT VENTURE Venture undertaken based on an express or implied agreement between the members, common purpose and interest, and an equal power of control.

MERGER The acquisition of one company by another, after which the acquired company ceases to exist as an independent entity.

Continued on next page.

MOTION TO DISMISS   Motion to terminate a trial based on the adequacy of the pleadings.

RECEIVERSHIP   Proceeding or condition whereby a receiver is appointed in order to maintain the holdings of a corporation, individual or other entity that is insolvent.

TENDER OFFER   An offer made by one corporation to the shareholders of a target corporation to purchase their shares subject to number, time, and price specifications.

■━━■

United States v. O'Hagan

Federal government (P) v. Attorney (D)

521 U.S. 642 (1997).

NATURE OF CASE: Suit alleging violations of §§ 109(b) and 14(e) of the Securities and Exchange Act.

FACT SUMMARY: O'Hagan (D) purchased call options of Pillsbury stock when his law firm was retained to handle a potential tender offer by Grand met for Pillsbury stock, and sold them for a profit following announcement of the tender offer.

🏛 RULE OF LAW
Criminal liability under § 10(b) may be predicated on the misappropriation theory.

FACTS: O'Hagan (D) purchased call options of Pillsbury stock when his law firm was retained to handle a potential tender offer by Grand Met for Pillsbury stock. When Grand Met announced the tender offer, he sold them for a profit of more than $4.3 million.

ISSUE: May criminal liability under section 10(b), be predicated on the misappropriation theory?

HOLDING AND DECISION: (Ginsburg, J.) Yes. Criminal liability under § 10(b) may be predicated on the misappropriation theory. Misappropriation satisfies the section's requirement that chargeable conduct involve a "deceptive device or contrivance" used "in connection with" the purchase or sale of securities. Misappropriators deal in deception. A fiduciary's fraud is consummated not when the fiduciary gains the confidential information, but when he uses the information to purchase or sell securities without disclosure. The securities transaction and breach of duty thus coincide. Reversed.

CONCURRENCE AND DISSENT: (Thomas, J.) If the relevant test here is whether the fraudulent act is necessarily tied to this securities transaction, then the misappropriation of confidential information used to trade no more than violates § 10(b) than does the misappropriation of funds used to trade.

▌ *ANALYSIS*

The Court also held that a person who trades in securities for personal profit, using confidential information misappropriated for securities trading purposes in breach of a fiduciary duty to the source of the information, is guilty of violating § 10(b) and Rule 10b-5 promulgated thereunder.

Quicknotes

FIDUCIARY Person holding a legal obligation to act for the benefit of another.

MISAPPROPRIATION The unlawful use of another's property or funds.

RULE 10b-5 It is unlawful to defend or make untrue statements in connection with purchase or sale of securities.

SECURITIES Instruments that reflect ownership rights in a company or a debt owed by the company.

SECURITIES EXCHANGE ACT § 10(b) Prohibits use of any "manipulative or deceptive device or contrivance" in connection with the purchase or sale of a security and in violation of any regulation adopted by the Securities and Exchange Commission.

TENDER OFFER An offer made by one corporation to the shareholders of a target corporation to purchase their shares subject to number, time, and price specifications.

Gollust v. Mendell

Shareholder (P) v. Shareholder (D)

501 U.S. 115 (1991).

NATURE OF CASE: Suit challenging the standing of a shareholder to maintain his action based on insider trading after a merger.

FACT SUMMARY: After Gollust (P) brought this § 16(b) action to recover short-term insider profits, a merger took place in which Gollust's (P) shares were exchanged for shares in the new parent company, prompting Mendell (D) to challenge Gollust's (P) standing to continue the suit since he was no longer a shareholder of the original corporation.

🏛 RULE OF LAW
A shareholder bringing suit under § 16(b) of the 1934 Securities Exchange Act must maintain a financial interest in the outcome of the litigation sufficient to motivate its prosecution and to avoid constitutional standing difficulties.

FACTS: Gollust (P) brought this shareholder action under § 16(b) of the Securities Exchange Act of 1934 to recover short-term profits for Viacom International, Inc. The profits were made by a group of shareholders, including Mendell (D), who held more than 10% of the company's stock. As a result of a merger which occurred while the suit was in progress, all shareholders of Viacom International became shareholders in its acquiror and parent company, Viacom, Inc. Mendell (D) then challenged Gollust's (P) standing since he was no longer a shareholder of Viacom International.

ISSUE: Must a shareholder bringing suit under § 16(b), maintain a financial interest in the outcome of the litigation sufficient to motivate its prosecution and to avoid constitutional standing difficulties?

HOLDING AND DECISION: (Souter, J.) Yes. A shareholder bringing suit under § 16(b) must maintain a financial interest in the outcome of the litigation sufficient to motivate its prosecution and to avoid constitutional standing difficulties. The only restrictions on the standing of a party to bring suit under § 16(b) are that he be the owner of a security of the issuer at the time the suit is instituted and that he own a security of the issuer whose stock was traded by the insider. Under Article III of the Constitution, a plaintiff suing in federal court must maintain a distinct and palpable personal injury and must retain a personal stake in the outcome of the litigation throughout its course. Congress understood and intended that an individual authorized to sue insiders on behalf of an issuer would satisfy the constitutional requirement. An adequate financial stake can be maintained when the shareholder's interest in the issuer has been replaced by an interest in the

issuer's new parent. Here, Gollust (P) has satisfied the statute's requirements by owning a security of the issuer at the time he instituted this § 16(b) action. After the merger, Gollust (P) retained a continuing financial interest in the outcome of the litigation and still stands to profit if this action is successful, just as he would have done if his original shares had not been exchanged in the merger.

▶ ANALYSIS

Section 16(b) imposes a form of strict liability on insider trading, which Congress chose to enforce by relying solely on the issuers of stock and their security holders. Unlike most of the federal securities laws, § 16(b) does not confer enforcement authority on the Securities and Exchange Commission. A security holder eligible to institute suit will have no direct financial interest in the outcome of the litigation since any recovery will inure only to the issuer's benefit. Attorney fee awards, however, provide the motivating factor behind such suits.

■═■

Quicknotes

INSIDER Any person within a corporation who has access to information not available to the public.

INSIDER TRADING Trading accomplished by any person within a corporation who has access to information not available to the public.

STANDING Whether a party possesses the right to commence suit against another party by having a personal stake in the resolution of the controversy.

■═■

CBI Industries, Inc. v. Horton

Corporation (P) v. Director (D)

682 F.2d 643 (7th Cir. 1982).

NATURE OF CASE: Appeal from recovery awarded in an action based on short-swing liability.

FACT SUMMARY: After Horton (D), who was a director of CBI Industries (CBI) (P), sold some of his own CBI (P) stock and then purchased CBI (P) stock within six months of the sale for a trust of which he was cotrustee, CBI (P) filed an action to recover short-swing profits.

🏛 RULE OF LAW
Section 16(b) of the Securities Exchange Act applies only to short-swing profits that provide a direct pecuniary benefit to the insider.

FACTS: Horton (D), a director of CBI Industries (CBI) (P), was also co-trustee of a trust created for the benefit of his two sons. The original assets of the trust consisted entirely of CBI (P) stock. While Horton (D) had the power to manage the trust, he did not have the power to divert the income of the trust to himself. Horton (D) sold 3,000 shares of his own CBI (P) stock on the open market. Within six months, he bought, on the open market, 2,000 shares of CBI (P) stock for the trust for less than the price for which he had sold his own stock. Alleging a violation of § 16(b), CBI (P) sued to recover the difference in price. That difference was $25,000, which the district court awarded to CBI (P). Horton (D) appealed.

ISSUE: Does § 16(b) of the Securities Exchange Act, apply only to short-swing profits that provide a direct pecuniary benefit to the insider?

HOLDING AND DECISION: (Posner, J.) Yes. Section 16(b) of the Securities Exchange Act applies only to short-swing profits that provide direct pecuniary benefit to the insider. Section 16(b) of the Securities Exchange Act provides that if a corporate director realizes short-swing profits by buying and selling shares in his company within six months, any profit realized by him shall be recoverable in a suit by the company. If Horton (D) had bought the shares for his own account, he would indisputably have violated § 16(b) and the company would have been entitled to his $25,000 "profit." However, Horton (D) was not a beneficial owner of the trust, and any profit he made did not become his to use as he wished but was for the exclusive use of his sons. To prevail, CBI (P) would have to show that the trust was a sham and that despite its terms Horton (D) was able to use income or assets of the trust to pay his personal expenses. CBI (P) has made no effort to prove a direct pecuniary benefit to Horton (D). The district judge can decide whether CBI (P) should be given a chance to prove liability under the standard adopted today. Reversed and remanded.

▶ ANALYSIS

According to the court, it is not enough that ties of affinity or consanguinity between the nominal recipient and the insider make it likely that the insider will experience an enhanced sense of well-being as a result of the receipt. Some economists believe that emotional relationships within the family can be expressed in economic terms. However, the court found it doubtful that the framers of § 16(b) would have wanted to complicate enforcement of the statute to this degree merely to make an already Draconian strict liability statute still more Draconian.

■══■

Quicknotes

INSIDER Any person within a corporation who has access to information not available to the public.

SHORT-SWING PROFIT An insider's profit on purchase and sale of a corporation's stock within a six-month period.

■══■

Feder v. Martin Marietta Corp.

Stockholder (P) v. Corporation (D)

406 F.2d 260 (2d Cir. 1969), *cert. denied*, 396 U.S. 1036 (1970).

NATURE OF CASE: Appeal from dismissal of a shareholder action to recover short-swing profits.

FACT SUMMARY: When Martin Marietta Corp. (D) bought and sold an additional 101,300 shares of Sperry Rand (Sperry) stock during the time Martin Mariettta's (D) president and chief executive sat on Sperry's board of directors, Feder (P) brought this § 16(b) action to recover the short-swing profits made by Martin Marietta (D).

🏛 RULE OF LAW
When an officer is deputized by his own company to represent its interests by serving on the board of directors of another company, the company which that officer represents will be considered a "director" of the company on whose board the officer sits.

FACTS: During the less than six months that Bunker, president and chief executive of Martin Marietta (D), sat on the board of directors of Sperry Rand, Martin Marietta (D) acquired an additional 101,300 shares of Sperry stock. Martin Marietta (D) later sold all of its 801,300 shares of Sperry stock within six months of purchase. Feder (P), a stockholder of Sperry, then commenced this § 16(b) action to recover for Sperry the short-swing profits realized by the purchase and sale of the 101,300 shares of Sperry acquired by Martin Marietta (D) while Bunker was sitting on the board of Sperry. Feder (P) alleged that Bunker was deputized by Martin Marietta (D) when he served on Sperry's board, thus making Martin Marietta (D) a "director" of Sperry within the meaning of § 16(b) of the Securities Exchange Act of 1934. The trial court dismissed the action, and Feder (P) appealed.

ISSUE: When an officer of a company is deputized by that company to represent its interests by serving on the board of directors of another company, will the company which that officer represents be considered a "director" of the company on whose board the officer sits?

HOLDING AND DECISION: (Waterman, J.) Yes. When an officer of a company is deputized by that company to represent its interests by serving on the board of directors of another company, the company which that officer represents will be considered a "director" of the company on whose board the officer sits. The logical inference from the wording of Bunker's letter of resignation to Sperry was that Bunker served on the Sperry board as a representative of Martin Marietta (D) to protect its investment in Sperry. While a Sperry director, Bunker had access to inside information relating to the short-range outlook at Sperry and admitted discussing Sperry's affairs with two

officials at Martin Marietta (D). In addition, Martin Marrietta's (D) board formally consented to and approved Bunker's directorship of Sperry. Finally, Martin Marietta (D) had representatives or deputies serving on the boards of other corporations whose functions were identical to Bunker's. All these factors are definite and concrete indicatives that Bunker was in fact a Martin (D) deputy. Reversed.

▶ *ANALYSIS*

Application of § 16(b) liability is automatic and attaches to any profit by an insider on any short-swing transaction occurring within the arbitrarily fixed time limits of the statute. The policy underlying the enactment of § 16(b) does not permit an expansion of the statute's scope to persons other than directors, officers, and 10% shareholders. However, through the creation of a legal fiction, the courts have managed to remain within the limits of § 16(b)'s literal language while expanding the Act's reach.

■■■

Quicknotes

INSIDER Any person within a corporation who has access to information not available to the public.

SHORT-SWING PROFIT An insider's profit on purchase and sale of a corporation's stock within a six-month period.

■■■

Glossary

Common Latin Words and Phrases Encountered in the Law

A FORTIORI: Because one fact exists or has been proven, therefore a second fact that is related to the first fact must also exist.

A PRIORI: From the cause to the effect. A term of logic used to denote that when one generally accepted truth is shown to be a cause, another particular effect must necessarily follow.

AB INITIO: From the beginning; a condition which has existed throughout, as in a marriage which was void ab initio.

ACTUS REUS: The wrongful act; in criminal law, such action sufficient to trigger criminal liability.

AD VALOREM: According to value; an ad valorem tax is imposed upon an item located within the taxing jurisdiction calculated by the value of such item.

AMICUS CURIAE: Friend of the court. Its most common usage takes the form of an amicus curiae brief, filed by a person who is not a party to an action but is nonetheless allowed to offer an argument supporting his legal interests.

ARGUENDO: In arguing. A statement, possibly hypothetical, made for the purpose of argument, is one made arguendo.

BILL QUIA TIMET: A bill to quiet title (establish ownership) to real property.

BONA FIDE: True, honest, or genuine. May refer to a person's legal position based on good faith or lacking notice of fraud (such as a bona fide purchaser for value) or to the authenticity of a particular document (such as a bona fide last will and testament).

CAUSA MORTIS: With approaching death in mind. A gift causa mortis is a gift given by a party who feels certain that death is imminent.

CAVEAT EMPTOR: Let the buyer beware. This maxim is reflected in the rule of law that a buyer purchases at his own risk because it is his responsibility to examine, judge, test, and otherwise inspect what he is buying.

CERTIORARI: A writ of review. Petitions for review of a case by the United States Supreme Court are most often done by means of a writ of certiorari.

CONTRA: On the other hand. Opposite. Contrary to.

CORAM NOBIS: Before us; writs of error directed to the court that originally rendered the judgment.

CORAM VOBIS: Before you; writs of error directed by an appellate court to a lower court to correct a factual error.

CORPUS DELICTI: The body of the crime; the requisite elements of a crime amounting to objective proof that a crime has been committed.

CUM TESTAMENTO ANNEXO, ADMINISTRATOR (ADMINISTRATOR C.T.A.): With will annexed; an administrator c.t.a. settles an estate pursuant to a will in which he is not appointed.

DE BONIS NON, ADMINISTRATOR (ADMINISTRATOR D.B.N.): Of goods not administered; an administrator d.b.n. settles a partially settled estate.

DE FACTO: In fact; in reality; actually. Existing in fact but not officially approved or engendered.

DE JURE: By right; lawful. Describes a condition that is legitimate "as a matter of law," in contrast to the term "de facto," which connotes something existing in fact but not legally sanctioned or authorized. For example, de facto segregation refers to segregation brought about by housing patterns, etc., whereas de jure segregation refers to segregation created by law.

DE MINIMIS: Of minimal importance; insignificant; a trifle; not worth bothering about.

DE NOVO: Anew; a second time; afresh. A trial de novo is a new trial held at the appellate level as if the case originated there and the trial at a lower level had not taken place.

DICTA: Generally used as an abbreviated form of obiter dicta, a term describing those portions of a judicial opinion incidental or not necessary to resolution of the specific question before the court. Such nonessential statements and remarks are not considered to be binding precedent.

DUCES TECUM: Refers to a particular type of writ or subpoena requesting a party or organization to produce certain documents in their possession.

EN BANC: Full bench. Where a court sits with all justices present rather than the usual quorum.

EX PARTE: For one side or one party only. An ex parte proceeding is one undertaken for the benefit of only one party, without notice to, or an appearance by, an adverse party.

EX POST FACTO: After the fact. An ex post facto law is a law that retroactively changes the consequences of a prior act.

EX REL.: Abbreviated form of the term "ex relatione," meaning upon relation or information. When the state brings an action in which it has no interest against an individual at the instigation of one who has a private interest in the matter.

FORUM NON CONVENIENS: Inconvenient forum. Although a court may have jurisdiction over the case, the action should be tried in a more conveniently located court, one to which parties and witnesses may more easily travel, for example.

GUARDIAN AD LITEM: A guardian of an infant as to litigation, appointed to represent the infant and pursue his/her rights.

HABEAS CORPUS: You have the body. The modern writ of habeas corpus is a writ directing that a person (body) being detained (such as a prisoner) be brought before the court so that the legality of his detention can be judicially ascertained.

IN CAMERA: In private, in chambers. When a hearing is held before a judge in his chambers or when all spectators are excluded from the courtroom.

IN FORMA PAUPERIS: In the manner of a pauper. A party who proceeds in forma pauperis because of his poverty is one who is allowed to bring suit without liability for costs.

INFRA: Below, under. A word referring the reader to a later part of a book. (The opposite of supra.)

IN LOCO PARENTIS: In the place of a parent.

IN PARI DELICTO: Equally wrong; a court of equity will not grant requested relief to an applicant who is in pari delicto, or as much at fault in the transactions giving rise to the controversy as is the opponent of the applicant.

IN PARI MATERIA: On like subject matter or upon the same matter. Statutes relating to the same person or things are said to be in pari materia. It is a general rule of statutory construction that such statutes should be construed together, i.e., looked at as if they together constituted one law.

IN PERSONAM: Against the person. Jurisdiction over the person of an individual.

IN RE: In the matter of. Used to designate a proceeding involving an estate or other property.

IN REM: A term that signifies an action against the res, or thing. An action in rem is basically one that is taken directly against property, as distinguished from an action in personam, i.e., against the person.

INTER ALIA: Among other things. Used to show that the whole of a statement, pleading, list, statute, etc., has not been set forth in its entirety.

INTER PARTES: Between the parties. May refer to contracts, conveyances or other transactions having legal significance.

INTER VIVOS: Between the living. An inter vivos gift is a gift made by a living grantor, as distinguished from bequests contained in a will, which pass upon the death of the testator.

IPSO FACTO: By the mere fact itself.

JUS: Law or the entire body of law.

LEX LOCI: The law of the place; the notion that the rights of parties to a legal proceeding are governed by the law of the place where those rights arose.

MALUM IN SE: Evil or wrong in and of itself; inherently wrong. This term describes an act that is wrong by its very nature, as opposed to one which would not be wrong but for the fact that there is a specific legal prohibition against it (malum prohibitum).

MALUM PROHIBITUM: Wrong because prohibited, but not inherently evil. Used to describe something that is wrong because it is expressly forbidden by law but that is not in and of itself evil, e.g., speeding.

MANDAMUS: We command. A writ directing an official to take a certain action.

MENS REA: A guilty mind; a criminal intent. A term used to signify the mental state that accompanies a crime or other prohibited act. Some crimes require only a general mens rea (general intent to do the prohibited act), but others, like assault with intent to murder, require the existence of a specific mens rea.

MODUS OPERANDI: Method of operating; generally refers to the manner or style of a criminal in committing crimes, admissible in appropriate cases as evidence of the identity of a defendant.

NEXUS: A connection to.

NISI PRIUS: A court of first impression. A nisi prius court is one where issues of fact are tried before a judge or jury.

N.O.V. (NON OBSTANTE VEREDICTO): Notwithstanding the verdict. A judgment n.o.v. is a judgment given in favor of one party despite the fact that a verdict was returned in favor of the other party, the justification being that the verdict either had no reasonable support in fact or was contrary to law.

NUNC PRO TUNC: Now for then. This phrase refers to actions that may be taken and will then have full retroactive effect.

PENDENTE LITE: Pending the suit; pending litigation under way.

PER CAPITA: By head; beneficiaries of an estate, if they take in equal shares, take per capita.

PER CURIAM: By the court; signifies an opinion ostensibly written "by the whole court" and with no identified author.

PER SE: By itself, in itself; inherently.

PER STIRPES: By representation. Used primarily in the law of wills to describe the method of distribution where a person, generally because of death, is unable to take that which is left to him by the will of another, and therefore his heirs divide such property between them rather than take under the will individually.

PRIMA FACIE: On its face, at first sight. A prima facie case is one that is sufficient on its face, meaning that the evidence supporting it is adequate to establish the case until contradicted or overcome by other evidence.

PRO TANTO: For so much; as far as it goes. Often used in eminent domain cases when a property owner receives partial payment for his land without prejudice to his right to bring suit for the full amount he claims his land to be worth.

QUANTUM MERUIT: As much as he deserves. Refers to recovery based on the doctrine of unjust enrichment in those cases in which a party has rendered valuable services or furnished materials that were accepted and enjoyed by another under circumstances that would reasonably notify the recipient that the rendering party expected to be paid. In essence, the law implies a contract to pay the reasonable value of the services or materials furnished.

QUASI: Almost like; as if; nearly. This term is essentially used to signify that one subject or thing is almost analogous to another but that material differences between them do exist. For example, a quasi-criminal proceeding is one that is not strictly criminal but shares enough of the same characteristics to require some of the same safeguards (e.g., procedural due process must be followed in a parole hearing).

QUID PRO QUO: Something for something. In contract law, the consideration, something of value, passed between the parties to render the contract binding.

RES GESTAE: Things done; in evidence law, this principle justifies the admission of a statement that would otherwise be hearsay when it is made so closely to the event in question as to be said to be a part of it, or with such spontaneity as not to have the possibility of falsehood.

RES IPSA LOQUITUR: The thing speaks for itself. This doctrine gives rise to a rebuttable presumption of negligence when the instrumentality causing the injury was within the exclusive control of the defendant, and the injury was one that does not normally occur unless a person has been negligent.

RES JUDICATA: A matter adjudged. Doctrine which provides that once a court of competent jurisdiction has rendered a final judgment or decree on the merits, that judgment or decree is conclusive upon the parties to the case and prevents them from engaging in any other litigation on the points and issues determined therein.

RESPONDEAT SUPERIOR: Let the master reply. This doctrine holds the master liable for the wrongful acts of his servant (or the principal for his agent) in those cases in which the servant (or agent) was acting within the scope of his authority at the time of the injury.

STARE DECISIS: To stand by or adhere to that which has been decided. The common law doctrine of stare decisis attempts to give security and certainty to the law by following the policy that once a principle of law as applicable to a certain set of facts has been set forth in a decision, it forms a precedent which will subsequently be followed, even though a different decision might be made were it the first time the question had arisen. Of course, stare decisis is not an inviolable principle and is departed from in instances where there is good cause (e.g., considerations of public policy led the Supreme Court to disregard prior decisions sanctioning segregation).

SUPRA: Above. A word referring a reader to an earlier part of a book.

ULTRA VIRES: Beyond the power. This phrase is most commonly used to refer to actions taken by a corporation that are beyond the power or legal authority of the corporation.

Addendum of French Derivatives

IN PAIS: Not pursuant to legal proceedings.

CHATTEL: Tangible personal property.

CY PRES: Doctrine permitting courts to apply trust funds to purposes not expressed in the trust but necessary to carry out the settlor's intent.

PER AUTRE VIE: For another's life; during another's life. In property law, an estate may be granted that will terminate upon the death of someone other than the grantee.

PROFIT A PRENDRE: A license to remove minerals or other produce from land.

VOIR DIRE: Process of questioning jurors as to their predispositions about the case or parties to a proceeding in order to identify those jurors displaying bias or prejudice.

Casenote Legal Briefs